SOCIAL ECOLOGY

Oxford in India Readings
in Sociology and Social Anthropology

GENERAL EDITOR
T. N. MADAN

SOCIAL ECOLOGY

Edited by

RAMACHANDRA GUHA

OXFORD
UNIVERSITY PRESS

OXFORD
UNIVERSITY PRESS

Oxford University Press is a department of the University of Oxford.
It furthers the University's objective of excellence in research, scholarship,
and education by publishing worldwide. Oxford is a registered trademark of
Oxford University Press in the UK and in certain other countries

Published in India by
Oxford University Press
22 Workspace, 2nd Floor, 1/22 Asaf Ali Road, New Delhi 110 002

First Edition published in 1994
Oxford India Paperbacks 1998
28th impression 2025

ISBN-13: 978-0-19-564454-8
ISBN-10: 0-19-564454-9

Printed in India by Manipal Technologies Limited, Manipal

for Anjan Ghosh and Shiv Visvanathan

OTHER BOOKS IN THE SERIES

Contents

Introduction

RAMACHANDRA GUHA

THE ENVIRONMENT DEBATE

In recent years, there has been a spectacular growth in public consciousness about the forms of environmental degradation in India. With an amazing but welcome rapidity, this awareness is being translated on the one hand into substantial media coverage, and on the other into the creation of new government departments concerned with different aspects of environmental management. From being treated barely a decade ago as a Western fad irrelevant to the Third World, the fate of our natural environment has emerged as one of the most hotly debated themes in public life.

Perhaps this new found concern is best illustrated by two well-known but contrasting episodes: the Chipko movement, that acclaimed initiative of the Himalayan peasantry towards forest protection, and the gas leak at Bhopal, that most devastating of industrial tragedies. If Chipko demonstrated the resilience and folk wisdom of the rural poor, Bhopal for its part revealed the dark side of modern technology.

Both Bhopal and Chipko are deeply imprinted in our consciousness, precisely because the public had (in a manner of speaking) been prepared for them. The two are dramatic illustrations of the social consequences of environmental degradation. At a day to day level, however, the majority of Indians are faced with more prosaic but equally significant environmental problems. Indeed, virtually every segment of Indian society has to cope with chronic shortages of natural resources. To take the forestry sector alone, there are acute shortages of forest land for shifting cultivators, fodder for pastoral nomads, fuel and small timber for peasant farmers, and raw material for forest based industry. There is also a serious crisis in the quality and availability of water, excessively high rates of urban and industrial pollution, and a continuing loss of biological diversity. We are faced with an ecological crisis of monumental proportions, whose most serious consequence is increasing social conflict, inevitable as different groups exercise competing claims on a dwindling resource base.

Both the *causes* and *consequences* of environmental degradation are, of course, research problems well within the purview of the social sciences. Yet it is notable that the environmental crisis has caught the social science community unawares. As yet, they have contributed little to the environment debate in India. By contrast, environmental journalists, social activists and natural scientists have contributed significantly to our understanding of the social implications of environmental degradation.[1]

In the West, too, social scientists have been rather slow to respond to the environmental dilemmas of their societies. Sociologists have ascribed this neglect to two factors: (i) the Judeo-Christian ethic of man's mastery over nature, and (ii) the fact of the social sciences themselves being formed in an epoch of unprecedented economic prosperity. These factors worked in unison to foster an illusion of man's independence of the natural world, an illusion reinforced by the discovery of new sources of energy and the colonization by Europeans of new lands which had an abundance of natural resources. (cf Catton and Dunlap, 1980).

Clearly, the roots of the indifference of Indian social scientists to environmental questions lie elsewhere. In retrospect, it is easy to claim that a concern for the sustainable use of natural resources should have been at the core of development theory and practice. Yet when the process of development formally got under way after Indian independence, it was viewed above all as a collective national endeavour to reduce the gap between India and the industrialized countries of the West. In the circumstances, any talk of ecological constraints to economic activity would have been regarded at best as irrelevant, and at worst, as a deviation from the primary task of rapid industrialization.

Here, the intellectual dominance of economics has been a major factor behind the neglect of ecological variables in development planning. For none of the three major schools of economic theory— neoclassical, Keynesian and Marxian—pays attention to biophysical

---

[1] This point can be illustrated by an examination of the sources used in the excellent citizens reports on the Indian environment (CSE, 1982 and 1985). See also Bandyopadhyay (1985).

realities (cf Martinez Alier, 1987, Chapter I). Moreover, the strong influence economists have exercised over both capitalist and socialist paths of industrial development has blinded them to its unpalatable features—rapid depletion of non renewable resources, deforestation, pollution, and their attendant human costs. On the methodological plane, their aversion to fieldwork has insulated all but the exceptional economist from the ecological consequences of economic activity (cf Singh, 1976; Nadkarni, 1987).

Ironically, there has for several decades been a vigorous debate among economists on the strategy of economic development most appropriate to India. These debates have focused on emulating the capitalist or communist model of industrial development; the suitability of labour or capital intensive technologies of production; the terms of trade between agriculture and industry; the role of foreign capital and technology, and so on. In unanimously advocating large scale, rapid industrialization, Indian economists have quarelled merely over the means to achieve these ends. Not surprisingly, their discussions have ignored the environmental consequences of economic growth as well as the finite nature of many natural resources.[2]

Economics has been referred to as the 'master discipline' of development (Banuri, 1989), and its own neglect of the ecological dimensions of human life has been reproduced within the other social sciences as well.[3] Consequently, the intellectual climate of independent India has been marked, in the main, by a profound indifference to human interactions with the natural environment. However, the writings of environmental journalists have made at least a few social scientists respond critically to the environmental dilemmas of the development experience. At the same time, the

[2] A flavour of these ongoing debates may be had by perusing the pages of the *Economic and Political Weekly* (EPW), formerly the *Economic Weekly*. Indian economists are regarded as being among the best in the world, and the debates in the prestigous EPW have had a major—but if my argument is correct, not always beneficial—impact on development thinking.

A major exception to this trend was the work of the Gandhian economist, J. C. Kumarappa, who explicitly incorporated natural resource constraints in his advocacy of the 'economy of permanence' and a 'village centred economic order'. Modern economists, and more surprisingly, modern environmentalists, are mostly unaware of his writings. See for example Kumarappa (1931, 1938 and 1945). Cf also Guha (1992).

[3] The most telling criticisms of the ecological poverty of economics have come from within the discipline. A notable example is Narindar Singh's *Economics and the Crisis of Ecology* (1976). While the book was respectfully reviewed when it first appeared, it has had almost no influence within economics. Indian economists have preferred to ignore Singh's work rather than face up to the challenges it poses for the normative basis and methodology of the discipline itself.

environment debate has led to the rediscovery of those Indian intellectuals of an earlier generation whose own work focussed on the ecological infrastructure of human society (see Mamkootam, 1980; Joshi, 1986; Guha, 1992). This Reader brings together a representative selection of such work on 'social ecology', both contemporary responses to environmental degradation as well as older and pioneering essays.

THE ELEMENTS OF 'SOCIAL ECOLOGY'

The dominant social science traditions in the West and India do share one assumption: that, to quote Durkheim, social facts can only be explained with reference to other social facts (see Catton and Dunlap, 1980; Buttel, 1986). True, for any particular social or historical process there are always competing explanations. Thus, in the most famous textbook example in sociology, the rise of capitalism was interpreted by Karl Marx as a consequence primarily of changes in the economy, whereas Max Weber was inclined to grant greater significance to the role of religious beliefs.

How then does an ecological approach modify the basic assumptions of the social sciences, and more particularly of sociology? It appears that sociologists implicitly work within a model of society as being divided into four broad bands: the *economy*, the *polity*, *social structure*, and *culture*. The economy incorporates, in the Marxian sense, the forces and relations of production, or from a more conventional viewpoint, questions relating to the production, distribution and allocation of goods and services. The polity refers to the relations of power and authority between different social groups, as well as to the institutions which regulate power relations—notably the law and the state. By social structure I mean those social arrangements that are critical to the reproduction of social units—for example, family and kinship (including gender relations), caste and community. Finally, culture embodies characteristic forms of collective self expression (e.g. ritual, music, art) as well as ideas and ideologies which influence social life, whether religious or otherwise.

This four-fold division is of course an analytical device used by the sociologist; society does not divide itself so neatly. However, this schema can explain the evolution of subdisciplines within sociology—e.g. 'economic sociology', 'political sociology', 'sociology of the family', and so on. One can just as easily demonstrate this framework's importance in comparative and historical sociology. Thus differences between two societies—or between the same society at two different points in time—may be explained by differences in family structure, or religious ideology, or the role of the state.

Essentially, an ecological perspective adds a fifth basic category to the scheme—the *ecological infrastructure* of human society—that is, soil, water, flora, fauna, climate, etc. While humans are unique amongst the earth's creatures in their elaborately developed culture(s), they do not stand above or apart from nature. It is true that to a considerable extent, social facts can be adequately explained with reference to other social facts alone. However, in many instances social facts can only be properly understood with reference to the natural environment within which humans, like any other species, live, survive and reproduce. The ecological infrastructure powerfully conditions the evolution and direction of human economic life, political relations, social structure, and ideology. At the same time, human intervention itself reshapes the natural environment in its own image. However, the intricate linkages of cause, effect and feedback in nature—of which even modern science has only a very imperfect understanding—can produce many unintended consequences of human intervention.

'Social ecology', then, rests on the awareness of the *interdependence* of the biophysical and sociocultural domains (cf Burch, 1987). Juxtaposing the ecological infrastructure to the economy, polity, social structure and culture gives us the following five-fold schema, labelled (for convenience) from A to E:

BASIC CATEGORIES OF SOCIAL ECOLOGY

E   CULTURE (the arts, religion, ideology)
D   POLITY (relations of power, law, the state)
C   SOCIAL STRUCTURE (family and kinship, caste and community)
B   ECONOMY (forces and relations of production, trade)
A   ECOLOGICAL INFRASTRUCTURE (soil, water, forests, etc.)

The task of an environmentally oriented sociology—or social ecology—is the study of the reciprocal relations between A on the one hand and B, C, D and E on the other. A new research agenda unfolds itself, as we look more closely at some of the problems which emerge from the following discussion.

Class and the use and Abuse of Natural Resources

In a widely noticed book, Bardhan (1984) argued that the ruling coalition in India comprised three social groups—industrial capitalists, rich farmers, and the bureaucracy. Bardhan used this model to understand how these three fragments of the ruling class influenced state policy through taxes, subsidies, and investment. However, neither Bardhan nor his reviewers showed any appreciation of the natural resource base of the Indian economy. Yet it is possible to extend the analysis to examine class influences on natural resource use and abuse: of how rich farmers, industrialists, and bureaucrats selectively channelize water, forests and other natural resources for their own benefit, but only at a substantial cost to the environment and disadvantaged social groups (for examples, see CSE 1982 and 1985).

Social Structure and Natural Resources

In the realm of social structure, research questions arise as to the role of traditional institutions in mediating human interactions with nature. Did, for example, the division of labour between the sexes in different peasant and tribal communities give rise to fundamentally different attitudes to nature on the part of women? Again, what were the responsibilities of caste and village institutions in regulating the use of forests, water and other common resources? What have been the effects of recent environmental degradation on gender relations, or on the autonomy of the caste and the village?

Conflict and Natural Resources

Conflicts over natural resources are an increasingly visible presence in the social landscape of contemporary India. At the time of writing, conflicts over forests—so prominent in the seventies and early eighties—are now being superseded by conflicts over water, in particular the popular opposition to large dams. The ongoing movement against the Sardar Sarovar dam on the Narmada River, that will displace tens of thousands of villagers, is a recent example of this. The Indian environmental movement has its genesis in these conflicts, in contrast to the West where aesthetic and biological concerns have been more important in creating a constituency for environmental protection. For the sociologist of conflict and social movements, past and present conflicts over nature are an important if neglected field of enquiry.

Culture and Environment

The relationship of culture to environment has been of some interest to anthropologists. For our purposes, it is useful to distinguish 'folk' culture from 'high' culture. Taking the former first, we may ask— what are the various representations of nature in folk cosmology and art? What kinds of knowledge have local communities had of their natural environments (ethnobotany, ethnozoology)? Are recent patterns of social and environmental change affecting folk cosmology and knowledge systems?

The realm of 'high' culture brings us to the environment debate proper—i.e. the study of the attitudes of different religious and political philosophies to nature, and the emergence of the new theories of environment and development. Thus there is a rich ideological debate on development options in contemporary India. At one end of the spectrum stand technological optimists who reject the notion of ecological limits to growth; at the other end, romantic environmentatists who wish India to turn its back on economic development altogether. There is in between a vast middle ground, occupied by those who would try to reconcile, through technical and institutional means, the often competing claims of environmental sustainability and rapid economic growth.

As these examples illustrate, an ecological perspective can considerably enlarge the scope of sociology and social anthropology. Although some scholars (notably Catton and Dunlap, 1980) have made exaggerated claims about the birth of a 'new ecological paradigm' in sociology, we follow Field and Burch (1988) in the belief that social ecology does not have a theoretical orientation, but a problem focus, albeit with important theoretical and methodological implications. In studying the reciprocal interactions of the biophysical world and the human social world, social ecology draws upon sociological theories of power, ideology, social organization, etc. as well as the concepts and findings of scientific ecology.

DISCIPLINARY TRADITIONS AND INDIAN PIONEERS

From a conceptual outline of social ecology, we now move to an examination of *existing* traditions of ecologically-oriented research in social anthropology and sociology.

If economics is, by general consent, the most anti-ecological of the social sciences, anthropology is certainly the most sophisticated in an ecological sense. Themselves embedded in the interstices of industrial society, most economists and sociologists have, till very recently, taken for granted its apparent independence of the natural world. In contrast, anthropologists studying small scale societies have traditionally exhibited a greater interest in ecological questions, relying as they do on methods of intensive fieldwork amongst peasant and tribal cultures so obviously dependent on nature. Moreover, indepth and empathetic studies of the social institutions of small scale societies have led anthropologists to develop a healthy respect for the ecological sensibilities of local communities (this again, is in sharp contrast to the contempt for non-modern systems of thought often expressed by economists and sociologists). Thus anthropologists have documented in great detail and in a variety of regions, the indigenous knowledge systems, conservation mechanisms, and adaptations to the biophysical world of tribal and peasant societies. They have also studied the ways in which a particular society's adaptation to nature influences its internal and external social relations. More recently, anthropologists have deplored the neglect of indigenous resource management institutions in development planning, and have stressed the importance of local control and knowledge in ensuring sustainable use of the environment (cf Orlove, 1980; Weiskel, 1983; Brokensha. 1987).

In an otherwise excellent review of the field, Orlove (1980, p. 237) makes the strange claim that ecological anthropology is a subdiscipline that is dominantly American in character. In fact, what is striking about ecological anthropology (or 'cultural ecology', as it is sometimes known), is its high place in the anthropological traditions of most countries. In America, the field was established early on by Franz Boas and his intellectual disciple, Julian Steward. In the fifties and sixties, this tradition was renewed and enhanced by work outside North America by American anthropologists—in particular the ecological studies of Southeast Asia by Conklin, Geertz

Rappaport, Vayda, and others.[4] In France, anthropology—like history—was influenced by the great French tradition of human geography. Independently, Emile Durkheim's emphasis on the symbolic side of social life gave rise to an extensive literature on the meanings which different social groups ascribe to nature—beginning with Durkheim and Mauss's own study of totemism as 'primitive classification' and culminating in Claude Levi-Strauss's wide-ranging studies on myth and folklore, which took close notice of the natural world.[5] In England, the major anthropologists of the generation following Radcliffe-Brown and Malinowski wrote monographs which highlighted the embeddedness of social institutions in their ecological surroundings—Evans-Pritchard on the Nuer, Raymond Firth on social life in the island of Tikopia, and Edmund Leach on sociopolitical systems in upland Burma.[6] In Scandinavia, a major influence has been the work of Frederik Barth, a Norwegian and a pioneer of ecological anthropology.

Mauss, Steward, Evans-Pritchard, Levi-Strauss, Firth, Leach, Barth and Geertz—this is a roll call of some of the seminal figures of twentieth-century anthropology. The studies of human-nature interactions by these gifted anthropologists strongly testify to the continuing vitality of ecological traditions in the discipline. At the same time, one must notice two important limitations of ecological anthropology as it has evolved over the years (Rambo, 1985): (i) while its strengths lie in studying the stable relationships of small scale societies, with a few exceptions (e.g. Geertz, 1963; Firth, 1959) it has shown little interest in historical change; (ii) it has studied mostly the human side of the human-nature relationship—the response of culture to nature—and has tended to ignore the environmental change that follows from human social activity.

As we have already noted, when compared to anthropology the discipline of sociology has been largely indifferent to ecological concerns. One reason has been its research focus on the developed industrial world, where environmental influences on social life are

[4] For a guide to the work especially of American ecological anthropologists, see Orlove (1980). See also Hardesty (1977), Rambo (1985) and Weiskel (1983) for a fuller overview of the literature.

[5] A pioneering French study of the influence of nature on culture is Mauss and Beauchat's *Seasonal variations in Eskimo societies* (first published in *L'Anne sociologique*, 1904–5, and more recently issued in an English translation), which was unavailable to me at the time of writing.

[6] A work of synthesis, once influential among anthropologists, was Darryl Forde's *Habitat, Economy and Society* (1934).

not so readily apparent. Thus, the two great intellectual traditions of sociology—those associated with the names of Karl Marx and Max Weber—have been largely unconcerned with the natural world, with Marxism tending to the belief that man is wholly independent of natural conditions (Bottomore, 1984). A notable consequence of the sociological dogma—that social facts are to be explained only by other social facts—is that the term 'environment' has a very different meaning from that used in this Reader. In sociology, it refers to the sociocultural environment external to an individual or group, not to the natural biophysical environment of human society (Catton and Dunlap, 1980).

Sociology's research interest in the environment is relatively recent (for an exception, see Firey, 1960); it is a direct response to the modern environmental movement in the West. Indeed, the subdiscipline of 'environmental sociology'—now accorded a formal status by the American Sociological Association—has focussed its attention almost exclusively on studies of the environmental movement. Using social movement theory, it has studied the evolution and articulation of organizations committed to environmental preservation. Using opinion polls, it has documented the growing support for environmental values in the post-industrial world, a support enhanced by the widening of opportunities for leisure and recreation. Using class analysis, it has argued that the dominant social support for the environmental movement has come from the middle class of service professionals, which unlike capitalists, workers and farmers is located outside the production process (cf Cotgrove, 1982; Lowe and Goyder, 1983; Hays, 1987; and for reviews, Buttel, 1986; Lowe and Rudig, 1987; and Field and Burch, 1988).

At least in the Anglo-American world, where it is primarily centred, 'environmental sociology' is more or less synonymous with the 'sociology of the environmental movement'. Some exceptional studies have taken a wider canvas, as for example William Burch's (1971) sensitive work on the vocabularies of nature in American society, or Raymond Williams's magisterial analysis (1973) of changing attitudes to land and nature in the transition to industrialization in England.[7]

What have been the traditions of environmentally sensitive

[7] Williams was by training a literary critic, but his historical and critical interests bring him close to sociology, and his work has always been accorded a warm reception by sociologists.

research within sociology and social anthropology in India? Despite the efflorescence of village studies in independent India, social anthropologists, whether Western or Indian, have paid scant attention to the ecological framework of rural life: their overriding concern has been with caste, kinship and religion. Yet an earlier generation of anthropologists—working on tribes rather than castes—had studied the influence of the natural environment on cosmology and ritual, as well as the impact of colonial forest laws on local economies. One may cite in this connection the work on different hunter-gatherer communities by Roy (1925), Ehrenfels (1952) and Furer-Haimendorf (1943a), as well as the latter's work on shifting cultivators in the Deccan (1943b).

The exemplar of such studies is Verrier Elwin's monograph on the Baiga (1939), a vivid and evocative portrayal of a community forced by the British authorities to abandon their traditional practice of shifting cultivation. Excerpted in this Reader, Elwin's study of the Baiga was, in its own way, a pioneering defence of the integrity of shifting cultivation as a way of life, an anticipation of the later work of American anthropologists like Harold Conklin (1954). In many other books, Elwin wrote movingly of the importance of forests in tribal life. As he demonstrated, the takeover of forests by the state (for commerical exploitation) represented an attack on the economic and cultural integrity of aboriginal life. His book on the Agaria (1942) documented the collective traumas of a community of charcoal iron makers, whose declining fortunes were closely related to restrictions on access to the forest. His later, policy-oriented work in northeast India likewise stressed the importance of forest rights for tribal identity and survival (Elwin, 1961).

Elwin's writings anticipated the concern of contemporary anthropologists with 'cultural survival'—viz. the threats to indigenous cultures, and the ecosystems they inhabit, from an expanding commercial-industrial economy. Yet his influence on later research has been negligible, as is the case with the scholar who may be considered the Indian pioneer in social ecology, Radhakamal Mukerjee. An intellectual polymath with wide-ranging interests—his corpus includes studies of the industrial working class and agricultural labour—Mukerjee also first outlined the theoretical possibilities of an ecologically oriented sociology. As Walter Firey (1978, p. 162) has remarked, it was Mukerjee who first showed an 'explicit interest in natural resources as an area of sociological enquiry'. Earlier sociologists—for example, the Chicago school of Park and Burgess—had used ecological concepts like niche and community as metaphors to explain social life. Mukerjee's work marked a major advance, in that he made ecological processes a fundamental part of his explanatory framework (cf also Burch, 1987).

In a series of books and articles written in the interwar period, Mukerjee fleshed out his theory of 'social ecology'. The influence of the Scottish ecologist, Patrick Geddes, and the French historian, Lucien Febvre, is visible in his early explorations of the regional basis of social life (Mukerjee, 1926). At the same time, Mukerjee kept pace with the developing discipline of scientific ecology, and was personally acquainted with pioneers like the British animal ecologist, Elton. He drew fascinating parallels between ecological influences on the plant, animal, and human worlds respectively. While eschewing ecological determinism, he illumined the influence of the 'web of life' on human economic, political and social relations (Mukerjee, 1942). Finally, Mukerjee tested his theoretical ideas through empirical studies of different geographical regions. Several studies (e.g. Mukerjee, 1938) focussed on ecological and socio-economic renewal of the Indo-Gangetic Plain, while another dealt with the princely state of Gwalior, whose peasants were plagued by soil erosion and declining yields (Mukerjee, 1946).

The intellectual styles of Elwin and Mukerjee were very different. Never formally trained as an anthropologist, Elwin was mostly out of touch with theoretical developments. He was however a marvellously evocative writer. In contrast, Mukerjee's prose style is both unwieldly and wooden, but he was working towards an integration of ecology with the social sciences that was considerably ahead of its time. The selections from their writings in this Reader give only glimpses of their varied and rich ouevre, and an extended reappraisal of their work appears to be overdue.

THE READER

This collection of readings brings together what, in my judgement, are some of the more interesting essays written on the social ecology of India. In contrast to other Readers in this series, it deals with a field in the making, not an established subdiscipline of sociology. Consequently, the sectional themes—Nature and Culture, The

Sociology of Resource Use and Abuse, Social Conflicts over Nature, and Towards Social and Environmental Renewal—may also be seen as indicating the major directions in which social ecology in India is likely to move. Thus, the ecological diversity of India can facilitate a plentitude of studies on the interactions between nature and culture; ongoing processes of environmental degradation—which affect the lives of millions of Indians—can only be understood through detailed case studies of resource use and abuse; conflicts over nature are likely to intensify in coming decades; and debates on the origins, trajectory, and possible resolutions of our environmental dilemmas will certainly be of great significance in intellectual and public life.

The Reader also draws rather more freely on the writings of scholars outside the disciplines of sociology and social anthropology. Only two sociologists and four anthropologists are represented here. The other contributors include three economists, two environmentalists with an academic background in technology, two scientific ecologists, an energy scientist, and a historian.[8] The criterion for inclusion has been the relevance of the contribution to sociological reflection and research, not the formal disciplinary affiliation of the author. Readers of this volume might notice that in the sectional introductions I have refrained from making any critical remarks about the essays, choosing instead to highlight their key arguments and original contribution to the field. This is not because I believe the articles chosen by me are flawless. Rather, the newness of the field as a whole renders premature a final judgement on individual essays. In a few decades, when 'Social Ecology' might well be a firmly established sub-discipline of sociology, the contributions to this volume can be more fully assessed for both their strengths and weaknesses. At the present time, however, I have felt it more appropriate to recognize these essays as pioneering forays into previously uncharted terrain.

Lastly, I should explain the omission of three important themes. The first is trends in population, a variable central to much work in scientific ecology. With respect to the human world, too, it is undeniable that trends in population density, growth and collapse have profound social and ecological implications. Indeed, there has in

---

[8] Keeping in mind the critical remarks in Section I of this essay, I should note that Jodha, Kurien and Sengupta—the three economists represented here—are among the handful of Indian economists who have conducted extensive fieldwork, a methodological preference which undoubtedly contributes to their sensitivity to the ecological fabric of economic life.

recent decades been a strong revival of Malthusianism, wherein
unchecked population growth, rather than technology or social
structure, is regarded as the prime cause of environmental degradation. Although none of the essays in this volume directly address
the population question and/or its relationship to ecological change, a
forthcoming Reader in this series will focus specifically on demography.

This Reader also does not explore the transnational and global
ramifications of the environment debate. As the lively controversies
around the Earth Summit of June 1992 underlined, economic growth
in one part of the world can, by causing atmospheric change, powerfully affect environments in areas far distant. Of increasing importance too are environmental conflicts between countries sharing
common borders or physical environments, particularly mountains and water bodies. Meanwhile, on the ideological plane a
sharp North–South divide has emerged within the environmental
movement. These are all issues to figure high on our research agenda
in coming years.

A third theme touched on only tangentially here is social policy.
Some of the essays in Section II and III do contain brief discussions
of the policy implications of their research findings. Again, the
selections in Section IV are programmatic, in so far as they outline
the directions social and environmental renewal ought to take.
However, in keeping with this series' stress on basic research,
none of the essays chosen are explicitly policy oriented. Nevertheless, I believe that social anthropologists and sociologists can contribute significantly to policy research in the area of social ecology.
This could take the form of studies of specific natural resource sectors
(see Gadgil *et al.*, 1983; Sengupta, 1985; Chambers, *et al.*, 1989) or of
planning for environmental renewal in a particular cultural-geo-
graphic region. For, as our premier social ecologist (Mukerjee, 1938,
p. 304), once noted, 'applied human ecology is the only guarantee
of a permanent civilization'.[9]

---

[9] I am grateful to André Béteille, Esha Béteille and T. N. Madan for their comments on an earlier draft of this introduction.

REFERENCES

Bandyopadhyay, J., ed.,
1985   *India's Environment: Crisis and Response*, Natraj Publishers
            Dehra Dun.
Bardhan, P.,
1984   *The Political Economy of India's Development*, Oxford University
            Press, New Delhi.
Bottomore, T.,
1984   *Sociology and Socialism*, Harvester Books, Hempstead.
Brokensha, D. W.,
1987   Development Anthropology and Natural Resource Manage-
            ment , *L'Uomo: Societa Tradizione Sviluppo*, Vol. 11, No. 2,
            pp. 225–47.
Burch, W. R.,
1971   *Daydreams and Nightmares: A Sociological Essay on the
            American Environment*, Harper and Row, New York.

1987   *Human Ecology and Environmental Management*. Mimeo,
            School of Forestry and Environmental Studies, Yale
            University.
Buttel, F. H.,
1986   Sociology and the Environment: The Winding Road
            Towards Human Ecology , *International Social Science Journal*,
            no. 109, pp. 337–56.
Catton, W. R. and R. E. Dunlap,
1980   A New Ecological Paradigm for Post-Exuberant Sociology ,
            American Behavioral Scientist, Vol. 24, No. 1, pp. 15–45.
Chambers, R., N. C. Saxena and T. Shah,
1989   *To the Hands of the Poor: Water and Trees*, Oxford and IBH,
            New Delhi.
Conklin, H.,
1954 [1969] An Ethno-ecological Approach to Shifting Cultivation , in
            A. P. Vayda, ed., *Environment and Cultural Behavior*,
            Anchor Books, Garden City.
Cotgrove, S.,
1982   *Catastrophe or Cornucopia? The Environment, Politics and the
            Future*, John Wiley, Chichester.

CSE,
1982   *The State of India's Environment: A Citizens Report*, Centre for
                Science and Environment, New Delhi.

1985   *The State of India's Environment 1984–5: A Citizens Report*,
                Centre for Science and Environment, New Delhi.
Ehrenfels, U. R.,
1952   *The Kadars of Cochin*, University of Madras, Madras.
Elwin, V.,
1939   *The Baiga*, John Murray, London.

1942   *The Agaria*, Oxford University Press, Bombay.

1961   *A Philosophy for NEFA.* Shillong: Adviser to the Governor of
                Assam.
Field, D., and W. R. Burch,
1988   *Rural Sociology and the Environment*, Greenwood Press,
                New York.
Firey, W.,
1960   *Man, Mind and Land: A Theory of Resource Use*, Free Press,
                Glencoe.

1978   Sociological Contributions to the Study of Natural
                Resources, pp 162–74, in Manorama Barnabas, S. K. Hulbe
                and P. S. Jacob, eds, *The Challenge of Societies in Transition*,
                Macmillian, New Delhi.
Firth, R.,
1959   *Social Change in Tikopia*, George Allen and Unwin, London.
Gadgil, M., Prasad, S. N., and Rauf Ali,
1983   Forest Management and Forest Policy in India: A Critical
                Review , *Social Action*, Vol. 27, No. 2, pp 127–44.
Geertz, C.,
1963   *Agricultural Involution: The Process of Ecological Change in
                Indonesia*, University of California Press, Berkeley.
Guha, R.,
1992   Prehistory of Indian Environmentalism: Intellectual
                Traditions , *Economic and Political Weekly*, 4–11 January
Hardesty, D.,
1977   *Ecological Anthropology*, John Wiley, New York.
Hays, S. P.,
1987   *Beauty, Health and Permanence: Environmental Politics in the
                United States, 1955–85*, Cambridge University Press, New
                York.

Joshi, P. C.
1986   Founders of the Lucknow School and their Legacy,
                Economic and Politicial Weekly, 16th August.
Kumarappa, J. C.,
1931   *An Economic Survey of Matar Taluka*, Gujarat Vidyapeeth,
                Ahmedabad.

1938   *Why the Village Movement?* All India Village Industries
                Association, Wardha.

1945   *An Economy of Permanence*, All India Village Industries
                Association, Wardha.
Lowe, P. D., and Jane Goyder,
1983   *Environmental Groups and Politics*, George Allen and Unwin,
                London.
Lowe, P. D. and W. Rudig,
1987   Political Ecology and the Social Sciences—The State of the Art,
                British Journal of Political Science, Vol. 16, No. 4, pp 513– 50.
Mamkootam, K.,
1980   *Radhakamal Mukerjee's Contribution to 'Man and his Biosphere'*.
                Mimeo, Indian Council of Social Science Research, New
                Delhi.
Mukerjee, R. K.,
1926   *Regional Sociology*, Century Co., New York.

1938   *The Regional Balance of Man: An Ecological Theory of
                Population*, University of Madras, Madras.

1942   *Social Ecology*, Longmans, Green and Co., London

1946   *Planning the Countryside*, Hind Kitab, Bombay.
Nadkarni, M. V.,
1987   Agricultural Development and Ecology: An Economist's
                View, *Indian Journal of Agricultural Economics*, Vol. 42, No.
                3, pp 359–75.
Orlove, B.,
1980   Ecological   Anthropology,   *Annual   Review   of
                Anthropology*,Vol. 9, pp 235–73.
Rambo, A. T.,
1985   *Conceptual Approaches to Human Ecology*, East-West
                Institute, Honolulu.
Roy, S. C.,
1925   *The Birhors*, GEL Mission Press, Ranchi.

18 *References*

Sengupta, N.,
1985   Irrigation: Traditional versus Modern , *Economic and Political Weekly*, Special Number, August.

Singh, N.,
1976   *Economics and the Crisis of Ecology*, Oxford University Press, New Delhi.

Von Furer Haimendorf, C.,
1943a   *The Chenchus: Jungle Folk of the Deccan*, Macmillian, London.

1943b   *The Reddis of the Bison Hills; A Study in Acculturation*, Macmillian, London.

Weiskel, T. C.,
1983   Rubbish and Racism: Problems of Boundary in an Ecosystem , *Yale Review*, Winter, pp 225–44.

Williams, R.,
1973   *The Country and the City*, Oxford University Press, New York.

1

Nature and Culture

As pointed out in the introduction, the dominant strands in social science research have been largely indifferent to natural processes. Disciplinary traditions have been reinforced by the conditions of urban life to which social scientists are accustomed, wherein society's dependence on nature is not so readily apparent as in the village or the forest. Not surprisingly, it is to these latter contexts that three of the selections in this section pertain.

We begin, however, with a methodological statement. Perhaps the most notable aspect of Mukerjee's essay is its date of publication—1930, or decades before ecological degradation and the modern environmental movement had helped make sociologists more aware of human-nature interactions. Impressive too is the range of authorities he cites, including geographers, ecologists, town planners and anthropologists. Mukerjee emphasizes that the relationship between nature and culture is both interactive and dynamic, with humans trying to mould the environment to their own ends but

always having to work within the limits set by nature. As he per-
ceptively notes, in their economic activities humans exterminate
many existing plant and animal species even as they introduce new
species from outside the region. Sometimes human intervention
is successful in establishing a new and stable balance between
society and nature; on other occasions, it is itself the cause of ecological decline.

While Mukerjee's essay is reflective and theoretical, our second
selection combines theory with empirical research. In accounting
for the persistence over several thousand years of the Indian caste
system, scholars have principally favoured one of two competing
explanations; some arguing that its basis lies in the close connection between caste and class (with upper castes controlling land
and other productive assets), others that caste has endured because
its ideology is widely accepted by those at the bottom of the social
hierarchy. In their essay, Gadgil and Malhotra propose an alternate,
ecological explanation for the stability of the caste system. Based
on field data from peninsular India, they show how different endogamous groups or *jatis* living in the same region had so organized
their use of natural resources as to minimize inter-caste competition.
Devices of resource partition and territorial exclusion ensured that
individual *jatis*, and often individual families or lineages within them,
had a monopoly over a specific resource in a particular territory.
The authors argue that these practices promoted the sustainable use
of natural resources (what they term 'prudence') thereby facilitating
the long term persistence of caste.

Where the focus of Gadgil and Malhotra's contribution is on purposive human action upon nature, Joan Mencher, in a fascinating
comparison between Kerala and Madras, is concerned more with
the influence of the ecological setting on social structure. Her essay
exemplifies the sensitivity to the ecological context in the best traditions of anthropology. With a heavy monsoon and high water
table, Kerala is abundant in water: by contrast, the relative scarcity
of water in the Tamil country has meant that agriculture has to rely
heavily on tank and canal irrigation, activities requiring a high
degree of co-operative labour and community organization. Where
in Kerala, settlements are characteristically dispersed, Madras con-
forms more to the pan-Indian pattern of consolidated villages with a
strong sense of unity. Mencher also innovatively uses differences
in the two regions' natural endowments to explore variations in

authority relations, caste practices, and forms of transportation. Our next selection takes us into the realm of the sacred. In a famous article entitled 'The Historical Roots of our Ecologic Crisis', first published a quarter of a century ago, Lynn White had claimed that the Judeo-Christian ethos, unlike Eastern religious traditions, was deeply inimical to nature worship. His thesis finds indirect confirmation in the Gadgil-Vartak essay, a study, set in Maharashtra, of a phenomenon that is, or was, in fact widespread throughout the subcontinent. The authors believe that sacred groves, mostly dedicated to mother goddess cults and preserved through strict taboos on the removal of wood, very likely originated in the hunting and gathering stage. The interpenetration of nature and culture are also finely illustrated in Michael Dove's essay, which concludes this section. In response to a celebrated book by the Sanskritist Francis Zimmerman, Dove clarifies the meanings of the terms 'jangal' and 'jangala' with reference to his own fieldwork in Pakistan. This essay nicely blends anthropological and historical approaches, textual and contextual analysis, in studying the dynamics of human interactions with nature over the long term.

Where many social scientists work under the assumption that social facts need to be explained with reference to other social facts, our selections here underscore the interpenetration of nature and culture. Given the ecological and cultural diversity of India, there is vast scope for studies of the reciprocal relations of the natural environment and human economic, social and religious life. At the same time, we must be careful to eschew environmental determinism—for as Mencher points out, variations in social structure cannot be explained by ecological factors *alone*.

An Ecological Approach to Sociology

RADHAKAMAL MUKERJEE

Ecological methods can be applied to many branches of sociology. They have been employed successfully, for instance, in the study of social evolution and adaptation. The works of the anthropogeographers, Ratzel and Vidal de la Blache, had contributed to promote among various subsequent writers the regional, or what has now expanded into the ecological outlook. The intensive methodical surveys of the Le Play school, in particular in France, clearly emphasize the importance of the physical environment in its relation to society, and especially in its effects upon occupation and family life. In the same country both Brunhes and his associate, Vallaux, have studied the physical landscape in so far as it has influenced human destinies, and also its exploitation or deformation as the measure of the power of human societies. Their influence has extended much beyond their country in eliciting meticulous local and regional studies. The German school, exemplified by Schlüter, Michotte and others, has stressed what has been called the anatomy and physiology of spaces and landscapes with a view to show the development of the cultural out of the natural landscape. Professor Patrick Geddes and his school, working both in Great Britain and recently in France, are not only using the regional survey method as a comprehensive tool of social study in definite regions and cities, but also have evolved a single, mathematical schema for presentation and co-ordination of their data. In America, Huntington has studied particularly the effects of the climatic factors on the distribution of human energy and the opportunities and limitations of civilization in different environments. The culture

Excerpted from Radhakamal Mukerjee, 'Ecological Contributions to Sociology', *The Sociological Review*, Vol. XXII, No. 4, October 1930.

area concept in the hands of Wissler, Kroeber and Herskovits, though onfined to anthropological data, also has influenced sociology notably through the writings of Willey. Through all this development of social theory, the ecological approach is gradually assuming significance. The conception that man and the region are not separate but mutually inter-dependent entities, plastic, fluent, growing has been emphasized in my *Regional Sociology*. It outlines a programme in which the region and the web of life within it are made the subject of a new division of Sociology. Man's mastery of his region consists not in a one-sided exploitation but in a mutual give and take, which alone can keep alive the never-ending cycle of the region's life processes. The region also is not a passive entity but a living organism which exhibits the harmonious working of different living systems such as the vegetable, the animal and the human worlds. These mutually influence one another establishing some kind of balance. Ecology, the science of the balance of species, the comprehensive physiology of life in all its forms, not only throws light on social origins but also gives the clue to an understanding of the regional balance of population. . . .

There is a balance between the natural and the vegetable and the animal environment, including the human, in which nature delights. It is maintained by chains of actions and interactions, which link man with the rest of his living realm, reaching up and down and all around as his invisible biological and social destiny. Such a balance assumes great significance in old countries like India and China. Here we can discern, especially in the mature, densely-peopled plains, every stage of the process by which the regional balance is kept stable and how it is upset both by natural fluctuations such as are caused by cycles of rainfall or changes of landscape and river, or by long continued human actions such as the destruction of forests, non-conservative agriculture, and artificial interference with natural drainage, . . .

Plant and animal ecology has shown the adaptation of plant and animal associations to the region, and also to one another. Says an ecologist,

The animals and plants of a region form a vast complex in which every organism affects every other directly or indirectly, and is in turn affected by all the others. Furthermore, all the organisms are influenced by their environment, and in turn affect the character of the environment. All the organisms are bound up with one another in an intricate network of interactions which the mind can only partially comprehend.'[1]

An important section of plant and animal ecology deals with the disturbances which human and animal populations bring about in the natural ordering of the array of different plants and animals formed in a given region at a particular time. Thus the ecological succession of plant and animal communities, and the interplay of the forces of the region and the animals and plants as well as of the biotic factors responsible for their development or retrogression have now come to the forefront.[2] In wild nature an abundance of rabbits leads in many parts of Europe[3] to the supersession of pine trees by heather and of heather by scrubby rushes, and of rushes by a mere carpet of grass. In the new world a heavy pressure from the small rodents as well as prairie dogs or kangaroo-rats when they form large colonies leads to the retrogression of vegetation and the initiation of secondary series. Similarly overgrazing and trampling by man's domestic stocks result in the complete destruction of the vegetable cover and the appearance of perennial or seasonal weeds in the river-plains of India. Man, by burning the forests and clearing the ground for farming, sets up a train of primary or secondary sequences in which an entire series of plant species and communities are implicated.

A notable instance of such complex sequences is found in the effect of man upon predatory animals. As population increases, and the frontiers of cultivation extend, the carnivores are ruthlessly exterminated. One result is that the rodent population enormously expands with a corresponding decrease in the yield of grazing range or cultivated field. As Weaver and Clements observe: 'the destruction of predatory animals which appears to be a simple and beneficial interference, tends to defeat in some measure the very purpose it was designed to promote—the greater production of cattle and sheep.' Normally the region which exhibits a definite sequence of the succession of plant and animal communities thus undergoes transformation.

Man by brand tillage, forest clearing, indiscriminate stock-grazing, and intensive farming alters the conditions of the environment to such an extent that a large number of plants and animals fail to

[1] J. W. Folsom: *Entomology with special reference to its ecological aspects*, p. 379.

[2] See, for instance, Tansley and Chipp: *Aims and Methods in the Study of Vegetation*; McDougall: *Plant Ecology*, and Ritchie: *The Influence of Man on Animal Life in Scotland*.'

[3] Richards: Studies on the Ecology of English Heaths, *Journal of Ecology*, Vol. 14.

survive this onslaught. He has, again, artificially improved and fitted plants to survive particular conditions of climate and soil and imported exotic varieties from similar regions, thus continually improving the yield of his cereals and extending the frontiers of cultivation. The plants which he does not tolerate are called weeds. These are ruthlessly exterminated and some of them have become man's pauperized dependents. Many weeds again, are imported from outside as a result of man's carelessness. It has been estimated that more than half the weeds in America have been imported from .Europe by the continual shipment of agricultural and horticultural products. A few prickly pears introduced into Eastern Australia, and water hyacinths into the delta of Eastern Bengal—both as botanical curiosities—have now covered thousands of miles and become a serious menace to agriculture, and communications. The intentional or unintentional introduction of exotic plants and domestic animals profoundly affects the flora and fauna of the region. A new plant and animal association is established, but it will be harmonious if the time that elapses is adequate for the working out of the forces of bio-economic equilibrium. Sir J. Arthur Thomson quotes the observation that in the mountains and forests of Central Europe every spot that has been used as a human abode can be identified by the plants that grow there and the animals that visit them, long after every trace of man's habitation and handiwork has disappeared. A large number of animals, some enemies, some allies, have been either entirely decimated or greatly reduced in numbers. On the other hand, in the broken balance of nature man creates more favourable conditions for certain species of animals than wild nature provides. Thus, in his cultivated fields, notably in areas where one particular crop like cotton, wheat or potato is grown over a vast expanse, man has nurtured through the supply of unlimited food, hordes of insect pests, parasites and fungi which it is difficult and often impossible for him to exterminate. . . .

The study of the so-called biotic and especially human interferences in ecologic succession has thus gradually been supplemented by the recognition of the harmful effects of man's unskilful and improvident interference with his organic milieu on his food-supply, health and living conditions. Elton is right in his criticism that human ecology has been concerned almost entirely with biotic factors, with the effects of man upon man, disregarding often enough the trees and animals, land and water. Owing to the fact that most workers in this subject are themselves biotic factors, an undue prominence has been given in history and economics to these purely human influences. The ecology of population will not only stress the importance of the intimate ecologic inter-relations of man, so grudgingly recognized by him, but in its applied aspects also demand his close alliance with the entire range of ecologic forces. It will highlight the need for his co-operation in the conservation of the land, in the use of water, in the management of forests and rivers, or in the domestication and use of his livestock and the control of insects, bacteria and parasites. A disregard of such co-operation, which is at once nature's law and wisdom, would spell man's social disaster. . .

Human, animal and plant communities are subject to similar rules, though shifting ones, which maintain a balance and rhythm of growth for all. Each community cannot appropriate more than its due place in the general ordering of life, from which nothing can be obtained without influencing everything else. Working symbiotically, they represent inter-woven threads of a complex web of life. No one thread can be isolated. None can be snapped or removed without the whole garment of the life of nature and human society being disfigured. The warp and the woof of the garment have become increasingly coherent as organic evolution has advanced. The inter-linkages of a fig-tree, an earth-worm, a rat and a bird are many, but the threads make much more intricate patterns as we reach the social economy of man. Though man often tears asunder the fabric through ignorance or selfishness, social progress no doubt consists in consciously weaving the forces of nature and society into finer and finer patterns of correlation and solidarity. It is the knowledge of and respect for the intricacy of the web of life which will guide man to his highest destiny.

The Ecological Significance of Caste

M. GADGIL AND K. C. MALHOTRA

1. INTRODUCTION

The Indian caste system has always fascinated students of human society. Their investigations have, however, hardly touched on the ecological implications of the system, being largely focused on the origin and development of castes, the social interrelationships amongst the various castes, and the impact of modernization on this institution (Dube 1955, Marriot 1960, Ghurye 1961, Karve 1961, Srinivas 1962, Bose 1967, Sinha 1967, Dumont 1970). In this paper we will explore the caste system from an ecological perspective, drawing on our own fieldwork in western Maharashtra. With its reproductive isolation and hereditary mode of subsistence, a caste population can be considered an analogue of a biological species and assigned an ecological niche (Hardesty 1972, Hardesty 1975). We will document that castes more directly dependent on natural resources had so organized their mode of subsistence as to avoid excessive overlap with other castes in their demands for various resources. Further, intracaste territoriality regulated competition among the lineages within a caste. We believe that this monopoly of lineages over particular resources in a given locality favoured the cultural evolution of social restraints on resource utilization, leading to their sustainable use. This was probably an important factor contributing to the stability of the caste system over the past several thousand years. We conclude by examining the implications for the caste system of the collapse of its natural resource base over the last couple of centuries.

Excerpted from M. Gadgil and K. C. Malhotra, 'Adaptive Significance of the Indian Caste System: An Ecological Perspective', *Annals of Human Biology*, 1983, Vol. 10, No. 5.

2. MATERIAL AND METHODS

The fieldwork reported here pertains to the western half of the state of Maharashtra in peninsular India. The state has an undulating coastal strip varying from 50 to 80 km wide, flanked by the hill chain of Western Ghats which rises abruptly to an altitude of between 1000 and 1500 m. The 15–20 km wide crestline of the Ghats is a region of heavy rainfall, in excess of 3000 mm a year. The society in this tract of low but stable agricultural and pastoral productivity is simple and made up of a few sedentary castes of cultivators, pastoralists and hunter-gatherers. Two of these, Gavlis and Kunbis, will concern us further (Table 1). The Western Ghats merge through a series of broken hills with the Deccan plateau at an elevation of 500 m. The annual rainfall in this tract decreases from 3000 mm

Table 1

Population size, language and traditional occupation of the seven castes under consideration.

Caste	Estimated population	Mother tongue	Distribution in Maharashtra (districts)	Traditional primary occupation
Kunbi	500 000	Marathi	Almost all districts	Agriculture
Gavli	100 000	Marathi	Kolaba, Kolhapur, Pune, Ratangiri, Sangli, Satara	Buffalo-keeping
Hatkar	573 000	Marathi	Ahmednagar, Akola, Amravati, Aurangabad, Bhir, Buldhana, Dhulia, Jalgaon, Kolhapur, Nasik, Nanded, Osmanabad, Parbhani, Pune, Sangli, Satara, Sholapur, Wardha, Yeotmal	Sheep-keeping
Tirumal Nandiwallas	3 000	Telugu	Pune	Bull-performance
Fulmali Nandiwallas	5 000	Telugu	Ahmednagar, Aurangabad, Bhir, Nasik	Bull-performance
Vaidus	1000 000	Telugu	Ahmednagar, Aurangabad, Pune	Indigenous medicine-men
Phasepardhis	150 000	Marathi	Ahmednagar, Aurangabad, Bhir, Kolhapur, Pune, Satara	Hunter-gatherers

at the crestline to 1500–1000 mm at the edge of the plateau. This tract provides productive agriculture with most of the land under cultivation. This region harbours a complex rural society with a number of artisan and service castes and has been the subject of two classic monographs in Marathi (Atre 1915, Chapekar 1933). The precipitation decreases further as one proceeds eastwards on the Deccan plateau, being less than 600 mm in a semi-arid tract of 100–150 km width. The agriculture in this region is really productive only in the river valleys. The large tracts of uncultivated land away from the valleys support pastoralism as well as hunting-gathering. The availability of uncultivated land, as well as the favourable nature of the terrain for sedentary existence during the four months of the monsoon rains, has favoured the establishment of the base villages of a number of pastoral as well as non-pastoral nomadic castes in this semi-arid tract. These nomadic castes operate in the higher rainfall tracts, both to the east and west of this semi-arid region, in the eight dry months of the year (Malhotra 1974). Five castes of interest to us, namely Hatkars, Tirumal and Fulmali Nandiwallas, Vaidus and Phasepardhis, have their base villages in this semi-arid region.

The information reported has been collected as a part of five different projects over a 12-year period from 1969 to 1980. For details, reference may be made to Malhotra (1974, 1979 a, b), Malhotra and Gadgil (1981), Gadgil and Malhotra (1982) and Khomne, Malhotra and Gadgil (1983).

3. Organization of the Indian Caste Society

Indian society is even today an agglomeration of numerous castes, tribes and religious communities. The tribal and caste groups are endogamous, reproductively isolated populations traditionally distributed over a restricted geographical range. The different caste populations, unlike tribes, have extensive geographical over-lap and members of several castes generally constitute a village. In a typical village, each caste, traditionally self-regulated by a caste council, used to lead a relatively autonomous existence. Each caste tended to pursue a hereditarily prescribed occupation; this was particularly true of the artisan and service castes and the pastoral and nomadic castes. The several castes were linked to each other through a traditionally determined pattern of barter of services and produce (Ghurye 1961, Karve 1961). These caste groups retained their identity even after conversion to Islam or Christianity. Each of the caste groups was thus the unit within which cultural evolution occurred, at least for the last 1500 years, when the system was fully crystallized and probably for much longer. Over this period the various castes had come to exhibit striking differences in cultural traits like skills possessed, food habits, dress, language, religious observances, as well as in a number of genetic traits (Sanghvi and Khanolkar 1950, Karve and Malhotra 1968, Malhotra, Chakraborty and Chakarvarthi 1977, Sanghvi 1978, Malhotra 1978, Chakraborty and Malhotra 1981).

One may then view the Indian society as being analogous to a biological community made up of a number of 'cultural species' or endogamous caste groups. These may be thought of as being organized in three trophic levels. The lowest trophic level is made up by cultivators, pastorals and hunter-gatherers directly dependent on land and its biological resources. In the second trophic level may be included artisans, entertainers and traders dependent on the populations of the first trophic level in a mutualistic fashion. In the third trophic level may be included military and priestly castes dependent on the two other trophic levels in a parasitic fashion. The trophic organization of a typical village in western Maharashtra may be illustrated by that of Badlapur (Chapekar 1933). In 1931, the village had a population of 1416 persons divided among twenty five caste groups with a minimum of five, a maximum of 214 and a median of fortyseven individuals per caste. The five cultivator castes made up a third of this population, eight artisan castes (carpenter, potter, leather-worker etc.) and five service castes (barber, washerman, village guard etc.) made up another third, and two castes of hunter-gatherers (who were largely farm labourers by 1931) and two castes of priests (who were largely landlords by 1931) the rest. In addition, such a village was visited by a number of nomadic castes. Atre (1915) lists thirty five such castes amongst which fourteen performed a religious function, twelve entertainment, four trade, four fabrication of tools etc, and one dispensation of medicine. Other hunter-gatherer castes, such as Phasepardhis that did not have an intimate relationship with the settled society, also used the tracts outside the village boundary.

In such a caste society, the cultivator castes may be said to occupy identical niches, but coexist through intra- and inter-caste territoriality in the form of ownership of cultivated land. The artisan and service castes dependent on them had diversified their niches in terms of their occupation, so that there were members of only one caste each of carpenter, potter, barber etc. in any given village. Furthermore, they regulated intracaste competition through the device of each household of an artisan/service caste having the exclusive right of dealing with a specific group of cultivator and other caste households. It is, however, the pastoralists and nomads that provide the most interesting examples of niche diversification, and the rest of the paper will be largely concerned with these castes.

4. Resource Partitioning

The relatively simple society of the high-rainfall tracts near the crest of the Western Ghats is largely made up of small, often single-clan settlements of Kunbis and Gavlis. Here the Kunbis lived (and still do) in the lower valleys, while the Gavlis lived (and still do) on the upper hill terraces. The major occupation of Gavlis was keeping large herds of buffaloes and cattle. They used to curdle the milk, consuming buttermilk at home and bartering the butter for cereal grains, produced by Kunbis, and other necessities. The protein requirements of the Gavlis were met from the buttermilk and they did almost no hunting. The Gavlis also practised some shifting cultivation on the upper hill terraces. The Kunbis on the other hand practised paddy cultivation in the river valleys and shifting cultivation on the lower hill slopes. They kept only a few cattle for draught purposes which produced very little milk. To meet their protein requirements the Kunbis hunted a great deal. Thus, the cultivation of valleys and lower hill slopes was restricted to Kunbis and that of hill terraces to Gavlis; maintenance of livestock and use of fodder and grazing resources was largely with Gavlis, while Kunbis had the monopoly of hunting wild animals (Gadgil and Malhotra 1982).

Another efficient instance of resource partitioning is provided by the hunting practices of the ecological guild (in the sense of Root (1967)) of three non-pastoral nomadic castes of Tirumal Nandiwallas, Vaidus and Phasepardhis. Between themselves these three castes used to do most of the hunting in the uncultivated tracts away from villages in the semi-arid region of western Maharashtra. The Phasepardhis were primarily hunter-gatherers, bartering some of the game for other goods. The Tirumal Nandiwallas and Vaidus had other primary occupations such as performance of bull play, dispensing herbal medicines, selling trinkets, midwifery etc., but hunted extensively for their own consumption.

We initiated an investigation of the hunting practices of these three castes with the presumption that they hunted much the same animals in the same tract. However, our investigations showed that the three groups differed markedly in the hunting techniques used. The Tirumal Nandiwallas specialized in hunting with dogs, the average number of dogs per household being five. These dogs were used in locating, chasing and killing much of their prey which predominantly included hyena, leopard cat, wild pig, hare and porcupine. The Vaidus kept a smaller number of dogs, an average of 1.5 per household. By contrast, they specialized in catching smaller carnivores like mongoose, toddy cat and domestic cat in traps baited often with squirrels. They also specialized in catching freshwater animals such as crabs, turtles and crocodiles in the past (Avchat 1981). The Phasepardhis never used dogs, but instead used a trained cow to enter a herd of blackbuck or deer, laying snares as they moved hiding behind the cow. They also used to snare birds, particularly partridges, quails and peafowl, on a large scale.

Table 2 provides the present-day estimates of the relative importance of different prey species for the three castes (Khomne *et al*, 1983). Admittedly, the exact quantitative estimates in this table are not to be taken literally, since our samples are small (2, 3 and 36 households for the three castes) and the abundance of prey has drastically declined in recent years. Nevertheless, the differences reflected in this table are very real, being based on the employment of very distinctive hunting techniques. What is striking is that while the hunting techniques employed do differ significantly none of them is so sophisticated as to preclude their adoption by another caste. Thus the Phasepardhis could have easily added the Vaidus' baited traps to their own snares. The fact that they do not do so points to a genuine cultural adjustment to reduce competition with other castes hunting in the same region.

This region had an ecological guild of four castes each concerned with displaying some domesticated animal to the villagers for entertainment or religious purposes, and an overlapping guild of two castes weaving and selling baskets. It is notable that they all used different species for these purposes. Thus, of the four castes displaying animals, the Darweshis used the tiger or the sloth bear, Nandiwallas the bull, Garodis the cobra and other species of snakes, and Makadwallas the bonnet macaque (Atre 1915). The Makadwallas also weaved baskets, exclusively employing leaves of the Palmyra

Table 2

Relative dependence in terms of percentage of reported biomass consumed of the different prey species by the three nomadic castes.

	Hunted animal species	Tirumal Nandiwallas	Vaidu	Phase-pardhis
I.	Small carnivorous mammals (e.g. toddy cat, mongoose)	8.94	41.09	0.28
II.	Large carnivorous mammals (e.g. leopard cat, hyena, fox)	24.99	7.86	0.07
III.	Small herbivorous mammals (e.g. hare, porcupine)	15.53	5.14	0.01
IV.	Blackbuck	1.19	0	70.43
V.	Wild pig	29.85	4.14	14.67
VI.	Birds (e.g. doves, quails, partridges, peafowl)	2.09	3.59	14.21
VII.	Monitor lizard	1.49	12.43	0.24
VIII.	Aquatic animals (e.g. fish, crab, turtle)	15.92	25.75	0

palm, while another basketweaving community, the Kaikadis, exclusively utilized the bamboos (Mane 1981).

5. COMPETITIVE EXCLUSION

We therefore have a number of instances of sympatric castes, i.e. castes which overlap in their geographical distribution diversifying their niches by specializing on different resources. The cultivator castes which otherwise occupy identical niches and have a broad geographical overlap managed to coexist by competitively excluding each other from particular pieces of land through land ownership. However, pastoral and nomadic castes which do not own land are not expected to tolerate geographical overlap with another caste identical in its ways of subsistence. An equivalent of Gause's principle of competitive exclusion, namely, that no two castes occupying identical ecological niches can coexist in a sympatric fashion, appears to hold.

The operation of this principle is nicely illustrated by two castes of Nandiwallas which had and largely continue to have an identical mode of subsistence. These two castes, Tirumal Nandiwallas and

Fulmali Nandiwallas, are both non-pastoral nomads, making a living by the display of the sacred bull, by selling trinkets and by hunting. They both originated from a common ancestral stock in Andhra Pradesh. The Tirumal Nandiwallas migrated into Maharashtra about 800 years ago, while the Fulmali Nandiwallas did so only 300 years ago. While they have developed complete reproductive isolation, their way of making a living and their culture has remained essentially identical (Malhotra, 1974, Malhotra and Khomne 1978). They thus exemplify castes with completely identical ecological niches.

It is, therefore, notable that Tirumal Nandiwallas and Fulmali Nandiwallas show no geographical overlap whatsoever. The base village of Tirumal Nandiwallas is Wadapuri in Pune district, while the 39 base villages of Fulmali Nandiwallas are distributed over the districts of Ahmednagar, Bhir, Aurangabad and Nasik (Malhotra, Hulbe, Khomne and Kolte 1983). Both these Nandiwalla castes used to and still largely do spend the rainy season in their base camps and then spread out over a dry-season territory to visit villages to display the bull and sell trinkets. There was and even today is a complete absence of overlap in the dry season migratory range of the two Nandiwalla castes.

6. INTRACASTE TERRITORIALITY

Different caste populations traditionally moderated or largely removed intercaste competition for limiting resources through diversification in resource use or territorial exclusion. It was noted above that sedentary artisan or service castes further moderated competition within the caste by assigning to individual households exclusive rights of dealing with specific households of other castes, while the cultivator castes did so by land ownership. The nomadic-pastoral as well as non-pastoral castes achieved this moderation of intracaste competition by assigning exclusive rights to move over certain territory to individual households.

Our first illustration of intracaste territoriality pertains to non-pastoral nomads. Every family of Tirumal Nandiwallas had and even today has an exclusive right to visit certain villages, respected by all other families of their caste, with heavy punishment levied by the caste council for any transgression of this convention. The rights are heritable and may be sold, but only to another family of the same clan within the caste (Malhotra 1974). The Fulmali Nandiwallas have a similar, if less well defined system.

Another instance of this phenomenon is provided by the pastoral-nomadic caste of Hatkars. About 18 per cent of the half-a-million total population of this caste still practises nomadic sheep-keeping, although the rest have taken to cultivation over the last few centuries (Malhotra 1982). These shepherds spend the rainy season in their base villages in the semi-arid tract and move over a wide territory during the eight months of the dry season to graze their flocks. The total caste population is divided into a number of groups of families, each of which has the exclusive privilege of grazing over a certain defined territory. This pattern is illustrated by the village of Dhawalpuri in Ahmednagar district. This village comprises four different settlements within a kilometre of each other. While setting out on the migration after the rains, each settlement leaves as a single band moving in a traditionally pre-determined direction. As the band moves, it continues to split along kinship lines into progressively smaller groups each moving in its own specific direction, till the group of families constituting the ultimate unit of the flock reaches its own territory. This composite territory of the small group of families is hereditarily handed down from generation to generation and may be encroached upon only with special permission in times of serious distress by other shepherd families.

7. PRUDENT PREDATORS

We have thus documented that castes within Indian society, particularly the pastoralists and nomads which directly depended on natural plant and animal resources, developed specific ways of utilizing these resources and which, coupled with territoriality, ensured that a particular limiting resource in a particular geographical region was more or less exclusively utilized by a particular lineage. The lineage would be aware that the resource had supported it for generations past and will have to continue to support it for generations to come. While we hope to return at a later date to the fascinating question of how these cultural practices must have evolved in the light of modern ecological theories as well as theories of cultural evolution (Roughgarden 1978, Wilson 1980, Cavalli-Sforza and

Feldman 1981, Lumsden and Wilson 1981), we would like to explore one significant consequence of these practices now.

The result of these practices would be to promote the evolution of cultural traditions of prudent exploitation of the natural resources. While exercising such prudence, any human lineage would be sacrificing some immediate use of the resource. It can be expected to do so only if it is assured of even greater benefit from the higher resource levels at a later date. For the system to operate the following conditions need be met:

(a) Some other lineage should not usurp the resource when it becomes available at a higher level at a later time.

(b) The resource should continue to be of value to the lineage adopting prudence.

Thus, a lineage should not shift to the use of some entirely different set of resources within a geographical region, or to some entirely different geographical region when the resource becomes available at a higher level at a later date.

The mode of resource utilization evolved by the Indian society clearly fulfils these conditions. We, therefore, expect the evolution of a number of cultural practices resulting in a sustainable use of natural resources by the caste groups which constitute not only the genetic but also the cultural units of the Indian society. Many such instances have been recorded, and we came across further evidence of these during the course of our own investigations. Thus the Phasepardhis reported that traditionally they did not kill a pregnant doe or a fawn caught in their snares, but let it loose. The same Phasepardhi lineage would of course be hunting the same blackbuck populations at a later time and would benefit from such prudence.

India, even today, abounds in examples of such traditions of prudence. In the Yamuna valley just upstream from Mussoorie the villagers poison the river with a drug derived from a herb just once a year at the time of a festival. All the fish killed by poisoning are then consumed in a communal feast to the accompaniment of barley wine. The fish may be caught at other times of the year but only with nets; anybody poisoning the river at any other time is socially outcast. The Dheevar caste of Bhandara district of Maharashtra never catch fish going upstream on spawning migration, although they are exhausted and easy to catch. There are entire sacred groves and ponds in which no plant or animal is damaged. Some species of plants and animals survive today only in such protected localities. Monkeys, peafowl, the banyan and other fig trees, and a variety of other plants and animals are regarded as sacred and protected widely over India. A detailed review of such practices is given in Gadgil (1983).

We therefore suggest that this organization of Indian society must have promoted prudent and sustainable use of natural resources, at least by the castes directly dependent on these resources. The consequent expected stability of the resource base, and the attendant moderation of competition amongst the different caste groups which were linked in a complementary fashion must have been a significant factor contributing to the stability of Indian society. . . .

8. IMPACT OF MODERNIZATION

The advent of British rule heralded the disorganization of this sytem. The British imposed much higher levels of demands on natural resources of the country to furnish the raw material for their economy. To avoid having to pay for the exploitation of these resources they took over as Government property vast resources which, until then, were owned communally. These resources were then rapidly depleted through commercial exploitation, a trend that has accelerated over the last three decades since independence. This had led to considerable impoverishment, and often complete collapse of the natural resource base sustaining many components of the Indian society.

Along with this collapse of the resource base, the replacement of old systems of barter by money economy has destroyed the traditional relationships amongst the various castes in the Indian society. The result of these two has not been a collapse of the caste system itself. Far from this being the case, restriction of marriages and limitation of the recognition of social responsibility within the caste group continues unchanged throughout rural India which makes up nearly 80 per cent of our population (Srinivas 1962). The persistence of the caste system, with a loss of its traditional complementarity has, therefore, led to an increasing level of conflict amongst different castes. We will end this paper with two illustrations of this phenomenon for the castes discussed above.

Traditionally, the Gavlis were pastoralists practising little shifting

cultivation on the upper hill terraces, while the Kunbis were cultivators maintaining very few animals in the valleys. The deforestation and consequent soil erosion in recent years have destroyed the
fodder base of Gavli animals who have been forced to reduce their
animal holdings and take increasingly to cultivation of more and
more hill slopes. Many Kunbis too have lost their fertile paddy fields
to river-valley projects and have been pushed up the hills. Their
prey has also dwindled with deforestation. At the same time, urban
milk schemes have created a market for milk. Consequently, the
Kunbis have also taken to keeping milch animals, and are no longer
willing to let Gavli animals graze in their fields after harvest. All of
this has led to serious conflicts between Kunbis and Gavlis, often
forcing the numerically weaker Gavlis to abandon their traditional
occupation and locality and migrate to city slums; some 10,000 Gavlis
have migrated to Bombay and are working as unskilled workers, and
some 8000 have moved to cities like Kolhapur, Satara and Pune
(Malhotra and Gadgil 1982).

The second example relates to Phasepardhis. This hunting-
gathering tribe generally stayed aloof from the settled villages, but
were sometimes employed by farmers to snare the blackbuck, deer
and other mammals raiding their fields. Even earlier, the Phasepardhis probably used to steal opportunistically. Recent decades have
witnessed mass destruction of their main prey, the blackbuck, and
declaration of all hunting by Phasepardhis as illegal. With this
loss of subsistence, they have taken increasingly to stealing. In
consequence, they now live in a very tense relationship with the
settled community.

The recent destruction of the ecological resource base has, therefore, rendered the once possibly highly adaptive organization of
the caste society largely maladaptive. In fact, it has now become an
impediment in coming to terms with new modes of resource utilization to which our society must adapt. But nurtured as it is by a
long history of what we believe to have been a successful ecological
adaptation, it is a very difficult task indeed to break out of the hold
of this now maladaptive system.

REFERENCES

Atre, T. N.,
1915   *Gaon-Gada—Notes on Rural Sociology and Village Problems*,
            Mote Publishers, Bombay (in Marathi).
Avchat, A.,
1981   *Manase*, Granthali Publishers, Pune (in Marathi).
Bose, N. K.,
1967   *Culture and Society in India*, Asia Publishing House, Bombay.
Cavalli-Saforza, L. L., and Feldman, M.,
1981   *Cultural Transmission and Evolution: A Quantitative Approach*,
            Princeton University Press, Princeton, New Jersey.
Chakaraborty, R., and Malhotra, K. C.,
1981   Dermatoglyphics and Genetic Distance: A Comparative
            Study of Variability between Populations, *Journal of the Indian
            Anthropological Society*, 16, 261–9.
Chapekar, N. G.,
1933   *Badlapur*, Aryasanskriti Publishers, Pune (in Marathi).
Dube, S. C.,
1955   *Indian Village*, Cornell University Press, Ithaca.
Dumont, L.,
1970   *Homo Hierarchicus: The Caste System and its Implications*,
            translated by M. Sainsbury, Weidenfeld and Nicolson,
            London.
Gadgil, M.,
1983   Social Constraints on Resource Utilization: the Indian
            Experience, in *Culture and Conservation* (edited by D. Pitts),
            I. U. C. N., Gland, Switzerland.
Gadgil, M., and Malhotra, K. C.,
1982   Ecology of a Pastoral Caste: the Gavli Dhangars of Peninsular
            India, *Human Ecology*, 10, 107–43
Ghurye, G. S.,
1961   *Caste, Class and Occupation*, Popular Book Depot, Bombay.
Hardesty, D. L.,
1972   The Human Ecological Niche, *American Anthropologist*, 74,
            458–66.

Hardesty, D. L.,
1975   The Niche Concept: Suggestions for its use in Human Ecology, *Human Ecology*, 3, 71–85.

Karve, I.,
1961   *Hindu Society: An Interpretation*, Deccan College Postgraduate and Research Institute, Pune.

Karve, I., and Malhotra, K. C.
1968   A Biological Comparison of Eight Endogamous Groups of the Same Rank, *Current Anthropology*, 9, 109–24.

Lumsden, C. J., and Wilson, E. O.,
1981   *Genes, Mind and Culture*, Harvard University Press, Cambridge MA.

Malhotra, K. C.,
1978   Natural Selection and Colourblindness: Fresh Data on Indian Castes, *Genetical Research*, 31, 203–7.

Malhotra, K. C.,
1979a   Inbreeding Among Dhangar Castes of Maharashtra, India. *Journal of Biosocial Sciences*, 11, 397–410.

Malhotra, K. C.,
1979b   Excommunciation as a Process Leading to the Formation of New Groups, *Eastern Anthropologist*, 32, 49–53.

Malhotra, K. C.,
1982   Nomads, in *State of Environment in India*, Centre for Science and Environment, New Delhi.

Malhotra, K. C., Chakarborty, R. and Chakarvartti, A.,
1977   Gene Differentiation among the Dhangar Caste-cluster of Maharashtra, India, *Human Heredity*, 28, 26–36.

Malhotra, K. C., and Khomne, S. B.,
1978   Social Stratification and Caste Ranking among the Nandiwallas of Maharashtra, *Proceedings of the Seminar on Nomads in India, Mysore*, pp. 1–36.

Malhotra, K. C., Hulbe, S. K., Khomne, S. B., and Koth, S. B.,
1983   Economic Organization of a Nomadic Community, the Nandiwallas, in *India*, edited by P. K. Misra and K. C. Malhotra, Anthropological Survey of India, Calcutta.

Mane, L.,
1981   *Upra*, Granthali Publishers, Pune (in Marathi).

Marriot, M.,
1960   *Caste Ranking and Community Structure in Five Regions of India and Pakistan*, Deccan College Monograph Series, no. 23, Pune.

Root, R. B.,
1967   The Niche Exploitation Pattern of the Blue-Gray Gnat Catcher, *Ecological Monographs*, 37, 317–50.

Roughgarden, J.,
1978   *Theory of Population Genetics and Evolutionary Ecology—An Introduction*, MacMillian, New York.

Sanghvi, L. D.,
1978   Nature of Genetic Variation in the People of Western India, *Journal of Human Evolution*, 7, 55–65.

Sanghvi, L. D., and Khanolkar, V. R.,
1950   Data Relating to Seven Genetical Characterisitics in Six Endogamous Groups in Bombay, *Annals of Eugenics*, 15, 52–76.

Sinha, S. C.,
1967   Caste in India: Its Essential Pattern of Socio-cultural Integration, in *Caste and Race*, edited by Devos and Roucek, CIBA Foundation, London.

Srinivas, M. N.,
1962   *Caste in Modern India and other Essays*, Asia Publishing House, Calcutta.

Wilson, D. S.,
1980   *The Natural Selection of Populations and Communities*, Benjamin and Cummings, Menlo Park, California.

Ecology and Social Structure:
A Comparative Analysis

Ecology, the study of the relations between organisms and their environments or of the organism-environment nexus, has been used as an independent variable in the study of aspects of simple or tribal societies. To what extent an ecological analysis is possible in dealing with complex civilizations still remains a question, although some attempts have been made in this direction (e.g., Geertz 1963: Harris 1965; Nicholas 1963). This paper represents an attempt to explore the reciprocal relationship between a limited number of aspects of ecology—regional topography, settlement pattern, patterns of land utilization and certain agricultural practices—on the one hand and some aspects of social structure such as inter- and intra-village organization and inter- and intra-caste relations on the other, in two neighbouring parts of South India, Kerala and Madras. It is not meant to be an argument for ecological or economic determinism, but rather to specify some of the links in the chain of causation between environment and social structure or, put another way, to indicate some of the ways in which ecological factors interdigitate with social ones.

These two areas were chosen for comparison because they share certain common features and at the same time exhibit today and in the past both cultural and structural differences. It is clear at least that, as far back as historical and literary records go, the same technology was known in both areas. Methods for constructing tanks and canals were known in Kerala as well as in Madras, but, apart from marginal areas, tanks were only built as private bathing pools

Excerpted from Joan P. Mencher, 'Kerala and Madras; A Comparative Study of Ecology and Social Structure', *Ethnology*, Vol. 5, 1966.

in Kerala,[1] where the abundant monsoon provided more than the requisite amount of water for cultivation. (Complete famines due to a failure of the rains never occurred in Kerala.)

Wheeled vehicles were known and occasionally used in Kerala, but they were simply not useful in the prevailing terrain; even today, apart from modern motorized vehicles, a man walking can usually reach his destination with far less effort and in about one half the time as a man in a cart. Food patterns were similar on both coasts, with some minor differences and one important one, namely, the place occupied by the coconut in Malayalee cooking. In both areas, however, rice was the dietary staple, and land was always devoted to rice cultivation if at all possible.[2] One only grew something else if the land was not suitable for growing rice, or if there was insufficient water.

Linguistically, both areas shared a common language until the middle ages. This spoken language diverged slowly between the ninth and the twelfth centuries, but during the first centuries of this era they shared a common literature known as the Sangam literature (Kanakasabhai 1956). Though the history of the two coasts has been different, there were certain common features. Both regions had a large amount of Jain and Buddhist influence, as is evidenced by both written accounts (S. V. Pillai 1956: 40–3; Sastri 1953: 72–4, 766–72) and archeological finds (Banerjee 1956: 32). Further,

---

[1] Since the completion of this paper, Unni (1965) has correctly pointed out that, in addition to the private tanks belonging to individual households, there were also tanks which belonged to wealthy landlords of high caste, who made them available to the residents of the neighbourhood. These included: (1) tanks located in rice fields in which any of the higher castes might bathe; (2) tanks of larger size used by untouchable castes and also by cattle to wallow in; (3) tanks with spring-fed wells, usually used by untouchable castes; and (4) shallow ponds with low embankments, usually used by washermen. (It is, however, significant to note that even these tanks were privately owned, though made available to other people of a small locality, sometimes in return for allegiance and services, whereas tanks in Madras were often owned by a village and not by any individual family, and their use was normally extended to at least everyone of a given village belonging to the appropriate castes.) Unni comments further that these four kinds of tanks were also used at times for irrigation. (It should, however, be noted that summer vegetables and third-crop paddy were only rarely found outside of certain parts of Central Kerala and in any case never figured in a major way in Kerala agriculture.) On the whole, tanks were used mainly for bathing or to water cattle.

[2] The exact date for the introduction of rice in South India, or for that matter in India in general, is not as yet known. The Sangam literature refers to rice or paddy, and Sankalia (1962: 103) notes: 'But the question that is vexing the minds of scholars—anthropologists, archeologists, and others—is the identity of these first rice-eaters of South India (as yet no evidence of these grains is available from this part of India, though rice has been found at Kolhapur in second century A D houses, and in Central India as early as the 12th century B C, besides Hasinapur where it can be dated to at least the eighth to ninth century B C).'

both experienced a strong Brahminical revivalist movement, which commenced with Sankaracharyya, a Namboodiri Brahmin from Kerala, at the end of the eighth and the beginning of the ninth centuries A D, and continued under many others on the two coasts. In addition, they were relatively free from outside intervention until a relatively late period historically (Sastri 1955a: 218ff.).

Structurally, in both areas there was a development of a highly complex and clearly articulated caste system, which during the middle ages came also to be rigidly and hierachically stratified (Sastri 1955b: 307; cf. also Raja 1953: *passim*; Stein 1961: 7). Even during the first centuries of our era there is clear reference to different social groups—in some instances what appear to be occupational castes (Minakshi 1938: 135; Kanakasabhai 1956), in others to what appear to be sub-regional communities.

In this paper, I hope to indicate the refractive effect of ecology in the two areas on the caste system, on the development of concepts of ritual purity, on the patterning of authority relations, and on the development of the machinery to deal with large-scale irrigation projects. I shall deal first with each area in terms of its own specialized ecology and then present the detailed comparison.

THE KERALA SYSTEM

The area comprising the state of Kerala is confined to the Malayalam-speaking territories on the southwest coast of India. It is a long and narrowshaped area bounded on the west by the Arabian Sea and on the east by the high ranges of the Western Ghats covered with rich primeval forests (Panikkar 1960: 1). According to Spate (1954: 627), a tripartite longitudinal division may be found in Kerala, consisting of (1) a narrow alluvial coastland extending only a few miles from the sea and mostly confined to the area south of Ponnani (the lower two thirds of the coast line), (2) low lateritic plateaus and foothills between 200 and 600 feet covered with grass and scrub, and (3) the highlands. Into the lateritic region project spurs of the higher mountains. The gap near Palghat, where the mountains form a pass at an elevation of 1,100 feet, and the narrower one in the south near Shencottah, plus the area at the very tip of the Indian peninsula, were and are today the prime avenues for contact bet ween the east and the west coast.

The central region, consisting of the low lateritic plateaus and hills, forms the main area of traditional village settlement, as well as the area for rice cultivation. The highlands formerly were the province of various tribal groups and now are the home of their remnants, as well as of large tea and, in the north, coffee estates. This region is not considered in this paper. Visually, the central region presents a picture of a continually undulating countryside, with long, narrow or winding paddy fields surrounded on each side by hills and slopes covered with thick vegetation. The land given over to dry cultivation is somewhat higher and gently undulating. Rice, the dominant crop, occupies about 45 to 50 per cent of the total sown area, though only about 30 per cent in parts of Travancore (Spate 1954: 629). According to Kuriyan (1942: 14–15):

Agriculture in India is mainly carried on with the aid of irrigation,[3] but Kerala forms an important exception to this rule. . . . The irrigated areas in Kerala are found (I) in Nanjinad in the south (with the canal system), and (II) in Shencotta, Chittur and Palghat (with tank systems). In these parts the distribution and incidence of rainfall are such that irrigation becomes necessary. These regions happen to be the very parts of Kerala where here is a maximum possibility of contact with Tamilnad. . . . Apparently therefore there exists a considerable amount of correlation between agricultural practices like the methods of ploughing, irrigation, etc. and linguistic and cultural distributions.

In the area behind the backwaters, i.e., in most of Kerala, methods of cultivation are based solely on the utilization of rainwater. Owing to the early onset of the rains, planting begins in April or May with a harvest in September. The continuance of the rains in October and November often permits a second crop, particularly on the lower lying lands, which is harvested in January. Occasionally a third crop is grown, though this must be carefully watered from nearby ponds and wells and involves much work; it is only seen in a few parts of South Malabar, as the yield hardly repays the cost of the labour involved, even to the owner-cultivator.

Rice is also grown on lateritic hills in parts of Cochin and Malabar after burning the jungle and making terraces. Apart from a few places

---

[3] An inaccuracy in Kuriyan's statement here has been pointed out by the geographer Schwartzberg (1965), who notes that there are abundant statistics to indicate the contrary, even for Madras. In relation to the argument of this paper, however, one might more correctly modify Kuriyan's statement to read: it is clear that production of basic cereals, particularly rice and wheat, in sufficient quantity to produce surpluses capable of feeding a large nonproductive and/ or nonagricultural population has in most of India (aside from Kerala and Bengal), owing to the unpredictability of the monsoon, necessitated the construction of irrigation facilities.

in the extreme north, these are seldom allowed to lie fallow for many years between plantings. This use of lateritic hills is rendered possible by the heavier rains of Malabar.[4]

There may be some barren rocks near the top of hills, but otherwise the only tracts of open land are either those which man has created for himself by dint of hard work, i.e., by clearing and then levelling a jungly tract or by building on what could have been good paddy land. With much land unavailable for paddy cultivation, people have usually been unwilling to use the level, low-lying paddy land for house sites. These are normally found in the undulating or high ground around the fields. . . .

V. K. J. Menon (1953) has shown in great detail how geographic features have exerted a striking influence on the distribution and pattern of settlement in Kerala. It is clear that the actual physical features of the country do not encourage the formation of compact settlements. The dispersed settlement pattern which is characteristic of Kerala is to be found in the coastal region as well as on the lateritic plateaus (Menon 1953: 45),

. . . where water is abundant and no co-operative effort is needed for cultivation . . . whereas nucleated settlements are confined to the more difficult regions of the gaps, southern Travancore, the foothills of the main ghats, and the highland regions. In the latter group of regions there is a dearth of water or conditions unfavourable to economic development which in turn necessitates co-operative planned effort. . . . A historical survey enables us to conclude that the original inhabitants of the country generally lived in dispersed settlements whereas foreigners from the east coast or from beyond the Arabian Sea have for reasons of security or occupation settled in nucleated villages or even urban centres.

The areas where nucleated settlement tends to be most common are also the areas contiguous to Madras. Menon (1953: 46) goes on to describe a Kerala settlement:

In general the settlement has no distinct core, nor is there any residential area or shopping street. . . . Here and there, there is a small hut, usually a one-storeyed building with a front yard. There is an occasional large house with a garden gate-house and out-houses probably belonging to an important landlord. In some cases there is a shop which supplies sweetmeats,

---

[4] According to Kuriyan (1942: 10), there is a steady increase in the yearly precipitation going from Trivandrum north, ranging from 64.40 inches in Trivandrum to 126.26 inches in Cannanore. According to reports available at the French Institute in Pondicherry, the precipitation is even higher inland, amounting to 154 inches, in the area around Irrikkur (26 miles from Cannanore). To some extent the poverty of rainfall in Travancore is offset by its more general distribution throughout the year.

lengths of cloth, provisions, etc. It might also be a tea-shop where some of the men might meet. There may be a temple, village tank, or court of justice but none of these form the core of the village which is altogether rather loosely knit.

The ideal Malayalee house is set in its own compound with its food-producing trees (coconut, plantain, and jackfruit), so that the 'dwelling space subtracts hardly anything from the cultivation space' (Spate 1954: 633). Even a Kerala temple, until recently, was usually located on top of a hill, at the edge of a lake, by the side of a stream, or in a field—in short, not surrounded by houses (K. P. P. Menon 1924: iv, 24). This pattern was described by Ibn Battuta (Gibb 1929: 231–2) as early as the fourteenth century:

Mulaybar, which is the pepper country, extends for two months journey along the coast ... there is not a foot of ground but what is cultivated. Every man has his own orchard, with his house in the middle and a wooden palisade round it.

There is little reason to question that this was the practice even earlier. The relatively high water table, coupled with the greater ease in boring through lateritic soils for wells, is another factor making dispersed settlements feasible. Digging a well in Kerala which can provide potable water is not the problem that it is in other parts of India.

A rural settlement in Kerala is not a village as in most of India. As Kuriyan (1938–39: 141–2) has described it:

The whole region along the coast is from one end to the other like a garden city where one can hardly walk a furlong without seeing some houses. . . . The villages in Kerala have no marked nodality.

It is the house and not the village which is the unit of settlement in this region. This was even clearer before the middle of this century, when family partition first became legal, but it is still true today. It is impossible for the ordinary Malayalee visitor to know when he has come to the edge of one village or entered another. A house may be only one furlong from a house said to belong to a different village but two miles from one that belongs to the same village. Sometimes one of the long, narrow paddy fields may mark the boundary between two villages, but at other times the house flanking one of these fields may belong to the same village. There is little geographic logic in the decision to consider an area part of one village or another.

Formerly the large Nayar house, set in its own compound with its walls for protection, was a veritable fortress. Namboodiri houses, known as *illam or mana*, and those of middle-class Tiyyar were built so that they could be used as fortresses from which the family and its dependents might be defended in case of attack.[5] Every home had a name, and the individuals of a particular Nayar *taravad* or Namboodiri *illam* were known by that name. (The word *taravad* refers to the unpartitioned matrilineal family group as well as to the family house itself; see Mencher 1965: 168–70). An individual Cheruman or Pulayan (former slave castes which now constitute the lowest class of agricultural workers and account for about 10 per cent of the population,[6]) was known by the name of the house for which he worked. . . .

The villages in Kerala were only loosely organized. Unlike Madras, there never has been a free village habitation area. Each family, in the present as in the past, lives on its own estate or that of a landlord and has no community of interest in land with its neighbours. Administrators, lawyers, judges, legislators and anthropologists have often debated what constitutes a village in Kerala. The answer depends largely upon how one defines a village. Clearly many factors are involved, such as the distribution of water, problems of space, and the social structuring of spatial relations, but a full discussion of this problem lies beyond the scope of this paper.

The question of what constitutes a village in Kerala was raised as soon as the British occupied Malabar. The 1881–2 report of the Government of Madras Malabar Special Commission (1881–2: 5) described the traditional units as follows:

We have already seen that the *Desam* was the territorial unit of the military

---

[5] This does not mean to imply that the thick windows and doors were built solely to resist attacks. Indeed, as Unni (1965) points out, 'One aim was that the house should outlive generations of descendants.' Unni further notes that the need for security was less in the period prior to the eighteenth century, when the northern part of Kerala was invaded by the Muslims from Mysore. Actually, he adds, most Nayar 'cared for local power, and as well to have enough physical prowess by training in gymnasium to ensure that one Nayar can ward off . . . an attack by several able-bodied non-Nayars. Black magic was also mastered by Nayar karanavans to claim themselves as incredibly powerful against enemies.' In any case, whatever the original motivation, it is clear that such *taravad* houses did sometimes serve as fortresses even prior to the eighteenth century.

[6] According to the census of 1871 for the Malabar District of Madras Presidency, the Cheruman alone numbered 12 per cent of the Hindu population and 9 per cent of the total population. According to the census of 1891–2 for Cochin State, the Cheruman plus the other 'slave castes which included the Kanakan, Kutan, Parayan, Pulayan, etc.' comprised one out of every ten people in the state. In the 1921 census for Cochin State, the Pulayan (with the Cheruman) and the Parayan numbered 9.5 per cent of the total population. Unfortunately, there are no clear recent statistics, but there seems no reason to assume any significant percentage change.

system, and that the *Tara* was the true equivalent of the Dravidian village. The council of *Karanavar* (elders) consisted of one male member from each *Taravad* (*tara*, village and *padu*, authority) house in the *Tara*. The *Tara* varied in size, but it frequently embraced several *Desams*. Perhaps the best way of illustrating the matter is to take an actual example. The present Kachcheri Amsam of the Calicut Taluk, comprising two *Desams*, constituted a *Tara*. The *Taravad* houses in it were the 1. Palan house, 2. Nilambara house, 3. Markat house, and 4. Mandut house. The *Karanavar* (elders) . . . constituted the council of the *Kuttam*.

The Malabar *tara* differed considerably from the villages found elsewhere in South India, apart from the areas of south Kanara and Coorg bordering on north Malabar, where dispersed settlements are also found. According to one Malayalee historian (K. A. Menon 1961: 292), 'within the historical period, the smallest political unit was a household.' In one sense each *taravad* in the Kachcheri Amsam referred to above could be considered as a meaningful political unit. A functional definition of a Kerala village would involve an analysis of land use, of patterns of interaction and authority, etc., and not just a simplistic correlation of the traditional *desam* or *tara* or the modern revenue-paying *desam* or *amsam* with the English word 'village,' but such an analysis is not essential here.

Land was always owned by either an individual, an unpartitioned family, or a temple (see also Gough 1961: 307–8). A given landlord family might own land in more than one locality, but it would normally reside in the locality where it owned the most land suitable for paddy cultivation. There was no land which belonged to the *desam* or *tara*. Even paths which passed through the property of a landlord were said to belong to the landlord.

Roads as such were practically nonexistent. In 1906, according to Innes (Innes and Evans 1907: 268), 'wheeled traffic was unknown and even pack bullocks were not used until recently.' The traditional modes of transport were by foot, including the carrying of headloads, by boat where feasible, by means of improvised litters, and, for the wealthy, by palanquin.[7] The famous Nayar soliders were foot soldiers. The first major construction of roads in Kerala commenced with the Mysorean invasions in the mid-eighteenth century, and most of the present roads were built during the nineteenth and twentieth centuries.

[7] K. P. P. Menon (1924: iii, 385) quotes Ibn Battuta as saying that 'no one travels in these parts upon beasts of burden . . . goods are transported on the backs of men', and notes that these conditions persisted until this century.

The bullock cart was practically unknown in traditional Kerala except in the extreme south. However, today the rural road system in Kerala is far better than in many other parts of India. For the most part, except in the extreme south, goods and people travel either by motorized vehicles or by foot across the hills and paddy fields. Since roads must of necessity take circuitous routes, avoiding winding paddy fields and sharp inclines, walking is more efficient than using vehicles drawn by animals. Since the lateritic soil absorbs moisture rapidly, even during the monsoon, a house or village is never isolated by the rains as in Bengal, despite the fact that the Kerala monsoon is more than twice as heavy. The Malayalee never consider a distance of ten miles by foot as far, and often set out on such a walk at a moment's notice. Traditionally, in many parts of south Malabar and Cochin, a Nayar husband might walk up to two miles each way on his nightly visit to his wife's house (Unni 1956: 37–56).

The lack of necessity for constructing irrigation works and roads requiring public expenditure may be correlated with the fact that until the Mysorean invasions no land revenue was collected in Kerala.[8] The local rulers in Kerala—from the largest ones like the Zamorin of Calicut or the Chiṟakkal Raja down to the petty chieftains—derived their income from the rents on their own farms, from duties on imports and exports, from succession fees in all Nayar and Namboodiri landlord families, and from gifts, fines, and escheat.[9]

Because there was no collection of land revenues there was no need for a village accountant, an office not established until the end of

[8] According to a letter written about the time of the invasion of Hyder Ally Khan (Madras Revenue Proceedings, Letters to the Board of Revenue, 50: 15, 26): 'At this time, it would appear that no direct taxes were laid on the land, although in the case of invasion as it had happened from the Canarese and the Portugese, a general contribution was levied equal to about 1/5 of the produce. But landowners who held feudal tenures from the Rajas were bound at all times to attend his summons for war with a stated number of vassals or dependents bearing arms.' A discussion of the entire land tenure system is beyond the scope of this paper (see Shea 1959b).

[9] According to the Census of India: Cochin State (1901: i, ixi): 'Like other Rajas of the coast states, the Cochin Raja made up his civil list by means of income derived from what is known as *Kandukrishi* (crown land), monopolies, customs, escheats, protection fees collected from rich proprietors, or temples, succession tax and various minor items. From some old papers, it is seen that a land tax was first levied in 937 M. E., A. D. 1762 chiefly to meet the increasing expenditure consequent on the wars with the Zamorin and Travancore. This is corroborated by the treaty with the Dutch in 1785 in which the Christian subjects who at first refused to pay the taxes agreed to abide by the rules which applied to other classes of the people. According to another version, it was during the occupation of the country by Haider and his men (about 950 M. E.) that a tax was first levied on land . . . whatever might be the exact period . . . it does not seem to have existed prior to 1760.'

the eighteenth century. Nor did one find in Kerala any of the other customary village officers found in Madras. Peace and order were insured in an area by the presence of the local Nayar militia. There were usually one or two temples in each *tara* or *desam*, and often in addition a *kalari* for military training, but on a day-to-day basis these were normally restricted to certain castes alone. Thus in one village dominated by the Namboodiri the temple was not even open to the Nayar. In Nayar villages, many temples were not open to people of the lower castes, though they might have some service to perform at the annual temple festival. As Miller (1960: 54) has shown,

... village unity in North Kerala is a somewhat nebulous conception. A physical, territorial unity may exist, but it is often not obvious, because of scattered settlement. Close neighbours may belong to different desams. ... Economic unity may be modified by the extension of caste obligations to several villages or in their restriction to a segment of a single village. .... Whatever internal self-subsistence there may have been in the desams of the 18th century and earlier, it is very difficult nowadays in Kerala to point to any unit as a clearly demarcated, coherent, independent village community.

Not only in the north, but also in Travancore, village organization existed only for the Nayar, in so far as it existed at all. According to K. M. Panikkar (1918: 256): 'For the purpose of communal life, other castes are outside the village organization.' In the past, the *desavazhi*, or head of a particular *desam*, was primarily the military chief of the area. He was responsible for providing the *naduvazhi*, the head of the next larger administrative unit, with a given number of Nayar soldiers. He was assisted by the leading men of his area, the *pramani*, who were normally the heads of the various landlord *taravad* in the *desam*. Oftentimes each large *taravad* maintained its own *kalari*. According to K. P. P. Menon (1924: ii, 380–1), the *desavazhi*, whose role was clearly limited,

... usually employed the lower classes, but no individual, even of the higher [classes], ever hesitated in performing whatever services he commanded ... he was always obeyed rather as the chief of the clan than the head of a village ... [The Raja] in some villages was owner of the lands, in others he had Desavali rights, and in still others owned some lands but the original landlord had Desavali rights.

Panikkar (1918: 256) goes on to note for Travancore, where there are many Christians, that even though a Christian house might be adjacent to a Nayar *taravad*, the Christians played no part in the village organization, such as it may have been; and the same held true for

Muslims, the members of the lower castes and of the small temple-servant castes, etc. Namboodiri Brahmins tended to live in villages which they controlled by virtue of the fact that they were the dominant landlords. Such villages had no *desavazhi* at all.

While there is some sense of unity in the Kerala village today, it is clearly weaker than in Tamil villages. The local school, post office, etc. have resulted in the inclusion of the immigrant castes (i.e., the groups coming originally from Tamilnad), the lower castes, and the Muslim and Christians in the 'we-group', notes Unni (1959), but he adds:

It is usually among the lower castes and the less well-to-do among the rest that the sense of pride in the social assets of the village (the well-employed, the powerful families, the new schemes of improvement) predominates.

The Namboodiri Brahmins, higher groups of Nayar, and even ordinary middle-class Nayar have hardly any need to move out of their residential compounds to meet their daily requirements. They have within their compound their own bathing pond, snake pit, small deity for daily worship, garden crops, and even cremation ground. Vendors make their rounds with additional foods, cloth for daily use, cooking utensils, etc. Furthermore, for the Nayar in south Malabar and Cochin, a woman's husband traditionally came to visit her in her own house. Thus there was and is even today 'little opportunity for individuals to have the experience of non-familial primary group life which characterizes the nucleated village' (Unni 1959).

There is some variation by caste in the degree of compactness or nucleation of settlement. In order of their observed preference for clustered settlement, notes Unni (1959), the lower polluting castes of Parayan and Nayadi come first, then the various immigrant castes from Madras, then the artisan castes, and finally the Tiyyar (known in some localities as Izhava, Tandan, or Chon) with a very slight tendency to cluster. However, when Tiyyar houses do form a cluster, each house is still set on its own small plot of land, and often one cannot see one's neighbours' houses, or at most can only see one or two, owing to the vegetation growth in between. Among the Christians, Muslims, Tarakan (one of the immigrant castes), and even the wealthier Brahmins from the east coast, many families live in their own substantial house in a spacious compound. Unni speculates that, among Hindus, the matrilineal castes have a greater tendency toward dispersed settlements, whereas, except for the Namboodiri Brahmins at the top and the agricultural Cheruman and

Pulaya at the bottom, the patrilineal castes tend to prefer nucleated settlements. The Cheruman and Pulaya, as serfs, had no choice in the location of their house sites, which were determined for them by their Nayar or Namboodiri landlords. It is significant that, by and large, the caste groups tending to dispersed settlement also tend either to be landlords or else to have superior tenancy rights.

There is also a significant correlation between the preference for dispersal and traditional rules relating to family partition. Thus those castes which did not permit family partition (Mencher 1962: 230–45) show a preference for dispersal. It may be suggested that the small clusters of Tiyyar or artisan houses actually consist of members of one *taravad*. Today, with the increasing partitioning of Nayar and Namboodiri families, there is also a tendency toward greater physical proximity between Nayar houses. Often a branch of a former large *taravad* will build a house close to the main *taravad* house so that they can share the same bathing pool and gate. The smaller size of the family, the high cost of construction today, and the sense of security in staying close to one's matrilineal kin play a part here (Unni 1959)

In some respects it may be said that there is a greater tendency for caste neighbourhoods to form today than in the past. Apart from 'royal' villages,[10] however, one still finds less segregation of dwelling areas by caste than on the east coast. Traditionally, there was a tendency for the higher-caste and landlord families in a village to build their houses close to the paddy fields, and for at least some of the low castes to live in the hilly areas farther away.[11] There were several reasons for this preference on the part of the higher castes. By flanking the open fields they were afforded a pleasant view and cool breezes during the summer months. Moreover, the land being somewhat lower, it was easier to construct large bathing pools in their own compounds, to keep an eye on the agricultural operations, and, because the land was normally more fertile, to grow their garden crops in their compound.

THE MADRAS SYSTEM

As opposed to Kerala, the traditional Madras or Tamil village was

---

[10] By royal village, what is meant is a village where either a branch of one of the ruling families, such as the Zamorin of Calicut lived, or else a village where one of the important Nayar chieftains lived.

[11] Some lower castes might live in the middle of the fields to watch the crops.

of the nucleated type. Among the reasons why people congre-
gated in such villages, certain ones are obvious, e.g., the necessity
for co-operation in clearing jungle areas and the need to locate
where water was available for domestic purposes the year around.
Above all, however, the nature of the land on this coast was such
that any type of complex agriculture was rendered possible only by
the construction of irrigation works. The construction of large-
scale water courses, tanks, etc. presupposes the organization of
groups of men through the help of at least a partially centralized
government (Iyengar 1916: 69). Wheeler (1959: 163) suggests that
in the Chingleput region the Megalithic people practiced agriculture with irrigation, and Sankalia (1962: 103) supports this view on
the basis of the relative location of tanks and villages. If we post-
ulate, as did Wheeler, that the Megalithic reached its climax in the
south after 300 B C, then we have a limiting date for some aspects of
the culture. But irrigation may predate the introduction of these
main hallmarks of the Iron Age in this part of India.[12]

Throughout the Madras area, people normally settled in an open
spot selected by the community, an area of high ground called the
nattam or *gramma-nattam*. According to Iyengar (1916: 69), a common feature of most villages on the east coast is such a central site
containing the habitations and surrounded first by cultivated (usually wet) lands, then dry lands, then waste. In some villages, however, the *gramma-nattam* is located on one edge of the irrigated wet
lands. The irrigated land is always given over to paddy cultivation,
but the non-irrigated land can be devoted to paddy only in years of
plentiful rainfall.

Occasionally a village might include a hamlet—a small village in
its own right though not large enough to be classified as a separate
village for administrative or revenue purposes. In addition, there
were normally separate quarters (*cheri*) for the houses of the lowest
castes, e.g., the Pariahs or the Chakkli (leather workers). Some
large villages had more than one *cheri* attached to them. Occasionally a village consisted of only a small *nattam* area and a large *cheri*
which was also attached to a neighbouring village. Some villages
had no *cheri* at all and were dependent on a *cheri* of another village.
The traditional east-coast village, and at least in Chingleput District
the modern Tamil village as well, had various kinds of lands set

---

[12] Information about irrigation in South India was provided in a personal communication by
K. A. R. Kennedy of the Department of Anthropology, Cornell University.

aside as 'village' or community property, such as the paths, roads, canals, tanks, and eris,[13] the banks of such waterworks, the threshing grounds, the community burial grounds, and cattle stands, as well as the habitation areas (Iyengar 1916: 69–71).

Though there is considerable regional diversity in Madras State,[14] the rainfall is everywhere extremely variable. Most of the precipitation falls between October and December, with a peak in November. In three districts of Chingleput, South Arcot, and Tanjore an additional 15 to 25 inches of rain may fall between June and September (Economic Atlas of Madras State 1962: 15, 21–2), though in some years these summer rains are negligible. In any case, the total annual rainfall seldom exceeds 55 inches and often is considerably less. This has led to a considerable elaboration of tank irrigation in all areas except Tanjore.

On the Coromandal plain, which includes the area around Conjeevaram as well as in Tanjore, between 70 and 77 per cent of the cultivable land is devoted to paddy.[15] The land which is not cultivated is mostly dry or rocky with little jungle coverage, and it is relatively flat with only rare contours. Even in areas where a smaller percentage of paddy is grown, because of dependence on tank irrigation and a perennial scarcity of water, the normal settlement is of the nucleated variety.[16]

The *gramma-nattan* or village site was always free of assessment. Villagers were expected to build their houses on this site and nowhere else. If they built a house elsewhere, they would have been expected to pay a tax on the land. If the *nattam* became too small to

[13] An eri is formed by throwing a mound or bank across a valley or hollow ground, so that rainwater or water from a canal leading off a river will collect in the upper part of the depression, from which it is let out into the lower part by sluices. A tank, on the other hand, is formed by excavating the earth; it is thus below the surface of the ground.

[14] According to the Economic Atlas of Madras State (1962), the state is divided into four physiographic regions: the coastal plains, the eastern ghats, the plateau area, and the western ghats. The coastal plains include three subregions: the northern plain, the Cauvery delta, and the southern plain.

[15] The Economic Atlas of Madras State (1962) notes that in Chingleput District 84 per cent of the irrigated land was given over to paddy, the other crops being millets (mostly ragi) and oil seeds (mostly peanuts). Of the non-irrigated land, only 48 per cent was devoted to paddy. However, my own statistics in one village in the district indicate that there is considerable variation in the amount of dry land devoted to paddy depending on the rainfall in a given year (see also Spate 1954: 697–719).

[16] The only place where one finds any tendency toward dispersion is in the sandy littoral strip of the Cauvery delta, which climatically resembles Kerala. We shall not concern ourselves with this region since it presents special problems and is populated by quite specialized groups (see Spate 1954: 724).

accommodate all of the people, then additional land surrounding it, or in some villages at a slight distance away, might be freed of assessment and people allowed to build on it. However, reserved sites never could be later converted into paddy fields without the express permission of the government, and then they were taxed. . . .

In the pre-British period, there was considerable variation in local village administration. In discussing the later Chola empire (between A D 850 and 1270) Sastri (1955b: 567) notes that there were some villages in which land was owned on a communal basis and the right to share was hereditary. In certain of these, sometimes referred to as *mirasi* villages, the produce is said to have been distributed in shares after deducting the shares of the King and the actual cultivators. In others, the land itself is reported to have been subject to periodic redistribution among the shareholders. In the northern part of Madras State, then known as Tondaimandalam, legend relates that these *mirasi* villages were originally colonized by groups of Vellala brought in by one of the early Chola rulers during the early Chola empire. By the time of the later Chola empire, however, there were also Brahmin *mirasidar*, and in Tanjore the *mirasidar* were primarily Brahmins. According to a 1799 report cited by Firminger (1918: iii, 149–67), there were still many *mirasi* villages in the Jaghire (as Chingleput District was then called), despite the effect of 200 years of Vijayanagar rule, of the invasion and rule by Maharattas, and of the depredations of Hyder Ali and Tipoo Sultan in the late eighteenth century. During the nineteenth century, however, the British replaced them by the *ryotwari* system (i.e., that of individual ownership of a particular plot of land). There were also the equivalent of *ryotwari* villages in Chola times—what Sastri (1955: 567, 571–3) calls a system of peasant proprietorship. Unfortunately, data are lacking as to the relative proportions of the several types of villages in particular areas.

Traditionally, village servants were given a certain amount of land in addition to such other payments as they might receive, and the same custom applied to the blacksmith and other resident artisans. If they did not cultivate this land, it could be taken back by the government. At the time of the settlement in the late nineteenth and early twentieth centuries, these plots were converted into 'service *inams*'—lands on which the owner paid only a nominal tax to the government so long as he performed his task and did not sell his plot to anyone else. If he sold it, however, or failed to perform his task, it reverted to ordinary government land and became subject to normal taxation.

According to Iyengar (1921: 76), the traditional roster of village officers in a Tamil village inculded: (1) a headman, called in the region around Conjeevaram the *nattanmeikaran* by non-Brahmins and the *manigar* by Brahmins; (2) the *karnam* or village accountant; (3) the *taliary*, whose duty it is to give information about crimes and offenses and formerly also to escort and protect people travelling from village to village; (4) the *vettiyan*, whose functions include guarding the crops, assisting in measuring them, and distributing the water of the streams and reservoirs;[17] (5) the boundaryman, who preserves the limits of the village and gives evidence in disputes. Other village offices include those of the Brahmin who performs village worship, the non-Brahmin priests, and the village artisans, barbers, washermen, leather workers, astrologers, etc. No village possessed in the past nor possesses today the full complement of officers, but all possessed the principal ones described plus usually a barber and a washerman.

After the advent of the British, another office was established—that of the *munsiff*, a kind of petty judge with functions partly overlapping those of the village headman. At first an unpaid office, it later became a paid one. ... The *karnam*, who had traditionally belonged to the Karnam or Kanakka-Pillai caste group, has become a government servant and may today be a member of any caste, though he usually belongs to a high non-Brahmin caste. There is some tendency to transmit the job to the son of the former *karnam*. The lower offices of *taliary*, *vettiyan*, etc. are hereditary, and are mostly held by Pariahs (one of the lowest groups of untouchables, formerly held as slaves, who claim to be the original or 'Adi-Dravida' owners of the land).

Alongside the formal village officers, a prominent role in village affairs has been played since earliest times by the village elders, the *nattameikaran* (colloquially *nattar*). In addition to assisting the people of their own streets in their personal problems, they convene from time to time in semi-formal meetings or councils to deal with the common needs of the community (Sastri 1955b: 486–94). It is this body that traditionally sets the time for communal fishing on the

---

[17] Previously the distribution of the water from streams and reservoirs was controlled by another officer, but today this function is performed by the *vettiyan*. In our sample village, for example, there are four *vettiyan*, two for each large eri. They also watch the crops in the fields and may at times serve as boundarymen. The *taliary* also assists in measuring the crops.

large eris, which depends upon the exact amount of water in the eri, the crop situation, etc. They likewise convene open-air meetings to discuss matters of public interest, such as the auctioning of fishing rights or the repair of a tank. To help repair a tank is considered a 'meritorious deed', and is thus sometimes paid for by wealthy benefactors, but such tasks may also be done by communal participation, each man playing his part according to his economic position.

The degree of communal activity was of course limited by caste roles, but in each village there was always one caste which was numerically and economically dominant, and it was this caste which took a lead in communal activities. Normally the village elders belonged to this caste (Srinivas 1959). If the Brahmins, the caste at the top of the ritual hierarchy, were wealthy, they might be the dominant caste even if they were not the most numerous. But often, as in the case of the sample village, they were quite willing to permit the dominant caste group to assume the leadership so long as they did not interfere in the life or activities of the Brahmins. Traditionally, in a village with a dominant Brahmin community which was also large numerically, as in Uttaramerur, there was a complex organization of Brahmin committees (Sastri 1955: 495–6).

A Tamil village displays a strong sense of unity as opposed to the outside world. This is not to say that there are no internal cleavages but rather that, in relation to outsiders, including people from neighbouring villages, the inhabitants stick together. This unity can even override caste barriers, so that a non-Brahmin may assist a Brahmin, or *visa versa*, in keeping matters of scandal from reaching the ears of outsiders.[18] Only when an offence becomes known to outsiders, e.g., if it occurs in another village or when people from another village are present, will people call in either the police in the case of a crime or others of their caste in the case of the breach of a moral law. . . .

COMPARISONS

I shall now undertake to present some further comparisons between Kerala and Madras and to relate these to the data previously set forth.

[18] I have even seen non-Brahmins who are strongly anti-Brahmin aid local Brahmins in keeping local scandal secret, not because of any affection or concern for the people involved but because it is after all their village as well.

I have chosen four points out of many possibilities for special elucidation: purity, the pattern of authority relations, subcaste proliferation, and the effect of irrigation and roads on social structure.

Ritual Purity

Regardless of whether one agrees with Leach (1960: 5) that 'A caste
can only be recognized in contrast to other castes with which its
members are closely involved in a network of economic, political,
and ritual relationships', or with Kroeber (1930), who stresses the
hierarchical and endogamous nature of the caste system, it is clear
that two important expressions of the caste system are the emph-
ases on occupational differentiation and on ritual purity. Both
obviously exist to a greater or lesser degree throughout the Indian
subcontinent and even on its peripheries; but in the south, particularly in Madras and Kerala, the concept of pollution is perhaps more
deeply ingrained and has been assigned even greater importance
than that of occupation. It is possible that the stress on purity was
elaborated during the period of the Brahminical revival (coinciding
with the downfall of Buddhism and Jainism in South India), though
there is literary evidence[19] that it appeared earlier.

In the period prior to European contact, there were both Tiyyar
and Namboodiri Brahmin soldiers in Kerala, though they were few
in number compared to the well-known Nayar soliders. Yet between these groups, at least when not at war (the records are silent
regarding actual military operations), the requisite distance had to
be maintained. However, a Namboodiri soldier, though lower in
rank than a Namboodiri who participated in Vedic recitation, was
still considered to be a Namboodiri and entitled to the various
privileges of his caste. He could still eat with other Namboodiri. It
is quite striking how today, in orthodox parts of Kerala and Madras,
a poor person may assume an occupation considered much lower
than that normal to his caste, but still not lose his or her caste status

[19] In speaking about the early Tamil literature, Kanakasabhai (1956: 114) notes: 'When men of
the higher classes passed on the streets, the lower classes made way for them. The *Pulayan* or
scavenger on meeting a nobleman bowed before him, with both hands joined in a posture of
supplication.' Again, in speaking of the attempts of the Brahmins to impose the Varna classification upon Tamilnad he states (p.116): 'But in the absence of the Kshatriya, Vaisya, and Sudra
castes in Tamilakam, they could not possibly succeed; and to this day the Vellala does not take
meals or drink water at the house of a Padaiyadchi, who calls himself a Kshatriya, or a merchant
who passes for a Vaisya.'

so long as purity is maintained in other ways.[20] Though it is true that Nayar of the middle and upper classes and Tamil Brahmins might not take jobs which were demeaning to their prestige, to do so reflected on the social status of one's individual family and not on one's caste position.

On the other hand, concepts of pollution and methods of maintaining purity have been more highly structured in South India than elsewhere and, as has been noted by many writers (e.g., Marriott 1960), have been particularly elaborated in Kerala. It is easy to see from the very ecology and geographical situation how this differential elaboration could have taken place.

In Madras the caste groups are arranged on streets. Certainly no Pariah from the *cheri* was permitted to walk down the main street of the Brahmin Agraharam, nor even the streets at the back of the Agraharam where they might see menstruating Brahmin women sitting on their back veranda. They were not allowed to use the wells in the village site, nor the ponds which were used by higher castes.[21] The Naicker, though the dominant caste group in the village, were not allowed to enter Brahmin houses except under special circumstances, and certainly, neither in the past nor today, were they allowed to go near the kitchen. This applied regardless of their economic position; even a wealthy Naicker landlord, for example, could not enter the kitchen of a middle-class Brahmin.[22] In Madras,

---

[20] Maintainance of purity in other ways includes not taking food while polluted, not taking food prepared by someone of a lower caste, changing one's clothes and taking a bath before entering a house upon one's return from work, etc. However, rules about purity have relaxed somewhat, as long as a job also carries a high remuneration. A Namboodiri who performs operations or who weaves is not polluted if he still observes the other rules in his private life. This pragmatic attitude towards caste occupation stands out in marked contrast to other parts of rural India, where there is normally an increased emphasis on not doing work beneath one's caste. In one village where I worked I observed a Tiyyar woman doing the work of a scavenger, and I saw both Nayar and Namboodiri weaving. In another, a carpenter woman was doing scavenging work. In none of these cases, nor in the many others like then, did this have any effect whatsoever on the 'caste status of the individuals concerned'. This same phenomenon has also been reported for Madras, though perhaps less frequently than in Kerala.

[21] From the 1912 land register, it is clear that the Brahmins owned only about 30 per cent of the land in the village. The Naicker were the dominant caste in the village, and in most matters it was their men who ran things. But the fact that the Brahmins were higher ritually speaking, plus the fact that they did live off the land, gave them greater authority than might otherwise have been expected. It might be suggested in this context that the village had two dominant castes, with the Naicker taking the lead in most matters.

[22] It is interesting in this context to note how modernization may at least temporarily assist in the maintaining of purity. Somehow, the machine remains essentially neutral in terms of purity. Thus, if one cannot get the proper service-caste individual to perform a task, one may use a machine without increasing the risk of pollution.

the layout of the village made it impossible to enforce more strictly the rules of distance pollution. A Brahmin house near the end of the road will obviously be approached more closely than one in the middle of the street or close to the temple. Nevertheless, the Pariahs assert that they would be beaten if they came near the Brahmin houses, and they are expected to maintain other status-demeaning symbols, e.g., not wearing an upper cloth, a good shirt or *dhoti*, or a headcover when a Brahmin was near. In some villages this started to break down during the rationing period of World War II, when the Pariah women had to come through the back streets of the main village to get their government ration. Whereas the Pariahs resided at a considerable distance from the main village site, the other lower castes merely lived on different streets. Though a Tamil village might have more than one pond for drinking water and for bathing, there were never many.

The layout of the higher-caste house compound in Kerala made it possible to elaborate upon the rules of distance pollution. Each house could easily have its own well and often even its own pond, thus avoiding the problem of sharing them. It also made it convenient for an individual to bathe upon returning from a trip away from the house compound. While extra bathing to remove pollution might be annoying, a bath in one's own pool after returning from outside was usually viewed with pleasure, and the problem with younger adults and children was often to get them to leave the pool and come inside.

Besides making it easier to remove pollution, the geography of the house compound facilitated the maintenance of the rules of distance pollution. Writers about Kerala commonly speak of distance pollution in terms of feet, conveying the strange impression of men walking around with footrules. In fact, the distances relate to places, e.g., the gate of one's compound, the courtyard, or the first step on the veranda. Thus a carpenter who did not have his tools with him was allowed to the gate of a Namboodiri *illam*, a Cheruma or Pulaya had to stay even farther away, and a Nayadi was expected to call out from the fields or from a particular stone in the hilly area. The term *tiyyapad* was used to refer to the distance usually kept by a Tiyyar in relation to a Nayar (Unni 1959). Such distance rules were not difficult to maintain.

When in the course of daily life they became onerous, methods existed to circumvent them. When a carpenter came to work in a

Namboodiri house, he was allowed inside, but placed a small leaf with a bit of grain on the floor to warn the older orthodox people not to approach that part of the house where he was working, and if they did, it only meant a bath. At the time of certain festivals in north Malabar, when a low-caste man was 'possessed by a god' (Mencher 1964: 10), he was allowed to come close to the people of the higher castes, and even his relatives might enter a house compound of the latter. The situational flexibility of these rules is perhaps relevant to their successful persistence.

The elaboration of distance pollution in Kerala may possibly be viewed as an extreme development of a structural ideal in a context which allowed it to develop. Put another way, it may be hypothesized that a particular principle of social organization or culture, here that of ritual purity, tends to achieve maximal expression if there is no ecological barrier to its doing so. The relative scarcity of water on the east coast might be viewed as such an ecological barrier. In Kerala, however, it was never necessary in the past for an individual to take water from a higher-caste well; and even today the necessity arises only occasionally in rural parts. Everyone had his own family well, or, in the case of poor people, perhaps three or four families shared a well. Except around a few of the famous temples, and then only on festival days, there were no public facilities which might provoke competition.

It is also possible to view distance pollution as a means of maintaining proper caste behaviour in a situation where there was only limited village unity, i.e., where the individual unpartitioned upper-caste household was the functional unit for day-to-day interaction and the maintainance of authority relations. In the Kerala village there was no complex organization of village functions by caste which might serve as a means of affirming caste. One did not find a member of one caste group in charge of records, another in charge of distributing water, another collecting revenue, or the like. Therefore, it might be suggested that the rules of distance pollution took the place of a complex village organization as a means of affirming intercaste relations. True, a temple festival might serve the same function (Miller 1960: 52), but these did not occur very often and, when they did occur, they were used as a means of affirming the rules of distance pollution. Thus it might be said that the loose village structure in Kerala necessitated a more rigid set of rules for

intercaste behaviour.[23] On the other hand, this looser village structure was adaptive to the ecology.

The Structure of Authority Relations

In Kerala, authority relations between higher and lower castes were
always directed from a given unpartitioned upper-caste landlord
family towards the families who either worked for them as tenant
farmers, coolies, or agrestic slaves, or with whom they maintained
one or another category of service relationship—the so-called
Avakasakkar and non-Avakasakkar castes, i.e., those who render
specialized service by hereditary right and those who do not (Unni
1959). One Nayar *taravad* or Namboodiri *mana* was quite independent of others in terms of its relationships with the members of
lower castes. Though a lower-caste man who did not owe something to his landlord might opt to leave him and seek the protection
of another landlord, often a rival of the first, there was no procedure for controlling a local landlord's relations with his inferiors.
Vertical ties were always stressed. The former *tara* organization
dealt with social, political, and military relations among the Nayar
but did not regulate relations between Nayar and those under
them. Even among Nayar the authority of the *tara* organization
was limited; it did not, for example, regulate behaviour between a
wealthy *taravad* and a poorer tenant of theirs, even if the tenant
belonged to the same subcaste. Namboodiri *grammam* similarly
dealt with Namboodiri affairs and only entered the arena of intercaste relations when there was a case of adultery or some other
offence requiring the outcasting of a Namboodiri. Economic and
authority relations between the dominant castes of Namboodiri
Brahmins and Nayar and those lower in the social hierarchy were
always a matter of individual family concern. Unni (1959), in speaking
about theft, willful pollution by approach, sorcery, threats of injury,
etc. at the intercaste level, notes:

The incidence of these is the minimum in villages with powerful *taravads*
for their power to control and maintain peace and order in every nook and

[23] In this connection, it might be noted that Dr Savitri Shahani, in a doctoral dissertation in the
Department of Anthropology of the School of Oriental and African Studies, University of London, is attempting to show the necessary correlation between the development and elaboration
of the caste system in Kerala and the looseness of the traditional Kerala kingdoms.

corner of the village is a threat to individuals. . . . There are instances, often quoted by informants, of police inspectors trailing culprits or coming to investigate complicated cases withdrawing from the scene leaving the situation to powerful *karanavans* of the village to handle.

Unni (1959) also shows how '*jenmis* of wealth and *taravads* of power play roles in keeping up the rather traditional pattern of relationships between groups.' If a lower-caste man was caught taking firewood from land belonging to a particular landlord or *jenmi*, or perhaps picking some of his mangoes or polluting his tank, there was no traditional village group to whom the landlord could bring his complaint. Normally, he would handle the case himself, or, if he was only a small landlord, he might bring the case to the leading landlord in his neighbourhood. Formally, the large landlords often inflicted very harsh punishments for such deeds, but today, primarily out of fear of the Communists who exploit such incidents, they are more lenient. In the case of larger offences, the *jenmi* today often call in the police. Since 1957, at least in some areas, the modern elected Panchayat has taken over some of the powers of the landlords, but such results of the modernization process lie beyond the scope of this paper.[24] In the past, most conflicts arising between families of a *jenmi's* dependents or with a dependent family were referred to the *jenmi* himself for adjudication[25] (see also Miller 1960: 51).

In many respects the relationship between the local Kerala landlord and his tenants or those who served him in other capacities resembled the type of patron-client relationship described for feudal Europe, though obviously modified by the caste system.

[24] The power of these Panchayats to curb the authority of a landlord is related to the amount of his land, i.e., the power and prestige remaining with a landlord after his family has juggled with land ceilings (cf. Mencher 1962: 234), as well as the extent to which he has been able to control the Panchayat elections and to keep 'party politics' out of his village. In villages where the Panchayat body is balanced between the two major political parties in Kerala, Congress and Communist, and members of polluting castes as well as high castes sit on the board, there is a considerable lessening of the power of the landlords. On the other hand, in villages where a large amount of land belongs to one wealthy family, this family may still have almost complete control over the lower-caste people living on its land.

[25] After the establishment of modern courts by the British, cases were often referred to government courts, particularly if they involved property disputes. However, it remained a matter of pride to a *jenmi* if no cases were brought to the courts by his tenants or servants. The number of cases brought to the courts increased sharply in the 1920s and 1930s following the passage of laws permitting the partition of family property. In Madras as well, after the courts were established, when people could not come to agreement, particularly in relation to the division of property, and did not like the decision of the village elders, they started taking their cases to the administrative courts. Such court cases drained many families of much of their wealth.

K. P. P. Menon (1924: iii, 337) speaks of this similarity on another level:

The petty chieftains more or less exercised the right, not simply of taking up arms between themselves, but also were so far free and independent as to wage war against their own feudal heads themselves.

Even today, authority relations in Kerala, or at least in Malabar and Cochin, are mostly between individual Nayar or Namboodiri houses (or sometimes a group of related Nayar houses, branches of a recently partitioned *taravad*) and those who serve them. While the sanction of gossip exercises control over some aspects of Nayar behaviour, the degree to which it is effective depends on the prestige, i.e., the economic and social status, of the *taravad* or *illam* involved. Concern about *taravad* prestige dominates other concerns and is often a source of fission within the village because today both poor and middle class *taravad* have members in other villages, towns, or even states. A Nayar is far more likely to refer to his *taravad* than to his village, or, if his *taravad* is not well known, then to the name of the famous landlord *taravad* or *illam* toward whom his family is in a subordinate position.

The localization of authority in the hands of individuals or individual families was never so striking in Madras. True, the local landlords had considerable authority. However, partly because partition of the land was always permitted and partly because landlords lived on streets with other landlords, authority tended to be localized in a caste group rather than in one man or his family (see also Gough 1955: 94–8). Both social and economic relations between groups were controlled by the village community. In Tamil villages, quarrels of any kind, whether between men of the same or of different castes, were normally settled by the council of elders belonging to the dominant caste. Thus, if a man did not allow his tenant to keep the agreed-upon share of the paddy after harvest, or if a man were caught polluting a tank or well, or stealing fish from a pond or grain from a field, the case was normally dealt with by the elders.[26] Despite complaints that the *nattar* are not listened to as much as formerly, in most villages cases are still regularly referred to them.

In Madras, the internal organization of caste groups extended over a moderately large area, at least as compared to Kerala. Though the

[26] Occasionally, in cases concerning only the Pariahs who live separately in their own *cheri* habitation area, quarrels are settled by their own elderly people and are not referred to the village council. However, anyone who is dissatisfied with the verdict can appeal to the village council.

breaking of caste rules was usually punished by members of the caste living in the offender's village, there was sufficient unity within the regional caste group to enforce the village punishment or to intervene if it was felt that the members of the caste in the offender's village had been negligent in their duty. For the larger castes, the effective local organization embraced between 20 and 35 villages; for very small caste groups, the number of villages was often larger and sometimes included small towns. Significantly, in Madras villages today, lower caste groups on occasion exercise and apply restraints over higher castes in an organized way. Obviously this marks some change in the role of caste groups, though it is unnecessary here to become entangled in the debate as to whether or not this constitutes caste behaviour (Leach 1960: 6–7; Srinivas 1962: 7). What is of interest is the fact that the former extra-village cohesion of caste groups may serve new needs. For example, if the Harijans of a given village wish to protest against members of the dominant caste in their village because of some grievance, and, therefore, refuse to perform their normal duties until the grievance is attended to, it would be well nigh impossible for the members of the dominant caste to enlist Harijans from a nearby village to do the work.

I have never seen this kind of organized behaviour of caste groups in Kerala. It is of interest here to note that Miller (1954: 416) has pointed for traditional Kerala:

The internal organization of castes was localized. Misconduct of caste members was punished by local elders of the castes. For the larger castes, such as Tiyyars, the effective group of local organization was often coterminous with the desam. The zone of caste-government for smaller castes seldom covered as many as half a dozen villages. . . . The only unifying features of a caste over a wide area were the common name and the overlapping zones of kinship and internal administration; and even these often ended abruptly at political boundaries.

Today there are some newly formed pan-Kerala caste organizations—one among the Izhava or Tiyyar and a growing one among the Nayar. But their field of activity is outside the village, in the small towns and cities and in schools and factories. These organizations do not provide an operational group *vis-à-vis* other groups within the village or in nearby villages. In one village in north Malabar, it is now becoming difficult to obtain men of the village belonging to the proper caste to provide firewood for a Nayar cremation. But people manage to find others to do it, of either the same or a lower caste. If people of one neighbourhood will not do something, someone from somewhere else will come forward, because there has never been a cohesive, horizontal organization of caste groups. Vertical ties have been stressed to such a degree that they override any horizontal ones.

One might say, at least as a first approximation, that in Kerala authority ran from individual landlord to individual tenants or workers, or at most from one family to a group of families. On the other hand, in Madras it ran from a higher-caste group to a lower-caste group. The Kerala village roughly resembles a pyramid with the large landlord family at the apex (see Gough 1960: 21), whereas the Madras village situation can be likened to a ranked series of rectangles, each representing a different caste group.

Relationship Between Settlement Pattern and Subcaste Proliferation

In considering the proliferation of subcastes in Kerala, it is essential to examine both geographical and census materials as well as social structural data. Obviously such a complex phenomena has multiple causes. The greatest proliferation of subcastes occurred in south Malabar and Cochin State. This has been, and still is, the area in which the Namboodiri Brahmins have been found in greatest number and where they at one time wielded considerable economic and indirect political power (Mencher 1964). Indeed, it was only in this region that one found small kingdoms ruled by Namboodiri, namely, Idapalli and Ambalapuzha (Raja 1953: 264). Though much has been said about subcaste proliferation in Kerala, this occurrred in actual fact primarily among the matrilineal castes. The Tiyyar or Izhava, who, extrapolating from earlier censuses, comprise between 36 and 42 per cent of the Hindu population and 27 per cent of the total population in Kerala,[27] were divided into large regional subgroups rather than into numerous subcastes. As K. P. P. Menon (1924: iii, 423) notes:

In fact there is no real subdivision into sects in the community, for Illuvan

[27] According to the census of 1921, the Tiyyar and Izhava constitute 42 per cent of the Hindu population in Malabar District of the Madras Presidency and 27 per cent of the total population. According to the Cochin government census for 1921, they constituted 36 per cent of the Hindu population and 27 per cent of the total population of that state. Among their subgroups, the Tiyyar are found north of the Korapuzha River and the Tandan near the coast in Ponnani taluk. Apart from these regional groupings, the only subcastes are those of the Tiyyar barbers and priests.

and Tiyyar are but designations denoting the same class inhabiting different localities.

Among the Namboodiri Brahmins, while there certainly were various sub-divisions, these were primarily based on wealth or the one
critical point of whether or not they had the right to recite Veda.
They considered themselves as belonging to one caste, and apart
from one or two degraded sub-groups, most Namboodiri would dine
with one another, though the females observed greater restrictions.
They never experienced the sectarian divisions characteristic of the
east coast.

The greatest amount of subcaste proliferation was found among
the Nayar, Ambilavasi, and Samandan, all matrilineal castes. The
Cochin State Census for 1891 lists fifty five Nayar subgroups,
seventeen Ambilavasi subgroups, and four Samandhan subgroups.
This subcaste proliferation is probably correlated with hypergamous
unions, and thus it is not surprising that this structural feature
occurred with greatest frequency in the area where there was the
greatest concentration of Namboodiri Brahmins. Unni has shown
that the matrilineal castes tended toward the greatest dispersal in
settlement pattern; each unpartitioned matrilineal family lived in
its own compound, cut off from others of their caste. In a chapter
dealing with caste and mobility, Unni (1959) shows how, even in
the apparently rigid social structure of Malabar, 'ascent in the
hierarchy was achieved, not by a regional caste but by a section of
it, which subsequently fissioned out and shaped itself as a new caste.'
He lists some of these processes for change, showing how sometimes
even a royal edict or moving to a new locality might help a new caste
to form. If a family was wealthy, notes Unni (1959), it was easier
to rise:

It was always families which were mobile in this manner and not a whole
local caste group achieving mobility as a corporate body . . . sections of patrilineal castes which changed over to be matrilineal and uxorilocal were
more successful in either achieving mobility or maintaining the achieved
degree of it.

What was required was for a family to break all connections with
any traditional occupation it might have followed, to start taking only
Namboodiri husbands for their women, then to begin employing
only high-caste cooks, and finally, after the family had contracted
many marriages with Namboodiri, to become vegetarian and to

model other family rites on Namboodiri custom. According to Unni (1959):

... in the process of mobility, Sanskritizing of practices and rituals was not so important as altering social relations and expressing the achieved degree of mobility in behavior of corresponding symbolic value. ... Once husbands came from higher castes or royal families, what was required was to curtail social relations with others of one's caste and pattern it on the principle of superordination-subordination as conspicuously as possibilities could permit. ... One procedure might be to assume a caste name of a higher caste in the same area.

Unni indicates that there have been rare instances of *taravad* belonging to low Nayar subcastes raising themselves in both secular and ritual status, so that even the males of the *taravad* could marry Nayar women of higher sub-castes. This also held true in the Zamorin's kingdom.[28] Comparable instances in the more distant past have probably been effectively disguised over time.

While fifty five Nayar subcastes were listed in the census of 1891 for Cochin State, only six had more than 10,000 members, and many so-called subcastes numbered only between twenty three and 200 individuals. Traditionally, not all of the major subcastes were found in every type of village. Thus Sudra Nayars appeared only in villages with Namboodiri landlords, Charnavar in villages ruled by Rajas and Stani Nayars, etc. Dumont (1964) presents an interesting argument about the Nayar castes, asking the question (Dumont 1964: 98):

Are the Nayar ... a caste, and are their subdivisions really castes or subcastes? ... Whether each of them is an old population which has adapted itself to Hindu influence by inner stratification and close combination with Hindu castes, or whether a name endowed with prestige ... and has become a blanket term for most of the native population, it is clear that we have to do with populations, not with castes. ... Among the Nayar in an exogamous lineage or cluster of lineages of a certain status cannot be called a subcaste. ... All these are actually status groups which may be absolutely (or practically) endogamous at the one end and exogamous at the other.

Certainly, the small groups which Dumont notes as comprising a single lineage or a small cluster of lineages, even if they choose to

[28] In one village where I worked in 1959–60, there was a Pallichan Nayar family which has risen in the social hierarchy by first marrying its females either to Stani Nayar or to male members of the Zamorin's family. Then, slowly as they accumulated wealth and education, they rose ritually by becoming more orthodox in other respects. Today, one male member of this *taravad* has married a Stani Nayar girl, from the same family as his mother's elder sister's husband. Obviously this would have been harder in the past, but if it had occurred, it would have been to the family's advantage gradually to claim not to be Pallichan.

call themselves *jati*, only make sense if they are thought of as status groups. Only rarely do such very small groups have specialized occupations. Some of those at the bottom of the hierarchy, e.g., the Veluthedan, who are the Nayar washermen, or the oil-pressers, may be groups which have risen to the status of a low-ranking Nayar over a long period of time. Most of the higher ranking smaller groups, however, had no specified occupation, nor did they tend to live in sociologically distinct areas. Certain specified tasks, however, were often assigned to the larger subcastes; thus the Pallichan Nayar were considered palanquin bearers for the Namboodiri and local royalty, the Attikurissi were ritual purifiers after death, the Anduran make a kind of pottery used by the Namboodiri, the Kiriyattil, and the Satani Nayar at funerals and other rites. True, most of these occupations appear to have occupied only a small amount of a *taravad* member's time. Many *taravad* certainly held land on lower forms of tenure (see Shea 1959b), which they either let out to tenants or had cultivated by coolies, and it further appears likely that many of the males of these groups were also warriors. However, they did follow specified occupations which functioned as a kind of badge to mark their position.

In addition, though historical data are meager, Unni (1959) points out that there is some indication that many of the larger Nayar castes have been in existence since the ninth century. If this is true, then most of the members of these groups could not have changed their statuses over time, and the groups would certainly qualify as subcastes though they might have originated as status groups. The numerous small subcastes can be thus distinguished from the larger groups in that among the former prestige is more critical in their ranking.

In South Malabar as well as Cochin, after the Mysorean invasions were repelled and the British had occupied and united the area, there was a significant movement of population which led to an increase in the number of subcastes present in any given village. The tendency for a village area to support a large number of subcastes was further accentuated during the second half of the twentieth century, when Nayar *taravad* partitioned, and subunits moved to different villages. While branches of a single *taravad* might choose to build in the same compound, sometimes a branch might move to property belonging to the *taravad* in another village, often one where their subcaste had not previously been residentially represented.

Two factors stand out as important in creating a social milieu permissive of subcaste proliferation, especially in the case of the small groups which Dumont calls status groups. These factors were (1) the presence of a matrilineal and usually matrilocal family system which stressed hypergamous unions and (2) the relative spatial isolation of the individual unpartitioned *taravad*, each economically independent of others of the same rank. The *taravad* in its 'ducal' isolation was freer to engage in the maneuvers described above. It is of interest that there is some correlation between the breakdown of the matrilineal family groupings, the decrease in the isolation of each unit, the end of hypergamy, and an increased stress on reciprocal cross-cousin marriage, on the one hand, and a present tendency to amalgamate the various higher and middle-range Nayar subcastes. This tendency is more pronounced in Travancore, but it is already observable in Malabar as well.

In Madras, subcastes among non-Brahmins were most commonly found in different regions, as among the Tiyyar in Malabar, or at least in different villages. Among Brahmins, it was rare to find members of the two major sects, Shaivites and Vaishnavites, in the same village,[29] but members of different subsects may reside together, particularly in a large village. However, subcaste differentiation among people living on the same street or adjoining streets was clearly retarded by group opinion. Furthermore, the practice of cross-cousin and uncle-niece marriages operated to keep a family from trying to raise itself. The only possibility of advancement was for an entire group to attempt it collectively, i.e., by giving up its traditional occupation, becoming sanskritized, etc. This was certainly more difficult to achieve than in Kerala.

Effects of Irrigation and Roads on Social Relations

One final striking difference between the two areas relates to the fact, noted above, that on the east coast it was never possible to develop a complex system of agriculture without recourse to irrigation. Many people (e.g., Wittfogel 1938; Lattimore 1963; Orenstein 1956) have dealt with the influence of the construction of irrigation works on social organization and structure. As ethnographic data

---

[29] After the arrival of the British, Shaivites and Vaishnavites occasionally lived in the same village, but usually one group was composed of the local landlords and the other of one or two families who worked in a temple.

indicate, small-scale methods of irrigation and/or drainage have certainly originated and been maintained by family labour.[30] However, any method which can drastically change the agricultural character of a region necessitates collective labour and an increased complexity in social organization (Lattimore 1963: 102). Madras, with its need to modify the environment by large-scale co-ordinated human effort, presented a sharp contrast with Kerala, where human efforts to modify the environment were traditionally limited to the boundaries of a given landlord's estate and involved only relatively small-scale construction works.

Obviously there is a complex interaction between ecology and social structure. It is not clear from the archeological evidence whether the nucleated settlements in Chingleput preceded the construction of irrigation tanks or the reverse. This question is really irrelevant to the present analysis, since it seems clear that the relationship between the two is circular rather than causal. In order to construct large-scale irrigation channels (as was done with each river emptying toward the east), as well as tanks and eris, some kind of centralized control was essential. In the village where I worked intensively, the two large eris, though partially fed by rainwater, received their water primarily via the Pampakkal canal from a series of winding channels connected to the Palar River upstream in the North Arcot District. Though this system was greatly improved by the British, who built a new anicut and straightened the channels between 1857 and 1877, it has been in existence from time immemorial. Many of the tanks and eris fed by the system date back to Pallava times.

Some tanks and eris have been built by wealthy donors, but others were constructed by the state. In relation to the irrigation system during the second Chola empire (from the ninth to the thirteenth centuries) Shastri (1955b: 583–4) notes:

The primary care of the village assemblies was to get the silt removed . . . from the tanks under their control in time for them to secure the proper depth needed to store the full supply for the next year. Often special endowments were created in relation to each tank to safeguard this important work from the neglect or the penury of village authorities. . . . The water-rights attaching to particular plots of land were often enumerated on the occasions when they changed hands by sale or gift. . . . About A D 1010

---

[30] Many ethnographic accounts refer to small-scale irrigation by tribal peoples based on family labour alone. This has been reported in all parts of the world. For India, it has been noted in tribal areas of the Central Plateau.

the sabha of Nemali . . . set apart certain incomes as eri-ayam for the maintainance of a local tank. . . . Popular tradition ascribed to the Pallava kings . . . the credit of having disafforested large tracts of South India and made them fit for agriculture and human habitation . . . epigraphy gives unmistakable proof of the deliberate efforts made from time to time and by easy stages, to increase the area under the plough and the enticements offered.

Politically, it is significant that in South India the Tamil kingdoms tended toward greater centralization and bureaucratization than those found in Kerala. Even the large pre-European state in Kerala, that of the Zamorin of Calicut (which was in the process of territorial expansion and consolidation when the Portugese arrived) was loosely organized and depended considerably on the allegiance of the various local chiefdoms. No attempt was made in these traditional kingdoms to set up a complex bureaucratic machinery of the type found in Madras.

Apart from the absence of irrigation, the absence of roads as a means of uniting a state is striking in Kerala. According to Shea (1959: 512), 'the extremely rugged terrain probably inhibited the development of large, well organized administrative units because of the communication problems which it engendered.' The importance of roads and of the development of complex networks of communication in influencing, and in turn being influenced by, social relations cannot be underestimated. In the southern part of Kerala, some reliance could be placed on the various inland waterways, but for much of the country the lack of roads meant some degree of local isolation, even though people might walk long distances across the fields and along paths.

In comparing the Kerala and Madras kingdoms, some correlation may be tentatively suggested between the requirements of large-scale irrigation systems and the type of society postulated by Wittfogel (1963) characterized by a highly centralized bureaucratic political organization. However, the Tamil kingdoms were never able to exercise absolute power over the population.[31] There are two possible reasons for this, namely, the fact that the irrigation systems for each river were to some extent separate from each other and were

[31] Raja (1953: 253) states: 'Like the church and baronage of Medieval Europe, the Namboodiris and Nayars so effectively checked royal authority that the autocratic systems of government which existed in contemporary Madura and Kanchipuram were conspicuous by their absence in Kerala'. By comparison with societies having fully developed 'despotic regimes', of course, the government in Madura and Kanchipuram (i.e., Madras) was less autocratic, although it is clear that there was more local autonomy in Kerala.

therefore relatively small in scale and, perhaps more important, that the caste system with its careful ranking and allocation of interdependent economic roles served to fulfill some of the social prerequisites which in a non-caste society could only be met by a kind of state which exercised absolute power. In other words, the power of caste rules and the control by higher castes of lower-caste behaviour militated against the development of absolute power in the hands of a monarch.[32]

I might suggest one other tentative correlation between Wittfogel's theory and this body of comparative data. Wittfogel (1935: 42–3, 48–9; 1938: 6–7) postulates that irrigation agriculture is associated with a society which tends to accentuate the nuclear family as against the joint family. Since we are dealing.with a situation rendered infinitely complex by the caste system, it might be meaningful to compare only the traditional land-owning castes in the two areas. If one makes this comparison, it is striking that, whereas the Tamil land-owning castes have always permitted partition of the family property and of the joint family itself, in Kerala partition was not sanctioned and occurred only rarely until the mid-twentieth century. Indeed, many of the reform movements in Kerala have dealt with just this issue, i.e., to get permission from the courts to partition ancestral estates. Whether the lack of an irrigation economy was responsible for the traditional rule preventing partition of property, with the concomitant tendency for large households to stay together, is difficult to establish. The correlation may simply be an accidental one devoid of meaning, but the association, nevertheless, remains tantalizing.

SUMMARY

It is clear that, both in the past and today, a complex and multifaceted relationship exists between aspects of the ecology and aspects of social structure in both these areas of South India. It is not possible

[32] In an illuminating comparison between traditional political structures in Kerala and the Punjab, Shahani (1965) shows clearly how the caste structure in Kerala did not allow for the development of large unified kingdoms and how it was only possible for Travancore to become a united kingdom of fairly large size when the Maharaja destroyed the power of the local Nayar chieftains by employing outside soldiers. She shows further that stronger states existed where caste distinctions were less stressed and that there is a positive correlation between Hindu ideals and weaker state formation.

to understand either system without reference to its place within the larger man-nature nexus. In a sense it might be said that ecological factors have led to an elaboration and development of a relatively constant caste system in somewhat different directions.

It has been shown that in Kerala, owing to ecological factors, the settlement pattern was of the dispersed type. A typical dwelling unit was placed in its own garden, set off from neighbouring houses. Middle and upper class houses had their own bathing pool and well, vegetable gardens, and fruit trees, all within the compound itself, which also served as the arena for daily interaction. For poorer people, the basic unit for daily interaction was the locality, and the focus of all their activity was the powerful family of their locality, often their landlord. Property was considered indivisible among the higher land-holding castes. All families were named, family name and prestige were highly stressed, and considerable compet- ition existed between such named family groups. Among the large matrilineal Nayar population, the practice of hypergamy, along with the geographic isolation of the individual *taravad* house, increased the opportunity for subcaste proliferation, or at least for the formation of new ranked status groups. On the whole, authority tended to run from the large landlord family to those under him, in a way reminiscent of the European feudal manor. Co-operation between workers never extended beyond those working for one landlord, and even among these was uncommon. The village organization was loose, with the main function of the Nayar *desam* being to attend to military matters involving only Nayar, and of the *tara* organization to attend to social and administrative matters involving the Nayar *taravad*. Since there was no need to construct either large-scale irrigation works or roads, there was no need for a complicated bureaucracy. Although states were formed, they remained small and never attained the level of complexity found on the east coast.

Madras, on the other hand, had a relatively flat terrain with an unpredictable monsoon often insufficient for cultivation and a scar- city of wells with potable water. Here the settlement pattern seems always to have been of the nucleated variety, with the houses of the caste Hindus built on a central *gramma-nattam* or village site, and often one or more separate *cheri* for the lowest untouchable castes. There was a highly developed system of irrigation, consist- ing of anicuts built on all of the rivers and of irrigation channels draining from the anicuts to the fields directly or to tanks which held the water until it was needed. Wherever feasible, large tanks were built by co-operative labour, and roads were constructed linking villages with administrative centres. Geographers report that the greatest amount of nucleation occurred with tank irrigation, indicating a significant relationship between the ecology and aspects of social structure. People lived on clearly demarcated streets with members of their own subcaste, who often belonged to a number of different lineages, not even remotely connected. There tended to be a strong sense of village unity *vis-à-vis* other villages. There was a set of village officers to attend to various village functions, and there were common threshing grounds, burial grounds, cattle stands, grazing land, and the like. To a large extent the importance of the joint family was limited by the fact that partition was always possible, even among the land-holding castes. Though the concept of pollution was as important in regulating intercaste relations as it was in Kerala, the fact that people lived on adjacent streets tended to limit the degree of its expression in day-to-day living. Subcaste proliferation was kept in check by the 'street'; indeed, it would have been very difficult for one family on a street to try to form a new subcaste or even a new status group. Marriage was with close kin, often from the same or an adjacent village, or else with a cross-cousin, and no distinction was made in the rank of bride-givers and bride-takers, who were always considered sociologically equal. Authority relations tended to run from a higher caste to a lower one on a group-to-group basis, unlike the more feudalistic pattern found in Kerala. While the caste system limited the development of absolute authority in the hands of the monarch, there was some development of bureaucratic organization of the kind found in other hydraulic states of the east.

Differences in the ecology thus played a part in the differential development of at least certain of the social institutions of these two areas. On the other hand, the different social institutions played their part in maintaining the delicate ecological balance in each area. In conclusion, it may be suggested that some of these differences may have profound implications for present-day programmes of directed social change, most of which seem to have the nucleated village as their model.

References

Banerjee, N. R.,
1956   The Megalithic Problem of Chingleput in the Light of Recent Exploration, *Ancient India: Bulletin of the Archeological Survey of India* , 12:12–34.

Barth, F.,
1956   Ecological Relationships of Ethnic Groups in Swat, North Pakistan, *American Anthropologist* , 58: 1079–89.

Braidwood, R. J.,
1960   The Agricultural Revolution, *Scientific American* , 203: 130–48.
     Census of India: Cochin State. 1891, 1921.
     Madras Presidency, Malabar District. 1871.

Dumont, L.,
1957   Une sous-caste de l'Inde du sud: Organization sociale et religion des Pramalai Kalar, Paris.

1964   Marriage in India: The Present State of the Question, Postscript to Part I-II: Nayar and Newar, *Contributions to Indian Sociology* , 7: 80–98.

Dupuis, J.,
1960   Madras et le nord du Coromandel, Paris.
     Economic Atlas of Madras State,
1962   National Council of Applied Economic Research, New Delhi.

Firminger, W. K., ed.,
1918   *Fifth Report from the Select Committee on the Affairs of the East India Company*, Vol 3. Calcutta.

Geertz, C.,
1963   *Agricultural Involution: The Process of Ecological Change in Indonesia*, Berkeley and Los Angeles.

Gibb, H. A. R., tr.,
1929   *The Travels of Ibn Battuta in Africa and Asia*, London.

Gough, E. K.,
1952a   Changing Kinship Usages in the Setting of Political and Economic Change Among the Nayars of Malabar, *Journal of the Royal Anthropological Institute* , 82: 71–88.

Gough, E. K.,
1952b   Incest Prohibitions and Rules of Exogamy in Three Matrilineal Groups of the Malabar Coast, *International Archive of Ethnography* , 46: 82–105.

1955a   The Social Structure of a Tanjore Village, *Village India*, ed. McKim Marriott. *Memoirs of the American Anthropological Association* , 83: 36–52.

1960   The Social Structure of a Tanjore Village, *India's Villages*, ed. M. N. Srinivas, pp. 82–92. 2nd edn New York.

1960   Caste in a Tanjore Village, *Aspects of Caste in South India, Ceylon and Northwest Pakistan*, ed. E. R. Leach, pp. 11–60. Cambridge.

Government of Madras, Malabar Special Commission,
1881–1882   *Malabar Land Tenures Report*, Vol 2, appendix 1. Madras, 1882.

Harris, M.,
1959   The Economy has No Surplus, *American Anthropologist* , 61: 185–99.

1965   The Cultural Ecology of India's Sacred Cattle, *Current Anthropology* (in press)

Innes, C. A., and F. B. Evans.,
1907   *Gazetteer of Malabar*, Madras.

Iyengar, S. S.,
1916   *Land Tenures in the Madras Presidency*, Madras.

Kanakasabhai, V.,
1956   *The Tamils Eighteen Hundred Years Ago*, Tinnevelly, Madras.

Kroeber, A. L.,
1930   Castes, *Encyclopaedia of the Social Sciences*, 3: 254–7. London.

Kuriyan, G.,
1938–9   Population and Its Distribution in Kerala. *Journal of the Madras Geographical Association* , 13–14: 125–46.

1942   Some Aspects of the Regional Geography of Kerala. *Indian Geographical Journal* , 17: 1–41.

Lattimore, O.,
1963   *Studies in Frontier History: Collected Papers, 1928–58*. London.

Leach, E. R.,
1960   Introduction, *Aspects of Caste in South India, Ceylon and Northwest Pakistan*, ed. E. R. Leach, pp. 1–10. Cambridge.

Mencher, J. P.,
1962   Changing Familial Roles, among South Malabar Nayars, *Southwestern Journal of Anthropology* 18: 230–45.

1964   Possession, Dance and Religion in North Malabar, Kerala, India. To be published in Collected Papers of the VII Congress of Anthropological and Ethnological Sciences, Moscow.

1964   Aspects of Social Continuity and Change in a Tamil Village. Paper delivered at the November 1964 Meetings of the American Anthropological Association.

1965   The Nayars of South Malabar, *Comparative Family Systems*, ed. M. F. Nimkoff, pp. 163–91. Boston.

Menon, K. A.,
1961   *Ancient Kerala: Studies in Its History and Culture*, Trichur.

Menon, K. P. P.,
1924   *History of Kerala*, Vol 4 Ernakulam.

Menon, V. K. J.,
1953   Geographical Basis for the Distribution and Pattern of Rural Settlement in Kerala, *Journal of the Maharaja Sayajirao University of Baroda* 2: 41–54.

Miller, E. J.,
1954   Caste and Territory in Malabar, *American Anthropologist* 56: 410–20.

1960   Village Structure in North Kerala, *India's Villages*, ed. M. N. Srinivas, pp. 42–55. 2nd edn. New York.

Minakshi, C.,
1938   *Administration and Social Life under the Pallavas*, Madras University Historical Series 13. Madras.

Nicholas, R.,
1963   Ecology and Village Structure in Deltaic West Bengal, *Economic Weekly* 15: 1185–96.

1964   Analysis of Process in Cultural Ecology: The Case of the Bengal Peasants. Paper delivered at the November 1964 Meetings of the American Anthropological Association.

Orenstein, H.,
1956   Irrigation, Settlement Pattern, and Social Organization. *Selected Papers of the Fifth International Congress of Anthropological and Ethnological Sciences*, pp. 318–23. Philadelphia.

Panikkar, K. M.,
1918   Some Aspects of Nayar Life, *Journal of the Royal Anthropological Institute* 48: 254–93.

1960   *A History of Kerala*, Annamalai University Historical Series 15, Annamalainagar.
Pillai, E. K.,
1961   *Kerala in Fifth and Sixth Centuries* [in Malayalam], Kottayam, Kerala.
Pillai, S. V.,
1956   *History of Tamil Language and Literature*, Madras.
Raja, P. K. S.,
1953   *Medieval Kerala*, Annamalainagar.
Sankalia, H. D.,
1962   *Indian Archeology Today*, New York.
Sastri, K. A. N.,
1953   *History of India, v. I: Ancient India*, Madras.

1955a   *A History of South India*, Madras.

1955b   *The Colas*, 2nd edn. Madras.
Schneider, D. M., and E. K. Gough.,
1961   *Matrilineal Kinship*, Berkeley and Los Angeles.
Schwartzberg, J. E.,
1965   Personal communication.
Shahani, S.,
1965   A Comparative Study of the Traditional Political Organization of Kerala and Punjab. Ph.D. dissertation, School of Oriental and African Studies, London University.
Shea, T. Jr.,
1959a   Barriers to Economic Development in Traditional Societies: Malabar, a Case Study, *Journal of Economic History* 9: 504–22.

1959b   The Land Tenure Structure of Malabar and its Influence upon Capital Formation in Agriculture, Ph.D. dissertation, University of Pennsylvania.
Spate, O. H. K.,
1954.   *India and Pakistan: A General and Regional Geography*. London.
Srinivas, M. N.,
1959   The Dominant Caste in Rampura, *American Anthropologist* 61: 1–16.

1962   *Caste in Modern India*, Bombay.

Stein, B.
1961   Social Mobility and Medieval South Indian Sects. Paper
              delivered at the March 1961 Meetings of the Society for
              Asian Studies.
Unni, K. R.,
1956   Visiting Husbands in Malabar, *Journal of the Maharaja Sayajirao
              University of Baroda* ,5: 37–56.

1959   Caste in South Malabar, Ph.D. dissertation, Maharaja
              Sayajirao University of Baroda.

1965   Personal communication.
Vayda, A. P, and R. Rappaport.,
1965   Ecology, Cultural, and Non-Cultural, *Introduction to Cultural
              Anthropology: Essays in the Scope and Methods of the Science of
              Man*, ed. J. A. Clifton (in press). Boston.
Wheeler, Sir M.,
1959   *Early India and Pakistan*, New York.
Wittfogel, K. A.,
1935   The Foundations and Stages of Chinese Economic History,
              Zeitschrift für Sozialforschung , 4: 26–60.

1938   *New Light on Chinese Society: An Investigation of China's Socio-
              economic Structure*, New York.

1963   *Oriental Despotism*, New Haven.

The Sacred Uses of Nature

MADHAV GADGIL AND V. D. VARTAK

INTRODUCTION

Present-day India still abounds in many forms of nature worship. All forms of life from hedges to fig trees, and from crabs to peacocks and tigers continue to be considered sacred and inviolable in relation to a variety of primitive cults. Amongst these varied religious practices, the most significant from an economic viewpoint are those relating to the preservation of sizeable patches of forests, sometimes as much as twenty hectares in extent, as 'sacred groves'. All forms of vegetation in such a sacred grove, including shrubs and climbers are under the protection of the reigning deity of that grove, and the removal, even of dead wood, is taboo. This preservation of the entire vegetation in association with a deity is quite a distinct phenomenon from the preservation of isolated specimens of sacred tree species such as peepal (*Ficus religiosa*) or umber (*Ficus glomerata*) which are often preserved and worshipped even without any association with a deity. The sacred groves harbour vegetation in its climax formation and probably constitute the only representation of forest in near-virgin condition in many parts of present-day India. The borders of such sacred groves tend to be distinct, even when surrounded by forest on all sides. The surrounding forest, suffering some interference, is likely to be different in composition, and to lack the tree and liana specimens of truly magnificent proportions that are apt to characterize the grove.

Such sacred groves occur in many parts of India, and in some other parts of Asia and Africa as well. They exist in Ghana (J. R. Karr. pers. comm.) Nigeria, Syria and Turkey (C. C. Townsend,

Excerpted from Madhav Gadgil and V. D. Vartak, 'The Sacred Groves of Western Ghats of India', *Economic Botany*, 30, 1976.

pers. comm.). In India they have been reported to us from Khasi Hills in Assam (A. G. Raddi, pers. comm.) in the northeast, Arvalli ranges of Rajasthan (I. Prakash, pers. comm.) in the northwest, all along Western Ghats in the southern peninsula, and Madhya Pradesh in central India (G. .G. Takle, pers. comm.). The only published reference to the phenomenon known to us (Kosambi 1962) deals with the sacred groves of Maharashtra, a state on the west coast of India. The account given by Kosambi is very brief, being based on a single site and his approach is mainly anthropological, being largely concerned with religious beliefs. Our own studies have been confined to the state of Maharashtra where we have been supplied with a considerable amount of data by the officials of the state Forest Department whose co-operation is gratefully acknowledged. This has been supplemented with intensive field studies by us in the crest region of the Western Ghats in the districts of Poona, Kolaba and Satara.

A CASE STUDY

Our field studies were conducted in the hilly regions of western Maharashtra. These areas still remain fairly inaccessible by road, and have retained forests and primitive religious practices to a much greater extent than other parts of the state. The altitude of this region ranges from 800 to 1500 m. and the entire region receives a rainfall of about 4000 to 6000 mm. during the southwest (summer) monsoon. The natural vegetation is a subtropical hill forest dominated by evergreen broad leaved species (Champion and Seth 1968). The whole of this area, locally known as *Ghatmatha* (the crest of the Western Ghats), is rich in sacred groves. We have chosen the catchment area of Panshet Dam which lies to the west of Poona at a distance of 40 km. as a representative area for a description of the phenomenon.

This area lies at the border of Velhe and Mulsi Taluks of the Poona district at a latitude of 18°25' N and a longitude of 73°25' E. A river, locally known as Mula originates at Dapsare and runs eastwards. It is dammed at Panshet. This has formed an extensive lake in the valley, flanked on either side by hills which rise 500 m. or so to an altitude of about 1300 m. The hill slopes are dotted by villages with populations ranging from 100 to 400. The villagers cultivate paddy on the flat land in the valley, most of which is now submerged under the reservoir, and practice shifting cultivation on the hill slopes. Hill slopes fairly remote from the villages are still covered by some forest. Until about twenty years ago the whole region was much better forested, particularly because the peasants left valuable trees standing even when they cleared a plot for cultivation. Notable amongst these preserved trees was Hirada (*Terminalia chebula*) whose nut is in great demand in the tanning industry. However, all of these trees on the land owned by shifting cultivators, as well as some forest, were cut down during the decade 1950–60. In consequence, most of the land in this region is now entirely barren and heavily eroded. The trees left around settlements, and the sacred groves, are the only arboreal vegetation left standing except for the reserved forest in the more remote hill regions. Even the latter is suffering continuous encroachment by cultivators as the productivity of their eroded fields is declining.

Table 1* provides a summary of the sacred groves of the entire region. An attempt has been made to include all of the sacred groves of this area. However some of the groves that were submerged when the reservoir was filled in 1961 and a few very small ones (i.e. less than 0.05 hectares in area) which are still standing may have been missed, since most of the groves were, in fact, not by the riverside, but a little distance further up the hill slope. Table 1 represents a fairly accurate account of the sacred groves of this region.

As may be seen from this table most of the cults around which the sacred groves exist are mother goddess cults. The images of the deities are generally uniconic, in the form of tandalas or stones of the shape of a rice grain, from 20 to 50 cm. along the long axis. They largely exist in the open, and many do not tolerate any shelter, punishing the misguided worshipper who tries to provide them with one. The cults are often associated with ancestor worship. Small round stones representing ancestors are generally set by the side of the deities. It is notable that apart from Kalkai and Wardani, the names given to the deities are all different from each other. Even two Kalkais of two villages are often considered as separate entities. The deities are very ferocious in nature, and mete out serious illness or death to any offender. They generally demand animal sacrifices to be placated, and stories of human sacrifices in the recent past are still current. The cult spots are rarely within a village, but lie at a distance

---

* *This table has been omitted here*. Editor.

of at least 0.3 km. in all cases. As Kosambi (1962) discusses, these features of the cults mark them out as primitive cults, dating from the hunting-gathering stage of the society. The villages are inhabited by milder male gods like Maruti who live tamely in a temple and are happy with the offering of a coconut.

The area under a sacred grove can vary to a considerable extent. Sometimes it is nothing but a clump of 5 or 10 trees, all of them often large specimens of considerable age. There are however several which are larger than 0.5 hectare in extent. When a grove reaches this size, it serves quite well to preserve many features of the primaeval forest which must have covered the entire area in the past. As befits monsoon forests, these groves are rich in the number of tree species, in climbers and in epiphytes. Thus, one sacred grove of five hectares lying a little outside the area under consideration that we completely enumerated for trees and climbers included twenty-six species of the former, and six species of the latter (Vartak and Gadgil 1972). The groves lie at all locations, ranging from the floor of the river valley, slopes at various distances to the top, plateaus at intermediate levels and the crest of the hill. Thus they serve to represent all sorts of vegetation from the stunted forest on the exposed hill crests to the tall luxurious growth in the ravines.

ORIGINS

As noted above, the nature of cults associated with the sacred groves indicated their origin in the hunting-gathering stage of the society. Since no specific sacred tree species such as peepal (*Ficus religiosa*) need be present in a sacred grove, the sacred grove does not appear to be totemic in its origin. Although this is pure speculation, we may suggest that the groves served to create the proper setting for the cult rites including human sacrifices. Kosambi (1962) mentions the occurrence of groves of mother goddesses of the Attonga tribe in West Africa, in which secret rites of the cult are performed by a sisterhood of priestesses. Any man entering the grove by accident is required to join the sisterhood and to dress and live like a woman for the rest of his life. There is a similar tale in Indian mythology of Manu's son, Ila who entered the grove of the mother goddess Parvati by mistake and was transformed into a woman.

Some of the sacred groves may also have had their origins in more secular causes, in particular for the preservation of a valuable tree or climber which was relatively rare in the locality. We encountered a possible instance of this in a sacred grove of the water deity, Sati Asara, at Bombilgani (Srivardhan Taluka, Kolaba district). This grove harboured a solitary, but well grown specimen of the liana locally known as Gaydhari or succourer of the cattle (*Entada phaseoloides,* Family Mimosae). We were informed that the bark and leaves of this climber were used in the treatment of snakebite of cattle. Since no other specimen of this liana occured at least within a radius of forty kilometers, people from a considerable area relied upon this one specimen in the sacred grove.

PRESENT–DAY FUNCTIONS

With deforestation proceeding at a rapid pace, the sacred groves are assuming a more and more important role in the daily life of the local population as the only remaining source of forest produce. Besides medicinal plants such as *Entada phaseoloides,* they supply deadwood for fuel and leaf litter for the initial burning of the plot in paddy culture. The sacred groves also occasionally supply timber in an emergency such as the destruction of an entire village settlement through fire. We came across many instances of such uses in our survey. In addition, one particular village, Gani in Kolaba district was dependent on the grove for its only perennial source of water for the cattle. Other formerly perennial springs in the vicinity had dried up with deforestation and soil erosion.

SANCTUARIES OF FOREST BIOTA

The sacred groves also have many potential economic uses as perhaps the last refuges of the forest vegetation and its associated fauna. We have come across many instances of the occurence in such groves of plant species absent from the entire region. Thus, the grove known locally as Dhuprahat in Varandha pass in Bhor Taluka has preserved two magnificent specimens of the Dhup tree (*Canarium strictum*) otherwise present only in the Canara forests about 200 km. to the south of this region. The forest department officials have informed us of the occurence of the valuable timber tree, teak (*Tectona grandis*) in sacred groves of Poona and Yewatmal districts while it has become extinct from the rest of the area. The Botanical Survey of India has discovered some rare species of orchids in sacred groves in the Khasi Hills of Assam (A. G. Raddi, pers. comm.).

The preservation of this biological diversity is clearly of much potential economic significance. Many of the species so preserved serve as sources of drugs used locally. The traditional knowledge of the uses of these plants will vanish forever if these plants were to become extinct. Besides the traditional drugs, many of these could also have unforeseen uses, as, for example sources of chemicals mimicking juvenile hormones of insects. The sacred groves may also be harbouring genotypes of possible significance in future programmes of forest tree breeding or fruit tree breeding. In addition, the sacred groves serve as sanctuaries for forest birds and arboreal mammals, particularly monkeys.

PRESERVATION

If the sacred groves have originated at the hunting-gathering stage of the society, as we suspect from the associated cults, then they have indeed been preserved now for several centuries, perhaps from before 6th century A D when agriculture was probably first introduced into this region. As befits the cults of hunter-gatherers, the deities are fierce and when aroused are apt to punish the offender with death. We have heard innumerable stories of people's experiences in this regard. About thirty years ago, some worshippers of Moleshwar in Javali Taluk in Maharashtra decided to construct a temple for the god. Although this deity tolerates a shelter, he could not tolerate the wood for the temple being procured by felling of a tree within the sacred grove. The worshippers nevertheless decided to take a chance and started felling a Jambul (*Syzygium cumini*) tree for timber. The tree came down much before expected and instantaneously killed all the three wood cutters. In the grove at Dapsare in Velhe Taluk, while a man was trying to smoke out a *Varanus* lizard from a hole in a tree trunk the tree caught fire accidentally and [the lizard] was killed. The person fell violently ill, and escaped death himself only by placating the deity with the sacrifice of a goat.

The protection extended to the vegetation in the grove by the reigning deity is, or at least used to be, quite absolute. No vegetable matter not even dead wood could be removed from the grove without incurring the wrath of the gods. The only possible exception was fallen fruit which may be gathered. This is the theory as related to us at almost every grove. How far these taboos were observed in the past in difficult to ascertain. There are however good reasons to believe that until recent times most of these taboos were complied with. The taboos may however have been violated under extreme duress, or by outsiders. Thus there are stories of the deity having permitted the felling of a tree for timber when the whole village of Manganv in Velhe Taluk was burnt down by fire some thirty years ago. Similarly, the grove at Ghol is reputed to have been felled a century ago by a timber merchant who propitiated the deity by the sacrifice of a number of animals.

The taboos have begun to weaken in recent times, especially since independence in 1947. Removal of dead wood and leaf litter is now a common practice everywhere, and in fact the villagers have often come to depend on the sacred grove as a source of fuel. Removal of live wood is still taboo in a number of groves. Even this taboo is becoming weak.

In fact, a look at Table 1 will reveal that a number of groves have already been completely destroyed. Some of these were so-called *inam* groves, i.e. groves in which no deity resided, but which were preserved for the use of the priests of the deity. The priests derived an income from the fruit and other produce collected from the grove, but did not disturb it otherwise. These inam groves seem to have been destroyed everywhere. What is far more alarming, however, is that not only inam, but even sacred groves are beginning to be cut down. Table 1 again shows that some of the largest groves in the region have been felled and converted into coal. The process seems to have been particularly intense around 1950s when all this region was being deforested to meet the demand for coal from the nearby urban centres. The demand now seems to have slackened temporarily. The realization of the economic value of the groves to the villagers as sources of fuel has also had a salutary effect and led to a resistance to the offers from the coal merchants. . . .

REFERENCES

Champion, H. G. and S. K. Seth,
1968   *A Revised Survey of the Forest Types of India*, New Delhi.
Kosambi, D. D.,
1962   *Myth and Reality*, Bombay.
Vartak, V. D. and M. Gadgil,
1972   Dev-Rahati: An Ethno-botanical Study of Tracts of Forest
              Preserved on Grounds of Religious Belief, *Proc. Indian Science
              Congress*, Sixtieth session (abstract only).

'Jungle' in Nature and Culture

MICHAEL R. DOVE

The ability to project symbolic universes may well be located in the structure of the human brain, driven—according to Levi-Strauss—to resolve
the irresolvable contradiction between Nature and Culture. Levi-Strauss
notwithstanding, however, this contradiction is dealt with not in pure
thought alone ('myth thinking man'), but in the active transformation of
nature through the social labor of human beings. Contrary to those who
believe that Mind follows an independent course of its own, I would argue
that ideology-making does not arise in the confrontation of Naked Man
thinking about Naked Nature; rather, it occurs within the determinate
compass of a mode of production deployed to render nature amenable to
human use. (Wolf 1982:388)

In CONTEMPORARY URDU (and in most local languages in Pakistan),
jangal is defined as 'a wood; a forest; a jungle' (Urdu-English Dictionary 1977:265). In classical Sanskrit, the cognate term, *jangala*, is
defined as 'arid, sparingly grown with trees and plants' (Monier-
Williams 1899:417). There is a major difference in meaning between the two terms: the latter denotes an open, arid savanna stage
of vegetation, while the former denotes a closed, tree-dominated
cover (with unspecified aridity).[1] Given this difference in meaning,
and since the common Sanskrit term for 'forest' is the completely
unrelated *arana*, some contemporary speakers of Urdu (or Hindi)
and students of Sanskrit deny that the term *jangal* has any Sanskrit
antecedents at all.

From Michael R. Dove, 'The Dialectical History of "Jungle" in Pakistan: An Examination of the
Relationship between Nature and Culture', *Journal of Anthropological Research*, Vol. 48, 1992.

[1] The Oxford English Dictionary (1989, vol. 8:313) notes this change of meaning in the word
'jungle' ('In India, originally, as a native word, Waste or uncultivated ground; then, such land
overgrown with brushwood, long grass, etc.') and compares it to a similar change that has
occurred in the meaning of the English term 'forest' ('from a waste or unenclosed tract to one
covered with wild wood').

Francis Zimmermann acknowledges the Sanskrit antecedents to *jangal* but maintains that they are 'erroneous'. In the preface to his remarkable book, *The Jungle and the Aroma of Meats*, Zimmermann (1987:vii) writes

An extraordinary *misunderstanding* [emphasis added] has overtaken the history of this word [jungle]. *Jangala* in Sanskrit meant 'dry lands', what geographers would call 'open' vegetation cover, but in the eighteenth century the Hindi *jangal* and Anglo-Indian *jungle* came to denote the exact opposite, 'tangled thickets', a luxuriant growth of grasses and lianas.

I suggest, on the contrary, that no misunderstanding has occurred. I suggest that *jangal* is derived from *jangala* in a meaningful way, that to deny this derivation is to deny the human ecological history of a large part of the sub-continent, and that to fail to understand this derivation is to fail to understand where relations between nature and culture have come from on the subcontinent and, thus, where they are going.

Zimmermann (1987:ix) states that the purpose of his book is to peel away the modern misconceptions of jungle and to 'reveal the jungle in its ancient sense.' The method that he employs to attempt this is a thorough exegesis of the concept of *jangala* in the classical Sanskrit texts. His approach is explicitly interpretive in nature: 'The theme of this book, which concerns the fauna, geography, and physical realities of ancient India, is not those realities themselves but the system of formulas used to classify them' (Zimmermann 1987:134–5). At the end of his study, he states that 'I have endeavoured to show in this study that a reality—in itself physical and biogeographical—also has a social significance and ultimately becomes a theme for religious prescriptions' (Zimmermann 1987: 218).

My interests are different: whereas Zimmermann is interested in the social meaning of physical reality, I am interested in the reverse— in the physical reality behind the social meaning. My thesis is threefold. First, I contend that the Ayurvedic formulas studied by Zimmermann are derived from the natural reality of the subcontinent: I suggest that the cultural classification of the natural world, as reflected in the Vedic texts, corresponds to meaningful divisions in this world. Second, I suggest that this linkage between cultural and natural systems is dialectical in nature: as changes take place in culture or nature, they provoke related changes in the other, and so on. Third, I suggest that this linkage—and the way that it is developed, in one direction as opposed to another—has implications for the political relationship between local communities and central governments, and that the perception and representation of this relationship have, in consequence, an ideological component.

FIELD SITE AND DATA

This study is based on three-and-a-half years' research and residence in Pakistan between 1985 and 1989. Most of the data that will be presented were gathered during a household survey focussing on farm economy and ecology paying special attention to the farmers' perception and classification of the rural environment.[2] Data also were gathered regarding the perception and classification of the environment by government officials, by means of participant observation during over three-and-a-half years of meetings, workshops, and field trips with federal and provincial foresters, and by analysis of official documents prepared by the Forest Department. Comparative and historical data were drawn from the contemporary, historical, and classical Sanskrit literatures.

This research was concentrated in the *barani* 'rainfed' region of Pakistan, comprising the Salt Range, Pothwar Plateau, and plains of northern Punjab Province and southern Northwest Frontier Province. This region is quite arid, receiving . . . as little as 20 to no more than 100 centimeters of rain per year. The climatic climax vegetation of this part of Pakistan (as indeed of most of the country) is tropical thorn forest, 'an open low forest in which thorny usually hard-wooded species predominate', which merges into dry subtropical evergreen forests in the hilly regions in the north and western parts of the country (Champion, Seth, and Khattak 1965:111). The potential robustness of this vegetative cover is reflected in the varied animal life that it formerly sustained. As recently as the seventeenth century, Moghul court records and European travellers document the presence of Asian elephant, rhinoceros, and lion in the Punjab plains (Bernier 1891:374–82; Gupta 1968:85; Rao 1957: 268–70).

[2] The survey sample ranged from 1,132 households in 118 villages to 13 households in 13 villages. The study comprised five successive stages: (1) group interviews focusing on gross village characteristics in 118 villages; (2) individual interviews on basic household characteristics in 1,132 households in 63 villages; (3) in-depth interviews on farm ecology and economics in 589 households in 40 villages; (4) in-depth interviews on village ecology with 40 groups of key informants and village mullahs in 40 villages; and (5) monitoring of daily activities for 18 months in 13 households of key informants.

Today, these plains are nearly devoid of natural vegetation, and all three of the aforementioned animals have vanished from this part of the subcontinent. The contemporary, natural vegetation in most of Pakistan's arid lowlands ranges from a 'scrub preclimax' . . . (Champion, Seth, and Khattak 1965:40) to rocky wastes . . . . The little true forest that remains occurs in oasis-like hazards [militate] against human cultivation or settlement; in government or tribal reserves, where the threat of sanction minimizes exploitation; and in holy shrines and cemeteries, where the same effect is achieved by the fear of supernatural sanction.

JANGALA

This picture of contemporary Pakistan is very different from the picture of ancient India drawn by Zimmermann in his elucidation of the *jangala* landscape.

The Ancient Concept of Jangala

One of the key citations in Zimmermann's analysis of the ancient concept of *jangala* is taken from a Vedic text, 'The Laws of Manu', and concerns the king's selection of a territory for himself. A part of the citation runs as follows: 'Let him [the king] take up residence in a *jangala* place, where cereals are abundant, where the Arya [Aryan colonists] predominate and which is free from disorders' (Zimmermann 1987:39). The gist of the verse is that the king should settle in the *jangala* 'dry lands' and avoid the *anupa* 'wet lands' (Zimmermann 1987:18, 39). Zimmermann (1987:4–7, 48) maintains that this distinction between *jangala* and *anupa* is one of the most fundamental polarities in early Brahminic beliefs and in the doctrines of the Indian medical science of Ayurveda.

Zimmermann assigns the following characteristics to *jangala*, based on his analysis of relevant Ayurvedic texts. First, it is located in the western part of the subcontinent, in the greater Indus River Valley, not in that of the Ganges to the east. (My study region—and, indeed, most of the rest of Pakistan—falls within the northwesternmost extent of the ancient zone of *jangala*).[3] Further, it is located

---

[3] This part of the subcontinent is today called (in both Pakistan and India) the *Punjab*, from the

in the central, flat part of this plain, not in the mountains on the periphery. It has an arid, not a moist climate, but with water (whether from well or rainfall) its soils are fertile and will support abundant crops. It is salubrious for humans (unlike the malaria and fever belts to the east) and encompasses their settlements in addition to their fields and fallow wastelands. The vegetative cover of the *jangala* is for the most part not closed forest, but rather open 'bush' or savanna. Of most importance, the *jangala* was 'pure' and the home of the Brahmin, whereas the non-*jangala* area was 'impure' and the refuge into which the Brahmin drove the barbarians.

Zimmermann suggests that the *jangala* was exploited primarily by pastoralists. . . . The suggestion that this environment is well suited to herding livestock is supported by the former isomorphism between the *jangala* and the subcontinent's then best-known ungulate and sacrificial animal, the Indian antelope (*Antilope cervicapra*). As reported by Zimmermann (1987:61), the ability of the antelope to live on the land was the ancient definition of the *jangala*, of the land appropriate for Aryan settlement and the propagation of Brahminic culture and religion.

The Development of Jangala

Zimmermann suggests that early Aryan society was not only adapted to, but in large measure was responsible for, the distinctive vegetative cover of the *jangala*. He states, 'Everywhere, the jungle is the product of the battle between the forest and the cultivated plain. It results from the degradation of the one and the abandonment of the other' (Zimmermann 1987: 44). He writes of a 'battle between man and forest. . . . encouraged by the overpasturing of livestock and the excessive exploitation of timber'. As to how specific practices affected specific types of forest in this battle he notes (Zimmermann 1987: 44) that slash-and-burn cultivation was responsible for the destruction of the wet *sal* (*Shorea robusta*) forest of the non-*jangala* zone; but regarding the original forest of the *jangala*, he says nothing. However, if Zimmermann is correct in arguing that human society created

---

Persian for 'five waters,' referring to the five rivers that here flow into the Indus: the Jhelum, Chenab, Ravi, Beas, and Sutlej. This land was the original *Arya-varta*, 'abode of the noble ones' (Moiner-Williams 1899:152), the heartland of the Aryan invaders. The Vedic texts discussed by Zimmermann and the author of the present study come from this people and this place.

the *jangala* and exploited it largely for animal husbandry, and I believe he is, then it follows that animal husbandry was responsible for the *jangala*.[4]

The thorn forests and dry deciduous forests of the *jangala* zone are especially vulnerable to livestock (Schaller 1967:7), so, significant degradation of the original forest cover through intensive use by early pastoralists is quite possible (cf. Allchin 1963:170–71). The natural forest would also have been felled (by axe) for its timber, and, of most importance, the forest was surely burned (cf. Zimmermann 1987:18). As Zimmermann (1987:44) writes, 'Brushfires and other phenomena, provoked essentially by the presence of man, bring about the degradation of the dry deciduous forest'. Data on the contemporary and historic use of fires suggest that early pastoralists would not merely have 'provoked' forest fires but would have purposefully set and used them to create grazing for domestic and feral animals, to prepare the land for periodic, low-intensity agriculture, and to drive game in the hunt.[5]

The initial opening of the thorn and dry deciduous forests would have been followed by the spontaneous growth of pioneering grasses and herbs, which are more palatable to herbivores than the mature vegetation of the forests. In the absence of further interference by people, this initial, herbaceous plant succession succeeds to bushy plants, which in turn succeed to young trees and eventually forest (the climatic climax vegetation).[6] (*Jangala* is not, therefore, the ultimate stage in vegetative succession on the Indian plains: it is an intermediate state [Champion, Seth, and Khattak 1965:27–8, 38–40; Spate and Learmonth 1967: 73–4; Whyte 1968: 167, 173, 174, 188].)[7]

[4] Agriculture also would have played a role, albeit a lesser one. Most contemporary pastoralists complement their animal husbandry with some agriculture, and there is every reason to believe that their forebears did likewise. A common pattern involves exploiting the alluvial *bet* lands along the rivers for cash crops, while exploiting the arid *bar* lands inland from the rivers for fodder (cf. Merrey 1983:83).

[5] Cf. Zimmermann's (1987:180) comment that there is 'no jungle without royal hunting'. Note that while the transformation of the ancient Indian landscape is being attributed primarily to pastoral Aryan society, some (lesser) role was played by the pre-Aryan, agricultural, urban-based civilization of the Indus Valley, which cut down forests for fuel for pottery making and copper smelting (Gupta 1968:79).

[6] For example, *Imperata cyclindrica*, which Zimmermann (1987:44) cities as an important savanna component, is well known as a colonizing grass that is rapidly succeeded by shrubs and bushes in the absence of continued intervention by man and fire (Dove 1986a:122–5, 1986b:164–5).

[7] In contrast, savanna is the climatic climax vegetation in the Central Asian steppes from which the Aryans originally came. I am indebted to an anonymous reviewer for pointing out that the Aryans re-created (artificially) in ancient India the natural environment that they left behind in Central Asia.

The further this succession proceeds, the less palatable the vegetation becomes to livestock. It is in the best interests of pastoralists to check this succession and maintain the vegetation in its initial grassy phase. Grazing by animals helps to achieve this, and Misra (1980: 146–7) maintains that once people have opened the forest, grazing was accompanied by burning. Periodic burning, especially when carried out before the rains, retards the growth of unpalatable woody species and destroys older and less nutritious grass, in addition to stimulating the growth of new grass.[8] The value of such burning to the herder is demonstrated in the persistence of annual summer burning of pastures within the boundaries of the capital city of Pakistan, Islamabad (as elsewhere in the country, cf. Ashraf and Akbar 1989:85), notwithstanding stiff opposition by the government.[9]

The Cultural-Historical Evidence

This analysis of the ancient land cover as an unstable, artificially maintained savanna is supported by ancient principles of land tenure. The 'Laws of Manu', for example, stipulate that an agricultural field belongs to whoever first cleared the weeds from the land (Ghoshal 1973:108). It is significant that this tenure is based on the clearing of weeds and not trees. Cultivators who live in and from the forest (such as swidden agriculturalists) customarily assign tenure to whoever clears the trees from the land. If tenure in a forested environment is assigned on the basis of tree clearing, then the assignment of tenure on the basis of clearing weeds or grasses suggests a grassy or savanna environment.

The effect of a one-time clearing of the land in a savanna environment is finite in duration. A constant effort is required to keep the land clear. When this effort ceases, the savanna vegetation will

[8] Cf. Champion, Seth, and Khattak (1965:38, 40) on the role of grazing and fire in creating contemporary 'preclimaxes'.

[9] The land being burned over lies mainly within the Margalla Hills federal park. The erection by the federal government of huge hurricane fences all around the perimeter of this park has greatly reduced (albeit not eliminated) the pressure of livestock on the local vegetation, and as a result, a robust natural vegetation—an incipient thorn forest—has sprung up. In just the two decades since Islamabad was founded and the park laid out, this vegetation has already surpassed in luxuriance almost anything else that can be seen on the plains of Pakistan. This example demonstrates that the barren vegetative cover over much of contemporary Pakistan is artificial, and it also demonstrates that the ancient vegetative cover was probably robust enough not only to support, but also to require, periodic burning in order to prevent the natural restoration of woody growth.

begin to reassert itself, and the recognition of tenure will lapse. As Zimmermann (1987:14) says, quoting from another transcription of ancient law ('The Code of Gentoo Laws'), 'Land waste [viz., unworked] for five years is called jungle.'[10] The implicit recognition in this tenet of the need for recurrent human activity to oppose the implicit tendencies of the land cover towards self-transformation is characteristic of savanna and, again, supports the identification of the ancient land cover as an anthropogenic savanna.

Finally, this identification is supported by evidence on the role of fire in Vedic religion. The Vedic literature is filled with impassioned paeans to Agni, described by some observers as the god of 'sacrificial fire' (Tyler 1986:47). In a pastoral society such as the one described here, however, the use of fire in sacrifice is a sideshow to the use of fire in creating and maintaining the basis of society's existence, the anthropogenic grasslands. In the *Rgveda*, the oldest of the classical Vedic texts (to which attention will be confined for reasons of space), Agni is mentioned not only in sacrificial contexts but also (and perhaps more commonly) in ecological ones: for example, 'He [Agni] eats the woods as a King eats the rich' (Griffith 1973:44). Agni's (implicit) impact in these contexts also is mentioned, including his impact on vegetation: thus, 'On thy [Agni's] way hitherward and hence let flowery Durva grass spring up' (Griffith 1973:639).

'Durva' is *Cynodon dactylon*, Bahama or Bermuda grass (Banerjee 1980:39; CSIR 1986:156), of which Burkill (1986:739) writes: 'In some parts of the tropics it is the most important of all fodder grasses. Vast amounts of hay are made from it in Bengal.' The role of fire in managing this valuable fodder grass is attested in (otherwise enigmatic) verses in the *Rgveda* about the protective and reconstitutive powers of fire. Thus, 'Cool, Agni, and again refresh the spot which thou hast scorched and burnt' (Griffith 1973:45) can be interpreted as referring to the growth of a 'fresh' (and thus more nutritious) grass cover on burnt-over land. Similarly, 'O Agni guard the spots that cattle love' (Griffith 1973:541) refers to the need for periodic burning to preserve the pastures favoured by cattle against the succession to nongrassy vegetation that otherwise inevitably

---

[10] Similar tenurial rules hold to this day among inhabitants of savanna environments, such as the Banjarese of southeastern Kalimantan, who farm fire-climax grassland by means of cattle-drawn ploughs. They say that when the grassy cover characteristic of cultivation begins to succeed to the more mixed cover characteristic of a fallow, as the result of noncultivation for too-long a period, all tenurial rights lapse (Dove 1986a:124).

Michael R. Dove

would occur.[11] The targeting of nongrassy, ligneous vegetation is explicit in verses such as 'And thou, O Agni, thou of Godlike nature, sparest the stones [soil?], while eating up the brushwood' (Griffith 1973: 639).

The linkage between burning and the growth of a new and more luxuriant grass cover throws light on the repeated use in the *Rgveda* of the metaphor of 'barbering' to describe Agni's impact: 'When through the forest, urged by wind, he spreads, verily Agni shears the hair of the earth [viz., grasses and shrubs]' (Griffith1973:639). Throughout South and Southeast Asia, in both historic and contemporary times, it has been the custom to shave babies' heads to stimulate the growth of a more luxuriant crop of hair. The purpose of 'shaving' the earth's vegetation with Agni's fire is identical.[12]

A final piece of corroborating evidence of the use of fire to manage the ancient savanna involves an analogy between Agni and flooding. Two natural forces in either ancient or contemporary Pakistan can suppress mature vegetative successions and stimulate depauperate ones with higher nutritive value to livestock: one is fire, the other is water. Annual floodwaters in the alluvial plains (*bela*) suppress mature vegetation and, when they recede, permit the growth of immature vegetation in its place. The fact that this same end is attained on dryland through the use of fire surely explains the coupling of fire and flood in such suggestive verses in the *Rgveda* as: 'Kin as a brother [Agni] to his sister floods', and 'Thy birth who seekest food is in the falling flood, Agni. . . .' (Griffith 1973:44, 639).

JANGAL

The contemporary concept of *jangal* is very different from that of *jangala*.

Historical Changes in Land Use

During the millennia that separate the Vedic period from contemporary times, the factors responsible for the development of the

---

[11] The conjecture by one commentator that this verse reflects concern to keep fire *away* from pasture (Griffith 1973:45n) shows how little comprehension there has been of the ecological underpinnings of Vedic beliefs.

[12] I am indebted to Carol Carpenter for this observation.

jangala have changed or disappeared, and new factors have come into play. One of the most important of these is population/land ratios,[13] which have increased as the result of not just demographic but also political-economic variables. Central governments prefer concentrated populations, which foster intensive and sedentary patterns of land use. These patterns, in turn, facilitate centralized political and economic control.[14] Successive central governments have directly supported the intensification of resource use through the development of irrigation and intensive agricultural technologies. In addition, by extending their control to include forests and so-called wastelands, they have curtailed exploitation of these lands under locally oriented and extensive systems of resource use, thereby favouring externally oriented and more intensive systems (cf. Buzdar 1992). The cumulative impact of these historical developments has been to shift the balance between animal husbandry and agriculture increasingly in favour of the latter and to replace the role of vegetative dynamics with human labour.

The labour saving practices of transhumance and pasture rotation—which use the natural dynamics of the vegetative cover to subsidize labour inputs into animal husbandry—have been replaced over time by labour-intensive practices of fodder crop cultivation and stall feeding. (A similar process has taken place in agriculture, with the function of the long fallow being replaced in most areas by soil tillage, fertilization, irrigation, weeding, and crop rotation.) One consequence of replacing vegetative dynamics with human labor is the disappearance of the vegetation itself. The intensity of land use has become so great, at least in the central plains of the subcontinent, that it does not provide sufficient time after each use of the land for secondary growth—viz., savanna—to establish itself.[15]

The Contemporary Concept of Jangal

The *jangala* has now disappeared, and its place has been taken by

---

[13] As Legris (cited in Spate and Learmonth 1967:74) correctly notes, 'Savannah results essentially from the regular passage of fire, but it presupposes a feeble density of human and cattle populations.'

[14] The tension between central government and rural farmer is reflected in the phenomenon of farmer flight into the forest, which is a recurrent feature of Indian agrarian history (Habib 1982a:64, cf. Dove 1985:15–8 on farmer flight in ancient Java).

[15] It is to this process that Gupta (1968:93) refers when he writes, 'It may therefore be safely said that Rajasthan desert, if not a "man-made desert" is surely a "man-maintained desert".'

the *jangal*. Contemporary Pakistani peasants use *jangal* (in Urdu and in most regional languages)[16] to refer to any distinct, contiguous block of trees—typically not the sparse scrub of *jangala*, but true forest, with taller, older, denser trees. The prevalence of this usage is reflected in the official name of the Pakistani Forest Service, *Mahkamah Junglot* (*junglot* being the plural form of *jangal*). The contemporary concept of *jangal* has lost the broad geographic referent that *jangala* had (viz., the connotation of the arid savanna lands of the west as opposed to the marshy lands of the east). *Jangal* does have a customary geographic association, but it is the reverse of ancient *jangala's*. While *jangala* developed where the forest was cleared, *jangal* is found only where the forest has not been cleared (or where it has been cleared and then grown back). *Jangal* is typically found not in the central plains, therefore, but in peripheral areas whose remoteness or some other characteristic (such as the slope of the land or susceptibility to seasonal inundation) makes them relatively less suited to agriculture. In practice, this means that *jangal* is found either in hilly regions or in seasonal floodplains.

The most important difference between *jangala* and *jangal* involves their respective relationships to society. Contemporary Pakistani farmers conceive of the *jangal* as uncultivated, as 'wild.'[17] For example, *jungli* in common usage refers to feral varieties of plants and animals, as in *jungli kikar*, 'wild Acacia'.[18] This characteristic of wildness is partly shared with *jangala*, but an associated characteristic of 'uncivilized' is not shared with it. The contemporary expression *jungli log*, for example refers to people—living in rural areas but not necessarily in the *jangal*—who do not obey the norms and laws of the country. The most well-known example is the *dacoits*, who to this day ply their kidnapping and banditry from the shelter of the riverine forests of the lower Indus. According to popular thought, the *jangal*,

[16] Cf. *jangal* in Punjabi: 'A Forest, a wood, a jungle, a desert, a forest land, any uncultivated ground' (Singh 1983: 478).

[17] This transition from *fallow* land (within the agricultural system) to *wild* land (outside it) is noted in *Hobson-Jobson's* entry for 'jungle' (Yule and Burnell 1903: 470):

> The native word means in strictness only waste, uncultivated ground; then such ground covered with shrubs, trees or long grass; and thence again the Anglo-Indian application is to forest, or other wild growth, rather than to the fact that it is not cultivated.

[18] A significant proportion of Pakistan's remaining forest cover is neither 'natural' nor 'wild', having been planted by the government Forest Service. According to both popular mythology and historical fact, even *jungli kikar* (which most often refers to *Prosopis juliflora*), while now growing wild throughout the arid plains of Pakistan, was initially introduced and sown from the air by the Forest Service. Thus, the meaning of *jangli* has more to do with the opposition of nature and culture than with the opposition of wildness and domesticity.

in addition to harbouring those who are not of society, harbours those who are not of this life: the *jangal* is thought to be the abode of *jin* 'spirits'. One farmer defined *jangal* as 'the place where one feels fear'. This feeling is enhanced by the fact that over much of Pakistan's desolate plains, the only remaining stands of trees are those protected by religious proscription within the walls of graveyards and shrines.[19]

Whereas *jangala* encompassed ancient civilization, contemporary civilization excludes *jangal*. To illustrate, the ancient barbarians were pushed *out* of the *jangala* (by the dominant Aryan society), but the contemporary equivalent (e. g., the dacoits) are pushed *into* the *jangal*. This disassociation of civilization and *jangal* has affected the broader relationship between civilization and nature. Whereas the 'wild' formerly encompassed the 'civilized' within the concept of *jangala*, the two (with all contemporary values of 'wildness' placed on *jangal*) are now distinct. Whereas civilized society was formerly seen as being part of nature, now it is seen as standing outside of nature. Further, while the 'wild' was once opposed to the barbaric or uncivilized (in the *jangala*/non-*jangala* polarity), the two are now collapsed together (in *jangala*). Thus, whereas nature once encompassed the values of civilized society, now it is seen as encompassing their antithesis.

THE RELATIONSHIP BETWEEN NATURE AND CULTURE

The contemporary *jangal* is, therefore, very different from the ancient *jangala*. The difference between the two is not the 'historical mistake' that Zimmermann believes. His errors stem from misunderstanding the dynamics of the *jangala* and the dialetical nature of the relationship between nature and culture.[20]

---

[19] This is so frequently the case that a subfield of silvicultural research has developed in Pakistan, which attempts to reconstruct an area's original vegetation based on the extant vegetation within cemeteries and shrines (e. g., Chaghtai, Shah, and Akhtar 1978; Chaghtai, Rana, and Khattak 1983; Chaghtai, Sadiq, and Shah 1984).

[20] Although today's barren landscapes do not suggest that man is engaged in a constant battle to suppress the natural vegetation, he still is. The balance between the regenerative abilities of the natural vegetation and man's agricultural management of it, what Mukerjee (in Lal 1985: 374–5) calls 'the balance between the progressive tendencies of vegetation and retrogressive influence of man', is responsible for maintaining what is left of India's savanna (cf. Misra 1980). However, with the immeasurably greater pressure of human population on natural resources today, the forces that would return the savanna to forest and the forces that would keep it under cultivation are far weaker and stronger, respectively, than they were in ancient times. The contemporary forces for cultivation are in some cases so great that they not only

Zimmermann's View of Nature-Culture Relations

Zimmermann's concept of *jangala* is well illustrated in his use of Kipling's short story 'Letting in the Jungle', although not in the way that Zimmermann intends. Kipling's story details the way that the jungle boy Mowgli took revenge for the mistreatment of his foster mother by the villagers of the Waingunga Valley. With the assistance of the jungle's 'Eaters of Grass' (viz., elephant, deer, pig, and nilghai [*Boselphus tragocamelus*]), the offending village was levelled, the inhabitants driven off, and the jungle 'let in' (Kipling 1990:208).[21] As this last phrase suggests, the jungle had been previously '*not* let in', had in fact been 'kept out' of the village and its surrounding agricultural lands by the unceasing efforts of the villagers. When the villagers were driven away—a more serious blow by far than the simple smashing of the village walls and houses—the heretofore checked natural succession of the tropical vegetation became unchecked. Kipling writes (1990:212), 'By the end of the rains there was the roaring jungle in full blast on the spot that had been under the plough not six months before'; or in Zimmermann's words (1987: 43), 'the abandoned land was literally transformed into savanna'.

However, if natural succession could produce 'roaring jungle' or 'savanna' in less than one year in this environment (in the dry deciduous forest zone of modern-day Madhya Pradesh), then— *assuming that the villagers did not return*—it would be likely to produce impenetrable bush forest on the site within a few years, young secondary forest in a decade or so, and mature secondary forest in several decades. True agricultural abandonment does not

---

check succession of the savanna to forest, but they also make it impossible to keep the savanna under cultivation: they (viz., overuse) turn the land into unproductive wasteland, which is so poor as to rule out (for the immediate future) either further cultivation or spontaneous reforestation.

This deflection of the normal processes of natural reforestation in the subcontinent has misled Zimmermann and others. In the face of this manifest challenge to keep savanna from degrading into wasteland, the suggestion that it requires an effort by society to keep savanna from progressing into forest may seem farfetched, but it is not. If the pressure from the rural population and their livestock is removed, then the tendency for savanna to degrade to wasteland will cease; and if the pressure from peoples and beasts is removed long enough, then the savanna will slowly begin its natural succession to forest. The contemporary evidence of the possibility of anthropogenic deflection of the savanna to wasteland does not, therefore, belie the necessity of human intervention to block the natural succession of the archaic savanna to forest.

[21] It is noteworthy that Kipling chooses the 'Eaters of Grass' to let the jungle in, since the natural habitat of this group of animals is the jungle, as opposed to the true forest, in which there is little or no grass to eat.

turn fields into savanna, it turns them—eventually—into forest (cf. Misra 1980:147). Only periodic human intervention can avert this process and keep the land under an intermediate, savanna cover. To use Zimmermann's own terminology: calamity produces forest wastelands, on-going exploitation produces productive *jangala*.

This understanding of the dynamics of vegetative succession yields a significantly different view of the relationship between ancient society and the savanna than Zimmermann's. Whereas Zimmermann regards the savanna as the product of the victory of the forces of nature over the forces of human society, I regard it as the product of a fine balance between the forces of society and the forces of nature. Whereas Zimmermann regards the savanna as the product of a *one-time* clearing of the forest for cultivation, followed by a subsequent 'abandonment' of the cultivated land due to some 'calamity' (Zimmermann 1987:41, 62), I regard it as the product of ongoing, periodic impacts by society. Zimmermann believes that the forest-savanna transformation is permanent, that cultivated fields can succeed to *jangala*, but *jangala* can never succeed to forest. He writes (1987:62), 'Who could forget in India the forests that have died out, and the dramatic expanse of wastelands, the lands once abandoned, the lands then desertified'. In fact, permanent abandonment of land has different biotic consequences than temporary fallowing in the course of a grazing or cultivating cycle: while fallowing for a fixed period results in a secondary vegetative cover, abandonment eventually results in a primary vegetative cover. In short, fallowing results in *jangala*, and abandonment results in forest.

This dynamic interpretation of the savanna actually supports Zimmermann's basic thesis—namely, that the early Aryan culture favoured the *jangala* environment—more than Zimmermann's interpretation of the Kipling passage does. According to Zimmermann, the *jangala* developed incidentally, as the result of the abandonment by the Aryans of their lands for unrelated reasons. According to my analysis, in contrast, the development of the *jangala* was purposeful, the result of society's conscious management of vegetative succession for its own ends. This conception of society's role in the creation of *jangala* also better explains the strong normative weighting placed on *jangala* in the classical texts, as elucidated by Zimmermann.

A Dialectical View of Nature-Culture Relations

Two forces have been at work here: on the one hand, society's use of livestock, fire, and axe to transform the forest into *jangala*, pasture, and fields; and on the other hand, the natural processes of vegetative succession returning pasture and fields to *jangala* and—in the absence of further intervention by society—to forest. The *jangala* was thus a zone of tension; it was the product of a balance between society and nature—a balance that was intentional on society's part. Understanding this balance helps to explain some otherwise problematic aspects of nature-culture relations in both ancient and contemporary times.

There is, according to Zimmermann (1987:38–8), a dichotomy in Brahminic thought between village and forest: the former is sociologically 'full', while the latter is sociologically 'empty'. The socioreligious distinction between the two is, he says, bridged by the ecological concept of *jangala*. This claim is not self-evident, so long as the *jangala* is regarded as the product of a one-time abandonment of the land. If the *jangala* is regarded instead as the product of periodic and continuing use of the land, however, then Zimmermann's claim is more comprehensible. As the site of an extensive system of land use, the *jangala* is sometimes inhabited and used and sometimes not. As a stage of vegetative succession, it is poised halfway between nature and culture. As the product of progressive natural forces and retrogressive human forces, it is a product of both society and nature. By virtue of being an *active* zone of tension between society and nature, therefore, *jangala* is a mediator between the two, between village and forest. Over time, however, this role was transformed.

The position of the jungle in the human geography of the subcontinent has undergone a profound historical change. The ancient pastoralists (*cum* agriculturalists) literally lived and worked within the *jangala*, the 'wild'. The *jangala* contained their pastures, fields, and villages, just as it contained the fallowed lands that were recuperating from use. The *jangala* encompassed the entirety of the land-use cycle. But this changed with the intensification of land-use practices. Pastures and fields are now largely outside the *jangal*, removed from the wild, removed from nature. Whereas extensive, long-cycle uses of the land obliged society to view agriculture and civilization within the bounds of nature, intensive, short-cycle uses do not. Whereas society once depended upon the natural dynamics of vegetative succession to restore the productivity of the land during fallow periods, society now views these dynamics as a threat. Whereas extensive practices caused society to honour nature and natural processes, intensive practices lead society to suspect and disparage natural processes—as implied in the contemporary use of the term *junglees* 'forest [people]' in derogatory fashion.

The changed relationship between cultural and natural dynamics, the changed dialectics between culture and nature, explains why society does not just disparage the *jangal* but—as mentioned earlier—fears it. The ancient *jangala* was not, in contrast, a place of fear.[22] It symbolized an achieved (and desired) balance between nature and culture, in contrast to which the *jangal* symbolizes either the lack or loss of balance. Whereas the *jangala* symbolized acculturation, the *jangal* symbolizes either nonacculturation or deculturation. The *jangal* is a reminder of how society's works are circumscribed or even undone. Therefore, the jungle became a place of fear when it came to represent not the 'working' of a natural landscape, but the nonworking or 'unworking' of a cultural one.

POLITICAL-ECONOMIC DYNAMICS OF 'JUNGLE'

The dialectical relationship between culture and nature involves not just local communities and their immediate environment; it also involves broader political-economic structures, including the state. Ancient, colonial, and contemporary governments all have participated in and passed judgment on the dynamics of 'jungle'. While the judgments vary from one case to the next, they all have one thing in common: they are all 'deflected' by the self-interests of the state.

State Views of Nature-Culture Relations

I began this study with Zimmermann's (1987:39) citation of an

---

[22] It was the other half of the Brahminic polarity, the wet forests of the Ganges (called *anupa* in Zimmermann [1987], that were feared. Shiva (1989:57) oversimplifies the complex relationship between society and environment and ignores both the ancient distinction between *jangala* and *anupa* and the contemporary distinction between *jangal* and non-*jangal*, when she writes, 'All religions and cultures of the South Asia region have been rooted in the forests, not through fear and ignorance but through ecological insight.'

ancient Vedic prescription for settlement in *jangala* 'savanna': 'Let him [the king] take up residence in a *jangala* place.' This prescription clearly implies that the *jangala* existed prior to human settlement and land use. There is no recognition in this or other relevant passages in the Vedic literature of the thesis that pastoralism was responsible for the transformation of the natural Indian forest to *jangala*. The Vedic literature presents the distinction between *jangala* and forest as one between the environment of civilization and the environment of barbarism, not between anthropogenic and natural environments (Zimmermann 1987).[23] This literature presents the *jangala* as land that is chosen because it is good, not land that has become (or been made) good because it was chosen. The state's conception of its environment as ritually pure militated against recognition of the *jangala's* anthropogenic character.

The British colonial government perceived the *jangala's* more recent manifestation in opposite, but similarly 'deflected', terms. Whereas the ancient Aryan state associated *jangala* with the presence of civilization, the British colonial government associated *jangali* landscapes with the absence of civilization; and whereas the early states conceived of *jangala* as natural, the British conceived of these landscapes as man-made. British interest in this matter was based on concern over afforestation of agricultural areas. Colonial observers claimed that whenever Moslem populations displaced Hindu ones, intensively cultivated 'good' landscapes were transformed into overgrown, sparsely cultivated, *jungli* 'bad' ones (cf. Heyne cited in Bartlett 1955:280–2). The British attributed this transformation to the Islamic system of agrarian taxation—dramatically referred to as the *damnosa hereditas*, 'legacy of loss'—which was said to penalize any long-term investment in the land because its limitations on the length of tenure discourged long-term planning and the heaviness of its exactions encouraged periodic flight (Moreland 1988:205, 207). In fact, the *jungli* landscape was a product not of a flawed sociopolitical system, as the British supposed, but of a rational land-use system. This system was characteristically associated not just with a particular religion but also with a particular environment (viz., arid or semiarid) and population

---

[23] Indeed, Vedic society appears to have reversed the actual status of forest and *jangala*, viewing the latter as natural and the former as artificial (at least in some cases). This reversal is reflected in injunctions in the Vedic literature for the state (especially a new state) to *plant* forests. Thus 'And he [the King] should establish forests, one for each of the products indicated as forest produce. . . .' (Kangle 1988:59).

density (viz., low), to which it was arguably well adapted.[24] The colonial government's view was self-interested, since extensive land-use systems, which produce *jungli* fallow covers, are inherently more difficult and less rewarding for governments to administer and exploit than intensive systems, which do not produce such covers.

The contemporary government of Pakistan adopts a similar, essentially cultural argument to explain not the rise but the demise of *jangal* 'forests'. The Forest Department attributes purported over-exploitation of tree products and deforestation of forested areas to the 'anti-tree' attitudes of the rural people (Dove 1992; cf. Agarwal 1986: 108). Up until recently, state foresters maintained that farmers were not merely the enemies of the forest (i.e., the state's forest), but that they were also opposed to trees per se (even on their own farms): the farmers were not 'tree-minded'. This belief was held in the face of the fact that virtually every farm in Pakistan contains naturally grown trees (whose existence attests to at least protection by the farmer), and 43 per cent (according to my studies) contain trees that actually were planted. The government's stance is (again) self-interested, because it construes conflict between forester and farmer as conflict between cultures, as opposed to competition between equally self-interested resource users. Such 'mystification' by the state of relations between society and the natural environment follows the same pattern as the colonial and precolonial states.

Reification of Nature and Culture

The error in these state interpretations of nature-culture relations can be illustrated with reference to the earlier-mentioned 'isomorphism' between the Aryan and the antelope. Vedic culture identified the proper range for Aryan settlement in the subcontinent as the range of the Indian antelope, whose preferred habitat was the *jangala* 'savanna'. However, if the *jangala* was, as argued here, anthropogenic in origin, the actual causal relationship must have been the reverse of that implied. The Aryans did not follow the antelope;

---

[24] The Islamic system of taxation may have encouraged more extensive land use, but this must be judged within the broader association of social system and land use. Through much of India's history, a basic dichotomy has existed between Hindu agriculturalists living in comparatively dense populations along rivers and in their floodplains and Moslem pastoralists and extensive agriculturalists living in the sparsely populated arid interior regions. Whenever a population pursuing one of these systems replaced a population pursuing the other, some intensification or extensification of land use is likely to have followed.

rather, the antelope followed the Aryans. This sequence is especially clear where the range of the antelope extended beyond the climatic dry zone, as Zimmermann (1987: 59) says occurred. The expansion of the antelope range followed the extension of the savanna into wetter parts of the subcontinent as the result of human land use. Here the savanna represented an even greater deviation from the natural vegetative cover. Failure to see this causal relation correctly can be attributed to an overly reified view of nature, as something completely distinct from human society.

The policies of the contemporary government of Pakistan reflect a view of culture-nature relations that similarly·suffers from reification. The Forest Service's previously mentioned explanation of deforestation and of farmers' purported 'anti-tree attitudes' is based on a reification of culture, just as its approach to reforestation is based on a reification of nature. The Forest Service holds it as an article of faith that the only way to reforest most barren land is by planting trees. This faith is illustrated by an example from the Forest Department of the Northwest Frontier province. Several years ago, this department fenced off a barren hillside in one district and planted it with seedlings of *Acacia modesta*. The biggest problem faced by the seedlings was competition from naturally growing weeds, and the Forest Department had to devote considerable resources to weed suppression. Eventually, outside observers discovered that the weeds in question were in fact also *Acacia modesta*, which had grown up naturally as soon as the hillside was fenced and browsing by local goats had ceased. As this example demonstrates, trees (and eventually forest) naturally and spontaneously grow over the plains of Pakistan whenever their suppression by people and animals ceases. The degradation, maintenance, and restoration of barren lands is, therefore, a question of relations between society and the physical environment, not a question of the physical environment alone.[25]

[25] The Forest Service's failure to acknowledge this point benefits it in a variety of ways. The reality of the natural vegetation—that it is straining to return would the human population and their animals but let it—and its corollary—that the key to successful afforestation is protection—directly conflict with the Forest Service's self-interests. Such protection is socially and politically difficult, demands a long-term commitment, and emphasizes social rather than silvicultural expertise. In contrast, the Forest Service's purported key to afforestation—the planting of tree seedlings—is straightforward, involves a short-term effort only, and emphasizes the value of silvicultural training. In addition, the raising of seedlings in nurseries for the purpose of reforestation offers a variety of financial rewards for forestry officers. The difficulty but also potential rewards of dealing with the reality of community-forest relations is evident in a program of 'Joint Forest Management' recently inaugurated by the Forest Department of India, which aims at promoting (mostly) natural regeneration of state forests solely by means of restricting use by

CONCLUSIONS

I conclude my study with a discussion of theoretical problems in the study of relations between nature and culture and of practical problems arising from obfuscation of these relations by the state.

Nature-Culture Relations

Zimmermann interprets the jungle not in terms of the way society interacts with it, but in terms of society's needs in some other sphere altogether. Thus, he writes:

> The jungle, like the human body, provides a favored context for a conceptualization of the relations between the outside and the inside, between wildness and culture, and, at an even deeper level, for a dialectic between the pure and the impure (Zimmermann 1987:218).

The implication is that the conceptualization of the jungle was not a response to the importance of the jungle to society in ecological terms, but a response to the metaphorical excellence of the jungle for articulating critical social dialectics.[26] In other words, Zimmermann treats nature as a 'given', something that is used by society as a ready-made symbol to think about culture.

This posture constitutes a reification of nature and a reductionist approach to the study of classificatory systems. Nature is *not* a given. It is, as the analysis here has shown, subject to modification by society, and this modification is central to the way that nature is conceptualized. The concept of the jungle has to do with neither nature nor culture, therefore, but with the relationship between them. The meaning of *jangala* is based not on one physical fact but on one physical fact and one social one: first, the vegetation on the subcontinent's arid plains grows back unless something is done to prevent it; and second, it was in the interest of early Aryan society to keep it from growing back. And a significant part of this society's pattern of land use was devoted to doing just that (viz., maintaining natural succession at the savanna stage), an effort which was acknowledged in the cultural value placed on the *jangala*.

Zimmermann does not appreciate the instrumental linkage

---

local communities, in exchange for a larger role in the management and exploitation of the forest by these communities.

[26] See Smith (1991) for an analogous interpretation of ancient Indian classification of fauna.

between land-use practices and cultural values. He writes:

Dryness, a flat terrain, sparse, scattered trees, mainly thorny ones: such are the physical features of the jungle given in the Sanskrit texts. They are not empirical observations, but norms (Zimmermann 1987: vii).

In fact, they are both: the physical features of the jungle given in the Sanskrit texts describe both the landscape that Aryan society desired and the landscape that it created. The normative values placed on these features refer less to a particular aspect of nature (viz., *jangala*) than to a particular type of relationship between culture and nature (that which creates and maintains *jangala*). In short, how society views nature is in part a function of how society has affected nature and how nature has affected society. Nature and the cultural conception of nature develop together; they co-evolve.[27]

As a result of his failure to fully perceive this co-evolution between nature and culture, Zimmermann falls short of one of his own major research goals, which was to explain the historical evolution of the concept of *jangala* to *jangal*. By the end of his analysis, he has proceeded no further than his initial statement that the change is an 'extraordinary misunderstanding' (Zimmermann 1987: vii). In contrast, by treating *jangal* and *jangal* as dialectical concepts that embrace both nature and culture, I have shown that the evolution of *jangala* to *jangal* represents not a misunderstanding, but, rather, an *understanding* of historical changes in the human ecology of the subcontinent. The former approach leaves us with a mistake, a historical accident; the latter leaves us with an explanation, a meaningful historical process.

Obfuscation and Degradation

A dialectical relationship between nature and culture may explain another aspect of Pakistan's ecological history, that pertaining to the role of the state. The relationship between nature and culture is so important that it draws the ideologically motivated attention of

[27] Cf. Norgaard (1984: 165, 1987: 118) and Thompson, Warburton, and Hatley (1986:132). Norgaard (1987: 118) says that knowledge of nature cannot be independent of relations with nature and suggests that only the tradition of objective knowledge makes us think it is. This distinction is well illustrated by Spooner's (1987) comparison of Native and Western ecological paradigms in Baluchistan: he concludes that Baluchi pastoralists focus on the *interaction* among the range, the livestock, and the people, whereas Western range scientists focus on the condition and welfare of the range alone.

the state. Each of the state systems discussed—ancient, colonial, and contemporary—customarily mystifies or obfuscates the character of this relationship. This obfuscation merits attention because the physical environment with which it is associated is one of the most degraded on the face of the earth today. Is this association coincidental, or is it, too, co-evolutionary? Is a history of self-interested misrepresentation of nature-culture relations by the state responsible (in whole or part) for the historical degradation of Pakistan's environment? If correct representation of environmental relations is a prerequisite for sound management of these relations, then this question bears raising. . . .

References

Agarwal, B.,
1986   *Cold Hearths and Barren Slopes: The Woodfuel Crisis in the Third World*, Md.: Riverdale Co. for Institute of Economic Growth.

Allchin, F. R.,
1963   *Neolithic Cattle-Keepers of South India: A Study of the Deccan Ashmounds*, Cambridge University Press, London.

Ashraf, M. M., and G. Akbar,
1989   Status of Desertification in Pakistan—A Review, *The Pakistan Journal of Forestry* 39(2): 79–87.

Banerjee, S. C.,
1980   *Flora and Fauna in Sanskrit Literature*, Naya Prokash, Calcutta.

Bartlett, H. H.,
1955   *Fire in Relation to Primitive Agriculture and Grazing in the Tropics: Annotated Bibliography*, vol. 1. University of Michigan Botanical Gardens, Ann Arbor.

Bernier, F.,
1891   *Travels in the Mogul Empire: 1656–1668* (trans. by A. Constable), S. Chand, Delhi.

Burkill, L. H.,
1966   *A Dictionary of the Economic Products of the Malay Peninsula.* 2 vols. Kuala Lumpur: Ministry of Agriculture and Co-Operatives, on Behalf of the Governments of Malaysia and Singapore. [Originally published 1935, London: Crown Agents for the Colonies, on Behalf of the Government of the Straits Settlements and Federated Malaya States.]

Buzdar, N. M.,
1992   The Role of Institutions in the Management of Commonly-Owned Rangelands in Baluchistan, in *The Sociology of Natural Resources in Pakistan and Adjoining Countries* (ed. by M. R. Dove and C. Carpenter), Vanguard Press for Mashal Foundation, Lahore.

Chaghtai, S. M., H. Shah, and M. A. Akhtar,
1978   Phytosociological Study of the Graveyards of Peshawar District, NWFP, Pakistan, *Pakistan Journal of Botany* 10: 17–30.

Chaghtai, S. M., N. A. Rana and H. R. Khattak,
1983   Phytosociology of the Muslim Graveyards of Kohat Division,
              NWFP, Pakistan, *Pakistan Journal of Botany* 15(2): 99–108.
Chaghtai, S. M., A. Sadiq, and S. Z. Shah,
1984   Vegetation around the Shrine of Ghalib Gul Baba in
              Khwarra-Nilab Valley, NWFP, Pakistan, *The Pakistan Journal
              of Forestry* 34(3): 145–50.
Champion, H. G., S. K. Seth, and G. M. Khattak,
1965   *Forest Types of Pakistan*, Pakistan Forest Institute, Peshawar.
CSIR (Council of Scientific and Industrial Research),
1986   *The Useful Plants of India*, Publications and Information
              Directorate, CSIR, New Delhi.
Dove, M. R.,
1985   The Agroecological Mythology of the Javanese, and the
              Political Economy of Indonesia. *Indonesia* 39: 1–36.
Dove, M. R.,
1986a   Peasant versus Government Perception and Use of the
              Environment: A Case-Study of Banjarese Ecology and River
              Basin Development in Kalimantan, *Journal of Southeast
              Asian Studies*,17(1): 113–36.
Dove, M. R.,
1986b   The Practical Reason of Weeds in Indonesia: Peasant vs
              State Views of *Imperata* and *Chromolaena*, *Human Ecology*,
              14(2):163–90.
Dove, M. R.,
1992   Foresters' Beliefs about Farmers: A Priority for Social Science
              Research in Social Forestry, *Agroforestry Systems*,17: 13–41.
Ghoshal, U. N.,
1973   *The Agrarian System in Ancient India*, Calcutta: Saraswat
              Library. [First published in 1929 by Calcutta University.]
Griffith, R. T. H., trans.,
1973   *The Hymns of the Rgveda*, Motilal Banarsidass, Delhi.
Gupta, R. K.,
1968   Anthropogenic Influences on the Vegetation of Western
              Rajasthan, *Vegetatio*,16: 79–94.
Habib, I.,
1982a   Northern India under the Sultanate: Agrarian Economy,
              Pp. 48–76 in *The Cambridge Economic History of India, vol. 1: c.
              1200–1750* (ed. by T. Raychaudhuri and I. Habib), Cambridge
              University Press, Cambridge, Eng.
Kangle, R. P.,
1988   *The Kautilya Arthasastra*. 3 vol. 2nd ed. Delhi: Motilal
              Banarsidass. [First published, 1969, Bombay University
              Press.]

114   *References*

Kipling, R.,
1990   *The Jungle Books*, New American Library, New York.
Lal, M.,
1985   The Settlement Pattern of the Painted Grey Ware Culture
                of the Ganga Valley, pp. 373– 9 , in *Recent Advances in Indo-
                pacific Prehistory* (ed. by V. N. Misra and P. Bellwood).
                Leiden: E. J. Brill.
Merrey, D. J.,
1983   Irrigation, Poverty and Social Change in a Village of Pakistani
                Punjab: An Historical and Cultural Ecological Analysis,
                Ph.D. diss., University of Pennsylvania, Philadelphia.
Misra, R.,
1980   Forest-Savanna Transition in India, pp. 141–54 in *Tropical
                Ecology and Development* (ed. by J. I. Furtado), The Interna-
                tional Society of Tropical Ecology, Kuala Lumpur.
Monier-Williams, Sir M.,
1899   *The Agrarian System of Moslem India: A Historical Essay with
                Appendices*, Kanti Publications [First published 1929], Delhi.
Norgaard, R. B.,
1984   Coevolutionary Development Potential, *Land Economics*
                60(2): 160–73.
Norgaard, R. B.,
1987   Economics as Mechanics and the Demise of Biological
                Diversity, *Ecological Modelling* 38: 107–21.
The Oxford English Dictionary,
1989   2nd ed, Clarendon Press, Oxford.
Rao, S.,
1957   History of Our Knowledge of the Indian Fauna through
                the Ages, *Journal of the Bombay Natural History Society*
                54(2): 251–80.
Schaller, G. B.,
1967   *The Deer and the Tiger: A Study of Wildlife in India*, University
                of Chicago Press, Chicago.
Shiva, V.,
1989   *Staying Alive: Women, Ecology and Development*, London:
                Zed Books.
Singh, B. M.,
1983   *The Punjabi Dictionary*, Vanguard Books, Lahore.
Smith, B. K.,
1991   Classifying Animals and Humans in Ancient India, *Man*
                26(3): 521–48.
Spate, O. H. K., and A. T. A. Learmonth,
1967   *India and Pakistan: A General and Regional Geography*, 3rd ed.,
                Methuen and Co., London

Spooner, B.,
1987   Insiders and Outsiders in Baluchistan: Western and Indi-
            genous Perspectives on Ecology and Development, pp.
            58–68, in *Lands at Risk in the Third World: Local-Level Percep-
            tions*, Westview Press for the Institute for Development
            Anthoropology, Boulder.
Thompson, M., M. Warburton, and T. Hatley,
1986   *Uncertainty on a Himalayan Scale: An Institutional Theory of
            Environmental Perception and a Strategic Framework for the Sus-
            tainable Development of the Himalaya*, Ethnographica, Lon-
            don.
Tyler, S. A.,
1986   *India: An Anthropological Perspective* [First published 1973.],
            Waveland Press, Prospect Heights, Ill.
Urdu-English Dictionary,
1977   Rev. ed., Ferozsons, Lahore.
Whyte, R. O.,
1968   *Grasslands of the Monsoon*, Faber and Faber, London.
Wolf, E. R.,
1982   *Europe and the People without History*, University of California
            Press, Berkeley.
Yule, H., and A. C. Burnell,
1903   *Hobson-Jobson: A Glossary of Colloquial Anglo-Indian Words
            and Phrases, and of Kindred Terms, Etymological, Historical,
            Geographical and Discursive*. 2nd ed. [First edition 1886.],
            John Murray, London.
Zimmermann, F.,
1987   *The Jungle and the Aroma of Meats: An Ecological Theme in
            Hindu Medicine*, University of California Press, Berkeley.

Further Readings for Section I

As indicated in the general introduction, anthropologists have long taken a keen interest in the influence of nature on human cultures. For a guide to the literature, readers are referred once again to the exemplary review essay on 'ecological anthropology' by Benjamin Orlove (*Annual Review of Anthropology*, Number 9, 1980). Of enduring worth too are two related works by the most celebrated anthropologists of the present day: Clifford Geertz's *Agricultural Involution: The Processes of Ecological Change in Indonesia* (Berkeley: University of California Press, 1963), an ecological and historical study of two different production systems, and Claude Levi-Strauss' *The Savage Mind* (Harmondsworth: Penguin, 1966), a comparative analysis of non-modern thought systems that pays close attention to human perceptions of the natural world.

Where anthropologists specialize in micro-studies, literary critics and historians have often taken a wider canvas. Two fine books that investigate the place of nature in a national culture (in both cases, England) are Raymond Williams' *The Country and the City* (Oxford: Oxford University Press, 1973) and Keith Thomas' less evocative, but equally well researched *Man and the Natural World: A History of the Modern Sensibility* (New York: Pantheon, 1983). Finally, those interested in the range of traditional conservation systems and the conditions under which humans exercise prudence in their use of nature may consult Madhav Gadgil and Ramachandra Guha, *This Fissured Land: An Ecological History of India* (New Delhi: Oxford University Press, 1992).

II

The Sociology of Resource Use and Abuse

The readings in this section offer a more sharply focussed perspective on the interactions of nature with culture. As the term *resource* implies, the emphasis is on the material uses of nature, the goods and services it provides for human society. But where economic sociology has primarily been concerned with relations of production within human society, the broader approach represented here examines relations between different social groups in conjunction with social relations around the use, and abuse, of nature.

The social relations around that key economic resource, cultivated land, have long been the staple of scholarly work. Our first selection—itself comprising two excerpts—investigates the sociology of an equally vital resource for the rural economy, namely water. Mukerjee shows how in many agrarian regimes the most effective use of water has characteristically relied on collective effort. The study of co-operative labour and community management, he suggests, may act as a corrective to those sociological theories which view the polarities of individual and state property as exhausting the forms of ownership over natural resources. In his case study of indigenous irrigation in south Bihar, Sengupta goes a step further in analysing the technology as well as social organization of water management. While the construction of artificial catchments and channels relied on a skilful use of the terrian, their management was undertaken through a division of responsibilities between landlords and cultivators.

Moving from 'traditional' to 'modern' forms of irrigation, the historian Elizabeth Whitcombe highlights some negative consequences of the great canal works built by the British in northern India. While encouraging peasants to shift to more profitable cash crops, these massive canals also brought in their wake new problems of soil salinity, water logging, and the spread of malaria. Whitcombe's contribution has a markedly contemporary ring, for the chain of large dams constructed in the past few decades have had similar effects on the environment.

From water, back to the land. The third selection deals with the role in the village economy of common property resources such as grazing grounds and forests. In an impressively thorough study spread over seven states and twenty-one districts, N. S. Jodha documents the relatively greater dependence of the poor on these resources. At the same time, he notes the decline in area and productivity of common property resources in recent years. While the author himself chooses to highlight the relevance of his findings for development planning and public policy, from a research point of view his essay also points to an area neglected by most analyses of agrarian society, with their focus on the cultivated field.

Although set in a single village, the following selection is likewise exemplary in its richness of data, sociological sensitivity, and attention to biophysical parameters. In his study of the 'Other Energy Crisis' (that pertaining to fuelwood), Vidyarthi documents the consequences for the poor of deforestation, the decline of patron-client ties, and changes in cropping patterns.

Our final selection deals with yet another common property resource, namely ocean fisheries. In an essay summarizing decades of field research, Kurien and Achari explore the causes and consequences of conflicts between artisanal fisherfolk and large trawlers off the Kerala coast. This conflict provides a chilling illustration of what can happen when one group's exclusive control over living resources is abruptly challenged by more powerful economic and political forces. Here the advent of trawlers has led inexorably to curbs on artisanal crafts, rapid overharvest of fish stocks, and increasing social tension.

Water, forests, pastures, fisheries—these are natural resources as important to economic and social life in India as agricultural land. As was the case in Section I, the essays excerpted here also point to an important but as yet largely unexplored field of research. A sociological and anthropological perspective, pinpointing the web of social and cultural relations around the utilization of these resources, needs to be complemented by an ecological understanding of the forces behind environmental degradation—i. e. of how and when resource use becomes resource *abuse*.

Water and Social Structure

I

THE BASIS OF COMMUNITY

RADHAKAMAL MUKERJEE

The partition of land is common everywhere but in some areas we find that water rather than land is the subject of careful partition and of a regular tenure on well understood conditions. This is the characteristic feature of the tenures in the North-West Frontier Province and in the districts in the south-west of the Punjab. In early tenures it is not so much the soil that is regarded as the subject of ownership as the produce. This may be the case, especially, where land is abundant and of little value until laboriously cleared of tall grass and jungle. A similar feeling regarding water arises in cases where the land, without means of irrigating it, would be absolutely useless. The principle of distribution depends on the amount of water available. When there is more than enough, every one extends his cultivation according to his means, and then gets water for the whole. But where the water is not superabundant, it is divided according to the inheritance-fraction which each holder represents in virtue of his place in the genealogical tree. Water-shares are in some cases (where the supply is very limited) sold quite independently of land. Thus, a man may have a piece of land dependent on rain only for its cultivation, and he may then buy a water-share, or perform labour and service to acquire it. Naturally such customs arise where cultivation is possible only by the aid of rainfall, but is so inferior, as well as uncertain, that an irrigation share is really the right which possesses the greater value. . . .

Water-Sharing and Human Solidarity.—In many parts of the world

Excerpted from Radhakamal Mukerjee, *Regional Sociology*, Century Co., New York, 1926, ch. VII.

we find men living in arid territories exploiting the water by means of an effective collective organization. Brunches observes:

'When men living in arid territories once wish to devote themselves to cultivation and seek to exploit the water they cannot but submit to that effective solidarity which water often imposes upon them. In several cases where the exploited water is furnished to them by a single source (spring, stream, canal or reservoir) and where this exploitation of the water has led them to ease and prosperity, they have clearly understood, or at least definitely accepted, this necessity of the collective union of individual interests.' . . .

In different regions the recognition of this common interest leads to those admirable 'hydraulic communities' of Valencia or of Msila; sometimes, as in Egypt or the Panjab to-day, the State is led to co-ordinate the interests of individuals . . .

In tropical Asia, too, the necessity for collective regulation of water-supply in the case of rice cultivation is an important factor which has contributed to the development and perpetuation of the economic and administrative organization of the village community. In Japan and Java, as in India, rice cultivation has encouraged a good deal of fluid communalism and association of labour and maintained the compact village communities for the common interests of agriculture. Everywhere rice cultivation demands a system of irrigation which can make good the loss of water by evaporation, by leakage and by the continual passing on of some of the water to other plots belonging to other farmers, which encourages co-operative habits of work. Thus there are in Japan, as in Java and parts of India, hydraulic engineering works, as remarkable in their way as those of the Netherlands, which have been the work of unlettered peasants working in co-operation. Tunnels for conducting rice-field water through considerable hills, aqueducts, reservoirs, etc., which are met with in Japan and, indeed, throughout the Far East, represent a vast amount of communal labour hardly to be met with anywhere else. There are also numerous irrigation societies (*suiri-kumiai*) and associations for the readjustment of fields (*kochi-seiri-kumiai*), etc., which had their origin in very remote times. Floods were of frequent occurrence. Hence the construction of dams and dykes was undertaken co-operatively. . . .

The above brief survey of the forms of property and their evolution in connection with natural conditions once again proves the need of introducing into economics the examination of the geographical environment, which will be found to be a corrective of abstract sociological theory. 'Human Geography', writes Georges Gariel, 'is destined to review all the sociological theories that speculate about some sort of abstract man'. For example, the study of the different forms of ownership of water here examined does away with all *a priori* and absolute theories, both those that lay down as a dogma that individual property is the only form of property acceptable to human reason, and those that tend to a conception of state ownership as applicable to all the countries of the earth.

II

TECHNOLOGY, MANAGEMENT AND CONTROL

NIRMAL SENGUPTA

The Indigenous System of Irrigation in South Bihar

Climatic and Topographical Condition

Average annual rainfall in Bihar varies from about 1,000 millimetres in Patna to 1600 millimetres or higher in the eastern extremes of the state. The variability of rainfall is also higher in the western districts. Within this drier zone, the areas lying north of the Ganges—the districts of Saran and southern parts of Muzaffarpur—are protected to some extent by the water-retaining capacity of the new alluvial type of soil. The southern part of this dry zone—the districts of Patna, Gaya, Shahabad, south of Monghyr and south of Bhagalpur, commonly known as south Bihar—is composed mostly of old alluvial type of soil with very little water-retaining property, which dries

Excerpted from Nirmal Sengupta, 'The Indigenous Irrigation Organization of South Bihar', *Indian Economic and Social History Review* Vol XVII, No 2, 1980
Notes and References Omitted. Editor

up very soon after the rains. The ground-water table is very low in south Bihar, excepting in those parts adjacent to the Ganges; and wells can be dug out only with much difficulty. Lastly, the area has a marked slope from south to north which causes quick flow of water. In fact, the natural conditions are so adverse that regular cultivation in most parts of south Bihar is not possible if left to the mercy of nature. Yet south Bihar has been the cradle of a very ancient civilization, and has continued to remain one of the most populous tracts in the world for a period stretching over two millennium.

As will be evident from Table 1, only in south Bihar was the major part of the gross cropped area irrigated in both the years shown. The data for Monghyr and Bhagalpur must be understood in the light of the fact that the irrigation facilities in these two districts are

Table 1

Districtwise Irrigation by All Sources

District	Percentage of gross irrigated area to gross cropped area 1931	Percentage of irrigated area to net sown area 1971
Patna	55.25	58.59
Gaya	48.87	59.37
Shahabad	40.25	64.41
Saran	15.62	25.42
Champaran	7.35	18.11
Muzaffarpur	8.59	5.65
Darbhanga	5.81	8.65
Monghyr	18.77	16.11
Bhagalpur	17.31	34.39
Saharsa	22.84	12.25
Purnea	1.53	8.61
Santhal Parganas	17.33	3.64
Palamau	11.59	16.02
Hazaribagh	1.43	2.09
Ranchi	0.19	2.15
Dhanbad	N.A.	2.06
Singhbhum	14.75	3.87
Total Bihar	17.92	19.55

Source: 1961 Census (*a*) District Census Handbooks, Tables AS—IV,
    All districts (*b*) Agriculture Census, Bihar, 1971.

concentrated mostly in the southern parts. Table 2 shows the relative importance of the different sources of irrigation in the dry zone area during the first quarter of this century. Under the soil and ground-water conditions in Saran district, well-irrigation, involving little dif-ficulties, was practised extensively. The Sone canal was constructed in the last quarter of the nineteenth century; and canal irrigation has replaced the old modes of irrigation in large parts of Shahabad district as well as in the eastern parts of Patna and Gaya districts. In the rest of south Bihar—in Patna, Gaya, south Monghyr and south Bhagal-pur—the major modes of irrigation were from regular tanks and two

Table 2

Area Irrigated by Various Sources of Irrigation

(in early twentieth century)

Sl. No.	District/region	Percentage of net cropped area irrigated by					
		Govt. canal	Pvt. canal (pynes)	Tanks & ahars	Wells	Other sources	Total
1.	Shahabad	22.28	3.83	10.26	4.85	0.70	41.92
2.	Patna	2.23	21.62	24.35	6.80	4.93	59.94
3.	Gaya	4.29	15.96	26.83	5.98	1.77	54.83
4.	South Monghyr	..	6.94	19.64	3.63	12.38	42.59
5.	South Bhagalpur	..	16.51	5.54	1.21	12.77	36.03
6.	Saran	..	0.38	2.80	10.86	1.10	15.14

N. B.: 'It is difficult to say how far the relative figures for private canals (i.e. *pynes*) and *ahars* are correct since in many cases the two are interdependent. . . . In comparing the percentage of irrigation from different sources certain allo-wances must be made. In South Monghyr (Final Report, paragraph 137) and South Bhagalpur (Final Report, paragraph 207) a certain proportion of area irrigated from other sources should have been included in the area irrigated from private canals and *ahars*. In Shahabad (Final Report, paragraph 314) a certain proportion of area shown as irrigated from private canals is really irri-gated from Government canals. It is probably judging from the figures given by the Canal Department reproduced in paragraph 41 of the Patna Final Report, that a similar mistake occurred to some extent in Patna also.

Source: Compiled from the different Final Reports of the Survey and Settlement Operations in South Bihar districts (1905–1918) by E. L. Tanner, *Final Report on the Survey and Settlement Operations in the District of Gaya, 1911–18*, pp. 136–7.

other systems peculiar to this area, namely *ahars* and *pynes* (called 'private canals' in the early statistics included in Table 2).

Description of 'Ahars' and 'Pynes'

Being bounded by Chhotanagpur Plateau in the south and the Gangetic valley in the north, south Bihar has a marked slope from south to north roughly at the rate of one metre per kilometre. Using this terrain condition, an *ahar* is made by erecting an embankment of a metre or two in height on the lower ground, generally the north side. From the two extremes of this embankment two other embankments are constructed so as to project towards the higher ground (generally the south), gradually diminishing in height as the ground-level rises, and ultimately ending at the ground-level. Thus constructed, an *ahar* resembles a rectangular catchment basin with embankments only on three sides. The fourth side—the highest ground—is left open for drainage water to enter the catchment basin following the gradient of the country. Unlike tanks, the beds of *ahars* are not dug out. Sometimes these are built at the end of drainage rivulets or artificial works like *pynes* further ensuring the supply of water. *Ahars* with sides more than a kilometre long and irrigating more than a thousand acres of land, are not by any means rare. But smaller ones are more common.

Pynes, on the other hand, are systems devised for utilizing the water which flows through the numerous hilly rivers flowing from south to north intersecting the whole country. For most of the days in the year these rivers remain almost dry, but turn rather suddenly into swollen torrents following heavy rainfall in the Chhotanagpur hills. But the slope of the country is so great, and the beds of most of these rivers are so sandy that the water is rapidly carried through the region or percolates down through the sand, within a few days returning the same old sandy look to those rivers. In order to prevent the waste of water in this manner, numerous artificial channels called *pynes* are led off from points facing the current of these rivers to the agricultural fields. Some of the biggest *pynes* are 20 or 30 kilometres in length, feeding a number of distributaries, and irrigating maybe a hundred villages. Since the beds of the sandy rivers of south Bihar are usually high, there is no need to make the *pyne* beds deep in order to divert the water into those. Further, because of the gradual slope of the country, within a few kilometres from its beginning, the beds of the *pynes* rise to near the level of the ground to facilitate irrigation of the adjacent areas, while still retaining sufficient fall to ensure the flow of water from the rivers into it. To raise the water level to field level the *pynes* are temporarily blocked at suitable length. In this way some of the small rivers of south Bihar never reach any of the main rivers like the Ganges or the Punpun, and are completely dispersed by several *pynes*. Sometimes *pynes* are impounded into *ahars* at the end, ensuring storage of any superfluous water. Alternatively, small *pynes* are also led from *ahars* for distribution of water. Both *ahars* and *pynes* generally carry water during the rainy season, from July to September, and guarantee against the untimely or scanty rainfall, frequent in south Bihar.

In the course of his Bhagalpur trip, Francis Buchanan was not much impressed by these irrigation works. He had felt that in comparison to similar works (i.e. tanks and *anicuts*) in Mysore, the works in south Bihar were 'vastly more imperfect' which he conceded had happened 'probably because the necessity is not nearly so great' in south Bihar. He had, of course, admired the economy of water use by impounding *pynes* into *ahars* as a 'judicious plan, so much neglected in Mysore.' As he proceeded further from Bhagalpur to reach Gaya, much of his earlier reservation vanished. His earlier characterization was that no attempt had been made to construct perennial works in the south Bihar system, and the intention was limited 'to supply the fields in intervals of fair weather that occasionally happen during the rainy season, and for the first month after these [rains] cease.' While in Gaya, he learnt that 'both canals and reservoirs contain also so considerable a supply, that they enable the farmer not only to bring the crop of rice to maturity, but, by the means of above mentioned [manual water-lifts], enable him to rear a winter crop of wheat, barley, &c.' Thus, although apparently crude, the *ahar-pyne* system is a remarkable indigenous system making possible the best out of a very unfavourable natural condition. Apart from the irrigation facilities there is still another utility of the system which has rarely been investigated. Being a region in between Chhotanagpur Plateau and the Gangetic valley, south Bihar is very prone to floods. But the abundance of storage works as *ahars* and the large-scale dispersion of torrential flood water into the *pynes* has minimized the rush and speed of the flood water passing through south Bihar.

The *ahar* and *pyne* system of irrigation attained its highest development in the district of Gaya. The first Irrigation Commission (1901–3) had noted that in total 1,670,000 acres—more than half of the total area of the district—was said to be watered in this way. As will be evident from Table 2, nearly three-fourths of the total irrigation facilities in south Bihar (excluding Sone canal command area) were from *ahars* and *pynes*. Among the other methods of irrigation, well-irrigation alone was of some importance. But wells were constructed, maintained and operated mostly by individual efforts and raised few social problems. The discussion here will be restricted only to the *ahar* and *pyne* systems.

Method of Cultivation and Irrigation

To a ryot of Eastern Bengal the country would seem utterly unsuitable for rice cultivation, both from the nature of the surface and the comparative throughly the plants begin to deteriorate at a steady rate. Thus, although the cultivators expect late rains during *Hathiya* no one will risk practising *nigar* hoping for a timely rain. The need for irrigation from *ahars* and *pynes* is mostly felt during *Hathiya nakshatra*, and even if there is good rain during this time and little artificial irrigation is actually practised, the irrigation works go far to increase the yield by encouraging the cultivators to undertake *nigar* operations. The late rains during *Hathiya* is crucial also for the sowing of the *rabi* crops. In case there is a failure in some year the cultivators exert their efforts to use up the last bit of water left in *ahars* and *pynes* for preparation of rabi fields for sowing, after irrigating the rice crop.

What great protection the *ahar-pyne* system of irrigation of south Bihar had lent to the tract can be understood from the fact that Gaya district, where the system reached its highest level of development, remained practically immune to famines while the rest of India suffered from several big famines. In the year 1866, the year of the so-called Orissa Famine, during the Bihar Famine caused by the untimely rain in 1873–4, and during one of the greatest famines in record, the famine of 1896–7, the district of Gaya required practically no relief, although the whole of the eastern region had suffered very badly. It is however significant that the immunity to famines began to disappear once the irrigation works began deteriorating. There were several years of scarcity in the thirties of this century. Gaya district, in particular Nawadah sub-division, was in the grip of severe droughts and famines in 1950–2 and 1957–9. Lastly the famine of 1966 struck Gaya district with the same severity as it struck other districts of Bihar. Today Gaya is regarded partly as a drought-prone area, no more as an area immune to famines.

Like famines, Gaya district was also immune to floods in the heyday of indigenous irrigation. But in recent years that immunity too has been lost.

A Note on Antiquity of the System

The effective settlement of the middle Ganges Plain does not seem to have begun until the eighth and ninth centuries BC. It is suggested that the dense forest cover had probably delayed settlement of this region. The first evidence of rice being grown on the margins of the Ganges delta dates from 700 BC. The effective occupation was even later. By then the settlers had probably known plough and iron axes without which settlement of this forest region would probably not have been possible. It appears that another invention—the characteristic irrigation system of this region—contributed greatly to, if not the original settlement, at least the extensive and dense settlement in this region. The *ahar-pyne* system of irrigation was already well in use during the time of the *Jatakas*. The *Kunala Jataka*, written in this area, mentions that canals were excavated communally and served sometimes as demarcation lines between two neighbouring properties, that the use of this commonly owned water often gave rise to keen dispute, that it was not uncommon for the course to be diverted in the direction of one village's fields at the expense of another's. In such cases violent quarrels resulted which developed occasionally into pitched battles between rival villages and the disagreement had to be brought before the local council for adjudication. The description sounds as if it is happening in a south Bihar village in modern times.

In the *Arthashastra* there is reference to *aharyodaka-setu* as a method used for irrigation. The word *para* (see *parabandi* later) is also found in the same book as a regulation for the violation of which persons shall be fined 6 *panas*. However, *para* and similar words (e.g. *wara* in Punjab) are still in use to describe the rotational arrangements in irrigation not merely in south Bihar but also in many other corners of India. Megasthenes' description too confirms the existence of closed canals in Bihar, from which water was distributed in the conduits for the purpose of irrigation. It must be understood that even if such earthworks had existed quite extensively in ancient times it would be impossible to find any trace of those in archaeological excavations. On the other hand, it may not be very surprising if some of the surviving works happen to be so old.

Social Organization

Such a society, with irrigated agriculture based on large irrigation works, has to accomplish several social tasks peculiar to irrigation. There is a set of technical tasks relating to planning, construction and maintenance of irrigation works. There is a set of relations necessary for the control and allocation of water among the users for meeting the cost and labour required in carrying out the technical works, for resolution of conflicts and even for organization of rituals, if any. Both Julian Steward and Karl Wittfogel had made the drastic generalization that the irrigation works in traditionally irrigated societies were centrally organized, requiring complete control over labour power. This gave rise to bureaucratic management, from which emerged a bureaucratic state power, despotic in its nature. Thereby resulted 'a state stronger than the society', and consequently, social relations were determined according to the needs of the despotic state, and were delegated to social classes by the state power. However various studies indicate that the social organizations in such irrigated societies are not as strongly modelled as suggested by Wittfogel, and that there are various aspects of social relations which deserve special attention. In this paper I will restrict my discussion to the production relations between the cultivators and their overlords, and only to those relations which arise because of the irrigation works. The relations among the individual cultivators, among the artisans, labourers and cultivators in the irrigated villages, among the residents of different villages using the same source of irrigation—all of which form interesting and important aspects of social relations—are not dealt with here. Further the availability of data imposes restrictions on the period of inquiry in this study. The discussion here will mostly be confined within the period of colonial rule. However, there is an interesting aspect within this period—there occurs a transformation of the social organization of irrigation in south Bihar. In the following section of the article that transition will be the major focus.

Physical Aspects of Organization

Hunt and Hunt inferred, from a review of the various studies on indigenous social organization of irrigation works, that the social organizations at higher levels are involved in matters of infrequent decisions, e.g. construction, repair of major areas of conflict including external conflicts. The areas of interaction between the village communities and the overlords—the *zamindars*, in south Bihar—with respect to irrigation works were more or less the same. During the *zamindari* days, the responsibilities of construction and maintenance of the *ahars* and *pynes* lay mainly with the *zamindars*, although there is no mention that they were responsible for similar works on the smaller distribution channels emanating from *ahars* and *pynes* and for distribution of irrigation water within the villages. Most of the *ahars* and *pynes* were very old and how these were constructed cannot be asserted, although officials have been emphatic that they were constructed by the *zamindars*, presumably inferring this from the records of construction of the few works undertaken in the nineteenth century. Fragmentary references to the modes of operation of the *zamindars* in matters of construction and maintenance are available. 'The expenses both of making and repairing the canals and reservoirs is entirely defrayed by the zamindars' observed Buchanan. Besides, there was a collective system called *goam* in which every cultivator had to supply one man per plough to turn out on certain occasions and carry out the physical works. But the *zamindars* had the responsibility of organizing such collective work by fixing and announcing the date of *goam* and even by forcing the unwilling to participate in such matters. The maintenance works need to be carried out regularly. If repaired regularly, these works do not involve very great effort either in manpower or in finance. But negligence results into quick deterioration of these crude works, so much that within a few years, even the trace of an old work may be difficult to locate. The smaller parts of these repair works, the negligence of which would affect only a few plots were probably done by the interested cultivators themselves. The responsibility of the *zamindars* lay more in organizing works which involved the interests of several villages.

Allocation of water within the villages was managed mostly by the cultivators themselves. Allocation between villages was a major source of conflict, and was a concern of the *zamindars*. Buchanan wrote that the *zamindars* would 'appoint proper persons to divide the water among the tenantry.' More detailed description is obtained for the later period. There was a system called *parabandi* by which the distribution of water among the villages from a common source (usually *pyne*) was regulated. Usually *parabandi* arrangements began in the month of *Aswin* (mid-September), when the demand was acute and the supply limited, and lasted for a month or two. At other times of the year it was usual to leave all branches of *pynes* open and let anyone use the residual water if one could. The *parabandi* arrangements consisted of more than one cycle of watering. Beginning from any one side of the *pyne* each village had its quota fixed either in the number of days or in the number of hours, thus assuring fair distribution to all the villages. After the completion of one cycle, the process was repeated in the same order (i.e. another cycle began) approximately after a gap of two weeks. In the principal *pynes* in Gaya district there were written regulations for *parabandi* arrangements. The Tikari Raj, the major *zamindar* family of Gaya, had in its possession an elaborate register called *lal bahi*, specifying the rights of each village enjoying irrigation facilities from such important *pynes*. For other smaller works, the regulations were mostly customary, until the beginning of this century. . . .

Canal Irrigation and Ecological Change in Colonial North India

ELIZABETH WHITCOMBE

... The great nineteenth-century developments in canal engineering were concentrated largely in the Doab. They began early, in the 1820s, with the building of the East Jumna Canal. This system, a radical re-development of an old Mughal canal line, was opened in 1830. It irrigated tracts in the Saharanpur, Muzaffarnagar, and Meerut districts. By 1878, its main and branch channels, together with distributaries, totalled 748 miles and irrigated 206,732 acres (as against the average of the preceding five years, 188,648). The cost of the works, excluding interest, came to £ 261,235. One of the most remunerative canals of British India, it paid nearly 23 per cent on the capital expended on it by Government.

Irrigation in the grand manner began, however, with the Ganges Canal. The works were begun under Government order on May 1847, water was admitted into the canal in 1854, and irrigation commenced the following year. In 1861–2, the area irrigated by the canal was officially set at 372,000 acres; in 1864–5, it was set at 350,000 acres (the area under canal irrigation had contracted in comparison with the figures for 1861–2 as a result of good seasons and adequate rainfall). By 1864–5, the canal works as completed comprised its main line (181 miles); the Fategarh Branch (82.5 miles); the Buland-shahr Branch (45 miles); the Cawnpore Branch (170 miles); and the Etawah Branch (170 miles)—a total length of 648.5 miles with 2,266 miles of distributaries. The total capital outlay thus far was £ 2,155,997—by 1866, capital expended on the canal stood at more

Excerpted from Elizabeth Whitcombe: *Agrarian Conditions in Northern India Vol I. The United Provinces under British Rule, 1860–1900*, University of California Press and Thomson Press, 1971, pp. 64–85.

Notes and References omitted. Editor.

than 88 per cent of total expenditure of British capital in the North
Western Provinces (NWP) since 1858. So far, only Upper Doab districts were served by the canal. In 1868, on the proposal of General
(later Sir) Richard Strachey, the construction of a Lower Ganges
Canal began, together with modifications in the completed channels.
By 1877–8, the area actually irrigated by the whole complex was set
at 1,045,013 acres (as against the average of the preceding five years:
906,036). Some 593 miles of main and branch lines had been completed by then in the Upper and Central Doab. With another 3,417
miles of distributaries, the total length of the channels constructed
ran into 4,010 miles, and the cost, excluding interest, stood at
£ 3,055,015.

In 1868, the first works—sanctioned for the purposes of famine
relief—began on the Agra Canal. In March 1874, the canal was formally opened and irrigation began the following *rabi* season. By
1877–8, it commanded an area of 375,800 acres altogether—114,200
acres in Muttra district and a further 113,100 acres in Agra made up
the proportion irrigated in the NWP. Smaller works in Bijnour, fed
by a stream in Moradabad district, covered an area of 4,000 to 5,000
acres. On a capital cost of £ 6,996, the Bijnour Canal paid 11 to 12
per cent: 'it has always been a remunerative little work', was R. B.
Buckley's comment. In Bareilly, a further group of some four channels, totalling 256 miles in length and known collectively as the
Rohilkhand Canals, irrigated a belt of country along the terai where
rice was grown extensively. The capital cost was £ 148,207, on which
only a small percentage had been realized by the end of 1870s. A
series of small watercourses in the Dun, and south in Bundelkhand,
fed by tanks and streams, completed the network of canals in the
NWP: some 5,601 miles of channels and distributaries, irrigating
in 1877–8 an area of 1,459,938 acres, by which time the cost of
their construction, excluding the payment of interest, came to
£ 4,338,384—all of it borrowed in England.

Works continued on the modifications and extensions to the
Ganges Canal, as projected. After 1878, further works for the protection of unirrigated tracts specially liable to drought were thence-
forward to be closely scrutinized by Government, 'in the light of
the latest knowledge', with rigorous attention to the 'financial
liabilities of the execution of works'. On these principles, General
Richard Strachey, as President of the Famine Commission of 1878–9,
recommended immediate and special enquiry into two schemes

which had not yet been implemented: the Sardah Canal to be constructed in Oudh and Rohilkhand, an elaborate project first prepared by Major (later Colonel) J. G. Forbes, R. E., in 1871, and a system of canals to be supplied from the rivers Betwa and Ken in Bundelkhand. The Sardah scheme was shelved in the face of opposition by both the talukdars of Oudh and the Chief Commissioner. Work on the Betwa Canal however, owing to pressure to provide relief for famine distress in the conventional form of temporary employment on public works was begun early in the 1880s.

Accurate statistics cannot be given of the overall increase in irrigated area owing to the canals. Acreages fluctuated with the seasons, the irrigated area expanding vastly with the threat of drought, to contract again in seasons of adequate rainfall. The question of payment of water rates also affected the area under irrigation during each season. In tracts where the cultivators were dependent on the canals, times in the *fasli* year when measurements were taken varied from district to district, pargana to pargana, and even mauza to mauza, thwarting any attempt at the compilation of a comprehensive statistical record. The period over which the increases in area were to be measured also posed a problem which was insoluble given the recording procedure used. Time limits were fixed according to the dates of revenue records compiled under Regulation IX of 1833: the period within which measurements were taken varied therefore from district to district, in the order of their settlement. In many cases, no statistics of irrigated area existed prior to the revision of settlements beginning in 1860. Further, both the earlier and revised settlements made no distinction between 'irrigable' and 'irrigated'. In 1884, W. C. Benett noted that an enquiry by the director of Agriculture and Commerce 'showed that [in several Doab districts] the settlement statistics are of no use in ascertaining the irrigated area, lands within irrigating distance of a well or tank being included in the actually irrigated area . . .'. Lastly, the problem of inadequate statistics is complicated by discrepancies in the percentage of increase in irrigated and in cultivated areas given in the various official sources.

Canal development was concentrated in those areas where facilities existed for it—that is, in western districts of the NWP. Those districts had a long-established and sophisticated pattern of farming, in which well irrigation particularly played a large part.

Colonel Baird Smith estimated that in 1848–9 the number of *pakka* (masonry) wells in the NWP came to some 137,337 of which 72,523 were in the Doab. Devastation during the 'Mutiny' brought this latter number down to close to 70,000, with each well having an irrigating capacity of approximately 4.5 acres per season. The corresponding number of the more common *kachha* (temporary) wells was estimated at 280,000, each with an irrigating capacity of 1.5 acres per season. From this, Baird Smith concluded that some 1,470,000 acres in the Doab were irrigated by wells in 1860–1. As the number of wells and their relatively low irrigating capacity would suggest, the Doab districts were densely populated by the latter part of the nineteenth century. Table 1 gives the density of population for selected canal-irrigated districts for which figures are available from the settlement reports.

Table 1

Density of Population for Selected Canal-Irrigated Districts

Canal	District	Population per square Mile[a]
Ganges, East Jumna	Muzaffarnagar (1872)[b]	415.9
Ganges	Bulandshahr (1865)	719.5
Ganges	Aligarh (1882)	548.0
Ganges	Etah (1872)	465.0
Ganges	Mainpuri (1872)	452.0
Ganges	Etawah (1872)	395.0
Ganges	Cawnpore[c] (1872)	442.0
Ganges	Fatehpur (1872)	419.0
Ganges	Farukhabad (1871)	534.0

[a] According to the census of 1872, the average density of population for the NWP was 381.24 per square mile.

[b] The dates in brackets are those of the various settlement reports used.

[c] Excluding Cawnpore city.

For its part in supplying this dense population, the well irrigation of the Doab was not regarded by Baird Smith and other official
observers trained in engineering as wholly inefficient. He himself
noted, significantly, that the effects of wells were 'less open to
doubt than those of canal-irrigation', whilst the labour required to
work the wells ensured the maximum use of water drawn; it was
clear also that 'the produce from land under well-irrigation is generally larger and better than that watered in any other way'. The
only trouble with the wells was that they did not produce enough.
The land had to be induced to produce more, and to achieve that
the canal system had to be expanded. Baird Smith confidently
anticipated that in time canal irrigation would show results comparable to those of the wells, and that over the enormously increased
area opened to irrigation by the canal system, 'existing differences
in relative value will disappear .

In Meerut, the richest of the Doab districts, irrigation prior to the
introduction of canals had 'naturally coincided very much with the
character of the soils', E. C. Buck noted in 1874 in reviewing the settlement report. As a general conclusion from the pargana reports,
it was clear that wells could be dug more easily, and lasted longer,
in proportion to their distance from the great natural drainage
lines: 'the best well tracts were on watersheds'. It was precisely
these tracts which the new canals covered most extensively—canals being 'only serviceable for irrigation along the watersheds of
the district'. The East Jumna Canal, opened in 1830, supplied the
'rich Jat country between the Jumna and Hindun with a close network of distributary channels'. The main line of the Ganges Canal,
opened in 1855, ran through the centre, level tract between the
Hindun and the Kali Nadi, whilst its Anupshahr Branch, opened
five years later, fed the comparatively narrow but fertile strip between the Kali Nadi and the Ganges. The division between areas
with high proportions of better soils and the poorer tracts intensified: parganas Puth and Gurhmukhtesur, where widespread irrigation by wells was impracticable owing to the predominance of
bhur ridges, also lay outside the range of canals and remained unreclaimed, whilst the extension of irrigation through the naturally
fertile areas—for example, the central tracts of parganas Jalalabad
and Baghpat—was reported by the end of the 1860s to have produced
immediate and extraordinary increases in production. Where the

soils were of the stiffest composition, well construction remained at least theoretically possible alongside the introduction of canals. In pargana Kotanah, to the north-west of the district, channels of the East Jumna Canal covered almost the entire area, yet good wells could still be readily constructed. This was reassuring: 'In case of any accident to the canal, there could not possibly be any danger to the imperial revenue, for temporary wells could be dug in every field at trifling expense.' The supersession of wells by the canals, which immediately commanded a much greater area was said to have saved Kotanah and neighbouring parganas—the core of the opulent estate of the Begam Sumroo—from the ravages of famine in 1860–1; indeed, 'the proprietors' (chiefly Jats) made enormous profits from the grain trade. To the south, pargana Dasnah benefited similarly from the Ganges Canal.

Elsewhere, however, disadvantages and even deleterious effects of the canals were already becoming noticeable by the end of the 1860s. The growing dependence on canal irrigation brought its problems. In 1866, W. A. Forbes noted that in pargana Chaprauli, which he, like Sir Henry Elliot thirty years before, agreed to be the finest in the district, the inroad of canals had left most wells in disuse and that well-sinking was now 'almost entirely abandoned. It would be fortunate', he cautioned, 'if the people would take further advantage of the natural facilities for well-irrigation, and thus guard against the uncertainties of canal-supply—a precaution some of the enterprizing Jat proprietors in the neighbourhood have already begun to recognize.' J. S. Porter noted the advantage the canal brought to pargana Sirdhana in that it enabled 'sugar and other more valuable products doubtless to be grown in greater abundance'. But against this 'is to be placed the uncertainty of the water supply and the utter dependence on the canal to which the people are reduced by the ruin of their wells'. Several villages in the pargana had already sustained loss from the canal's (or its distributaries) interference with natural drainage: two had lost their entire *kharif* owing to flood water which had swamped the fields because its outlets had been obstructed by the canal; a considerable part of another mauza just beneath the canal bank was so swamped by percolation as to be unfit for cultivation. In other areas—parts of Baghpat, for instance—puddling was the inevitable consequence of the volume of water made available from the canal, far exceeding that supplied by wells and distributed by flush irrigation. Problems of soil saturation were imminent. Buck, however, noted with reassurance in 1874 that it was 'entirely within the Government's power to alleviate or entirely remove these evils'.

Wherever canal irrigation had been introduced, the same—or similar—benefits accrued, as well as the same problems. If the driving principle behind the construction of the canals was the achievement of increase, without which no real prosperity could be envisaged, this aim was certainly satisfied, even if its exact measure remains out of reach. But in which products was this increase realized?

The overwhelming majority of the population—the peasantry—relied on the *kharif* millets, principally *jowar* and *bajra*, and the various pulses for staple food grains. These and fodder for draught beasts were generally grown on the wider areas of middle- and even poor-quality soils dependent for their moisture on periodic rainfall; irrigated land, of better- and top-quality soils, was used for the heavier and more valuable crops which required careful attention and a number of waterings in addition to rainfall for good yields. The expansion of irrigated and irrigable areas through the introduction of canals resulted in the increase in production of these 'valuable' crops—principally cotton, indigo, sugar cane, and wheat.

In the trans-Jumna parganas of Muttra district before the building of the Agra Canal, the principal *kharif* crops were *jowar*, *bajra*, and cotton, and the chief *rabi* staples were barley, gram, and *bejhar* (mixed barley and gram). The canal was confidently expected to alter this, in favour of the 'richer' crops. Whilst the area under cotton would be little affected, the pattern of cereal cultivation would show significant changes—'the substitution of irrigated wheat [encouraged by the relative richness of soils in these parganas], bejhar or barley for either *jowar*, *bajra* or unirrigated *rabi* crops.' The next stage would be the introduction of sugar cane, indigo, and opium—all hitherto almost unknown in the area—and an increase in *kachhiyana* (garden produce); double-cropping would become prevalent. 'There will then be not only an improvement in the quantity but also in the quality of the produce,' that is, the balance of the crop pattern would turn against the coarse staple food grains. These anticipations were realized. Two or three years later, R. S. Whiteway recorded in the settlement report that sugar cane had in fact been planted extensively along the canal distributaries; the coarser *kharif* crops, such as *jowar*, had in fact been 'greatly superseded by the more valuable ones', including cotton, and even indigo had been sown in some villages. Of the canal-irrigated area of the parganas, 69.4 per cent was recorded under *rabi* crops in the year of revenue survey as against 26.4 per cent under *kharif*: wheat occupied 26.2 per cent, *barley* 12.3 per cent, and *bejhar* 21 per cent, compared with *kharif* staples of *jowar*, now only 9.7 per cent, and *bajra* 4.1 per cent. Throughout, the valuable crops of cotton, wheat, and barley alone accounted for some 39 per cent of the canal-irrigated area; in the cis-Jumna parganas, untouched by the canal, these crops aggregated a mere 23 per cent of the total cultivated area. Etah district, too, showed a crop pattern generally characteristic of canal-irrigated areas, which were most extensive in the Meerut and Agra divisions of the NWP: the best districts, supplied now by an abundance of canal water, went over to producing larger quantities of the most saleable crops. In Etah's *kharif* harvests sugar cane, cotton, and indigo predominated, and in the *rabi*, it was wheat, barley, and bejhar once again. In pargana Mahrehra—the best in the district—the Cawnpore Branch of the Ganges Canal had brought an immense stimulus to indigo growing: almost every village had its factory.

The distribution of wheat itself became one of the clearest indications of the direction in which the stimulus of canal irrigation was applied. In 1876–7, the total area under wheat throughout the NWP and Oudh was officially estimated at 5,902,770 acres, with 2,257,344 acres in the Ganges-Jumna Doab, as against 2,695,730 in the considerably larger area between the Ganges and Gagra which was barely watered by canals. That year, the acreage under wheat for the whole of Oudh was recorded as some 1,904,798 acres; and in Meerut Division alone, one of the great canal-irrigated regions of the NWP, wheat was said to be grown on no less than 1,371,103 acres. It was well known that wheat was 'not the food of the masses. They live either on the millets of the autumn crops or the coarse mixed grains (barley, gram, and peas) of the spring harvest. The urban population undoubtedly do consume a large proportion of wheat for their numbers; and the richer proprietors or tradesmen in the villages also use wheaten flour. But to the millions wheaten flour is a luxury, untasted perhaps from birth to death or only at high festivals and holidays.'

Given these conditions, we may ask what sort of protection the canals offered in the event of drought. When the summer rains failed, it was the staple *kharif* grains and fodder crops which suffered; where the winter rains were insufficient, it was the poorer *rabi* crops. Canals were used to redress the balance only in dire emergency, and the growing of *kharif* foodgrains on canal-irrigated lands was never sustained once the immediate pressure of severe scarcity had eased. The famine years of 1868 and 1869 in the NWP exhibited a pattern which was to reappear whenever the rains failed. At the beginning of the drought, Government issued a circular encouraging the sowing of grain and fodder crops in canal-irrigated areas. This resulted, according to Frederick Henvey, in a considerable increase in areas cultivated with miscellaneous grains, 'though cultivators at first were very reluctant to water food-crops at the expense of other more remunerative produce'. It was not until August 1868, when the destruction of the *kharif* harvest was clearly imminent, that a rush for water took place. 'The fact is, as has been stated in the Irrigation Report for the year 1868–9, that farmers will only take canal-water to save, not to improve, the coarser grain-crops.'

The disastrous failure of the summer rains of 1877 in most districts of Meerut, Agra, Rohilkhand, Sitapur, and Lucknow divisions, and in parts also of Allahabad, Jhansi, and Rae Bareli districts, destroyed the *kharif* food and fodder crops. The enormous deficiencies in out-turn could not be supplemented by canal irrigation, even where such existed, since, 'at the sowing season, cultivators could not foresee the terrible drought that was to prevail, and did not avail themselves of canal-water for this class of crop, the canal-irrigated lands being principally devoted to sugar cane, indigo, and cotton'. W. R. Burkitt saw how, in Etawah, sugar cane and indigo were gradually ousting food grains in the canal tracts and why this should give cause for alarm rather than the enthusiasm for increase so commonly expressed amongst his colleagues in the service: 'During the late drought [in 1877], when I was out inspecting the condition of the country, it was to me a most melancholy sight to see acre upon acre of magnificent indigo and sugar cane, while hardly a blade of any food-grain was to be seen. The same remarks apply, though in a very much less degree, to cotton.' Crop patterns in canal-irrigated areas persisted with their preponderance of 'valuable' crops, as did the consequent lack of any effective remedy for recurrent dry seasons. Again in 1880–1, an official report noted that 'highly cultivated crops (sugar, wheat) suffered as might be expected least damage while the drought was felt most by peas and gram and the other pulses . . . sown on inferior localities and out of reach of water'. The fact was that, except for crops sown before the onset of the monsoon proper, irrigation in the *kharif* was practically inconsiderable and, as was clearly stated by the highest officers of Government in the provinces, 'must always be more or less so'. When the rainfall failed entirely or almost entirely, canals and wells could not take its place.

Only in those few areas where canal irrigation combined with excellent soil conditions to make wheat the chief grain staple was the threat of scarcity least felt. As previously mentioned, the Jat proprietors of pargana Kotanah, Meerut district—a by-word for fertility—not only were saved by the East Jumna Canal during the drought and famine of 1860–1 but made enormous profits by supplying grain to stricken districts of the NWP famine tract. Generally speaking, canal irrigation did, and could do, little to decrease the ravages of scarcity by expanding the sources of staple food supply; indeed, its effect tended to be the reverse, to contract them—a process which tended to worsen with the added stimulus of the export trade in grains, particularly wheat, beginning in the late 1870s. In addition, the canals incited the cultivators to load the land with an unrelieved burden of crops year after year, disrupting the regular practices of fallowing. As we have seen, Colonel William Sleeman reported double-cropping and consequent deterioration of the land through exhaustion to be conspicuous in certain Doab districts at least by 1850. A sizeable area of *dofasli*, or double-cropped, land was generally taken by field officers as a sign of local prosperity. A. B. Patterson however agreed with Sleeman and drew attention to the dangers of gross deterioration from the obvious over-cropping in Fatehpur district, where, he warned, cultivation was increasing in area and intensity with a disregard for the necessary relief to the soil. He admitted further to hearing from 'men familiar with Oudh' that there the same distressing tendency was now evident also: 'the *pax Britannica* [as Patterson's report obligingly states] has worked its natural effect in inducing a dense population to keep as much land as possible constantly under cultivation, and ... the "Garden of India" has already lost some of its relative superiority in fertility.'

This tendency was encouraged by the canals. Auckland Colvin noticed it as early as 1864, in pargana Thana Bhawan in the canal tract of Muzaffarnagar district:

... the chief danger in the canal area is overcropping. The land is rarely allowed to rest. For example, cotton is sown in a field in autumn, and wheat follows as the next crop; chari will be sown the following autumn, succeeded by wheat, then cotton as before and so on. The only crop for which the land is rested is sugar cane, and not for more than one season. In ordinary villages, this system is kept within bounds, not more than 10 per cent of the cultivated area 'do-fuslee' but on the canal, it is carried to excess. The cane is very much deteriorated.

According to Lieutenant-Colonel A. F. Corbett, whose *Climate and Resources of Upper India*, published in 1874, was the first outspoken technical criticism of the Government's zeal in promoting canal irrigation at all costs, over-cropping in itself was only a superficial explanation of the noticeable decline in productivity in certain canal tracts. A more fundamental cause could be found in the increase of irrigated area under the stimulus of the canals. By irrigation, as Corbett explained,

... the whole surface-soil is brought into the condition of sun-dried bricks; the more water that has been applied to the land the harder the soil becomes, and while its powers of absorption and radiation are reduced, those of reflection and retention of heat are increased; and we find also that the power of capillary attraction possessed by the land is increased, and that the soil so compacted will sooner become dried up than soil left loose and open, partly from the fact of the interstices between its particles having been reduced in size, thus increasing its capillarity, and partly from the increased heat of the surface . . . .

This hardening of the upper soil by irrigation coincided with the consolidation of a '*pan*' in the sub-soil

by the treading of cattle in ploughing . . . This causes shallower ploughing, the roots of plants have less depth of soil in which to search for food, and cannot force their way into the hardened pan; and there is the alternate soaking and drying of the land, during which the natural salts of the earth are gradually brought nearer the surface by capillary attraction.
This process may go on for some years before the land shows any excessive amount of *reh* (saline efflorescence) on the surface; but the soil is steadily being poisoned by its accumulation in the upper soil, which accounts, together with the increased hardness of the soil, for the diminished fertility of lands some time under irrigation.

Why did this not happen with the large numbers of irrigation wells worked in the Doab districts? C. H. T. Crosthwaite explained the reason for the decline of canal—as against well-irrigated—land as follows:

... wells require a large livestock and great labour. The soil reaps two benefits therefrom: more manure saved from burning, and the tendency to overfarm checked. If a farmer has to work his well, he cannot sow more sugar and wheat than he has time to irrigate but when he is relieved from all well duty he has nothing to keep him within bounds. He sows more of these crops, and has less manure . . . The extraordinary large produce of the first years of canal irrigation calls forth all the powers of the soil but if not backed up by a due supply of other food, it leaves exhaustion behind it.

Meanwhile the over-watered, unmanured soil was still ploughed up with bullock teams. Problems of double hardening inevitably followed, and an ominous increase in the barren and frequently *reh*-infected land known as *usar*.

Crosthwaite had reported with some alarm the spread of *reh* in pargana Phapphand, Etawah district—irrigated by the Ganges Canal—as early as 1871. Although *reh* was as yet by no means widespread, as G. H. M. Ricketts, then Officiating Commissioner of Agra Division, was at pains to point out when commenting on Crosthwaite's report, it was nonetheless an evil 'demanding an immediate remedy'. Seven years later, and two years after Corbett's careful examination of the *reh* problem, the condition had become far more obvious—sufficient now to cause serious, if somewhat academic, concern on the part of Government officers. A committee was appointed to investigate the problem thoroughly, on the basis of reports—chiefly from a Mr David Robarts, a substantial zamindar of pargana Sikandra Rao, Aligarh district—of the disastrous spread of *reh* in parts of Aligarh, Meerut, and throughout the Kali Nadi valley. In each case some hundreds of acres, which in these populous districts represented thousands of livelihoods, had been put out of cultivation; in each case, the damage was directly attributable to excessive irrigation by canal water. In introducing the final report of the Reh Committee in 1878, Buck, then Director of Agriculture in the provinces, warned that these and similar cases noted elsewhere, brought to light at the last minute and even sometimes by accidental observation, were 'the first and earliest outcome of the introduction of a canal system' (it was now four years since the publication of Corbett's treatise), and that the same disturbing influences might be slowly at work in many areas.

The findings of the Reh Committee amounted, in substance, to little more than a corroboration of Corbett's assertions. Its enquiry was far from adequate. No account, for instance, was given of the extent of *usar* tracts in the provinces: they were said to cover 'immense areas', without details as to acreage. No agricultural chemist was appointed to the committee nor even consulted during the investigations. However, the committee's final report made it clear that the chief cause of the increase in *usar* had not gone unnoticed: they condemned the 'vicious system' (in Buck's words) of swamping the fields for irrigation, which was the direct result of the accessibility of 'flush water'. The 'true remedy' was stated equally categorically: a greater economy in the distribution of water, to be achieved by the raising of rates charged by Government on flush irrigation. This was more than the Canal Department could provide. Since flush rates were already high, an increase would deter farmers altogether with disastrous results for the revenue accruing from canal charges. The committee itself realized that a remedy which it acknowledged to be inferior would have to be applied and recommended accordingly that lift irrigation should be substituted for flush irrigation as far as possible—'a waste of labour for a waste of water', sighed the president. He was encouraged solely by the realization that the waste of water was by far the more serious evil, leading as it so clearly had done to swamping, thence to deterioration of the soil and of the health of the people, thence to a diminution of their income, and ultimately, it was certain, to a reduction in the land revenue. For the rest, the committee recommended that experiments in reclaiming *usar* tracts which had begun in 1874 under the supervision of the newly created Department of Agriculture should be continued. These consistently showed that *usar* could be brought back into cultivation only by careful watering accompanied by intensive manuring. Nothing however was done on any significant scale to increase the local supply of manure near these tracts in order to keep pace with the increase in irrigation from the canal. When Dr J. A. Voelcker, the first agricultural chemist to be appointed by Government to report on Indian agrarian conditions, toured India in 1891, it is hardly surprising that he found 'enormous tracts, especially in the plains of Northern India', affected by *reh*. In the NWP alone, it was estimated to cover between 4,000 and 5,000 square miles. In the midst of this desolated *usar* land, patches of 'valuable' crops—opium, sugar cane, wheat, castor-oil plant, and cotton—stood out 'like oases in the salt-covered desert around them'.

The contrast between the benefits and drawbacks of canal irrigation was not always so clear to the eye. In Etawah, for example, the indices of prosperity in the form of extensive cultivation of 'valuable' crops dominated the scene. The drought of 1868–9 had brought a stimulus to irrigation from the Ganges Canal. The falling-off in the use of the canal water after these dry months was however 'chiefly confined to cotton and ordinary kharif crops which would not benefit by irrigation', whilst the area under indigo began rapidly to increase, as did canal-irrigated sugar cane. The rest of the picture was filled in from the complaints of local farmers, recorded in this instance by Crosthwaite, when on settlement work in the district. They complained of corruption by the authorities administering the canal (standards seemed to vary with the character of the successive district canal officers). They complained of uncertainty in the supply of canal water and of its inferiority as a fertilizing agent. They complained, as might be expected, of the deposits of silt and *reh* and the consequent deterioration of the soil. Kachhis, the skilled gardener-cultivators, and even the officers of the Government Opium Department were reported to have a marked preference for wells. But the real disadvantage of the canal was, as 'universally asserted in Etawah', that 'after the first two to three years, the crops do fall off'. Along with all this, the canal disrupted the farmer's former pattern of work. Far from firing him with the much-heralded spirit of industriousness which increase was assumed to bring, canal irrigation required less by way of labour than his well had demanded. As Crosthwaite went on to note,

. . . the great relief from labour given by the canal probably goes as far as anything else with an ordinary peasant in directing his choice when it is possible for him to choose [between canal and well]. When a man has no sons or male relatives to help him, or when he has to keep more bullocks for irrigation than he wants for his plough, he may realize that he actually saves money by employing the canal. But ordinarily it strikes him the other way. The expenses of well-irrigation disbursed by degrees consists [sic] largely of the consumption of the cultivator's own produce. The canal rate has to be paid in cash, and in a lump sum, and by a stated time, its collection attended by all the annoyance of a tax. To the average cultivator the canal appears an expensive business more costly than his well, but . . . he is swayed by his being saved an infinity of toil, and his ability to irrigate a much larger area of land . . . .

It was not always a matter of choice for the farmer. He had to use canal water where the canal had put local wells out of use, especially where it had made well-digging impracticable by the rise in the water table which it had caused. Whiteway made enquiries as to the situation in Muttra in the hot weather of 1878—a difficult season—and discovered that all *kachha* wells in villages through which the main (Agra) canal passed and from which more than 5,000 acres had previously been irrigated were now useless, owing to the rise in spring level. He concluded with caution that the canals therefore were, very possibly, a failure as an insurance against famine owing to their indirect effect on indigenous methods of cultivation. The Secretariat noted the following year that Whiteways' remarks were 'deserving of attention'.

Deleterious effects of canals on wells were by now widely noted. Saturation of the sub-soil was especially common in *bhur* irrigated by the canals, and this in turn caused the sides of *kachha* wells to fall in and made the continued construction of them to any depth out of the question. In Bulandshahr, according to R. G. Currie, a general rise of some six feet in the water level all over the canal area had resulted in the *kachha* wells being almost entirely superseded. A similar situation was reported from Mainpuri, and W. H. Moreland later collected further examples of this destruction of *kachha* wells in canal tracts from Aligarh and Agra. The only remedy was to construct a *pakka* well. Its cost in materials and labour, however, made it inconceivable as a viable alternative for the majority of farmers.

The problems that canals caused or, more often, aggravated were not restricted to over-cropping, salination, and the destruction of wells. Percolation from main channels or *rajabahas* (distributaries) could create swamps. In the Budh Ganga valley area of Etah district, the entire sugar cane crop of 1878–9 was ruined by this. The Canal Department provided the sum of Rs. 4,150 in compensation, but it did not undertake to drain the swamp. More widespread and serious swamping arose from the canals' obstruction of natural drainage lines where an insufficient number of syphons had been built to carry the canals beneath these natural watercourses. The obstruction caused by canal embankments led to swamping, the worst consequence of which was the aggravation of malaria. During the 1870s, the incidence of the disease increased alarmingly throughout the canal-irrigated districts where the saturation from flush irrigation coincided with the obstruction of natural drainage lines. In spite of a series of minor drainage operations begun by the Irrigation Department, fever continued to be a frequent cause of death and, worse still for a larger number of cultivators, a frequent cause of debilitaton, especially in districts with large irrigated areas.

According to Alan Cadell, even the climate in Muzaffarnagar had
grown worse, in terms of an increasingly unhealthy humidity,
'than it was before irrigation from the canal became so general and
the cultivation of rice [an export staple] so much extended'.

A farmer in a low-lying area irrigated by a canal might therefore
have had to face a number of setbacks with which he was hardly
equipped to deal. His fields might become salinized. If they lay
close to an irrigating channel, he might have had the (often doubt-
ful) benefit of easy access to the water supply or the prospect, alternatively, of swamping from drainage obstructions. Such drainage
channels as were built to take excess water off the land ran into the
same problem with the natural lines; a farmer might therefore oppose
their construction, with reason. The obstruction or inadequacy of
drainage facilities increased the dangers from seasonal flooding.
Excessive rain in the early *kharif* would turn his irrigated fields into
a lake and drown his 'valuable' crops. Meanwhile, his well might
have fallen into disuse, leaving him no alternative but the canal for
his irrigation. With the expansion of cultivation of 'valuable' crops
into land formerly occupied in part by staple cereals and with the
increase in population, his food supply became more precarious.
Not only food, but fuel and fodder were also threatened: 'Since the
introduction of canal-irrigation on an immense scale in this part of
the country, the conditions of agriculture have been almost revolu-
tionized,' William Crooke, then manager of the Awa estate in Etah
district, declared in reviewing the situation in the Central Doab
towards the end of 1881. 'A great part of the culturable waste lands
had been broken up, and the supply of firewood and grass seriously
diminished. The consequences would have been more serious had
not the use of canal-water enabled the cultivators to dispense with
a large number of their plough cattle.' This, however, as Crooke
went on to show, was of little genuine assistance for the farmer in
dealing with this sudden revolution in his environment, especially
since his techniques remained unadapted to the changed circumstances. 'The number of cattle now maintained is, in comparison with
the area under cultivation, inadequate. This has led to a slovenly
system of cultivation, and has greatly reduced the manure supply.'

Early in the century, *dhak* jungle (*butea frondosa*, a fine timber tree
which also provides excellent charcoal when burned) had covered
much of the Doab. With the extension of agricultural settlement,
the jungle had been largely stripped away, leaving bare *usar* patches

by the time when Crooke was writing. As a result, forage and fire-wood for the cultivator had already become scarce and costly—a condition which was now aggravated by the canals. Fire-wood, according to Crooke, cost a rupee for four *maunds*, assuming it could be bought, and dry grass for cattle was sold at from two to four *maunds* a rupee. The condition of cattle, especially during the thin period prior to the rains when no fresh fodder was available, was 'miserable in the extreme'. Cattle starvation and concomitant dis-eases (rinderpest, foot-and-mouth disease, fever) became regular ocurrences which were aggravated by, rather than originating in, years of severe drought.

Could this be remedied? Crooke himself advocated a scheme which would combine the reclamation of *usar* tracts in the Central Doab with the establishment of fuel and fodder reserves. Exhaus-tive discussions over the next three years by the Revenue Depart-ment, however, revealed the 'material difficulties' which pre-vented the implementation of this project and other proposals to buy up waste land and enclose it for emergency reserves: the cost was too great for Government. These same schemes went forward for discussion by the Revenue and Agricultural Department of the Government of India, and were wrecked on the same rocks:

The expense of taking up as reserves even a small proportion of waste lands now used as pastures would be enormous. For example, a reserve of some 6% of the grazing grounds of Bareilly would cost for acquisition alone Rs 1 1/2 lakhs [Rs 150,000]. The experiment of acquiring and enclosing 954 acres of usar land in Aligarh is to cost Government more than Rs 10,000. Without multiplying illustrations, it may be briefly said that in those fully settled districts, where pressure on the available pasturage is felt, no reserves could, by fencing, planting, and re-foresting waste and *usar* land, be created which would have an appreciable effect, except at an outlay so enormous as to place the measure at present beyond the means of the Government to undertake . . . a small experiment in reclaiming and plant-ing *usar* has been in progress in Cawnpore since 1882. The results so far demonstrate the necessity of great caution in undertaking any large expenditure on the formation of grass preserves in such soil . . . .

Meanwhile, the contraction of fodder areas in the Doab had a direct effect on the pastoralists who supplied cattle to the agricul-tural communities. In pargana Lonee, Meerut district, the expan-sion of cultivation was rapidly converting the traditionally pastoral Gujars into settled agriculturists, a transformation described by the Settlement Officer, Forbes, as in the 'spirit of industry'. The

same transformation was taking place in pargana Dadri, Buland-
shahr district, where the Gujars, according to the Settlement Officer,
had begun to 'recognize the value of property': they 'have benefited
considerably', Currie wrote, 'by greatly increasing their cotton
cultivation in the last two years'. But here too there were problems.
Most Gujar settlements were situated in the low-lying *khadir* areas—
the river valleys—where the constant threat of inundation meant
little regular *kharif* cultivation could be hazarded, whilst pasture
lands were extensive, with long grass flourishing in the moist soil
conditions. Gujars therefore derived their regular livelihood from
grazing and from the sale of thatching grass, and their food supply
from *rabi* grains since these were sown when there was no threat of
flood. When conditions prevented cultivation, they could resort to
cattle thieving. Thus, with the expansion of cultivation into the
khadir, the Gujars benefited from *rabi* cultivation, though the *kharif*
crops were still precarious. But with the conversion of the Gujars
into agriculturists, the supply of cattle to the cultivators necessarily
contracted; for this reason, cultivators had to rely on their own,
often deteriorating, stock. Meanwhile, Gujars in areas outside the
range of the canal developments remained obstinately unmoved
by the 'spirit of industry'. In Muzaffarnagar, Auckland Colvin
noted in 1864 how the Gujars of pargana Bedauli derived their chief
support from cattle. 'This', he wrote, 'supplies them with a motive
for maintaining large tracts of uncultivated land, and materially
diminishes their necessity for cultivating land'. It was assumed that
this regrettable situation could be changed only by the realization
of enormous gains from an increase in cultivation. 'Nothing, I
believe, will outweigh this motive but some agent not only bringing
greater profits than cattle-stealing and cattle-breeding, but profits
sufficiently great to supplant the old pleasant habits of indolence
and theft by the laborious habits of toil and agriculture.' Such an
agent was to be found in Colvin's view in the form of canal water.
Crosthwaite's observations on the labour saving consequences of
the canal lead one to doubt a priori that Colvin's vision would ever
be realized. . . .

Common Property Resources
and the Rural Poor

N. S. JODHA

I

INTRODUCTION

An important factor completely disregarded by development
policies and programmes in India is the role of common property
resources in the economy of rural people, particularly of the rural
poor. Common property resources (CPRs), broadly speaking are
the resources accessible to the whole community of a village and to
which no individual has exclusive property right. In the dry regions of India, they include village pastures, community forests,
waste lands, common threshing grounds, waste dumping places,
watershed drainages, village ponds, tanks, rivers/rivulets, and river-
beds, etc.[1] Despite their significant contributions to the economy of
rural people, these resources have seldom received enough attention
from planners. The important reasons are: (i) Rural development
planning has largely emphasized private property resource (PPR)
centred activities, be it the promotion of high-yielding crop varieties,
or distribution of cross-bred cattle, or supply of electricity for ground-
water lifting devices;[2] (ii) Inadequate understanding of the survival

Excerpted from N. S. Jodha, 'Common Property Resources and Rural Poor in Dry Regions of
India, *Economic and Political Weekly*, Vol. XXI, No. 27, 5 July 1986.

[1] Ground-water is also often regarded as a CPR, although it may not (unlike other CPRs considered by us) belong to any identifiable community.

[2] The neglect of CPRs in the process of rural development has been so great that even when
some programmes are directed to these resources, they are adopted more as physical measures
and have little concern for their CPR context. For instance, efforts in terms of research and
development activities relating to forests and grasslands or measures to harness runoff and
ground water, are seldom adopted in the framework of CPRs. Even in the programmes connot-
ing group orientation, e.g. rural co-operatives or community development projects, the 'community' is usually bypassed due to the PPR orientation of development activities (Jodha 1973).

mechanisms used by the poor as well as the complementarities between CPRs and PPR-based activities in rural areas; (iii) The contributions of CPRs are not only numerous and varied but they are often available as a matter of routine. Consequently, they often go unnoticed by rural researchers as well as by development planners. This paper, based on household and village data from twenty one dry tropical districts in seven states in India, attempts to quantify some of the contributions of CPRs with special reference to the rural poor whose dependence on CPRs (excluding water-based CPRs used through irrigation) is greater than that of the well-to-do villagers. The paper also examines the changing status of CPRs, especially its impact on the rural poor.

After commenting on the methods used for selection of areas and collection of field data in Section II, the paper briefly describes in Section III general benefits accruing to the rural people from CPRs. Section IV presents evidence on rural households' dependence on CPRs, as well as on employment and income generated by CPRs. Section V deals with the changes in the status of CPRs, particularly the decline in the areas of selected CPRs, and how it has affected the rural poor.

II

Method and Material

This paper is a part of a larger study on CPRs initiated in 1982 to understand their role in the farming systems in the dry tropical regions of India. That investigation, besides indicating strong complementarity between CPRs and the PPR-based farming systems, revealed a number of important issues that are relevant to both anti-poverty programmes and strategies for development and management of waste lands in the dry regions. The present paper, however, is addressed to the specific theme of CPRs and the rural poor.

The study covers 21 districts in dry tropical regions spread over seven states. Table 1 provides additional information about the coverage of the study. The areas were selected purposively. Two considerations that had to be satisfied were: (i) representation of zones with different soils, agro-climatic features, and population densities; and (ii) availability of local co-operators to help in the field work. The latter was a logistic requirement imposed by the nature of the study. The study of CPRs, unlike routine agro-economic surveys, required greater flexibility and use of unconventional methods for gathering information. This involved greater reliance on investigators who have lived for a long time in the study areas and had knowledge of the local language as well as oral history of the villages. Pre-existing close contacts with the villagers and an ability to record participant observations along with other numerical data were other attributes of the potential collaborators in the field work. The identification of relevant co-operators (investigators) from different agroclimatic zones, therefore preceded the purposive selection of study areas.[3]

Information on physical features and population pressure and on the extent of the CPR lands in the study villages is given in Table 1[4] In the study villages, the proportion of CPR land to total village area ranged from 9 to 28 per cent (Table 1). The extent of CPRs is affected by several factors including physical conditions, institutional environment, and demographic pressures. Though there is not a one-to-one correspondence between lower population pressure on land and higher extent of CPR lands, Table 1 indicates that in the villages of 10 districts where proportion of CPRs to village area was 15 per cent or higher, the population densities were also lower, ranging from 73 persons per sq km to 115 persons per sq km.

Respondent households for the study were selected in the following way. First, the households were stratified into three groups: (i) landless labourers and small farmers (<2 ha of dryland equivalent), (ii) large farmers (i e, top 25 per cent of the households on the basis of land they owned in each village), and (iii) medium farmers (i e, other than those covered by (i) and (ii) above). Final selection of the sample household was made randomly from these categories. The respondents from category (i) are described as 'poor' and those from category (ii) as 'others' throughout the study unless mentioned

[3] They included local school teachers or other village-level functionaries, elderly villagers, persons from voluntary agencies, educated youth in the villages and workers of some research organizations engaged in the field investigations in the areas covered by our study.

[4] Information on the extent of CPRs at taluka or district level was difficult to assemble. The secondary data or official records on land utilisation while reporting the extent of forest, waste land, etc., do not provide any indication about their ownership status (e g, whether owned by government, private individuals or a village community, etc). Hence, it was impossible to estimate the extent of CPRs in the total area reported at taluka level.

otherwise.[5] On some specific aspects such as monitoring of grazing on CPRs, and acquisition or disposal of privatized CPR lands, the selection of households was dictated by other factors that will be described while discussing these aspects. For detailed case histories, households were selected purposively. The procedures used for collecting specific data will also be described while discussing the results.

Information collected for CPR studies was supplemented by more detailed data from ICRISAT's village level studies (VLS) that have been conducted in 10 villages in four states. Under the VLS, resident investigators collected information on various aspects of traditional farming systems from panel households regularly with an interval of 20 to 30 days (Jodha *et*. 1977, Binswanger and Jodha 1977, Singh and Singh 1982, Singh *et al*. 1984).

III
CPRs and Their Contributions to Rural Economy

To understand the significant role played by CPRs in the life and economy of rural people, we briefly highlight the general benefits offered by CPRs. The way in which these benefits and contributions emanate from different CPRs, is elaborated by me (1985a) and are briefly indicated in (Table 2).

(a) Through supply of fodder and grazing space some CPRs help individuals in saving their land for crops. Put differently, these CPRs help in sustaining a number of animals for draft and livestock production which would not have been permitted on . . . land owned by individuals, especially for small farmers.

(b) CPRs like dry beds of rivers/tanks used for off-season cropping and rivulets, tanks used to collect irrigation water, play an important resource-augmenting role in the private property resource (PPR) based farming system.

(c) The traditional farming systems in dry areas partly derive their stability and viability through an integrated production strategy involving crops, livestock, trees/bushes, the latter being less sensitive to temporal variability of rains. Village forests, grazing lands,

---

[5] Information from medium farm households (ie, category (iii)), was collected only from some and not from all the villages. Hence it is not reported in this paper.

Table 1

The Location and Agro-Climatic Features of the Areas Covered by the CPR Study in the Dry Regions of India[1]

State/District	Taluka/Tehsil	No of Villages	Rainfall[2] mm	Soil Type[3]	Proportion of CPRs to Total Area of Villages (Per cent)	Density of Rural Population[4]		
						Persons/Km² of Total Area in		Person/10 ha of CPRs Area in the Village
						Taluka	Villages	
Andhra Pradesh								
Anantapur	Anantapur	2	563	A-L, G	15	90	106	71
Mahbubnagar	Athmakur, Kalvakurthi, Mahbubnagar	5	721	A-D, A-L	9	124	162	186
Medak	Medak	3	834	A-D, V-D	11	177	158	145
Gujarat								
Banaskantha	Kankrej, Vadgam	5	655	S	10	210	201	205
Mehsana	Sidhpur, Vijapur	5	633	S	11	340	332	301
Sabarkantha	Prantij	5	739	S, V-M	12	238	253	208
Karnataka								
Bidar	Bhalki, Bidar, Humnabad	3	907	A-M, A-D	12	162	137	113
Dharwar	Kalghatgi	3	691	A-M	10	134	156	154
Gulbarga	Gulbarga	3	702	V-M, A-D	9	106	129	146
Mysore	Gundulupet	3	680	A-M	18	106	103	55
Madhya Pradesh								
Mandsaur	Mandsaur	4	847	V-M	22	142	116	51
Raisen	Gairatgunj	6	1181	V-M	23	82	91	41
Vidisha	Vidisha	4	1134	V-M, V-L	28	91	98	38

State/District	Taluka/Tehsil	No of Villages	Rainfall[2] mm	Soil Type[3]	Proportion of CPRs to Total Area of Villages (Per cent)	Density of Rural Population[4]		
						Persons/Km² of Total Area in		Person/10 ha of CPRs Area in the Village
						Taluka	Villages	
Maharashtra								
Akola	Mangrulpir, Murtizapur	5	840	V-M	11	116	145	130
Aurangabad	Aurangabad	4	727	V-M, G	15	128	114	76
Sholapur	Akkalkot, Mohol, Sholapur	4	667	V-D, V-M	19	122	111	59
Rajasthan								
Jalore	Sanchor, Bhinmal	5	421	S	18	67	98	54
Jodhpur	Jodhpur	3	319	S	16	68	81	50
Nagaur	Jayal	3	389	S, G	15	71	73	48
Tamil Nadu								
Coimbatore	Coimbatore, Palladam	4	718	A-L, S	9	250	361	402
Dharmapuri	Dharmapuri, Pennagaram	3	844	A-L, S	12	286	210	169

Notes: 1 Based on district, taluka and village records and field work in the villages during 1982–85.

2 Average annual rainfall of the nearest rain gauge stations of the study villages.

3 Soil types: S = Sandy and/or sandy loam, G = Gravelly, A = Alfisol (red soils), V = Vertisol (black soils), D = Deep, M = Medium deep, L = Shallow.

4 Population and area data relate to 1981.

Table 2

Benefits from Village Common Property Resources[1]

Benefits	Contributions to Farming Systems[2]	CPRs[3]						
		A	B	C	D	E	F	G
Physical products:								
Food	e,c	√		√				
Fodder	a,c,d,e	√	√		√			
Fuel/timber, etc	a.e.	√	√	√	√	√		
Water	b,c,d				√	√		√
Manure/silt/space	b,c	√	√	√			√	
Supplement income/employment:								
Off-season activities	e,d	√				√	√	
Drought period sustenance	d	√	√				√	
Additional crop activities	b,d				√	√	√	√
Additional cattle	b,d	√	√					
Petty trading/handicrafts	d,c	√					√	
Social gains:								
Resource conversion	f	√	√					
Drainage/recharge of Groundwater	f,d,b			√	√	√		
Sustenance of poor	e							
Stability of farming systems	–	√	√	√				√
Renewable resource supply	a,b	√	√	√				√
Better micro-climate/environment	d	√	√		√			

Notes: 1 Table adopted from Jodha (1985a).

2 The benefits can be regarded as contributions to private property resource (PPR) based farming systems and can be classified under categories (a) Resource saving for PPR based farming systems, (b) Resource augmentation for farming systems, (c) Fuller use of environment, (d) Seasonal buffer and stability of farming systems, (e) Rural equities and nutrition, and (f) Importance in resource-centred technology.

3 CPRs A Community forest, B Pasture/waste land, C Pond/tank, D River/rivulet, E Watershed drainage/river banks, F River/tank beds, G Groundwater.

rivulets, and watershed drainages play a significant role in this strategy.

(d) CPRs, as sources of both physical supplies as well as employment and income, cushion dryland farmers' welfare during crisis periods, eg, droughts.

(e) Rural inequalities generated by the PPR-based farming system are partly reduced by CPRs as the resource-poor households (unlike the rich), significantly supplement their income from CPRs. CPRs also greatly contribute to the poor man's nutrition by facilitating his food gathering from forests, ponds, and other sources and strengthening his self-provisioning system.

(f) Management of CPRs should be an integral component of resource-centred prospective technologies and development strategies directed at conservation and better use of waste lands and the environment in the dry regions.

IV
CPRs AND RURAL POOR

Before initiating the discussion, a few clarifications are in order. Firstly, ground-water as a CPR is not covered by this study at any stage. Secondly, as far as the data regarding dependence on employment and income from CPRs are concerned all CPRs (except ground-water) are considered. However, while discussing the status of CPR's (e g, decline in their area, extent of privatization, etc) only village forests, pastures, waste lands, catchment as well as filling areas of ponds, river banks, and watershed drainages are covered. The 'rural poor' for this study, as indicated in the last section, includes landless labourers and small farm (< 2 ha of dryland equivalent) households. The dependence of the rural poor on CPRs is greater than others. To highlight this fact, the rural poor's situation has been compared with that of the large farm households, indicated by 'others' under each Table. In the dry regions the large farm households too may not be very rich, but they are certainly better off than the 'poor'. The information is presented by district along with the number of villages as well as number of households wherever necessary.

Rural Poor's Dependence on CPRs

Dependence of a community on CPRs can be indicated in several ways. They include the proportion of households making use of CPRs, per household average number and type of benefits derived from CPRs, or actual extent of benefits in cash or kind received from CPRs.

Table 3 summarizes some details that indicate the dependence of rural households on CPRs in the study villages.[6] Between 84 and 100 per cent of the poor households gathered food, fuel, fodder, and fibre items from CPRs. In contrast, just 10–28 per cent of large farmers depended on CPRs for these items. However, a greater proportion of large farmers collected items like silt from CPRs, e g, ponds to enrich soils of their fields, and timber (mature trees from the village forest that are not legally allowed to be cut) for their private use. Though not indicated in the Table, the households who freely used water from rivulets for irrigating their land did not include 'poor' households.

The number of CPR-based activities as well as the number of CPR products collected[7] by respondents, as reported and physically verified in most cases, were also higher for poor households compared to the rich households (Table 3).

The greater dependence of the poor on CPRs compared to the rich, i e, large farm households, as captured in Table 3, implies that poor households derive more of the benefits indicated in Table 2, from CPRs. Both negative and positive features of poor households' resource endowment compel or induce them to make greater use of CPRs.

Firstly, the poor households have high man-to-land ratios and in most cases high animal-to-land ratios, and CPRs indirectly provide an important means for adjusting factor proportions in farming systems. CPRs, through grazing space and cut fodder/fuel, help the poor households to devote all of their land area to food or cash crops rather than sparing part of it for fodder/fuel supplies. Similarly, the CPRs' role as a cushion during the crisis situation, noncrop season or drought period, is greater for the poor households, as unlike the rich, they do not have many other adjustment mechanisms (Jodha 1985a).

Secondly and more importantly, the dependence of poor households on CPRs is reinforced by some degree of match between the

  [6] Details about rural households, dependence on CPRs, and their employment and income gains from CPRs for Raisen and Nagaur districts as reported in this paper may slightly differ from the preliminary results about the same districts reported earlier (Jodha 1985a). This is due to the availability of additional information and exclusion of medium farm households from this paper. This also applies to employment and income details reported in the paper.
  [7] The highest number of CPR items recorded from a small farm household in a village in Raisen district of Madhya Pradesh was 22. For a similar account of product collection and dependence of the rural poor on CPRs in the irrigated areas of Uttar Pradesh and tribal areas of Andhra Pradesh, see, Dasgupta (1985) and AERC (1985) respectively.

Table 3

Indicators of Rural Households' Dependence on CPRs in the Study Villages in Dry Areas of Seven States of India[1]

Details	States (Study Districts, Villages)													
	Andhra Pradesh (2,5)		Gujarat (3,6)		Karnataka (3,7)		Madhya Pradesh (3,7)		Maharashtra (3,6)		Rajasthan (3,7)		Tamil Nadu (2,4)	
	Poor[2]	Others[2]	Poor	Others	Poor	Others	Poor	Others	Poor	Others	Poor	Others	Poor	Others
Category of households														
Number of households	65	41	84	62	64	33	98	72	102	64	72	64	48	23
Per Cent households collecting CPR products: Food items	95	10	96	16	84	14	100	18	98	13	100	23	93	12
Fuel, fodder, fibre	99	15	100	19	100	18	100	11	100	16	100	28	100	17
Timber, silt, etc	37	59	29	83	41	78	21	84	19	90	31	89	92	42
Per household average number of: CPR based activities[3]	4	2	5	2	5	3	6	3	3	2	5	2	4	3
CPR items Collected[4]	7	4	8	3	7	4	12	5	7	3	10	5	6	3

Notes: 1 Based on field surveys during 1983–85.

2 'Poor' households include agricultural labourers and small farms (< 2 ha of dry land equivalent) households. 'Others' include large farm households only.

3 Activities included product collection, grazing, processing and handicrafts based on CPR products and marketing of CPR products.

4 Items included fuel, fodder, various wild fruits and flower, roots, leaves and skin of plants and trees, honey, gum, fish, small game, silt etc. For more details (including prices of these items) see Jodha (1985a).

characteristics of CPR-based activities and features of the labour endowment of the poor. For instance, the extraction cost or cost of using CPR's, except the lifting of water from rivulets or wells, is quite low and the main input required in the process is human labour. This matches very well with the labour surplus resource position of the poor. Furthermore, because of over-use and degradation, the returns from CPRs to individual users, in most cases, are not very high and are unattractive for the rich. However, poor households, with surplus labour and low opportunity cost, readily accept the low pay-off activities possible through CPRs. Additionally, most of the CPR-based activities, except collection of seasonal fruits and spices, are neither time bound nor fulltime jobs and workers can engage in them without sacrificing alternative employment opportunities. Specific skills for harvesting CPRs are not required, except in the case of collection of honey, fish from ponds, and game from forests, and even unemployable members of the family such as young children and old people can help. Thus, a self-selection process of CPR users, governed by low pay off from CPR use and still lower opportunity cost of labour of the users, initiates and perpetuates the poor's dependence on these resources.

The oral histories revealed that in the past, until CPRs became very 'unproductive', large farmers' dependence on CPRs was also greater. Even today in areas like Madhya Pradesh, where CPRs continue to be more productive, proportionately more of large farmers depend on CPRs than in many other regions.

Table 3 also reveals considerable interregional differences in households' dependence on CPRs in terms of the number of CPR items collected and CPR-based activities followed. Without information on volume or value of these entities, they are at best crude indicators of relative dependence of households on CPRs in different regions. Yet, they do indicate considerable interregional variation, eg, Madhya Pradesh or Rajasthan compared with Maharashtra or Tamil Nadu. Several factors individually or jointly help explain the above differences. Factors operating on the supply side of CPR products include:

(1) overall greater size of CPRs (as in the case of Madhya Pradesh and Rajasthan);

(2) higher productivity of CPRs, in terms of type and quantity of produce, as in the case of Madhya Pradesh where village forests and waste lands offer good supplies;

(3) availability of high value products like honey, gum, spices, soapnuts, and fish as in some villages of Madhya Pradesh, Maharashtra, and Karnataka; and

(4) coinciding of CPR-product availability with the labour surplus period, e g, in Rajasthan when a number of wild fruits like *ker* and *sangari* become available in the summer.

The factors operating on the demand side of CPR products include the general inadequacy of the household's own resources to sustain the family, as seen in many poor families of Madhya Pradesh, Tamil Nadu and Andhra Pradesh in particular; greater profitability of PPR-based activities that are supported by CPRs, e g, poor man's dairying in Gujarat and sheep/goat rearing in Rajasthan; easy marketability of CPR products, like minor forest products, fuel, fodder, etc. in Tamil Nadu, Karnataka and Maharashtra; distress caused by drought or crop failure which compelled people to depend on CPRs to a greater extent as in some villages of Rajasthan, Tamil Nadu and Karnataka.[8]

CPRs as Source of Fuel

Table 3 gave broad indications of poor people's significant dependence on CPRs for collection of fuel and other supplies. Information about fuel requirements met from CPRs and other sources is presented in Table 4. Actual fuel consumption (kg of dry weight) by a limited number of households was monitored for one week during each of the three seasons in VLS villages. Though family size was more or less the same, the average quantity of fuel consumption by large farm households was substantially higher, ranging from 185 to 219 kg for three weeks compared to poor households, ranging from 104 to 185 kg for three weeks.[9]

The results in Table 4 further show that poor households met 66–84 per cent of their fuel requirements from CPRs. The corresponding

[8] In view of the situation-specific relative role of these factors in different villages, it is difficult to explain the regional differences in the dependence of people on CPRs with reference to specific factors. This limitation will also apply to the regional differences in quantified benefits reported in the following discussion.

[9] Large farm households used fuel for multiple purposes, e g, cooking food and animal feed, making tea quite frequently, heating water for bath, etc. They consumed small quantities of kerosene as well. The poor used fuel mainly for cooking food and often only once a day. In most cases the fuel requirement was higher during the rainy season, partly because of the reduced fuel use efficiency due to humidity.

Table 4

Some Details about Fuel Consumption by Households in the Study Villages in Selected Districts of the Dry Regions in India, 1984–85[1]

District (State)	Household Categories	Per Household Average Consumption of Fuel during One Week in Each Season (Kg)				Proportion (Per Cent) of Fuel From:			
		Monsoon	Winter	Summer	Total	CPRs	Crop Byproduct[2]	Dung	Fuelwood and Others
							Own Sources		
Mahbubnagar (Andhra Pradesh)	Poor (13)[3]	42	36	41	119	84	8	9	—
	Others (7)	74	67	49	190	13	20	41	26
Akola (Maharashtra)	Poor (13)	38	34	32	104	79	18	3	—
	Others (7)	72	65	48	185	13	43	24	20
Sholapur (Maharashtra)	Poor (13)	36	37	43	119	72	14	12	2
	Others (7)	77	63	65	205	10	38	34	18
Sabarkantha (Gujarat)	Poor (20)	62	65	57	184	66	9	25	—
	Others (1C,	70	74	69	213	8	46	28	18
Raisen (Madhya Pradesh)	Poor (20)	66	61	58	185	74	6	11	9
	Others (10)	79	74	66	219	32	15	29	24

Notes: 1 Based on data (including through selectively weighing the items) from the panel households covered by ICRISAT's Village Level Studies (VLS). Average size of household was 4–5 persons.

2 They include stalks of cotton, pigeonpea (tur), castor and sun hemp, groundnut shells, and empty maize cobs mainly.

3 Figures in parentheses indicate number of households. For definition of 'Poor' and 'Others' see note 2, under Table 3.

figure for large farmers ranged between 8 and 13 per cent except in Raisen in Madhya Pradesh, where large farmers also gathered and used considerable amount of fuel from CPRs. The poor households collected fuel material (including dung) from CPRs in small quantities almost throughout the year. Large farmers cut and collected bushes from CPRs at the end of the monsoon, initially for purpose of fencing and using them as fuel subsequently. Of course, unlike the rural poor the large farm households have a relatively self-sustaining fuel supply system where crop by-products and animal dung play an important role (Table 4).

Dependence for Animal Grazing

After fuel, fodder is the major item for which practically every poor household depends on CPRs. However, the extent of dependence on CPRs for fodder will be far greater if animal grazing, along with the collection of fodder, is also considered. Accurate recording of information on the extent of grazing is a complex and difficult task. Nevertheless, monitoring of animal grazing for a small number of households was attempted in the selected villages for one week in each season. That information is summarized in Table 5. The procedure used for monitoring animal grazing days and their conversion into animal unit grazing days is described in footnote 3 of Table 5.

Except in Jalore and Nagaur districts of Rajasthan, where livestock raising was a major occupation, poor households had fewer animal unit grazing days than the large farm households. However, the proportion of animal unit grazing days provided through CPRs for poor households was two to three times higher compared to the large farmers in all districts except Raisen. Jalore, Nagaur and Raisen are the only areas where CPRs were used to meet more than 35 per cent of the grazing requirements of large farmers. Availability of better grazing material or larger grazing space besides the limited extent of stall feeding practised in the areas, determined these interregional differences in grazing on CPRs by large farmers (Jodha 1985b). Mehsana and Sabarkantha were at the other extreme, where large farmers' dependence on CPRs for grazing only reached 15 per cent. In these areas, dairying was well developed and livestock management, involving higher extent of stall feeding, was also improved. Consequently, dependence on degraded common

Table 5

The Extent of Dependence of Households on Common Property Resources for Animal Grazing in the Study Villages of Selected Districts in the Dry Regions of India[1]

District and No of Villages	Type and No of Households	Per Household Average Number of Animal Unit Grazing Days and the Proportion of CPR Grazing There during 3 Weeks a Year[2]		
		Animal Unit Grazing Days[3]		
		Total (No)	On CPRs	(Per Cent) On CPRS
Aurangabad (2)	Poor[4] (11)	63	43	69
	Others[4] (10)	125	34	27
Mehsana (2)	Poor (12)	89	70	78
	Others (12)	118	18	15
Sabarkantha (2)	Poor (16)	68	57	84
	Others (10)	102	12	11
Mandsaur (2)	Poor (12)	117	94	80
	Others (11)	198	55	28
Raisen (2)	Poor (10)	91	70	77
	Others (10)	168	71	42
Jalore (2)	Poor (12)	231	180	78
	Others (13)	189	71	38
Nagaur (2)	Poor (16)	240	213	89
	Others (12)	205	77	37
Mysore (1)	Poor (12)	68	56	83
	Others (9)	112	33	29

Notes: 1 Based on household interviews and participant observation during the field work during 1982–85.

2 Data relate to one week each in three seasons during 1983–84.

3 A grazing day implies that the animals remained in the grazing land/field at least for 6 hours in a day and no stall feeding (except concentrates) was given. The number of grazing days using the above procedure were first recorded for each animal owned by the respondent household during the reference weeks. Animal grazing days (no of animals x number of grazing days) were changed into animal unit grazing days by converting all animals into animal units on the following basis: 1 animal unit = 1 bullock/cow/he or she buffalo/camel/horse/2 calves or buffalo/5 sheep/goat.

4 For definition of 'Poor' and 'Others' households see note 2 under Table 3.

grazing lands had significantly declined. Moreover, in Gujarat, as in some other areas, privatized CPR lands received by large farmers were used for grazing only.

The poor households' greater dependence on CPRs for grazing is mainly because they do not own grazing land. Furthermore, they owned a larger proportion of currently unproductive animals, including those through the salvage system[10] such as young stock, dry milch stock, which were sustained through free grazing on degraded pastures. Moreover, poor people also owned more sheep and goats which were able to survive on degraded pastures, on which cattle could barely subsist.

Employment Generation

CPRs are not only a source of physical supplies for the rural people. CPRs also greatly contribute to employment and income of the rural people. Depending on the type of worker, the CPR based activity, and the season, employment through CPRs may be both a continuous or an irregular activity. To highlight the contribution of CPRs towards employment of rural people we use the following four sets of data:

(1) Time spent by different household members on collection of CPR products in different seasons.

(2) Number of CPR employment days of individual workers during the whole year; these data have been collected under the Village Level Studies (VLS).

(3) Share of CPR-based activities in the household workers' total labour time allocation. These data were recorded through participant observations and interviews under the VLS.

(4) CPR-activities during days of involuntary unemployment. That information was available for the VLS-panel households.

CPR product collection: The time spent on collecting CPR products varies between members of households. We prepared an inventory of total CPR products collected during the week preceding the interview day in each season. Next, we recorded amount of time

---

[10] Though varying in its extent, the practice of 'salvaging' unproductive animals was observed in practically all the study areas. Large farmers gave their unproductive animals to the poor for maintenance as it was costly to maintain them, at their own farm, using the feeding standards followed by the large farmers. When such animals became productive they were returned to the large farmer and net additions to the value of such animals (after becoming productive) was shared by the two parties. Depending on the type of animal, necessity of seasonal migration of animals due to fodder/water scarcity, and marketability of animals, the terms and conditions governing this practice differed from region to region. In areas like Gujarat and Rajasthan such herding was an important source of income for the rural poor.

spent by family members, separately for adults and children, on collecting CPR products. Two hours of child labour were set as equal to one hour of adult labour.[11] We thus obtained total adult labour hours spent on CPR product collection by a household. For the poor, the total employment generated by CPRs, during the 3 weeks, ranged between 120 and 200 hours per household (Table 6). Large farm households spent less time on CPR product collection than the poor. We used 8 hours to convert the above information into employment days. CPR product collection during the 3 weeks created 15–25 days of work per household for the poor. The corresponding employment for large farm households ranged between 4 and 10 days.

Owing to factors like weather, changing availability of CPR products, changes in the availability of other work and hence the opportunity cost of labour, etc, the pattern of employment revealed during the 3 reference weeks may not represent CPR employment in all the weeks in the year. Yet, by assuming that during the rest of the weeks of the year employment created by these activities is at least 50 per cent of the average reported for the 3 reference weeks, one can hazard a guess about employment during a year. Under the above assumption, employment per household may range between 128 and 204 days per year or 36–64 days of work per worker per year in the poor households. An important limitation of these estimates is that they also include pooled observations on small and irregular time intervals devoted to the collection of CPR products and that they do not reflect sustained employment for whole days.

The time spent on CPR product collection indicated very minor seasonal differences (Table 6), though the type, value and quantity of CPR products collected during different seasons do differ.

Employment days through all CPR-based activities. Employment information about each adult worker in the VLS-panel households was regularly recorded with an interval of 20–30 days for several years. Collecting CPR products is only one component of CPR employment. Other important components are processing of CPR products and herding[12] on CPRs. Inclusion of these components on CPR employment (Table 7), does not change the relative position

[11] We did it quite reluctantly as the productivity of child labour in terms of collection of a number of CPR products was often equal to or higher than that of adults.

[12] The grazing employment days may involve some under-reporting, as only those cases were included where grazing on CPRs (as against private lands) were clearly detectable from the worksheets of investigators.

Table 6

Employment Provided by CPR-Product Collection Activities in the Study Villages of Selected Districts in the Dry Regions of India[1]

District and No of Villages	Per Household Average Number of Hours Spent on CPR-Product Collecting in One Week during:								Estimated Total Employment[3] (Mandays) in		
	Monsoon		Winter		Summer		Total		3 Reference Weeks		Whole Year[4]
	Poor[2]	Others[2]	Poor	Others	Poor	Others	Poor	Others	Poor	Others	Poor
Aurangabad (2)	39	9	35	18	36	13	120	40	15	5	128 (36)[5]
Mehsana (2)	58	21	64	26	52	25	174	72	22	9	187 (46)
Sabarkantha (2)	62	25	71	32	58	21	191	78	24	10	204 (51)
Mandsaur (2)	36	7	50	17	43	10	129	34	48	4	153 (40)
Raisen (2)	70	20	78	28	52	17	200	65	25	8	212 (64)
Jalore (2)	44	16	51	17	46	18	141	51	18	6	153 (45)
Nagaur (2)	54	28	60	20	49	17	163	65	20	8	176 (54)

Notes: 1 Based on field work during 1982–85. Information relates to the week preceding the interview day during different seasons.

2 For definition of 'Poor' and 'Others' see note 2, under Table 3.

3 Mandays of employment arrived at by dividing number of hours by 8.

4 Extent of employment during the whole year is worked out by using 50 per cent of the employment rate of the 3 reference weeks as a rate of employment on CPR-product collection per week in the year.

5 Figures in parentheses in the last column indicate the number of employment days per worker.

of poor and rich households as revealed by Table 6.

For the poor, CPRs provided exclusive employment for 43–89 days per household or 18–31 days per adult worker during the reference year. This was marginally higher than their employment on their own farms. Large farm households, in all districts except in Raisen, were occupied with CPR activities only to a small extent. Furthermore, even if only 10 per cent of the time of the partial employment days (in parentheses in Table 7) is assumed to have been spent on CPR-based activities, another 9–18 days of employment would be derived from CPRs.

Table 7

Employment in CPR-Based Activities in the Study Villages of Selected Districts in the Dry Regions of India[1]

District and No of villages		Per Households Average Number of Employment Days in a Year (1982–83) Created by:			
		CPR-Based Activities:[2]		Own Farm Work	
		Poor[3]	Others[3]	Poor	Others
Mahbubnagar	(1)	53	5	50	209
		(112)[4]	(40)[4]		
Akola	(1)	48	4	42	375
		(93)	(34)		
Sholapur	(1)	89	12	86	289
		(187)	(51)		
Sabarkantha	(2)	43	7	44	301
		(155)	(69)		
Raisen	(2)	56	25	47	237
		(124)	(66)		

Notes: 1 Based on employment data collected under the VLS project of ICRISAT.
  2 CPR-based activities include product collection and marketing, handicrafts based on CPR-products and animal grazing on CPRs. Data relate to household members and exclude hired grazers. Household members having regular paid jobs are not covered by the Table.
  3 For definition of 'Poor' and 'Others' households see note 2, under Table 3. The number of 'Poor' and 'Others' households respectively, in the study areas were as follows: Mahbubnagar, 18, 8; Akola 16, 9; Sholapur 17, 8; Sabarkantha 30, 17; and Raisen 33, 18.
  4 Figures in parentheses under columns 3 and 4, indicate number of employment days when CPR-based activities were undertaken casually while doing other jobs.

Time allocation: The data on time allocation collected under the VLS, indicated that CPR activities accounted for around 10–20 per cent of total daily time of the poor in all villages (Table 8). Large farmers

Table 8

Share of CPR-Based Activities in Daily Time-Allocation of Households in the Study Villages of Selected Districts in the Dry Regions of India[1]

Year	Proportion (Per Cent) of CPR-Based Activities in the Total Time of Activities Covered by Daily Time-Allocation by Household Members in					
	Mahbubnagar		Sholapur		Akola	
	Poor[2] (40)	Others[2] (20)	Poor (40)	Others (20)	Poor (40)	Others (20)
1975/76	17	1	16	6	13	1
1976/77	12	4	12	7	8	1
1977/78	15	9	15	3	12	2
1978/79	22	9	11	6	11	2

Notes: 1 Based on interviews and participant observation on time-allocation by each working member of the household for 1 day (i e, the day preceding the day of interview) with an interval of 20–30 days during the year. Such information collected under the VLS project of ICRISAT, covers time-allocation details for 12–15 days in a year for each worker.
2 For definition of 'poor' and 'other' households see note 2, under Table 3. Figures in parentheses indicate number of households under each category.

allocated only little time to CPR activities. In some cases, particularly among the poor households, there was significant inter-year variability in the proportion of time allocated to CPR activities. These changes can be explained by weather and emerging employment and income opportunities, which modify people's relative dependence on CPRs.

The data in Table 8 provide information for only 12–15 days per year for each adult worker. But they are likely to be more precise compared to other recall-based data because the former were recorded through participant observation or a recall of barely 10–20 hours. Their real significance lies in confirming the broad patterns about the rural poor's employment through CPRs, already revealed by the preceding Tables.

Follow-up activities during involuntary unemployment: Special investigations of activities of workers who could not get wage employment in the village labour market were conducted under the VLS. A significant proportion of such workers resorted to CPR activities. Workers of the large farm households were not involuntarily unemployed to a significant extent. Adults of poor households were involuntarily unemployed for 28–69 days during the reference year (Table 9). CPR employment in most districts accounted for 23–30 per cent of the total days, for which adults of poor households otherwise would have been involuntarily unemployed (item 'e', Table 9). If the CPR-based activities taken up along with other activities are also considered, the employment contribution of CPRs during the involuntary unemployment period would increase further (item 'f', Table 9).

CPRs are an important source of employment opportunity for the rural poor that can be exploited at times when no alternative employment is available. This is highlighted by greater self-employment in CPR activities during the off-season, especially after the crops are harvested, during poor crop years, and during the days of involuntary unemployment in the labour market. In some cases, self-employment of poor households in CPR generated employment was often higher than the employment created by a number of anti-poverty rural development programmes.[13]

Income Generation by CPRs

It is quite difficult to translate all the supplies and services offered by CPRs into income flows. Furthermore, since most of the CPR-based activities have a low pay-off, their contribution to monetary income may not be high. However, the importance of income received from the use of CPRs should be evaluated more in terms of its temporal and situational contexts, rather than in terms of its magnitude alone. Only two components of CPR-based income are

[13] George (1984) reported per household 125 mandays of additional employment, generated by IRDP in his study villages in Rajashtan. A study by NABARD (1984) reported additional employment of 109–163 mandays per beneficiary family due to various schemes (except tailoring) covered by IRDP in eight states. PEO (1985) reports 13–69 per cent increase in employment due to IRDP schemes in different areas. However, absolute number of mandays of additional employment were not reported.

Table 9

Details Indicating the Role of CPR-Based Activities During the Days of Involuntary Unemployment in the Study Villages of Selected Districts in the Dry Regions of India, 1982–83[1]

| Details | Involuntary Unemployment and Follow Up Activities in the Case of Different Groups of Households in | | | | | | | | | |
| | Mahbunagar | | Sabarkantha | | Raisen | | Akola | | Sholapur | |
	Poor[2]	Others[2]	Poor	Others	Poor	Others	Poor	Others	Poor	Others
Total households (number)	21	1	31	7	27	—	31	2	33	8
Total Workers (number)	49	1	58	13	38	—	68	5	57	14
Per worker average number of days of:										
a Involuntary unemployment[3] (number)	43	35	63	32	28	—	34	26	69	50
b Employment through follow up activities during (a) (number)	32	35	43	8	22	—	31	23	55	38
c Share of exclusively CPR-based employment in (b) (per cent)	35	83	33	0	38	—	9	0	34	18
d Share of partly CPR-based employment in (b) (per cent)	50	17	30	0	13	—	26	0	20	22
e (c) as proportion of (a) (per cent)	26	83	23	09	30	—	8	0	25	14
f (d) as proportion of (a) (per cent)	37	17	17	0	10	—	24	0	15	17

Notes: 1 Based on data on involuntary unemployment and follow-up activities of panel households covered by the VLS for 1982–83.
2 For definition of 'Poor' and 'Others' households see note 2, under Table 3.
3 Involuntary unemployment is defined as an event when the worker tried to seek wage employment in and around the village and failed to get it.

discussed here. They are income from CPR product collection[14] and proportion of income from animal husbandry that is attributable to grazing on CPRs.[15] CPR's contribution to household income and its stability, through their support to PPR-based crop farming, and processing and marketing of CPR products, are not considered. The income data in Table 10, therefore, considerably underestimate the total income contribution of CPRs.

Average annual income of poor households from CPRs ranged from Rs 445–Rs 830 during the reference period. CPR income of large farmers did not exceed Rs 300, except in the Rajasthan and Madhya Pradesh villages. A substantial share of this income originated from CPR product collection in most regions. The exceptions were large farm households in Nagaur, Jalore, and Mandsaur district where livestock production is important. Except in the Akola and the Aurangabad villages, the CPR-income accounted for 15–23 per cent of total income from all other sources, for the poor households. The corresponding proportions for large farm households were 1–3 per cent only.

In 6 of the 12 study areas, average annual income from CPRs per poor household exceeded Rs 700. CPR income constituted more than a fifth of poor households' income from all other sources in these districts (except Mehsana). In the case of two districts at the bottom, this figure was less than Rs 550. The regional differences in the income from CPRs can be explained in terms of the extent and productivity of CPRs and major activities supported by them. For instance, high CPR income areas like Raisen, Jalore and, to an extent, Nagaur are endowed with larger extent of CPRs (Table 1). Similarly, availability of high-value CPR products such as gum, honey, fruits, and game, contributed to higher CPR income in Raisen and Dharmapuri. Poor man's animal husbandry, sustained mainly through CPRs, was responsible for higher CPR income of the poor in households

---

[14] Income from CPR products was estimated by first making an inventory of the total products collected by respondent households during different seasons and then calculating their value on the basis of the village-level prices of the products. These prices were much lower than the corresponding prices even at the taluka town level.

[15] Estimation of livestock income attributable to CPR grazing is based on data on animal-husbandry practices (e g, stall-feeding, grazing including on CPRs) and on composition of livestock income. Apportioning of animal income to CPR grazing was simple for sheep, goats, and currently unproductive animals that were almost totally maintained through CPR grazing especially by the poor. In the case of animals involving both stall-feeding and open grazing only dung income was apportioned between CPR-grazing, private resource grazing and stall-feeding on the basis of animal-unit days involved. This, however, resulted in considerably underestimating animal income attributable to CPR grazing.

of Nagaur, Mehsana, Sabarkantha and Jalore. Limited area of CPRs and limited number of CPR products on the one hand and greater availability of agricultural employment opportunities due to cotton and paddy dominated cropping patterns on the other, may explain the lower CPR incomes of the poor in the Akola and the Mahbubnagar villages.[16]

Reduction in Income Inequalities

The pattern of inter-class differences in CPR income suggests that CPRs help reduce the rural inequalities. The inequalities of the VLS-household incomes, measured with the Gini coefficient, are reduced when CPR income are included in household income (Table 11). The values of the Gini coefficient varied from 0.37 to 0.50 in

Table 11

Impact of CPRs on Inequality of Household Incomes in the Study Villages of Selected Districts in the Dry Regions of India*

District and Number of Villages		Mean and Gini Coefficient of Household Incomes from			
		All Sources		All Sources Excluding CPRs	
		Mean (Rupees)	Gini Coefficient (Per Cent)	Mean (Rupees)	Gini Coefficient (Per Cent)
Mahbubnagar	(1)	7443	0.41	6777	0.50
Akola	(1)	9549	0.40	8928	0.48
Sholapur	(1)	6989	0.32	6008	0.37
Sabarkantha	(2)	9249	0.33	8205	0.45
Raisen	(2)	5186	0.34	4150	0.44

Notes: * Based on data (for 1983–84) from panel households covered by the VLS. The panel of 40 households from each village included 10 households from each category namely, landless labourers, small farmers, medium farmers, and larger farmers.

[16] Levels and the regional pattern of CPR incomes (Table 10) may change if income from CPR-product processing and marketing is considered. This was indicated by rough calculations based on limited cases of processing, marketing, and handicrafts based on CPR-products in different areas. They included soapnut in Aurangabad; forest products for basket, *pattal*, and mattress making in Mysore, Dharmapuri, Mandsaur and Raisen areas; sisal and other products used for making rope and other fibre in Akola, Sholapur and Mahbubnagar areas; wild fruits for making pickles and medicine in Nagaur and Raisen. These activities could add about 9–21 per cent to the already reported CPR-income in different areas.

Table 10

Average Annual Household Income from CPRs in the Study Villages of Selected Districts in the Dry Regions of India[1]

| District[2] | Per Households Annual Average Income in the Case of[3] | | | | | | | |
| | Poor | | | | Others | | | |
	Households (Number)	Value of CPR-Products Collected (Rupees)	CPR-Share in Livestock Income (Rupees)	Total (Rupees)	Households (Number)	Value of CPR-Products Collected (Rupees)	CPR-Share in Livestock Income (Rupees)	Total (Rupees)
Mahbubnagar	15	382	152	534 (17)[4]	10	109	62	171 (1)
Mehsana	26	421	309	730 (16)	24	88	74	162 (1)
Sabarkantha	35	432	336	818 (21)	19	111	97	208 (1)
Mysore	26	534	115	649 (20)	11	112	58	170 (3)
Mandsaur	23	400	285	685 (18)	18	113	190	303 (1)
Raisen	37	568	212	780 (26)	15	283	185	468 (4)
Akola	16	342	105	447 (9)	9	85	49	134 (1)
Aurangabad	22	405	179	584 (13)	21	110	53	163 (1)

Per Households Annual Average Income in the Case of[3]

District[2]	Poor				Others			
	Households (Number)	Value of CPR-Products Collected (Rupees)	CPR-Share in Livestock Income (Rupees)	Total (Rupees)	Households (Number)	Value of CPR-Products Collected (Rupees)	CPR-Share in Livestock Income (Rupees)	Total (Rupees)
Sholapur	24	443	198	641 (20)	9	143	92	235 (2)
Jalore	24	447	262	709 (21)	27	170	217	387 (2)
Nagaur	32	473	358	831 (23)	25	143	295	438 (3)
Dharmapuri	30	530	208	738 (22)	11	112	54	164 (2)

Notes: 1 Based on field work during 1982–85.

2 Number of villages covered in Mahbubnagar, Akola, and Sholapur was one each. In other districts it was two.

3 CPR income was estimated by valuation of CPR-products collected by the households on the basis of village level prices of those products. Livestock income attributed to CPRs was estimated on the basis of contribution of CPR grazing to total livestock maintenance. The procedures used, briefly mentioned in the text, tended to underestimate the contribution of CPR grazing to livestock income. In the case of villages in Mahbubnagar, Akola, Sholapur, Sabarkantha, and Raisen, all incomes were estimated on the basis of cost accounting method, while in others they were based on recalls during three seasonal rounds of field work.

4 Figures in the parentheses indicated total CPR-based income as per cent to total income from other sources.

different areas when income from all sources excluding the CPRs was considered. However, once CPR-based income was included in household income, the value of the Gini coefficient declined and ranged between 0.32 and 0.41 in different areas.

In view of the fact that CPRs contribute more than a fifth of the incomes from other sources for the poor, they should be recognized as an integral part of programmes directed towards reduction in rural poverty and inequality. In fact, the CPR-based income works out to Rs 112 per worker in an area like Akola and Rs 243 per worker in Nagaur, even when not all components of CPR-related income have been quantified here. If the unaccounted income components are added, CPR-based income could be much higher in many areas than the per household income generated by a number of antipoverty programmes.[17]

V

CHANGING STATUS OF CPRs

Investigation into the village-level records and oral accounts of the recent past in the study areas indicated that the contribution of CPRs towards the income of the rural poor as well as rural equity was probably much higher in the past than it is at present. Both the area and physical productivity of CPRs, in terms of quantity and quality of products, have declined. We tried to document this change by comparing total CPR output in the early 1980s with the early 1950s, when following independence, land reforms were introduced.[18] For both periods physical productivity of CPRs and their area were recorded. The CPRs covered are village pastures, village forests, waste lands,[19] unoccupied, catchments of ponds, tanks, river banks, watershed drainages, and community threshing grounds.

[17] A study by NABARD (1984) reported that for 10 per cent of the beneficiary households per household incremental income from IRDP in different states was upto Rs 500. For another 13 per cent it ranged between Rs 501–1,500. According to a PEO (1985) study, the per household incremental income from IRDP schemes ranged from Rs 1,069–Rs 2,770. However, in several areas the incremental income from different schemes was less than or around Rs 600 per family. Kutty Krishnan (1984) reported that 39 per cent of the participants in IRDP schemes in his study village in Kerala did not have any change in their income. Another 29 per cent of the families got incremental income of less than Rs 400 per family.

[18] Land reforms served as an important event to facilitate the recall of the past by the people. Moreover, the status of CPRs was greatly affected by various by-laws and side effects of land reforms (Jodha 1985a, 1985b). Hence it was quite convenient to gather details from oral history and records before this change.

Decline of CPRs

Decline of CPRs can take three forms:

(i) Physical loss of resources, such as the submersion of grazing land in a newly constructed irrigation dam or area of CPR covered by roads and buildings.

(ii) Deterioration of physical productivity of resources, as revealed by degradation of pastures or forest lands.

(iii) Re-assignment of usage and property rights as indicated by transfer of CPR lands to private ownership.   -

As mentioned earlier, the following discussion is confined to the last category of the decline of CPRs.

In the dry areas we studied, CPRs mostly occupy sub-marginal land with undependable water supply. With increased resource scarcity, it can however be expected that common property rights will be infringed on or substituted by *de jure* or *de facto* private property rights. In the areas covered by this study, the above substitution of property rights has taken place on a large scale. For instance, during 1982–4, the extent of CPR lands in the study villages ranged from 9–28 per cent of total area (Table 12). These proportions ranged between 15 and 42 per cent in 1950–2. The area of CPRs during the last three decades has thus declined by 26–52 per cent.

Details of technological, institutional, and demographic circumstances causing decline in the area of CPRs, and also their physical productivity, have been discussed elsewhere (Jodha 1985a, 1985b). Here we will confine our discussion to those aspects of the decline of CPRs that affect particularly the rural poor. The main form of decline is the privatization of CPRs.[20] Under various welfare programmes CPR lands had been distributed to people for private use. CPR lands had also been illegally appropriated often with subsequent legalization. The stated intention of privatization of CPRs was to give land to the poor who were landless or who had

---

[19] All the village waste lands unlike other CPRs listed here do not fall under the jurisdiction of a village or village panchayat. They belong to State Revenue Departments. However, since they are common access resources, for the concerned village community they are village CPRs for all practical purposes. Historically, these commons were categorised as wastelands not on the basis of their extent of biological or economic productivity. Being uncultivable (or uncultivated in some cases), they were non-revenue generating lands. Hence, the colonial government classified them as 'wastelands'. For some implications of this categorization, see Shiva (1986).

[20] In some cases, area of CPRs declined due to transfer of land to institutions (e g, milk co-operative, village school, public works department, forest department, etc.). For a brief account of causes and consequence of transfer of forests to state control, see Singh (1986).

N. S. Jodha

Table 12

Extent and Decline of CPR Land in the Study Villages of Selected Districts in the Dry Regions of India[1]

State and District	Number of Villages	Area of CPR-Lands (ha)[2]	CPRs as Proportion (Per Cent) of Total Village Area		Decline in the Area of CPRs since 1950–52 (Per Cent)
			1982–84	1950–52	
Andhra Pradesh					
Anantapur	2	221	15	24	36
Mahbubnagar	5	408	9	16	43
Medak	3	198	11	20	45
Gujarat					
Banaskantha	5	167	9	19	49
Mehsana	5	224	11	17	37
Sabarkantha	5	198	12	22	46
Karnataka					
Bidar	3	297	12	20	41
Dharwad	3	242	10	18	44
Gulbarga	3	291	9	15	43
Mysore	3	335	18	27	32
Madhya Pradesh					
Mandsaur	4	327	22	34	34
Raisen	6	770	23[3]	42	47
Vidisha	4	338	28[3]	38	32
Maharashtra					
Akola	5	192	11	19	42
Aurangabad	4	304	15	21	30
Sholapur	4	422	19	25	26
Rajasthan					
Jalore	5	639	18	29	37
Jodhpur	3	591	16	38	58
Nagaur	3	619	15	41	63
Tamil Nadu					
Coimbatore	4	187	9	17	47
Dharmapuri	3	225	12	26	52

Notes: 1 Based on village-level records and field work during 1982–5.
2 CPRs included are village pastures, village forests, waste lands, unoccupied catchments of ponds/tanks, river/rivulet banks, watershed drainages, and community threshing grounds, etc, which are used for free animal grazing and collection of fuel, fodder, and other items.
3 In Raisen and Vidisha villages large area of CPRs initially taken over by the forest department but now available for use by the villagers is included with CPRs.

very little land. Hence, from the days of land reforms in early 1950s to the present day, programmes such as the 20-Point Programme, allotment of land titles to the poor of CPR lands, already used collectively by the poor, was an important measure. The consequent decline in the area of CPRs, and the resultant overcrowding and the degradation of CPRs have led to a considerable reduction in the overall quantity of CPR benefits for the poor. However, it is quite possible that the losses the poor suffered collectively, might have been compensated by the individual gains from possessing more private land. This balance could be examined by comparing the magnitude of the decline in CPR-based income of the past with the returns from privatized CPR lands owned by the poor. A few studies investigating the losses and gains have been initiated and await completion.

Alternatively, one may analyse the changes in the land resources base of the poor following the privatization of CPRs.

Privatization and Distribution of CPR Lands[21]

It is evident from Table 13 that, although the privatization of CPRs was promoted in the name of helping the poor, very little land was received by them. For 10 of the 19 areas covered, the proportion of poor households in the recipients of CPR lands was higher than the proportion of other farmers (Table 13, col 6 and 7).[22] However, in 16 of the 19 regions, the share of the poor in the privatized lands was lower than the share of all other farmers (Table 13, col 4 and 5). The poor received between 0.8 and 1.6 ha per household, whereas other farmers received 1.5–4.9 ha per household. The comparison of landholding size before and after the privatization of CPR lands indicates that those who had relatively more land also got more

[21] The details on this aspect were collected in the following manner. First, the land parcels (currently privately owned lands that had CPR status in the past) were identified. Then the households, which received ownership of the land under various welfare programmes or through grabbing were identified. Information about the resource position of these households was collected. Current ownership and use status of these lands were also recorded. For understandable reasons it was not possible to cover all privatized CPR land. The extent of the land left out broadly ranged between 18–32 per cent in different villages.

[22] 'Others' in Tables 13–15 do not necessarily include only large farmers unlike the data reported by rest of the Tables. In the latter, 'large farmers' indicated by 'Others' were deliberately selected. In the case of privatized CPR lands, the primary step was selection of land parcel and then an enquiry into who got it. The recipients of CPR-land parcel included people other than large farmers also.

Table 15

Some Indicators of Factors Causing Dispossession of CPR Lands Given to the Rural Poor in the Study Villages in the Dry Regions of India[1]

Details	Some Attributes of CPR Lands (A) Retained and (B) Given Up by Poor Households in the Study Villages of[2]													
	Andhra Pradesh		Gujarat		Karnataka		Madhya Pradesh		Maharashtra		Rajasthan		Tamil Nadu	
	A[3]	B[4]	A	B	A	B	A	B	A	B	A	B	A	B
Total land area (ha)	139	108	39	27	83	69	114	35	71	48	99	51	189	34
Total households involved (number)[5]	208	88	53	22	75	56	103	24	76	43	113	42	147	32
Proportion of lands (under A and B) through: Welfare programmes[6] (per cent)	12	68	38	63	22	72	43	91	24	83	35	78	19	70
Illegal grabbing (per cent)	88	32	62	37	78	28	57	9	76	17	65	22	81	30
Proportion of sub-marginal lands to lands (under A and B)[7] (per cent)	9	45	0	37	6	45	0	37	9	25	35	39	20	47
Bullocks (per cent)	27	0	66	0	43	7	64	8	39	0	62	7	27	6
Heavy dependence on labour income (per cent)	24	70	13	82	48	71	10	62	24	81	25	76	28	78
Proportion of households giving up land due to: Inability to develop/use the land (per cent)	—	48	—	77	—	71	—	88	—	74	—	91	—	100

land. Thus, transfer of CPR land had not helped the poor to improve their resource position in relation to the better-endowed farmers.

In 7 of 19 regions more than 40 per cent of CPR lands received by the poor was no longer owned by them at the time of field work.[23] Land was sold, mortgaged, or leased on long-term basis as a first step towards eventual sale (Table 14).[24] In 9 districts the rural poor had lost control over 20–40 per cent of the CPR lands they had received. In more than half the districts 10–20 per cent of the CPRs land received by rural poor were fallowed. Thus the actual extent of privatized CPR lands cultivated by the rural poor was much less than the area indicated by Table 13. For other recipients, i e, large and medium farmers, the extent of privatized CPR land being given up was negligible. A substantial part of the new land acquired by large farmers was fallowed.

Disentitlement of the Poor

The complete process of privatization of CPRs as it affected the rural poor involved three stages: (i) they were deprived of their right to collectively use the CPRs, (ii) they were given individual title to small parts of privatized CPRs, and (iii) the circumstances disentitled them of the newly received lands.

According to Table 15, 63–91 per cent of the land distributed to the poor under welfare programmes subsequently changed owners. In contrast, the proportion of land that was later transacted away was only 9–37 per cent for land that was illegally appropriated initially. The appropriation of land in a way reflected the effective and felt need for acquiring land and hence after acquiring it, people kept it at any cost. The CPR land distributed under welfare programmes may have been regarded as a dole by the poor. The latter parted with these lands to satisfy their other needs and priorities.

Furthermore, in several areas, unlike the appropriated land, the land distributed under welfare programmes was often poor and sub-marginal. The low quality of the land may also explain why the

[23] This suggests that poor people's approach to land is not different from other assets given to them under various anti-poverty programmes. Based on more than a dozen evaluation studies of IRDP, Rath (1985) summarizes the extent of current non-possession (22–72 per cent) of the assets initially distributed to the rural poor under the integrated Rural Development Programme in different states.

[24] Since in most of the areas there were legal restrictions on purchase of land from economically and socially backward groups, leasing of land was used as a cover for acquiring such lands.

(Continuation of Table 13)

1		2	3	4	5	6	7	8	9	10	11	12	13
Maharashtra													
Akola	(3)	101	100	39	61	58	42	0.7	1.5	1.0	1.6	3.1	4.6
Aurangabad	(2)	83	55	30	70	42	58	1.1	1.8	1.1	2.2	6.4	8.3
Sholapur	(3)	132	72	42	58	53	47	1.5	2.3	0.7	2.2	3.4	5.6
Rajasthan													
Jalore	(2)	83	27	14	86	37	63	1.4	4.9	0.3	1.7	7.2	12.5
Jodhpur	(2)	405	318	24	76	35	65	0.9	1.5	0.4	1.3	2.3	3.8
Nagaur	(3)	147	81	21	79	41	59	1.2	3.1	1.3	2.5	2.4	5.2
Tamil Nadu													
Coimbatore	(4)	206	145	50	50	75	25	1.1	2.9	0.8	2.5	3.8	5.8
Dharmapuri	(3)	241	127	49	51	55	45	0.9	2.1	1.0	1.9	4.6	7.5

Notes: 1 Based on field work during 1982–85.
   2 For definition of 'Poor' and 'Others' households, see note 2 under Table 3.
   3 Before and after receiving CPR land.

Table 14

Current Status of the CPR Lands Given to the Rural Poor in the Study Villages of Selected Districts in the Dry Regions of India, 1982–85[1]

State and District and Number of Villages	Total Land Given (ha)	Poor Households[2] (Number)	Proportion (Per Cent) of the Received Land		
			Sold/ Mortgaged/ Leased[3]	Fallowed	Cultivated
Andhra Pradesh					
Mahbubnagar (3)	209	262	50	3	47
Medak (2)	38	34	10	9	74
Gujarat					
Banaskantha (3)	14	11	26	—	74
Mehsana (2)	17	23	59	10	31
Sabarkantha (3)	35	41	45	12	43
Karnataka					
Bidar (3)	34	35	21	14	65
Gulbarga (3)	48	30	25	8	67
Mysore (4)	70	66	41	13	46
Madhya Pradesh					
Mandsaur (2)	54	41	30	20	50
Raisen (4)	48	49	18	10	72
Vidisha (4)	47	37	21	15	64
Maharashtra					
Akola (3)	39	58	21	—	79
Aurangabad (2)	25	23	54	15	36
Sholapur (3)	55	38	48	9	43
Rajasthan					
Jalore (2)	14	10	44	—	56
Jodhpur (2)	97	112	33	15	52
Nagaur (3)	39	33	30	3	67
Tamil Nadu					
Coimbatore (4)	103	109	21	6	73
Dharmapuri (3)	120	70	13	3	85

Notes: 1 Based on field work during 1982–85.
2 For definition of 'Poor' and 'Others' households see note 2, under Table 3.
3 Lands leased on long-term basis (similar to mortaged lands) are included here.

poor parted with it so easily. This reasoning is supported by the high proportion (37–47 per cent) of sub-marginal lands in the land given up (Table 14). Thus the quality of land and the manner of obtaining it seemed to have complemented each other.

Some more factors that directly or indirectly impinge on effective desire for land can be examined in terms of resource endowments

Table 15

Some Indicators of Factors Causing Dispossession of CPR Lands Given to the Rural Poor in the Study Villages in the Dry Regions of India[1]

Details	Some Attributes of CPR Lands (A) Retained and (B) Given Up by Poor Households in the Study Villages of[2]													
	Andhra Pradesh		Gujarat		Karnataka		Madhya Pradesh		Maharashtra		Rajasthan		Tamil Nadu	
	A[3]	B[4]	A	B	A	B	A	B	A	B	A	B	A	B
Total land area (ha)	139	108	39	27	83	69	114	35	71	48	99	51	189	34
Total households involved (number)[5]	208	88	53	22	75	56	103	24	76	43	113	42	147	32
Proportion of lands (under A and B) through: Welfare programmes[6] (per cent)	12	68	38	63	22	72	43	91	24	83	35	78	19	70
Illegal grabbing (per cent)	88	32	62	37	78	28	57	9	76	17	65	22	81	30
Proportion of sub-marginal lands to lands (under A and B)[7] (per cent)	9	45	0	37	6	45	0	37	9	25	35	39	20	47
Bullocks (per cent)	27	0	66	0	43	7	64	8	39	0	62	7	27	6
Heavy dependence on labour income (per cent)	24	70	13	82	48	71	10	62	24	81	25	76	28	78
Proportion of households giving up land due to: Inability to develop/use the land (per cent)	—	48	—	77	—	71	—	88	—	74	—	91	—	100

(Continuation of Table 15)

Cash needs of the family (per cent)	—	52	—	23	—	29	—	12	—	26	—	9	—	—
Poor quality of land (per cent)	—	50	—	58	—	57	—	61	—	58	—	63	—	52

Notes: 1 Based on field work during 1982–85.

2 Details are presented by pooling data for different districts for each state presented in Table 14.

3 A = CPR lands received and retained by the recipients.

4 B = CPR lands received and subsequently given up by the recipients.

5 The households included under category (B) include all those who had partly or fully given up their newly acquired lands.

6 Under the programmes ranging from introduction of land reforms in the early 1950s to the new 20-point programme in the early 1980s, land was distributed to the rural poor as a part of the welfare programme.

7 Lands were illegally encroached initially, the possession was regularised subsequently by revenue authorities.

8 Rocky/gravelly/steep and completely eroded lands, and the lands with problem soils (eg, saline soils) etc, are included under this category.

and capacities of the recipients of the CPR lands. Resource endowments are differentiated in terms of possession of land, bullocks,
and other complementary resources including experience in farming. Only a small proportion of the households who gave up the
newly acquired land owned complementary resources (Table 15).
Mere distribution of land, particularly of sub-marginal land, without the provision of necessary complementary resources was not
sufficient to develop and cultivate the land. The situation differed
dramatically for those households that retained the newly acquired
lands (Table 15). More importantly, family labour capacity as indicated by a household's dependence on labour income was the
major asset of 62–82 per cent of the households who gave up their
new lands. Rather than sticking to a small piece of land that could
not be developed and used for want of other resources, these
households preferred to sell or mortgage the land and concentrate
on wage earnings.

Inability to develop and use the land was the reported reason for
giving up the land in 48–100 per cent of the cases in different areas.
Immediate cash needs of the family compelled 9–52 per cent of the
households to sell out, mortgage, or lease out their land. Poor quality of land was reported as a reason for not retaining the land by
more than 50 per cent of the households.

To sum up, our analysis shows that privatization of CPRs as a
strategy to help the rural poor yielded a negative result. The collective
loss of the poor from a decline of CPRs has not been compensated
by acquisition and retention by the poor of privatized CPRs. Alternative strategies to help the poor are needed. One strategy could
be to develop CPRs and improve their use through technological and
institutional interventions. However, it may be pointed out that
growth in the CPR productivity alone may prove counter-productive.
At present the process of self-selection of CPR users, tend to induce
mainly the poor to depend on these resources. CPR activities are
low pay-off options. The poor chooses them as the opportunity
cost of their labour is lower than the returns from CPR activities.
An increase in CPR productivity will induce greater demand on
CPRs through (i) increased number of users, (ii) pressure for
privatization including through illegal appropriation, and (iii)
encroachment by government in the form of handing over of more
paying CPRs to contractors as has happened in the past. The consequence in all cases would be reduced benefits to the rural poor.

Hence, the management or regulated use of CPRs is as important as any measure directed to raise their prodictivity. Identification and evaluation of intervention measures, to meet these objectives, form a part of our ongoing work on the subject.

REFERENCES

AERC,
1985   *Minor Forest Produce in the Tribal Economy in Andhra Pradesh*,
                Waltair, AP, India: Agro-Economic Research Centre, Andhra
                University (Limited distribution).

Binswanger, H. P., and Jodha, N. S.
1978   *Manual of Instructions for Economic Investigators in ICRISAT's
                Village Level Studies*, Patancheru, AP, India: Economics
                Programme, ICRISAT (Limited distribution).

Das Gupta, Monica,
1985   *Informal Security Systems and Population Retention in Rural
                India*, New Delhi: NCAER Working Paper No 2, National
                Council of Applied Economic Research (Limited dis-
                tribution).

George, K. M.,
1984   Rural Development Programme: Its Strength and Weak-
                nesses, *Indian Journal of Agricultural Economics*, 39(3): 434–43.

Jodha, N. S.,
1973   Special Programmes for Rural Poor: The Constraining
                Framework, *Economic and Political Weekly*, 8(13); 633–639.

Jodha, N. S., Ashokan, M., and Ryan, J. G.,
1977   *Village Study Methodology and Resource Endowment of Selected
                Villages*, Patancheru, AP, India: Occasional Paper 16,
                Economics Programme, ICRISAT (Limited distribution).

Jodha, N. S.,
1985a   Market Forces and Erosion of Common Property Resources,
                pp. 263–77, in *Agricultural Markets in the Semi-Arid Tropics*,
                Proceedings of the International Workshop, October 24–28,
                1983, ICRISAT Centre, India. Patancheru, AP, India:
                ICRISAT.

Jodha, N. S.,
1985b   Population Growth and the Decline of Common Property
                Resources in Rajasthan, India, *Population and Development
                Review*, 11(2): 247–64.

Kutty Krishnan, A. C.,
1984   A Case Study of Integrated Rural Development Prog-
                ramme in a Kerala Village, *Indian Journal of Agricultural
                Economics*, 39(3): 419–26.

NABARD,

1984 *Study of Implementation of Integrated Rural Development Prog-ramme*, NABARD (Limited distribution), Bombay, India.

PEO,

1985 *Evaluation Report on Integrated Rural Development Prog-ramme*, New Delhi, India: Plan Evaluation Organisation, Planning Commission, Government of India.

Rath, Nilkantha,

1985 'Garibi Hatao': Can IRDP Do It?, *Economic and Political Weekly*, 20(6): 238–46.

Shiva, Vandana,

1986 Coming Tragedy of the Commons, *Economic and Political Weekly*, 21(15): 613–14.

Singh, R. P., and Singh, S. B.,

1982 *Features of Traditional Farming Systems in Two Villages of Gujarat*, Patancheru, AP, India: Progress Report 35, Economics Programme, ICRISAT (Limited distribution).

Singh, R. P., Jain, B. L., and Rao, V. B.,

1984 *Features of Traditional Farming Systems in Selected Villages of Madhya Pradesh*, Patancheru, A P, India: Progress Report 61, Economics Programme, ICRISAT.

Singh, Chhatrapati,

1986 *Common Property and Common Poverty: India's Forests, Forest Dwellers and the Law*, Oxford University Press, Delhi, India.

Energy and the Poor in an Indian Village

VARUN VIDYARTHI

INTRODUCTION

Locally available non-commercial fuels form the principal source of energy for cooking for most rural inhabitants in the economically less developed countries. This constitutes the major and the most important component of energy used by the rural poor.[1] With increasing scarcity of these fuels, this section of the population is faced with an energy crisis, that threatens to be a serious impediment to the efforts aimed at improving their living conditions.

Concern with this crisis has led to considerable effort aimed at development and promotion of energy systems based on the use of decentralized renewable sources,[2] e.g. production of biogas from local residues or plantation of energy forests with fast growing tree species. However, it is being learnt that despite such a focus, there may be little impact on the energy situation of the poor.[3] An

Excerpted from Varun Vidyarthi, 'Energy and the Poor in an Indian Village', *World Development*, Vol. 12, no. 8, 1984, pp. 821–36.

[1] For example, a study of an agricultural village in Karnataka showed that cooking and heating of water accounted for 92 per cent of the total input energy to different end-uses. Refer to: Government of India, *Report of the Working Group on Energy Policy* (New Delhi: Planning Commission, 1979), p. 90.

[2] It is now well recognized that decentralized renewable sources have a major role to play in meeting the energy needs of rural areas, especially for basic needs like cooking, in a self-reliant and environmentally compatible manner. See: A. Makhijani, *Energy Policy for the Rural Third World* (Washington, D. C.: International Institute for Environment and Development, 1976); A. K. N. Reddy, 'Energy Options for the Third World', in Nautilus Inc. (ed.), *Southern Perspectives on the Rural Energy Crisis* (California: 1981).

[3] E.g. it is seen that in spite of encouraging subsidies, individual ownership of biogas plants is by and large restricted to the rural elite. See: T. K. Moulik, U. K. Srivastava and P. M. Shingi, *Biogas Systems in India: A Socioeconomic Evaluation* (Ahmedabad: Indian Institute of Management, 1978); Planning Research and Action Division, *Janata Biogas System: An Evaluation* (Lucknow: State Planning Institute, 1981). Social forestry programmes have been seen to benefit industry with negative effect on the rural poor. See: Vandana Shiva, H. C. Sharatchandra and J. Bandyopadhyay, 'Social Forestry—no Solution within the Market', *The Ecologist*, Vol. 12, No. 4 (July/August 1982), pp. 158–68.

awareness of this is leading to increasing emphasis on proper assessment of felt needs and technology alternatives in the design of solution approaches.[4] Direct participation of people is considered essential for the implementation of desired improvements.[5]

In this context, however, little attention has been paid to the energy problems of the poor, as determined by the manner of resource allocation and use at the local level. Changes in village social structure[6] could significantly affect the energy resource availability and use opportunities of different groups of villagers. On the other hand, desired changes could be restricted due to conflicting objectives and interests of the different interacting groups, in spite of the stated participation of all.[7] The dynamic relationship of such factors to the energy problem is clearly brought out in some recent village studies,[8] which also illustrate the importance of in-depth analysis of village situations in order to understand the different dimensions of the energy problem and to arrive at more realistic strategies of intervention.

The present study was undertaken to examine the energy alternatives in a village in northern India. This paper includes part of

[4] See: A. K. N. Reddy and D. K. Subramaniam, 'The Design of Rural Energy Centres', *Proceedings of Indian Academy of Sciences*, Vol. C2, Part 3 (September 1979); S. Siwatibau, *A Survey of Domestic Rural Energy use and Potential in Fiji*, a report to the Fiji Government and the International Development Research Centre (Ottawa: IDRC, 1978); A. Barnett, 'Rural Energy Needs and Assessment of Technical Solutions', in A. Barnett, M. Bell, and K. Hoffman, *Rural Energy and the Third World: A Review of Social Science Research and Technology Policy Problems* (Pergamon Press, 1982).

[5] See: FAO, *Proceedings of the Workshop on Rural Energy Planning in the Developing Countries of Asia* (Rome, 1983); R. Morse and others, 'Converting Rural Energy Needs to Opportunities', in M. N. Islam, R. Morse and M. H. Soesastro (eds.), *Rural Energy to Meet Development Needs: Asian Village Approaches* (Westview Press, 1984); Bina Agarwal, 'Diffusion of Rural Innovations: Some Analytical Issues and the Case of Wood-burning Stoves', *World Development*, Vol. 11, No. 4 (1983), pp. 359–76.

[6] For example, it is noted that the Indian village has been undergoing important changes in design and character, especially during the last few decades, due to changes in the social relations between villagers. See: A. Béteille, 'The Indian Village: Past and Present', in E. J. Hobsbawm *et al* (eds.), *Peasants in History, Essays in Honour of Daniel Thorner* (Calcutta: Oxford University Press, 1980).

[7] It is argued that participation, even in 'developmental' terms, tends to be political in nature and it is essential to ask the question as to who is participating and for what purpose? For more discussion, see: John M. Cohen and Norman T. Uphoff, 'Participation's Place in Rural Development: Seeking Clarity Through Specificity', *World Development*, Vol. 8, No. 3 (1980), pp. 213–35. Also see: A. Bhaduri and Md. Anisur Rahman (eds.), *Studies in Rural Participation* (New Delhi: Oxford Books and Stationaries, 1983), pp. 1–13.

[8] E.g. see: J. Briscoe, 'Energy Use and Social Structure in a Bangladesh Village', *Population and Development Review*, Vol. 5, No. 4 (December 1979), pp. 615–41; D. Bajracharya, 'Fuel, Food or Forest? Dilemmas in a Nepali Village', *World Development*, Vol. 11, No. 12(1983), pp. 1057–74.

the work, in which an attempt has been made to understand the energy problems in relation to important changes that have been affecting the lives of villagers in the recent past. The focus is on problems of the poor, including factors affecting their cooking fuel supplies.

The paper is divided into five sections. This section includes a brief description of the study village and the fieldwork. Section 2 gives a historical account of the land systems and social relations, before and after the abolition of Zamindari, together with the usage and access to fuels during those periods. In the next section, the present social and economic conditions are discussed together with the factors affecting supplies of different fuels. In the fourth section, the future prospects are examined together with village experiences on alternatives. The final section presents the general observations and conclusions.

The study village

Garhi is located about 60 km north of the city of Lucknow in northern India. It can be reached from the nearest town, Sidhauli, by traversing 5 km. of a lonely metalled road and 2 km. of mud path. Sidhauli acts as the main market, health and entertainment centre for the villages around. It is an important centre of trading, but does not provide any significant employment opportunities.

Garhi comes under the block Gondlamau of Tahsil Misrikh, a region having a population density of more than 700 persons per sq. mile. This region has no significant industry and agriculture is the main occupation of most of the population. Despite fertile alluvial soils and a hot dry climate, many farmers sow one or two crops only. This is because, in many parts, farming is done under rainfed conditions. There are few alternative employment opportunities other than trading. As a result, poverty is widespread and the region is notorious for criminal activities.

Garhi is a typical village of the region. A large proportion of its inhabitants consists of low-caste Harijans, who eke out a living from subsistence agriculture. There are no state-owned tubewells or canals for irrigation. There is no electricity or drainage system either and access to the village becomes difficult during rains. A research team stayed in this village in a hired cottage for a period of

18 months up to April 1983, collecting data and experimenting with alternatives, e.g. energy plantations, improved stoves, etc. The researcher, a native of the state, stayed there intermittently during the period.

Fieldwork

The fieldwork consisted of two types of activities:
DATA COLLECTION
Data were collected by several methods over different sample sizes. These included:

(a) *Village Census* including information on own and sharecropped land together with living space and other assets owned like cattle, pumpsets, trees and bullock-carts. The figures for landholding were checked with official records.

(b) *Agricultural Survey* including information on crop rotation, inputs and produce was carried out on 25 per cent of the families from different landholding classes.

(c) *Fuel Survey* including occasional measurements of fuels consumed in cooking on sample days spread over 10 months (excluding October and November). This was done for 10 per cent of the families of different landholding classes. The choice of days was irregular, determined by convenience, the total number of days of fuel survey varying between 30 and 40 for the different families. On these occasions, data was also collected on the time spent in fuel and fodder collection. Several meal tests[9] were also done in the course of regular cooking of households.

(d) *Long detailed discussions* were held with several villagers on important events in the past together with changes affecting their lives and relations with others. These were supplemented with information from an official historical record of the village[10] and participant observation during the period of study.
EXPERIMENTAL INTRODUCTION OF ALTERNATIVES
Improved smokeless stoves and solar cookers were introduced among some families on an experimental basis. Saplings of 'Subabul' (*Leucaena leucocephala*) were also distributed to villagers. Several

[9] These included detailed measurements of food and fuel, including the amount of water used in making a full meal.

[10] Zild Bandobasta, Mauza Garhi Kherwa, Pargana Gondlamau, Tahsil Misrikh (March 1871).

group meetings were held in the village to discuss, among other technologies, possibilities of introducing a community biogas plant.

These activities were accompanied by (1) organization of tutorials for children after school hours and (2) establishment of a dispensary for giving simple medicines. These involved minor costs in terms of fund or man-hour involvement, but were helpful in maintaining the interest of villagers in the on-going research.

AN HISTORICAL ACCOUNT

In this section, the fuel supplies of villagers are discussed in relation to the land system and social relations before and after the abolition of Zamindari.

Period before Zamindari Abolition (1950)

LAND SYSTEM AND SOCIAL RELATIONS

Social relations during this period were largely determined by the nature of rights over land. In this respect, there were broadly two types of tenure holders in Garhi: (1) the proprietors, known as 'Zamindars', who held the land and acted as intermediaries between the state and the cultivators. Their rights were permanent, allowing them to use the land any way they liked, the only obligation being payment of land revenue. It included all village land including inhabited sites, cultivable and uncultivable land, as well as village common land; (2) the tenants, known as 'Kashtakars', who cultivated the land based on a system of sharecropping whereby, using their own agricultural inputs and implements, they had to give 50 per cent of the estimated produce to the Zamindar.

Towards the end of the Zamindari period there were two Thakur Zamindar families[11] and about fifty families of other castes, mainly Harijans. Each Zamindar family was associated with about half-a-dozen families each of permanent labourers, watchkeepers, tenant cultivators and the service castes, i.e. Nais, Dhobis, Bhurjis, etc. Most of the permanent labourers known as 'Harwahas' belonged to the Raidas community (caste Harijan). They tilled the land, tended

---

[11] Henceforth we shall use the terms Thakurs and Zamindars interchangeably, as although there was one Thakur family which was not a Zamindar, it did not play a significant role in the affairs of the village and has therefore been kept out of the discussion.

the cattle, did house repairs, cleaning, etc. They were considered the poorest members of the village who worked full time for the Zamindars for which they received food, clothes and pocket money. Most of the tenant cultivators or Kashtakars also belonged to this community. They were relatively more independent but suffered a great deal at the hands of the Zamindars. As mentioned earlier, these cultivators using their own agricultural inputs and implements had to give 50 per cent of the estimated produce to the landlord. The estimate of produce, known as the 'Kankut', was made much before the maturing of crops and involved considerable uncertainty, related both to the estimate itself and to the season. This usually allowed the Zamindar and his associates to humiliate a tenant at will. Forcing him to plough or irrigate the fields of a Zamindar was common. Refusal often meant physical beating or unreasonably high Kankut and even risk of termination of tenancy.

The watchkeepers and bodyguards, known as 'Beesardars' were relatively better off in this respect. Nearly all of them belonged to the 'Pasi' community (caste Harijan). Their job was mainly to protect the village crops and the property of Zamindars for which they received one-twentieth of the grains harvested from the Kashtakars' share and the usual food, pocket money and gifts from Zamindars. Members of the service castes, i.e. Nais, Dhobis and Bhurjis, worked as barbers, washermen and grain roasters respectively. Although they worked for the whole village, for which they received payments in kind at the harvest and later (known as 'Lehna' and 'Tihai'), a considerable part of their time was spent in working for the Zamindars, especially by the Nais who also did massaging and acted as messengers for them. The Kahars generally worked as their domestic servants. Payments by the Zamindar generally included food and gifts. As the villagers say, their contribution of Lehna and Tihai was uncertain.

The above description gives a rough indication of the roles of families of different castes. In reality, these roles were often mixed. For example, some families of the service castes and the Beesardars combined their roles with cultivation. Many Raidas families also did leather work, their traditional occupation which was considered degrading by status, but improved their economic position considerably. Some villagers worked as agricultural labourers, though there was limited scope for such work beyond the Zamindar families. Notwithstanding these variations, an overriding fact was the one-sided dependency of most families on the Thakur families who had most of the resources at their command, by virtue of their rights over land and otherwise. Such dependency was reinforced by the fact that most villagers were illiterate (Harijans were not allowed to send their children to school) and important circular letters had to be taken to the Zamindars to be read. Credit was available at a very high interest rate (24 per cent) from the Zamindar himself or the local money lender. Failure to pay in time meant confiscation of grains or worsened service conditions. Kashtakars hardly reached a situation that permitted selling of grains. There were no alternative employment opportunities. Settling in another village was of little help as the same conditions prevailed elsewhere. As a result, few villagers could make useful investments in other ventures, say in animal husbandry or trading. Among important assets, at most some Kashtakars had a pair of bullocks or a pony and cart. Buffaloes, which were relatively costly, were owned by the Zamindars only.

Access to Energy and Consumption Patterns

We have already seen that many families of permanent labourers, watchkeepers and service castes ate food at the Zamindars' house every day. Cooking for them was done on a grand scale in kitchens known as 'Bhandaras' by Nai women assisted by Kahars. By one estimate, more than 25 per cent of the village population ate at the Bhandaras all year round. These families had practically no independent energy need for cooking or for any productive enterprise. The energy consumption pattern of others was determined by their rights over forests and orchards in the village. The 'Zild Bandobasta' gives a brief account of these rights. As mentioned there, if a Kashtakar chose to plant an orchard, he had to give a quarter of the fruit sold to the Zamindar. If any tree fell, the Kashtakar could use only half of the wood and fruit. In regular use, he could use the wood from one tree only. However, there is no record of Kashtakars owning orchards. Most of the wood came from forests that covered several acres of village land. The villagers were allowed to gather firewood for cooking, but had no right to the wood in the forest otherwise, and had to request wood from the Zamindar during festivals, for house construction or burning of the dead. According to the Zild Bandobasta, 'The Zamindar generally arranged for sending of the wood for such purposes without being asked.' This clearly indicates a form of patronization that is probably symptomatic of the nature of relationship between the Zamindar and the villager.

It is interesting to note that the cooking fuels used included both firewood and dung cakes, even in a Zamindar house. Clearly, the use of dung cakes could not be explained by the shortage of firewood, which was available in abundance in the forests. Instead, the Zild Bandobasta mentions that, 'It was a tradition to burn dung cakes'. According to a Thakur woman, who often supervised the cooking activities during Zamindari, there were two types of heating arrangements in the Bhandaras—a big stove using firewood and an open fire of dung cakes. After initial heating, the cooking vessel was placed on the slow fire of dung cakes for simmering. In other households, dung cakes and firewood were burnt simultaneously in the same stove. The dung cakes served a dual role of providing a method of heat control and supplementing the firewood.

Period after Zamindari Abolition

CHANGES IN THE LAND SYSTEM AND SOCIAL RELATIONS

At the abolition of Zamindari in 1950, three types of tenure were created—Bhumidari, Sirdari and Asami. All land under the personal cultivation of the ex-Zamindars including groves was recognized as their Bhumidari by conversion, with permanent, heritable and transferrable rights. There was provision also for the acquisition of Bhumidari rights by any tenant by lump-sum payment of ten times the former annual rent. Tenants who could not pay this sum were declared Sirdars, with permanent and heritable right but excluding the right to transfer. There was some negligible amount of land held under Asami rights, which were not permanent and are excluded from discussion here. All land other than the land under any holding or grove, including cultivable land, waste land, forests, tanks, pathways, etc. was vested in the state under control of a village committee known as Gaon Sabha.

The Kashtakars, having thus obtained permanent rights over the land cultivated, were able to establish themselves as independent peasants. This is also true of others who had chosen to play a mixed role during the Zamindari period, i.e. as Kashtakars and Beesardars or Kashtakars and Nais. However, those formerly attached to the Zamindar families as permanent labourers, Beesardars or domestic servants only were relegated to the position of landless labourers or marginal landholders and continued to be the weakest groups economically. These constituted nearly 50 per cent of the total households (Table 1).

Zamindari abolition should have affected the Zamindars, i.e. the Thakurs, most. This is both true and untrue. It is true because the Thakurs lost the influence and privilege they had earlier, being left with land under personal cultivation together with their groves only. Their rights to land were further curtailed by the imposition of the Ceiling on Landholding Act of 1960.[12]

However, it is also true that there was no significant change in their social status or relations with villagers. In spite of the mentioned legislation, the Thakurs continued to own a large proportion of the village land (nearly 45 per cent). As cultivation was done by animal power, it involved a large number of labourers, many of whom were attached on a permanent basis. A significant proportion of the land was rented out to sharecroppers due to difficulty in the management of scattered holdings. As a result, a number of families remained attached to the Thakurs as permanent or semi-permanent labourers, watchkeepers and sharecroppers. As there were no alternative employment opportunities, most of these families continued to have a dependent relationship with them.

In general, therefore, although some families were able to establish themselves as independent farmers, there was no significant change in the social structure of the village.

ACCESS TO ENERGY AND CONSUMPTION PATTERNS

It has been reported that in anticipation of the legislation which provided for state control over forests, most of the village forest was destroyed by the Zamindars, who felled the trees and sold the wood. Others had also taken part in the process, receiving partial support from the local political party for occupying and cultivating such lands. Similar fellings have been noted in several other places.[13] The effect of destruction of the forest was felt mainly by the poor, as few trees remained on the village common lands. The Thakurs still owned several acres of orchards, which were not vested in the

---

[12] This restricted the size of holdings to 40 acres going up to a maximum of 64 acres for large size families. However, land under groves was exempted from the operation of land ceilings.

[13] Vandana Shiva, 'People and Forests: Crucial Fight Ahead', *Economic and Political Weekly*, Vol. 18, No. 13 (March 1983), pp. 497–8.

Table 1

Land distribution in Garhi

	1960s*				1982			
	Total households†		Landholding		Total households		Landholding	
	Number	%	Acres	%	Number	%	Acres	%
Landless and marginal (up to 2.5 acres)	41	60.2	37.5	11.9	116	77.8	93	28.7
Small and medium (2.5–10.0 acres)	19	28.0	97.5	31.0	24	16.2	91	27.7
Large (above 10.0 acres)	8	11.8	179.0	57.1	9	6.0	142	43.6
Total	68	100.0	314.0	100.0	149	100.0	326	100.0

* The figures for the sixties are based on aggregation of landholdings of brothers in 1982. It is assumed that individual holding magnitudes were not affected by the process of land consolidation in the intervening period. Some surplus land, available as a result of imposition of Land Ceiling Act in 1960, was distributed to the landless in the seventies. This accounts for the increase in the total holdings magnitude in 1982, as compared to that in the sixties. No other transactions in land were reported during the period.

† Households have been defined on the basis of people eating from a common kitchen. The basis of categorization of the households has been discussed in Note 16.

state and were also exempted from the purview of the Land Ceiling laws. For the poor, access to firewood from these orchards was obviously restricted. Perhaps this also led to a change in the fuel consumption pattern, i.e. towards increased use of agricultural residues and dung cakes. Such a change is indicated by the following:

1. Traditionally, dung cakes were made during the period between the festivals 'Dusshera' and 'Holi' corresponding to the months of October and March, respectively. For the remaining period, i.e. between March and October, the dung was composted. The practice has since changed in favour of a much increased allocation of dung to dung cakes, as now they are made all through the year except during the rains, i.e. between July and October, when it becomes almost impossible to dry them.

2. There has been a change in the value of crop residues. A village Thakur could clearly remember an occasion in the past, when no one was interested in picking up residues of 'Bajra' (spiked millets) from his field. This has now become a common cooking fuel for the poor and is very much in demand.

Cultivated land and cattle were thus becoming important sources of cooking fuels—land as a source of agricultural residues and cattle for dung cakes. Although these resources were distributed unevenly over the population, there was a mechanism for redistribution of fuels, as indicated by the following:

1. Several families, who were attached to the Thakurs as permanent labourers, watchkeepers or domestic servants, had free access to their stock of agricultural residues. These were always in surplus as the Thakurs themselves preferred to use firewood, which was available to them in abundance.

2. A significant proportion of the land owned by the Thakurs was sharecropped.[14] The terms of sharecropping were: sharing of seeds, fertilizer, irrigation cost and produce including grains and residues on a fifty-fifty basis. This formed an important source of agricultural residues for many villagers.

3. Milch cattle, i.e. cows and buffaloes, were generally grazed.[15] Villagers were allowed to pick up the dung dropped during grazing. The problems created by deforestation were, therefore, nullified by the availability and the redistributive mechanism of other fuels.

[14] By one estimate, this could be as high as 40–50 per cent of their cultivated land.

[15] A rule which applies even in the present situation. Milch cattle are grazed to give them exercise which also increases the yield of milk. Bullocks, on the other hand, are generally stall-fed.

PRESENT SITUATION

Economic Condition of Different Villagers[16]

LANDLESS AND MARGINAL LANDHOLDERS

In Garhi, the landless and marginal landholders have been increasing in number and proportion. This is essentially due to the process of division of land between heirs when transferred from one generation to the next. Thus, in 1982, nearly 80 per cent of households were in this category (Table 1), as compared to about 60 per cent a generation earlier. Most of them (77 per cent) were in the agricultural occupation with few alternative sources of income, other than goat rearing or making of ropes from the local tall grass known as 'Moonj Patawar'. Returns from agriculture were at best sufficient to meet subsistence needs, as a large proportion of their land remained unirrigated (Table 2). Only a small proportion (about 8 per cent in the case of marginal landholders) was devoted to the production of cash crops(in this case, groundnuts). Nearly all these families indicated agricultural labour as the primary or the second most important source of income and an average of more than two months of unemployment. Those in the non-agricultural occupations included barbers, tailors, washermen, petty shopkeepers and cycle-rickshaw drivers. They did not appear to be significantly better off, although there was an important difference in that they had an assured income throughout the year. In any case, there appeared to be limited scope for such alternative employment. A few (less than 1 per cent) families had migrated to towns. There

[16] Villagers have been categorized in a manner similar to that followed by the villagers themselves, i.e. as poor, better and rich. This corresponds closely (with few exceptions) to the landholdings of the villagers. Thus the poor villagers correspond to landless and marginal landholders (having land up to 2.5 acres), the better ones to the small and medium landholders (having land from 2.5–5.0 and 5.0–10.0 acres, respectively) and the rich ones to the large landholders (having land above 10 acres). The terms 'marginal', 'small', 'medium' and 'large' landholders, as applied to different landholding classes, are commonly used in Indian planning and administration and have been retained as such. It may be noted here that the landless and marginal landholders have been grouped into the same category. This is due to the fact that while some landless families are seen to own bullocks, enabling them to rent-in land, there are several marginal landholders who prefer to rent-out their land and work as agricultural labourers, because they do not find it economic to keep a pair of bullocks. In general, the economic strength of a family was seen to depend on factors like co-operation between brothers or non-farm income. In this respect, while the distinction beween the landless and marginal landholders was more or less superficial, there were significant differences when this category was compared to the small and medium landholders, for example in terms of assets owned or living space.

was practically no seasonal migration. The poor economic condition of these villagers is clearly indicated by the relative lack of living space and their small proportionate ownership of some assets considered important in the village (Table 3).

SMALL AND MEDIUM LANDHOLDERS

It is seen that the number of small and medium landholders did not change significantly as compared to that in the past. Interestingly, nearly all of them came from Harijan families whose ancestors were tenant-cultivators during the Zamindari period and had suffered the most at the hands of the Thakurs (with the exception of some Pasi families who had played dual roles as Beesardars and Kashtakars). All these families reported agriculture as their main occupation and no other significant source of income other than occasional work as agricultural labourers. Among them, some of the Raidas familes had formerly done leather work, but were forced to discontinue in the face of social boycott by their relatives who considered it degrading in status. Most of these families faced an uncertain future, having made no useful investments other than a tubewell boring for irrigation, by some. Although relatively better off, they seemed destined to join the ranks of the less fortunate as a result of further division of land in future.

LARGE LANDHOLDERS

The large landholders, all Thakurs by caste, owned nearly half of the village land, most of which was irrigated (Table 2). They were all in the agricultural occupation[17] producing mainly for the market. Most of them also had significant non-farm income from sources like fishing contracts in the nearby river or hiring of tractors for agricultural work and transport outside the village. The higher standard of living of these families is apparent when one compares their living space and assets with the rest.

Change in Social Relations

Since the 1960s, there have been considerable changes which have affected the social relations in Garhi. An important event in this regard was the land consolidation programme that led to a significant thrust towards mechanization. Although, under the impact of

[17] Except those who had migrated to towns. Their land was being looked after by their brothers.

Table 2

Irrigation and cropping pattern

Landholding class	Unirrigated land (%)	Kharif crops (July–November)						Rabi crops (November–April)					
		Bajra*	Arhar†	Urad Lobia‡	Ground-nut	Other misc.	Un-cropped	Wheat	Barley	Gram	Arhar	Other misc.	Un-cropped
Marginal	57	18.2	13.6	15.2	7.8	15.7	29.3	28.3	14.8	5.4	13.6	—	37.1
Small and medium	43	11.0	14.5	25.3	9.8	12.4	27.0	35.9	5.2	6.1	14.5	—	38.3
Large	13	2.9	7.4	8.3	20.9	7.4	53.1	49.3	1.4	8.9	7.4	7.5	25.2
Total	35.8	8.6	10.8	14.7	14.9	9.0	40.5	40.9	5.4	7.4	10.8	3.7	31.6

* Spiked millets. ' Pigeon pea. ‡ Pulses.

Percentage calculated in terms of cultivated land.

Several crops are planted as mixed crops, especially by the poor farmers. In such cases, land has been divided equally between components of a mixed crop.

Those components recorded as sprinkled lightly, e.g. peas, are excluded.

Other miscellaneous crops include paddy, Jowar (small millets) and green chilly in Kharif; potatoes and mustard in Rabi.

Uncropped area in Kharif consists mainly of 'Chomasa' area, i.e. that ploughed regularly for four months for conservation of soil nutrients and moisture.

A large portion of the uncropped area in Rabi consists of fields of Arhar from which other mixed crops have been harvested in Kharif. (Arhar occupies the land in both the seasons.)

Table 3

Living space and assets (mean per family)

Landholding class	Living space			Some important assets				
	Rooms (incl. kitchen)	Thatched verandas	Tractors	Diesel pumpsets	Chaff cutting machines	Bullock carts	Cycles
Landless and marginal	1.5	2.3	—	0.02	0.18	0.14	0.31
Small and medium	2.6	2.4	—	0.12	0.37	0.21	0.46
Large	5.0	7.6	0.22	0.66	0.66	0.11	0.44

the Green Revolution, at least one private diesel operated pumpset was installed in Garhi in the 1960s, the real incentive to mechanize came only after land consolidation in the early 1970s.[18] Consolidation means the rearrangement of holdings in a unit among several tenure holders in such a way as to make their respective holdings more compact. Prior to consolidation, many farmers had their plots scattered in distant locations. Consequently, there was not sufficient land in contiguous units for pumpset investments to be attractive. After consolidation, several landholders, mainly the large ones, invested in pumpsets and two even purchased tractors. A number of families that were earlier attached to them, as permanent and semi-permanent labourers, were affected as a result.

The process of land consolidation and mechanization also led to a much reduced incidence of sharecropping. As explained earlier, one of the main reasons for a high incidence of sharecropping during the earlier period was the difficulty in the management of cultivation of scattered holdings with animal power. With self-driven tractors and assured irrigation from diesel-operated pumpsets, there is an increasing shift towards self-cultivation. Discussions with these landholders showed that some of the important reasons for 'retaking' the land from a sharecroper were: differing crop perferences, low productivity due to inadequate investments by the sharecropper and increased ability of the owners to cultivate it themselves.

Such a trend towards mechanization and self-cultivation has led to significant changes in social relations clearly seen in the extent of resource transactions between families of different classes. Land and irrigation water are seen as important resources by a Garhi farmer, which he hopes to hire or share if inadequately endowed with them himself. An analysis of the transactions in these resources (Table 4) showed that the number of transactions between the large landholders and others was far less than that between others, indicating a much diminished role of large landholders as patrons. Patron-client relationships were thus being replaced by contractual relationships. These were marked by increasing expression of distaste for the former patrons or clients, which seemed to be sharpened by increasing competion for labour during the peak agricultural seasons.

---

[18] Although the Act for consolidation of holdings was passed in 1954, consolidation was actually carried out in Garhi only in the 1970s.

Varun Vidyarthi

Table 4

Sharing of resources in Garhi (1982–83)

Resources	Between large landholders and others	Among others
Land		
Area rented (acres)	25.0	30.5
Number of incidents	9	24
Irrigation water		
Area irrigated (acres)	13.5	29.0
Number of incidents	20	40

Fuel Consumption Patterns

VARIATION IN CONSUMPTION MAGNITUDES

An analysis of fuel consumption patterns showed that the consumption magnitudes are affected by: (1) family size—the correlation coefficient between the average daily fuel consumption in the sample families and the number of members in those families is 0.89,[19] and (2) economies of scale—meal tests in different households indicated considerable economies of scale in the preparation of chapatis (bread) and dahl (pulses).[20] Significantly, there was no systematic difference in the per capita fuel consumption across classes.[21] This may be explained by the fact that, in a relatively good harvest year like the study year of 1982–3, the per capita cereal consumption of the poor households may not be less than that of the richer households. As regards noncereals, however, one could easily expect the richer households to be consuming relatively more in amount and variety and hence consuming more fuel. But here too, one cannot be sure because, as revealed from the meal test, the poor may be using much greater proportion of water

[19] For calculating the number of members in a family, those above the age of 14 years were treated as adults. Children between 3 and 14 were treated as half-adults.

[20] Relationship between fuel consumption (y, kg of agricultural residues) and flour cooked as chapatis (x, kg): $y = 0.38 + 0.6x$ (with a standard deviation of 0.31). Relationship between fuel consumption and dahl (x_1, kg): $y = 0.7 + 0.15x_1 + 0.87x_2$ (with a standard deviation of 0.35).

[21] Based on conversion values given earlier, the mean per capita daily fuel consumption for the poor, medium and rich was 7830, 8060 and 5660 kcals, respectively.

in the preparation of dahl or vegetable.[22] This increases the fuel consumption significantly.

VARIATIONS IN FUEL SOURCES AND TYPES

In Garhi, essentially three types of fuels were in use—firewood, dung cakes and agricultural residues.

(a) *Firewood*. Most of the firewood used in the village came from privately owned trees.[23] As seen from Table 5, most trees belonged

Table 5

Fuel-producing assets

Landholding class	Land		Cattle		Trees	
	Mean	Median	Mean	Median	Mean	Median
Landless and marginal	0.8	1.0	1.1	0	2.9	0.0
Small and medium	3.8	3.2	1.6	0	23.6	3.0
Large	15.7	11.0	1.5	0	128.0	79.0

to the large landholders. Others did own a few trees that were planted in their courtyard or on a bad patch of land. However, wood from such trees was used only on special occasions or emergencies, e.g. a marriage feast or burning of the dead. Only those who had a substantial number of trees lopped branches from them in regular course. Few families other than those of the large landholders could do so. A village tree census showed that only 10 per cent of the families owned more than 10 trees (Table 6). This gives a good indication of the number of families that may be using logs or thick branches. Most others relied on gathering twigs from the orchards of large landholders. Gathering of twigs, seeds and flowers[24] was generally allowed, but restrictions were imposed sometimes in the fruit-bearing season. Villagers did not dare to break branches, but some amount of stealing was unavoidable. In general, supplies of firewood were uncertain for most villagers who depended more on crop residues and dung cakes. There was no report of purchase of firewood for cooking purposes.

[22] In the preparation of dahl, a common food item, the grain to water ratio was seen to vary from 1:1.6 to 1:7.1.

[23] There were a few trees on village common lands (about 2 per cent of the total).

[24] Seeds of 'Neem' tree are crushed for making non-edible oils, used in the soap industry. Flowers of 'Mahuwa' tree are used for making liquor.

Table 6

Families owning trees

Number of trees	Families	
	Number	Percentage
Above 50	8	5.4
10–50	6	4.0
Up to 10	55	36.9
None	80	53.7

(b) *Dung cakes.* Cattle are distributed more equitably among the villagers. This is because many families had bullocks which were essential for farming. To be able to do so, some farmers were seen to trade in them—buying a younger stock at the beginning of the ploughing season, using it in agrciultural operations while nurturing it over the year, and then selling it at a higher price at the beginning of the next ploughing season. This interesting adaptive process, indicative of the resource management skills of a poor farmer, had allowed several families to own cattle which, though generally lean and small in size, provided them both draft power and dung. Those without cattle obtained their dung supplies by collecting the droppings of grazed cattle.

(c) *Agricultural residues.* Many types of agricultural residues were used as cooking fuels, but the preferred residues were stems of 'Arhar' (pigeon pea) and 'Bajra' (spiked millets), locally known as 'Jhakar' and 'Bajri', respectively. These give better sustained heat as compared to others and were most commonly used. Bajri is available at the end of the kharif season in November. The top portion of the crop was also used as fodder. Jhakar, on the other hand, is available at the end of the Rabi season, in April. Jhakar stems are thicker and harder, hence they cannot be used as fodder. They were used in making roof frames. That did not affect the supplies, however, as Jhakar was then obtained from the old replaced frames.

Land under the crops Arhar and Bajra determined the availability of these residues. Interestingly, both these crops are traditional rainfed crops. These were more popular among the poor sections, who had a large rainfed area (Table 2). Large landholders, who had assured irrigation, had much less proportional area devoted to these crops. But it did allow them to build up considerable stock of agricultural residues.

The above differences in fuel supplies account for significant differences in the type of fuels used by different villagers (Table 7) which is also indicative of their fuel problem. The large landholders had little to worry about with assured firewood supplies. They often burned firewood in combination with Jhakar and dung cakes depending on the amount of heat required. Dung cakes give slow

Table 7

Fuel consumption during the study period

Landholding class	Percentage of total consumption			
	Agricultural residues	Dung cakes	Firewood	Spring plants
Landless and marginal	44.7	34.2	14.4	6.6
Small and medium	59.8	27.0	7.6	5.5
Large	22.6	4.7	72.7	—
Total	44.5	27.0	23.2	5.2

Percentage figures are arrived at after converting fuel consumption magnitudes to their energy equivalent.
Conversion values[25]
Dry firewood logs (used by large landholders):   4700 kcal/kg
Thin stems and twigs of wood (used by others):   4000 kcal/kg
Agricultural residues and spring plants: 3000 kcal/kg
Dung cakes (made with about 10 per cent straw):   2500 kcal/kg.

heat, useful for simmering, while Jhakar stems being thinner than the firewood logs, burn up quickly giving more heat. Their use therefore provides a good method of heat control.

Their predominant use by others, however, was more because of need than convenience. The small and medium landholders, who were better endowed with land, consumed greater quantities of agricultural residues. This allowed them to spend less time in gathering other fuels (Table 8) which formed a relatively small proportion of their total fuel consumption.

[25] Tests could not be carried out to determine the calorific values of the different fuels. The figures used here are based on values reported in earlier energy surveys. See: National Council of Applied Economic Research, *Rural Energy Consumption in Northern India* (New Delhi: 1978), p. 121; Centre for Application of Science and Technology to Rural Areas, *Rural Energy Consumption Patterns, A Field Study*, mimeo. (Banglore: 1980), pp. 48, 73.

Table 8

Time spent in fuel and fodder collection

Landholding class	Fuel collection (Av. person hr/day)	Fodder collection (Av. person hr/day)
Landless and marginal	1.3	4.0
Small and medium	0.9	2.6
Large	0.0	0.0
Total (excluding large)	1.2	3.6

Those in the lowest landholding category should have minimum supply of agricultural residues. However, it is seen that the residues still form the most important component of their fuel consumption. This is explained by the following facts: (1) Farmers owning bullocks are able to rent in land and thereby have a share of the residues produced. (2) About 15–20 per cent of the pigeon pea crop is generally destroyed.[26] This leaves dry Jhakar stems standing with the unaffected crop in the field. Such stems are plucked by the foraging villagers. This is generally permitted. There is some amount of cheating also, but it is difficult to stop it. (3) Those maintaining good relations with the large landholders are able to borrow agricultural residues from them. This makes a significant difference in consumption, as brought out in Table 9. A member of family A works as a permanent labourer for one of the large landholders. He has free access to the large landholder's stock of agricultural residues which is clearly reflected in the high proportion of residues burned by this family in comparison with that of family B which relies on greater use of spring plants and gathered firewood. At the time of study, not more than 5 per cent of the families had such a relationship with the large landholders. But other families in their good books, were also able to borrow sometimes.

A fourth type of fuel, that is gradually becoming more important among most families other than those of the large landholders, is a spring plant known as 'Behaya' (*Ipomoea fitulosa*). This is best described as a tall weed with relatively thick stems that grows in abundance in the area. The stems of this plant are generally cut and left to dry in the open for about a month before actual use. However, Behaya produces a lot of smoke, which is said to be harmful for the

[26] It is not clear why this occurs. Villagers say that it is due to the attack of pests.

Table 9

Comparative fuel consumption of two landless households

Family	Percentage of total consumption			
	Agricultural residues	Dung cakes	Firewood	Spring plants
A	61.8	34.3	—	3.8
B	41.4	19.8	25.7	13.0

eyes.[27] Therefore it is among the least preferred fuels and its use by several families is a clear indication of the increasing fuel problem.

IDENTIFYING THE FUEL PROBLEM

In Garhi, the fuel scarcities do not seem to have affected the consumption magnitudes. Instead, as noted earlier, the problem is seen in terms of increasing dependency on less preferred and possibly harmful fuels. Two related issues that clarify the problem will be discussed now.

(a) *Seasonality.* Fuel consumption data of the landless and marginal landholders (Table 10) indicate that the fuel problem is probably most severe during the months December—March when a significant proportion of the fuel consumed is accounted for by Behaya. Gathered firewood is also seen to be relatively more important during these months. Bajri harvested in November constitutes the main agricultural residue consumed in the same period. The use of agricultural residues jumps up in the following months when Jhakar becomes available. Jhakar then continues as an important fuel in the remaining months, together with dung cakes. It may be noted that the consumption of dung cakes is highest during the rainy season (June–September), when in fact they are not made at all. This is because dung cakes are generally stored along with Jhakar for the rainy season. The process of storage of dung cakes starts as early as the preceding month of November and continues right through the dry months of winter and summer, when the dried cakes are kept systematically in 'bathias' (small mounds) visible to any visitor passing through north Indian villages. This in fact suggests that the fuel problem is maximum during the rains, for

---

[27] A survey showed that 18 women from about 12 per cent of households had 'Motiabind', an eye disease, which the villagers associate with smoke from lowgrade fuels like Behaya.

Table 10

Seasonal variations in fuel consumption of landless and marginal landholders

Months	Percentage of total consumption			
	Agricultural residues	Dung cakes	Firewood	Spring plants
Dec.–Jan.	17.3	43.4	22.4	16.7
Feb.–March	41.7	11.2	29.3	17.6
Apr.–May	72.8	8.7	18.4	—
June–July	47.7	41.5	7.1	3.5
Aug.–Sept.	42.5	54.8	2.6	—
Total	44.7	34.2	14.4	6.6

which the villagers stay prepared in advance. This can be better appreciated if one visits the house of a poor villager during rains. The lack of space (see Table 3) often prohibits proper storage, allowing the fuel to pick up moisture that leads to improper combustion, with a lot of smoke. An alternative fuel during rains would cut down the need for storage, improving the fuel situation in other months.

(b) *Opportunity cost of collection.* The opportunity cost of collection is often used as an indicator of the fuel problem. In Garhi, it was observed that several families were also involved in the collection of fodder. Accordingly, data were collected for both the activities. Table 8 gives the average time spent by different families in fuel and fodder collection. It is seen that while fuel collection took an average of 1.2 hours per day per household, fodder collection involved three times the number of hours. Women played a major role in both these activities.

Activity	Man hr.	Woman hr.	Children hr.
Fuel collection	1.1	1.6	1
Fodder collection	1.3	2.1	1

Significantly, the two activities were not necessarily exclusive. Participant observation by a woman investigator indicated that women from different families generally moved out of their homes in groups. Different members of a group could have different and often mixed purposes for such an outing—grazing goats, fodder collection or fuel collection. Generally, fodder collection entailed the maximum time and effort, as green grass had to be chiselled out root-by-root. Relatively speaking, collection of fuel was considered a subsidiary activity.[28]

This suggests that the figures for collection hours that were based on interviews, are only indicative, and that it may be impractical to present actual opportunity costs of fuel collection in isolation from other economic costs incurred in such multipurpose outings.

The Future

The future holds little promise for a poor Garhi inhabitant as regards energy supplies. This is because the fuel resources threaten to decimate further as a result of the factors discussed below.

A Trend Towards Felling of Orchards

As noted earlier, orchards constitute much of the remaining tree cover in Garhi. In 1982, the orchards occupied 30 acres (about 9 per cent) of the village land. Most of them were owned by the large landholders, who had a definite motivation in maintaining them, as they were exempt from the purview of the land ceiling laws. However, such an incentive does not hold once the landholding falls below ceiling limits, say with the division of land between brothers. This has already started happening in Garhi where, in at least one case, felling of an orchard was reported. Felling was supposedly enticed by the need to pay back a loan used for purchasing a tractor.

As more farmers seek alternative investments, the tree cover is threatened with obliteration due to such fellings. Although the law makes it obligatory for the owners to plant two trees in the place of each one felled,[29] it would be difficult to ensure this, unless there is

---

[28] In the process of collection, the group members often got scattered. But they made it a point to meet at one place later, for rest and gossip. In fact, the outing was seen as a useful opportunity for socialization.

[29] Government of Uttar Pradesh, *Uttar Pradesh Protection of Trees in Rural and Hill Areas Act*, 1976 (Lucknow: Eastern Book Company, 1976), p.3.

also a commercial motive to do so. Availability of fuelwood would also depend on the species planted. In the case mentioned above, the farmer chose to plant Mango (*Mangifera indica*), a fruit-bearing species, having a relatively slow growth rate.

Shift in Cropping Pattern

As mentioned earlier, the crops Arhar and Bajra produce residues that are used as cooking fuels. Both these crops are traditional rain-fed crops. The cropping pattern of Garhi (Table 2) shows that the large landowners, having greater area under irrigation, have much less land devoted to the production of these crops as compared to others (about 10 per cent as compared to 25–30 per cent by the rest). Instead, a higher proportion of their land is devoted to the production of cash crops—groundnuts and wheat.

Studies in Indian agriculture confirm that coarse grain crops including Arhar and Bajra get replaced by other 'high value' crops with the improvement of the resource base of an area.[30] In Garhi, agricultural residues constitute more that 40 per cent of the total fuel consumption. As more area is brought under irrigation, a shift in cropping pattern would reduce the availability of such fuels substantially.

The above changes would have greater effect on the poor who rely heavily on agricultural residues and gathered firewood. Earlier, when the forests were destroyed, the existence of orchards and such crops together with a redistributive mechanism, possible through continued ties with the large landholders, allowed them to have access to these fuels. In the future, however, both the availability of and access to these fuels is threatened.

Alternatives

To assess the potential role of some alternative energy systems, individual and group discussions were held with villagers on several

[30] See: N. S. Jodha and R. P. Singh, 'Factors Constraining Growth of Coarse Grain Crops in Semiarid Tropical India', *Indian Journal of Agricultural Economics*, Vol. 37, No. 3, Conference No. (July–Sept. 1982), pp. 346–54. In this paper, analysing the production of millets and pulses, including Bajra and Arhar, the researchers note that when the resource base of an area traditionally allocated to the production of coarse grain crops improves (e.g. through a new irrigation facility), rather than harness the potential of these crops, farmers replace them with high value crops.

occasions. Some, e.g. tree plantations, improved stoves and solar cookers, were introduced on an experimental basis. Details of these interactions are presented elsewhere.[31] Some observations, pertinent to the present discussion, are given in brief here.

(i) *Biogas*. There was relatively little enthusiasm among the poor villagers for biogas plants for cooking. This was due to several reasons: (1) most of them did not have sufficient inputs to own a family plant; (2) they felt unsure of participation at village level to organize a community plant; (3) they preferred to make investments in schemes that could raise their incomes. This applied to women as well, who were very clear about their priorities: 'We would prefer an irrigation system.' This, however, did not apply to large land-owners, who were eager to have a biogas system for cooking.

(ii) *Improved stoves*. A trained woman worker made several improved mud stoves that showed lower fuel consumption as compared to the traditional one.[32] The women were quite enthusiastic about these stoves. However, they were unwilling to invest in material worth Rs 20 for making it. For the same reason, solar cookers costing Rs 500 did not receive serious attention either. According to a survey covering nearly 90 per cent households in Garhi, while 99 per cent of the women felt that the improved stove was useful only about 13 per cent were willing to invest in it. The corresponding figures for solar cookers were 94 and 1, respectively. Instead, many families were more willing to purchase and some actually did purchase 'charkhas' (a hand-operated cotton-spinning device) costing about Rs 20, that allowed them to earn money by selling the yarn produced.

(iii) *Tree plantation*. Most villagers did not have sufficient land to undertake plantation on private land. Although the law encouraged tree plantation on common lands, most villagers refrained from doing so because of uncertainty of rights over such lands. It appeared that these rights were determined more by the use of force, that gave a definite advantage to the large landowners in the utilization of such lands. There was no willingness among decision makers, including the village head, to allot some portion of the village common land for purposes of plantation, that allowed

---

[31] V. Vidyarthi, 'Participatory assessment of rural energy needs and alternatives: case study of an Indian village', *Economic and Political Weekly*, August, 1985.

[32] Though not always. A lot depended on the cooking practices.

families to have individual control over trees.[33]

The first two responses indicate that, in spite of increasing fuel problems, most poor villagers see poverty as their main problem and would prefer to invest in projects that generate income. The third example illustrates the complexity of the issue of use of common lands. In general, it was clear that alternatives could not be seen in terms of straightforward technical interventions, and that any useful change would depend on the ability to deal with more difficult social and economic problems.

GENERAL OBSERVATIONS AND CONCLUSIONS

Indian villages have been a scene of several changes that have affected the lives of poor villagers in the recent past. The most significant events in this respect were those associated with changes in the land system and agriculture, that provided the basic conditions determining the economic opportunities and social relations. Observations in Garhi indicate the manner in which these changes have been affecting the energy availability to the poor.

Before the abolition of Zamindari, the traditional ties between the patron-Zamindars and the client-villagers, provided security to the latter in respect of a resource like firewood, which was available in abundance. Even after the destruction of the forests, continued ties between the two allowed the latter to have access to the woody agricultural residues, that served as alternative cooking fuels. Animal based farming and large incidences of sharecropping provided the basis for these ties. With increasing mechanization and self-cultivation of holdings, however, these ties have been giving way to contractual relationships, characterized by minimum sharing of resources between the large landholders and the poor, affecting the supply of agricultural residues of the latter.

Fuel supplies of the poor are also seen to be affected by (1) shifts in cropping pattern towards crops that do not provide woody agricultural residues and (2) further loss of tree-cover presently

---

33 The usual method of carrying out village forestry plantations is different. In such programmes, the responsibility for protection of the trees and the distribution of benefits lie with a village committee especially formed for the purpose. The plantation is undertaken with paid labour. To overcome the plantation costs and the future distribution problems, it was suggested that families, individually or as a group, be given the right over trees including the responsibility of planting and protection.

provided by the orchards. In Garhi, the effects of these changes are likely to be felt more in the future, as these phenomena spread.

All these changes point towards increased fuel problems for the poor, who are already seen to use least preferred and possibly harmful spring plants as cooking fuel. It is of interest to note that none of them reported purchase of cooking fuels and few had the willingness to invest in a fuel-saving device. Lack of purchasing power was clearly an important element of their problem. This could be linked in part to the poor agricultural conditions, the lack of alternative sources of income and the increasing number of landless and marginal land holders.

The problem origins and linkages discussed here are of a general nature, the essential components of which would be typical of many villages in the region and elsewhere. From the point of view of the poor, the energy problem can be seen as a problem of decreasing availability of local fuel resources and access to them: the former stemming from changes in land cover and cropping pattern, and the latter being affected by the changing social relations. Clearly, remedial measures need to ensure both fuel availability and access to be of relevance to the poor. Attempts at intervention generally tend to emphasize the former through the introduction of new techniques, i.e. by tapping new resources or improved utilization of existing resources. The Garhi experience suggests that there may be scope for improving availability of local fuels also through appraisal and correction of existing trends in private land use and cropping pattern. For the poor villagers, however, the question of access would still pose a difficult problem. Its resolution appears to lie mainly in simultaneous development of their capabilities, i.e. through measures to strengthen their social and economic position. Only energy programmes planned in *conjunction* with activities contributing to the development of such capabilities[34] can lead to desired improvements in the energy situation of the poor.

---

[34] E.g. by methods to ensure the rights of different villagers over village common land and property, as a prelude to introduction of forestry plantations on the common lands; by planning biogas programmes in conjunction with schemes to give loans for cattle and biogas-powered machinery to the poor, with innovative methods of obtaining loan security from them (e.g. group collaterals instead of individual securities).

Overfishing the Coastal Commons: Causes and Consequences

JOHN KURIEN and T R THANKAPPAN ACHARI

INTRODUCTION

In developing countries, use of common property resources is closely related to the survival and sustenance of a vast population of persons such as pastoralists, forest dwellers and fisherfolk. This paper highlights how a *combination* of economic, technological and social factors interacting in a specific context results in overuse of a commons—the coastal sea eco-system and the fish therein—leading to its near ruin. It points to the fact that the ensuing detrimental economic consequences are by no means equitably distributed.

The paper is divided into seven parts. In Section II a background sketching the relevant aspects of the history of the fishery development process in Kerala is given. Section III enumerates the various factors leading to overfishing; Section IV provides evidence of overfishing; Section V assesses the impact of overfishing on the various social groups depending on the resource; Section VI analyses their responses to the effects of overfishing; and Section VII examines possible ways of resolving the crisis.

BACKDROP

Fisheries as an economic sector gained importance with the initiation of economic planning in India. The long coastline and the

Excerpted from John Kurien and T. R. Thankappan Achari, 'Overfishing along Kerala Coast: Causes and Consequences', *Economic and Political Weekly* , 18 September, 1990, pp. 2011–18.

productive continental shelf gave fisheries the status of a sector capable of accelerating the growth of the rural economy of the country. Accordingly, planned marine fisheries development had the multi-faceted objectives of increasing the fish harvest, improving socio-economic conditions of fishermen, augmenting export earnings and generating new employment opportunities. These objectives were to be achieved through initiatives promoted by the state and private efforts. To achieve them the 'modernization growth-oriented' model of development, largely premised on the experience of the more developed temperate water maritime countries, was accepted. This approach primarily implied the superimposition of a modern, capital-intensive, specialized technology over the existing traditional base which was largely labour-intensive and of great technical diversity. It assumed that this base was a hindrance to development and had to be either transformed or completely phased out.

In Kerala, the leading maritime state of India, the approach to fisheries development was initially radically different. The state's fishery policy in the first decade of planned development—1956 to 1966—can be summarized as having been based on 'the judicious exploitation of marine resources by effectively and gradually raising the productive capabilities of the existing facilities giving primacy to the accumulated skills of the fishermen' [Kurien 1985]. During this phase increased fishing effort was applied by the artisanal fishermen using their traditional non-mechanized craft and a wide array of fishing gear and tackle. There was a rapid change from cotton to nylon nets. The overall fish harvest, and that of species like prawns, also increased substantially.

This approach did not last long. By the mid-sixties the 'modernization/growth-oriented' model came to be introduced in Kerala. The single most important factor responsible for this was the rising demand for prawn in the international market. The waters of Kerala, being one of the world's richest resource for the penaeid prawns, virtually became the main 'breeding ground' for this model. Fisheries development in Kerala soon became synonymous with increasing prawn harvest and earning foreign exchange. With the phenomenal rise in the number of small trawlers—introduced initially by the former Indo-Norwegian Project—the prawn harvest and export earnings increased steadily. The earlier caste-bound nature of the fishery sector ceased to be a barrier to entry. The main investors involved in the new development model were non-fishermen [Kurien 1985]. For a decade, i.e. until mid-1970s, it was smooth sailing. The direction of the tide changed after 1974. The levels of overall fish and prawn harvest began to fall. By the end of the seventies the marine fishery sector of the state was heading towards an ecological crisis of overfishing.

The artisanal fishermen who were only peripheral beneficiaries of this modernization model responded to this crisis at two levels. The more rapid, widespread and vocal response was in the form of organized protest demanding state regulation of what they perceived as destructive fishing methods [Kurien and Achari 1988]. The slower response was in the form of adoption of new technologies for propulsion of their fishing crafts and greater investments in fishing gear in a desperate attempt to enhance their share of falling harvests. This response further aggravated the level of overfishing particularly after 1984.

Overfishing not only implied a fall in the fish harvest but led to a very skewed distribution of the benefits and costs in the fish economy. This in turn came to attain larger socio-political implications which today plague the state. It is customary to distinguish between two types of overfishing: economic and biological. Economic overfishing occurs when marginal costs of an additional unit of fishing effort are higher than marginal revenues. The economy experiences loss (even though total fish catch may still increase) because of a misallocation of capital and labour which might have produced higher economic yields in alternative activities. Biological over-fishing occurs when the marginal yield of an additional unit of fishing effort is negative.[1] At such a level of effort the fish population stock is prevented from generating its maximum sustainable yield.[2]

The sea off the south-west coast of India, comprising the maritime states of Goa, Karnataka and Kerala, forms a relatively homogeneous aquatic eco-zone. The inshore or coastal waters (upto a depth of 50 metres) of this region measure 23,400 square kilometres and have a

---

[1] In tropical multi-species fisheries, biological overfishing may occur even though total catch is still increasing because the decline in yield—or complete extinction—of one or several species may be compensated through higher yields of other species.

[2] Biologists further distinguish between 'growth overfishing', and 'ecosystem overfishing' depending on the most important factor preventing full recovery or growth of the stock [Pauly, 1979].

maximum sustainable yield (MSY)[3] of 7,00,000 tonnes [George *et al.* 1977]. The average fishery productivity potential of these waters works out to 30 tonnes per square kilometre (or 300 kg for every hectare) compared to 12.5 tonnes for all-India making it the most productive fishing zone in India. Kerala accounts for 12,570 sq kms of this coastal sea area which has an estimated MSY of 4,00,000 tonnes. The fishery resources in the tropical seas off Kerala are marked by a multitude of species attaining varying sizes at age of maturity. They are widely dispersed in the coastal commons. Each species is available in relatively small quantities. There are complex prey-predator relationships between them as well as competition for food.

These characteristics differ distinctly from the characteristics of fish resources of temperate waters. There one finds a relatively small number of species which grow to larger sizes and each species is available in teeming millions. The inter-species interactions are also less complex than what obtains in the tropical waters making it easier to 'target' fishing operations to specific species.

For the purpose of data collection the numerous fish species of Kerala have been clubbed under about fiftyfour broad names. The fish harvest pattern of 1984–5 indicate the important species to be: oil sardines, mackerels, anchovies, ribbon fish, carangids (all pelagic), perches and catfish (all demersal).[4] Of these, oil sardines, mackerels and penaeid prawns have traditionally been considered the three prime economic species. Their MSY's are estimated to be 1,26,000 tonnes, 56,000 tonnes and 56,000 tonnes respectively.

FACTORS CONTRIBUTING TO OVERFISHING

There are several factors contributing to excessive fishing effort in a fishery. We will restrict our assessment to five major areas: (a) the

[3] The maximum sustainable yield (MSY) is subject to changes due to biological and ecological factors. Hence, MSY estimated for a year need not be the same for all years. The estimates quoted in the article are taken from George *et al.* 1977 and are the only available and comprehensive estimates made so far.

[4] Fish species are generally divided into two broad categories in accordance with the niche that they generally inhabit in the marine environment. Pelagic species are the predominantly surface dwelling fishes. The demersal species are those that generally inhabit the bottom of the sea. The behaviour and life cycles of pelagic species are more prone to influence of oceanographic conditions like changes in water temperature, salinity, dissolved oxygen content and so forth. Demersal species remain largely unaffected by such changes.

open access nature of the fishery, (b) the use of inappropriate technology, (c) the demand-pull factors that create galloping prices, (d) financial subsidies offered by the state which encourage investment and, (e) the pressure of population on the coastal commons.

Open Access Nature

When traditional technologies and the custom-bound organization of the fish economy predominated, the common property nature of the marine fish resource did not pose a major problem. Technical barriers, such as the need to have fishery specific skills, and social barriers like fishing being the occupation of a lower caste, prevented free entry of capital and persons from outside the traditional fishing communities into the fishery. The introduction of mechanized boats and the perceived profit opportunities in prawn exporting changed this scenario considerably. The mercantile capital class of Kerala took the initiatives to break these barriers. They shifted some of their capital from such ventures as coir and cashewnut processing and exports to prawn fishing and its processing and exports. Rapid entry was facilitated by the free access to the sea: mechanized boats could be operated without any form of licence or registration. There was also no regulation limiting the ownership of fishing assets only to those who were active fishermen. As a matter of fact, entry into the fishery was given greater impetus by the state. As a result, the post-1966 period witnessed a considerable influx of non-fishermen owners of fishing assets particularly mechanized trawlers. Between 1966 and 1985 the number of trawlers increased from a couple of hundred to around 2,800.

Use of Inappropriate Technology

Traditional fishing technologies (nets, tackle and the methods of fishing) were in general evolved to suit the particular ecological context of the fish. Deserving special mention is the selective nature of fishing nets (a special mesh-size/share for catching a specific species of fish) and the 'passive' nature of fishing operations (allowing fish to get entangled in the net rather than going in hot pursuit of them or catching them by disturbing their milieu).

As indicated earlier, the 'modernization' phase of fisheries development was premised on the need to introduce fishing crafts, gear and methods which were proven efficient in the temperate water milieu. These tended to be 'active' fishing techniques using single gear combinations innovated for the fishery resources of the temperate waters. Trawling (the method of scraping the sea bottom with a bell shaped net to catch demersal fish) and purse-seining (the method of quickly encircling whole shoals of pelagic fish) were two such techniques introduced after the decade of the sixties. Both these techniques were very capital-intensive and initially raised the labour productivity. In the short-run harvesting costs were low and given the high prices of certain species of fish (see below), the profits to owners were very high. This led to a rapid increase in numbers and the extensive use of these techniques. This contributed very significantly to overfishing by destroying the sea-bottom eco-niche (trawling) and by indiscriminate and non-selective fishing of whole shoals of pelagic fishes (purse-seining).

Booming Demand

The introduction of trawlers into Kerala was a response to the rise in demand for prawns in the international market. This was spurred by factors such as the enhanced growth of the US and Japanese economies and also the former's loss of access to supply from China. These demand-pull factors were outside the control of the local economy and it was also difficult to insulate the fishery resources from being harvested in response to them.

From a commodity used to manure coconut palms, prawns grew to become the 'pink gold' of marine exports from India. In 1961–2 the beach price of prawns was only Rs 240 per tonne—less than even the price of mackerels which were considered the 'poor man's protein'. In 1971–2 prawn prices reached Rs 1,810 per tonne. Between then and 1984–5 it increased nearly sevenfold while the prices of oil sardines and mackerels rose by 184 and 213 per cent respectively (Table 1). In the case of the domestically consumed fish species—oil sardines and mackerels—there is evidence to show that the increased prices were the result of the inability to enhance the harvest in keeping with the growing demand for fish from the local population [Kurien 1978]. Purse-seiners were first

Kurien and Achari

Table 1

Trends in Prawn and Fish Prices in Kerala

(Current Prices; Index: 1971–72 = 100)

Year	Prawns		Oil Sardine		Mackerel	
	Rs/Tonne	Index	Rs/Tonne	Index	Rs/Tonne	Index
1961–62	240	13	90	24	340	38
1971–72	1810	100	380	100	890	100
1976–77	7260	401	850	224	1600	180
1984–85	14120	780	1080	284	2790	313

Source: GOK, department of fisheries, *Administration Reports* (several years)

introduced in Kerala in 1976. Until then oil sardines and mackerels were caught exclusively by fishermen using traditional crafts and gear.

State Subsidies

Following the adoption of the 'modernization path' to fisheries development, the state became actively involved in promoting the direction of investments in the sector. It invested in the capital-intensive and long gestation infrastructure facilities like harbours, landing centres, etc. It also provided training facilities and gave subsidies to the owners of modern crafts. As much as 25 per cent of the cost of the hull of the boat and 50 per cent of the cost of its engine were provided as grants. The remainder was treated as a loan to be repaid in 64 instalments over a period of eight years at 7 per cent interest. In theory all the 1,200 mechanized boats so issued by the state between 1961–2 and 1977–8 were to fishermen co-operatives or genuine groups of fishermen. In practice however this hardly happened as is evident from the evaluation of these co-operatives by a government report which concludes:

The failures in the operation of the scheme of distribution of mechanized boats were due to the fact that the fishermen co-operatives to whom or through whom the boats were issued were all *benami* (under false name) co-operatives almost without exception. The rich and influential among the fishermen sponsored and controlled the co-operatives [Krishna Kumar 1981].

It was this realization which prompted the dropping of a similar scheme drawn up for the Sixth Five-Year Plan (1980–1 to 84–5) which envisaged providing subsidies and soft loans for the introduction of purse-seiners. Although the state dropped the scheme, the private entrepreneurs went ahead with finances provided by commercial financing institutions. State subsidies for mechanized boats were completely withdrawn in 1973. From 1985 onwards, following the rush of artisanal fishermen to obtain outboard engines, the state extended subsidies at the rate of Rs 3,000 per engine and Rs 2,600 per craft and gear. Though late, for the first time state subsidies were enjoyed by genuine fishermen. The rapid increase in outboard engines in Kerala from a handful in 1982 to as many as 8,000 in 1988, is to a small extent due to these incentives.

Population Pressure on In-shore Waters

One characteristic of tropical water fisheries is that overuse of even low productive, passive fishing gear can affect the renewability of stocks [Pauly 1979]. The pressure exerted by increasing numbers of fishermen using increasing amounts of fishing equipment within the limited area of the coastal waters has this effect. The active fishermen population has been increasing at a rate of about 2.3 per cent per annum. In 1961 there were 80,700 active fishermen in Kerala. Given Kerala's coastal sea area of 12,570 sq km, the population density was about 6.4 fishermen per sq km ensuring that on the average each fisherman had 16 hectares of coastal commons to fish. By 1985 the population increased by 65 per cent to 1,34,000, increasing the fishermen population density in the coastal sea area to 10.6 per sq km. This reduced the average coastal commons per fisherman to nine hectares as against 30 hectares for all of India.

With the increase in the number of fishermen their fishing assets also increased. Traditional fishing crafts increased from around 21,000 in 1961 to over 27,000 in 1986. More important are the increases in the quality and the quantity of fishing gear. During the last two decades practically all the fishermen have shifted over from using cotton to nylon nets. Though no aggregate estimates are available, evidence from village studies indicates that the quantum of fishing nets and other tackle has increased significantly [Achari 1987a]. This fact became most evident with the post-1982

outboard motorization drive which was induced by declining productivity due to overfishing of the coastal commons. This popula-
tion-induced increase of fishing pressure can certainly be viewed
as an issue which will exacerbate the extent of overfishing if the
present trend continues.

THE EVIDENCE OF OVERFISHING

Considerable data is now available to indicate that the above mentioned factors have in combination led to the ecological crisis in the
coastal waters of Kerala. The evidence with respect to some parameters is substantial but scanty in the case of others. The total picture that emerges however points undoubtedly to a scenario of
strong tendencies towards overall economic and ecosystem overfishing with biological overfishing clearly established in regard to
the most valuable species namely prawn.

Biological and Eco-system Overfishing

Kerala has been the leading maritime state contributing between
20 to 35 per cent of the total marine fish harvest in India between
1956 and 1985.[5] The total marine fish harvest in Kerala during this
period fluctuated between 1,52,200 tonnes in 1956 and 4,48,300
tonnes in 1973. Within this the harvest of pelagic species ranged
between 89,900 tonnes in 1956 and 3,57,000 tonnes in 1971 and that
of the demersal species between 48,000 tonnes in 1957 and 1,98,000
tonnes in 1975.

One can discern two distinct phases in this time span of three
decades: a phase of steadily increasing harvest—1956–73—and a
phase of stagnating or declining harvests—1973–85. This broad
periodization is valid whether one considers the total harvest, the
harvest of pelagic and demersal groupings or the major economic
species—oil sardines and mackerels and prawns. This is evident
from the growth rates shown in Table 2 for the two periods mentioned above.

To establish that a decline in fish harvest points to biological

---

[5] Output figures in this and other parts of the paper (unless otherwise mentioned) are taken
from the published data of the Central Marine Fisheries Research Institute. Price data is taken
from the *Administrative Reports* of the Department of Fisheries.

Table 2

Compound Growth Rates of Fish Harvest of Kerala State

Species Groups	Period I 1956–1973	Period II 1973–1985
Total Marine Fish Harvest	3.23*	− 1.79*
Total Pelagic Fish Harvest	3.19*	− 0.18
Total Demersal Fish Harvest	3.52*	− 4.60*
Total Oil Sardine and Mackerel Harvest	5.01*	0.60
Total Prawn Harvest	6.21*	− 8.30*

Note: Estimated using semi-log function.
* Significant at 5 per cent

overfishing conventionally requires that at least two more indicators exhibit a downward trend. These are (i) the catch per unit (fishing) effort (CPUE), and (ii) the size of the harvested fish species. In a multi-species fishery these indicators can only be measured with respect to a particular species. In our case we have such data only with regard to penaeid prawns which is the most important economic species and the most controversial one in regard to the overfishing debate.

In the main prawn landing centre in Kerala (Neendakara in Quilon district) the catch per unit effort (CPUE) declined from 83 kg/hr of fishing effort in 1973 to 20 kg/hr in 1984 [George 1988]. Taking the three most important centres where trawler operations are concentrated (Neendakara, Cochin and Calicut) the CPUE for 1973 and 1984 are 50 kg/hr and 20 kg/hr respectively. Also it has been reported that the size of prawns caught has been declining over the years [George 1988]. Another overall indicator, pointing at least to the possibility of eco-system overfishing, is the decline in the catches of the demersal species of fish. As indicated earlier, these bottom dwelling species are largely unaffected by nature induced changes in their eco-system. Hence, both the increase and the decline in their harvest can be attributed to man-induced interventions in the form of fishing. Between the years 1971–5 and 1981–5 the harvests of nearly all the important demersal species registered a sharp decline [See Table 3] This can largely be attributed to excessive or destructive fishing—particularly the use of trawlers.

Kurien and Achari

Table 3

Demersal Fish Harvest in Kerala

(000 tonnes)

Species	1971–75	1976–80	1981–85	Per Cent Change over 1971–75	
				1976–80	1981–85
Catfish	22	11	10	(50)	(55)
Perches	10	16	7	60	(30)
Sciaenids	10	9	5	(10)	(50)
Leiognathus	11	4	5	(64)	(55)
Prawns	59	41	29	(31)	(51)
Others	36	30	38	(17)	6
Total	148	111	94	(25)	(36)

Note: Figures in ( ) indicate percentage decline
Sources: Paul (1982); Government of Kerala (1985)

Economic Overfishing

That economic overfishing had set in by the beginning of the eighties is evident from the profitability calculations made for the trawler fleet at different points in time. In 1968–9 trawlers in Kerala (above 10m length) operated on an average for 160 days and landed 30 tonnes of fish valued at Rs 34,500 incurring a total operating cost of Rs 26,700. Net income after depreciation and interest worked out to Rs 7,800 or a 14 per cent return on the investment [Government of India 1971]. In 1978 an enquiry conducted by the Kerala State Planning Board indicated a net return on investment from trawling boats of 8.6 per cent [Government of Kerala 1979]. Results from an FAO/UNDP-sponsored study indicated that in 1980–1 trawlers operated on the average for 157 days and landed 19 tonnes of fish valued at Rs 92,300 but incurring a larger total cost. This resulted in a negative rate of return [Kurien and Willmann 1982].

Despite 'average losses' it is reckoned that as much as a third of the fleet was operating profitably. This fact, coupled with the fluctuating nature of fortunes from fish harvests, provides a strong incentive for marginal loss makers to continue in the fishery because they operate on the basis of the expectations of a bumper catch which could wipe out their accumulated losses. Apart from this there is the role of state subsidy. Having initially obtained subsidies and long-term loans from the state, the owners of several boats have defaulted in their repayments. In fact, since most of them have appropriate political connections the repayment of loans seems more closely correlated to one's contacts rather than the economics of operation of one's boats. This makes the *private* return from the boats to the owners still lucrative when calculated on the basis of their *own* investments. In March 1986 a provisional estimate of the government of Kerala, assessed the total accumulated arrears on loan repayments due from mechanized boats (mostly trawlers) issued by it to stand at Rs 75 million. Of this Rs 58 million was the principal amount—or Rs 42,000 per boat which on the average was about 30–40 per cent of the investment cost. The experience of the commercial banks in this regard is unlikely to have been very different.

An expert committee appointed by the government of Kerala to study the question of resource depletion and overfishing was of the unanimous opinion that investment in Kerala's coastal waters was far above the desirable optimal levels. From the above calculations it was estimated that the extent of over-capitalization in the fishery was of the order of Rs 530 million, an amount equal to the total development assistance given by the state to the fisheries sector in Kerala during the three decades of planned development [Achari 1987b].

Table 4

Estimates of Excess Fishing Craft in Kerala

Craft Type	Existing Number	Committee Recommendation	Excess	
			Number	Per Cent
Trawlers	2807	1145	1662	59
Purse-seiners	54	Nil	54	100
Motorised Crafts	6934	3690	4244	61
Non-motorised Crafts	20170	20000	170	negligible

Sources: Department of Fisheries (personal request—September 1986. Mechanised gill-net boats not accounted here); Kalawar, 1985.

IMPACT OF OVERFISHING

The overfishing of the coastal marine fishery resources of Kerala seem to have adversely affected the working fishermen as well as the poorer sections of consumers for whom fish forms a major source of nutrition.

Productivity and Incomes of Fishermen

The productivity of the working fishermen dropped significantly with overfishing. Incomes however did not plunge to abysmal levels because shore prices of fish exhibited considerable increases. They rose from around Rs 1,260/tonne in 1974 to Rs 2,300/tonne in 1982. The trends in productivity and income were similar for both the workers on the mechanized trawlers and the artisanal fishermen working with their traditional crafts. Taking 1974 as the base we see that productivity and income levels declined across the board. Trawler crew who harvested 10 tonnes of fish in 1974 landed only 7.7 tonnes in 1982. Their real per capita incomes during this period fell by 45 per cent from around Rs 2,700 to Rs 1,500. In the case of the artisanal fishermen the extent of setback was similar. Productivity registered a 50 per cent decline between 1974 and 1982—falling from 3.3 tonnes to 1.6 tonnes. Real per capita incomes also dropped from Rs 850 to Rs 420 during this period (see Table 5).

Table 5

Productivity and Income of Fishermen in Kerala

(Income per capita in 1960–61 prices)

Year	Fishermen on Trawlers		Artisanal Fishermen	
	Productivity (Tonnes/yr)	Income (Rs)	Productivity (Tonnes/yr)	Income (Rs)
1961	NA	NA	3.54	330
1965	NA	NA	3.82	380
1969–70	5.15	790	3.34	630
1974	10.04	2700	3.20	850
1979–80	7.54	2630	1.78	540
1982	7.70	1560	1.62	420

Source: Kurien and Achari (1988)

Recent estimates made by the state government also indicate that the per capita state domestic product (SDP) is increasing faster than the per capita fishery sector product (FSP). In 1973–4 when the SDP was Rs 811, the FSP was 18 per cent lower. By 1980–1 the gap increased to nearly 30 per cent and quick estimates for 1986–7 place the SDP at Rs 2,371 and the FSP at Rs 1,415—a difference of 40 per cent. Though the population growth of the fishing community is higher than the state average, this increasing disparity is primarily due to the slower rate of growth of the fishery sector product. This is due to the change in the composition of fish harvests towards species commanding lower market values following the overfishing of high value species.

Income Disparities between Workers and Owners

Overfishing has not only reduced the income levels of the working fishermen but has also increased the level of disparity between them and the non-worker capitalist owners of mechanized boats. From a small share of 12 per cent of the total value of output of the sector in 1969 their share of output increased to 27 per cent in the boom period of 1974. Thereafter, with the phase of overfishing setting in, their share increased further. It reached 43 per cent by 1982 (see Table 6)

With the increase in the number of mechanized boats between 1969 and 1982 the number of owners has increased. This partly explains the increase in their share. However, assessments of

Table 6

Distribution of Value of Output of Fish between Workers and Owners

(In Rs million)

Year	Workers*		Owners of Mechanized Boats	
1969	144	(88)	19	(12)
1974	392	(73)	143	(27)
1982	428	(57)	314	(43)

* Artisanal fishermen (workers and worker-owners) and workers on mechanized boats. Figures in ( ) are the shares.
Source: Kurien and Achari (1988)

profitability [Government of India 1971; Government of Kerala 1979; Kurien and Willmann 1982] indicate that until 1980–1 the *net* returns on investment on mechanized boats on the *average* were positive and that the *private* returns were lucrative.

Less Fish for the Masses

Fish was at one time considered to be the poor man's protein in Kerala. It is no more so. Viewed from the perspective of the fish eating population of the state *more* investments for fisheries development have yielded less fish for domestic consumption. The availability and quality of fish sold in the markets have deteriorated and the retail prices have increased faster than the general cost of other food items [Kurien 1984]. There is evidence to indicate that middle and higher income households are shifting to more readily available and cheaper sources of protein [Nair 1978]. The poorer consumers do not exhibit easy changes in diet patterns and are therefore the ones most affected by this scarcity of fish. Per capita availability of locally consumed fish has decreased from around 19 kilograms in 1971–2 to around 9 kilograms in 1981–2 [Kurien 1985].

RESPONSES TO OVERFISHING

Responses to the overfishing crisis have come from several quarters. We shall here deal with only the responses of the key actors—the fishermen, the boat owners and exporters, the state, and the scientific community. Understanding the nature of their reactions and the logic behind them is crucial to any attempt to resolve the crisis.

Responses of Fishermen

There were two types of responses by the fishermen; one at the political level and the other at the level of technology. The first, beginning in 1979, was more vocal and publicly visible. Decline in productivity and drop in incomes began to get correlated in the minds of the artisanal fishermen as a direct result of the destructive fishing by mechanized boats. Isolated physical conflicts at sea between trawlers, purse-seiners and fishermen using traditional craft were on the increase. Soon there were strong waves of organized dissent by the artisanal fishermen. They demanded that anarchic and destructive fishing by trawlers and purse-seiners be stopped. They wanted zoning of the coastal waters in what can be considered a plea for state regulation of the commons by the creation of distinct fishing zones. This would compel the mechanized boats to fish in deeper waters. They also demanded a total ban of trawling operations during the monsoon months of June, July and August which is the breeding season for many fishes. This socio-ecological movement extracted rich dividends from the left-wing dominated government in power at that time. Most important was the legal enactments providing for comprehensive measures restricting and regulating fishing activities in coastal waters.[6]

From 1981 onwards the ides of May brought the onset of the monsoon in Kerala and along with it the organized struggles of the fishermen. Until 1983 it was an independent trade union (i.e. one which had no affiliation to any political party—an anomaly in the Kerala context) which spearheaded the fishermen's agitation. In 1984 all the major political parties in Kerala created (and in a few cases revived) their own fishermen unions and joined the fray. The movement developed from strength to strength and reached its zenith that year. The movement's slogans and its non-violent agitational tactics brought it into the limelight of the national information media. It received the support of many environmentalists and ecology groups all over the country (see Kurien 1988a).

The technological response was slower. Since 1981–2 fishermen began to use outboard engines on their traditional crafts. These artefacts were to reduce the drudgery of their work, provide flexibility to fish in deeper waters and, hopefully, catch more fish. What started as a cautious experimentation soon acquired the proportions of a tidal wave and had the tacit support of the new right-wing government in power.

However, for both these objectives to be *simultaneously* realized entailed a significant rise in operating costs. This fact, combined with the unfamiliarity with deeper waters, led to continued fishing in the coastal waters for longer periods of time and with more fishing

---

[6] The Kerala Marine Fishing Regulation Act (1980) provided for the comprehensive measures for registration of all fishing craft. It also restricted fishing by mechanized boats—in particular the trawlers and the purse-seiners—to a depth outside the 20 fathom depth contour line in the coastal sea. The zone on the shore-side of this contour was reserved exclusively for the non-motorized and motorized craft.

gear. Mechanical power provided the flexibility to use more active fishing techniques including smaller versions of trawl nets and purse-seine nets.

The political upheaval of the fishermen was basically a response to being deprived of their traditional, historical, communal rights over the coastal commons. The state legislations of 1980 zoning the coastal waters was an *ipso facto* recognition of these rights. Their subsequent widespread and anarchic expansion of investment and fishing effort within this zone was basically succumbing to a crisis of survival brought about by declining productivity and incomes. Engulfed in the euphoric wave of the new technology, they did not stop to think of the long-term implications of their pursuits. The potential gains from zoning the coastal commons was almost totally lost by these actions [Kurien 1988].

Responses of Boat Owners and Export Lobby

Opposing the agitation of the fishermen was the economically strong, and politically influential boat owners' associations and export processors' lobby. They had strong connections with both the left and the right wing coalition governments. They contested the ecological views of the artisanal fishermen as being based on myths and argued forcefully that a ban on monsoon trawling would result in a major drop in the foreign exchange earnings from prawns. The unemployment implications of a three-month trawling ban was also highlighted. They argued that this would create an explosive social situation in the overall context of high unemployment in Kerala. The boat owners' associations also went to court questioning the validity of government promulgations regulating and restricting their free access to the coastal commons. They deemed fishing in the commons their fundamental right enshrined in the Indian Constitution. The High Court ruled in their favour. It held that while the state did have a right to regulate the coastal commons, it could take action to exclude persons from it only if sufficient scientific evidence was available to substantiate that these persons' activities were socially or ecologically harmful and against the interests of the majority in society. Such unambiguous evidence could not be mustered up by the state government.

This was a victory for the boat owners and the exporters. Despite fresh legislations enacted by respective governments making amends for the loopholes in the law, in reality the *status quo* prevailed: the coastal commons continued to be open to all.

Response of the Government

The state began to recognize the issue of overfishing only after the social upheaval in the coastal areas in the late 1970s became widespread. Thereafter, irrespective of the political colour of the government in power, the conflicts between the traditional fishermen and the trawlers at sea created intense pressure on the political system. In a parliamentary democracy with a multi-party system and a predominance of coastal electoral constituencies, no political party could take the restive fishing community for granted.

A left-wing dominated coalition was in power in the state in 1980. They were in basic sympathy with the movement of the artisanal fishermen who were a big vote-bank. However they could not overlook the economic interests of the boat owners and the exporters. In a democratic polity functioning in the overall capitalistic framework of society, the vote-bank strength as well as the economic clout of the various interest groups involved must necessarily be carefully balanced. The left-wing dominated coalition therefore (as mentioned above) enacted legislations to regulate and manage the commons. They also postponed taking hard decisions, which would necessarily be biased, by constituting an expert committee composed of scientists working in fishery institutions located in the state, government bureaucrats and representatives of fishermen and the boat owners, to examine the ecological and economic aspects of the issues raised. The onus of suggesting remedies was also bestowed on the committee.

Elections in 1982 brought a more conservative right-wing-dominated coalition government into power. However, the swing in the coastal votes towards the left did not go unnoticed by them. They realized the gravity of the situation and its future electoral implications. The fact that the chief minister himself chose to hold the hitherto insignificant fisheries portfolio was a clear indicator of this.

When the fishermen announced renewal of their monsoon agitation in 1984, this government was firm about its stand. It was unwilling to negotiate with the fishermen and tried its best to break the agitation using strong arm tactics. It also attempted to wean away sections of the fishermen through the influence of religious leaders. These met with only limited success. When this failed, the 'carrot and stick' approach was tried and with considerable success. The government warned against militant unionization and divided the ranks of the fishermen by placating those under its political influence with direct financial assistance—subsidies and loans—as well as access to intermediate technology. Implicit in this strategy was the tenet: 'if you can't beat the trawlers join them with your outboard engines!' With this the private initiative of some fishermen on this score got a big boost. Further, the government conceded to the demands of the unions to appoint a second committee to re-examine the issues regarding overfishing and destructive fishing. The committee was to consist only of reputed scientists and the government vouched to accept its recommendations. Such a committee was appointed in 1984 and was expected to give its recommendations within a year.

Responses of the Scientific Community

None of the fishery scientists in their wildest dreams had imagined that the question of where and when fishes in Kerala laid their eggs and breed would become a hot political issue! When it did, they were at a loss on the position they should take. Most of them being in highly bureaucratic and hierarchical institutions had little academic freedom. When confronted by the fishermen representatives who on occasions did point to inconsistencies in scientific publications, they had little choice but to get defensive.

In the first expert committee appointed by the government in 1981, one of the most reputed fishery scientists in India failed to participate at meetings on the plea that the fishermen's demands were 'more political than scientific'. He thought it best to leave it to the bureaucrats to resolve the diametrically opposing positions of the fishermen and the trawler owners on the fishery-ecological issues. This committee, not surprisingly, could not arrive at any consensus.

The second expert commitee appointed in 1984 consisted of only three fishery experts, all from outside Kerala. This report cautioned the government about the impending crisis which could affect the coastal waters if the existing configuration of fishing assets and fishing effort continued to grow in an unregulated fashion. They did not approve of the need for a monsoon trawling ban but favoured a drastic reduction of the fleet size of the trawlers to half the then current level. They recommended the use of more passive fishing techniques of the type used by artisanal fishermen; were in strong favour of a total ban on purse-seiners; cautioned the government and the artisanal fishermen about the massive motorization drive; and highlighted the need for active fishermen's participation in managing the coastal commons.

RESOLVING OVERFISHING

The conflicting motivations and actions of the capitalist boat owners and traditional fishermen provide the basis for the unequal bargaining power of the two classes and the rationale for the state to regulate the coastal marine waters. The objective of any programme of action must be two-fold: (a) to revive the sustainability of the coastal commons, and (b) to ensure that it provides a basis for a decent livelihood and inexpensive food for as large a population as is possible. To ensure the achievement of these objectives demands a policy approach in which development and management of the marine resources and the fish economy are seen as two sides of the same coin.

The scale and type of harvesting technology should be in consonance with the known biological and ecological parameters of the resource. Small-scale fishing crafts using multiple sources of energy, selective fishing gear, and operations from decentralized centres along the total length of the coastline should be encouraged. Economically efficient but ecologically destructive fishing artefacts should be strictly controlled irrespective of the user.

The ownership of harvesting technology—fishing craft and gear—should be restricted exclusively to those who are willing to fish. An aquarian reform of sorts to ensure this needs to be enacted by the state. Such a community of workers and working-owners should be entrusted with the collective rights and responsibility of managing the coastal commons within the jurisdiction of their decentralized operations at the micro and meso levels.

Conscious efforts to enhance the biological productivity of the coastal waters should be given adequate encouragement. Attempts such as the collective creation and establishment of fish aggregation devices in coastal waters are good examples of this. Moving to the hitherto unfished deeper waters is an essential step to reduce the pressure on the coastal commons. This is an arena for diverting some of the excess investments presently in the coastal waters. Making fresh investments in the deep sea should be preceded by thorough resource estimation surveys and economic viability studies. These need not be excessively preoccupied with export potentials. Subsidies to those who move out to these waters may be more economically and socially justifiable.

The above options with regard to (a) conserving and enhancing the fishery resource, (b) the choice, ownership and operation of the technology and (c) the creation of social institutions for management of the resource provide the basic framework for a fresh policy approach. This will be required to pull Kerala's fish economy out of its ecological crisis and provide a sustainable future for the fishery resources in the coastal commons and the commoners—the fishworkers as well as the poorer consumers.

Postcript

Fish production continued to drop in Kerala after 1985. The political and technological responses of the fishermen continue unabated. The state played to both the tunes. In 1988, responding to the continued demands of the fishermen's unions for a monsoon ban on the operation of trawling boats, the government, dominated by left parties, promulgated a partial ban. All the trawler-operating centres in the state—except the largest one, Neendakara—were ordered closed for the months of July and August. The reason given for not closing Neendakara was that the heavy concentration of a marine prawn (P. Stylifera) in the in-shore area during these months would perish if not harvested (mainly by the trawlers) resulting in loss of foreign exchange and employment. The partial ban turned out to be ineffective. It could not prevent trawlers from the other centres operating from out of Neendakara. The boat owners also went to court charging the government of discriminatory treatment of trawlers located in different parts of the state. The traditional fishermen's unions were also unhappy with the situation. There seemed to be no significant political, economic or ecological gains from this management measure.

By 1988 the motorization wave had swept through every fishing village in the state. Power propulsion of traditional fishing craft was here to stay. Motorization of traditional crafts did result in fishing in deeper waters leading to an increase in physical productivity and harvesting of new species. This was however at a much higher investment and recurring cost. In the central and northern regions of the state, motorization gave a big boost to the use of fine meshed encircling nets called 'ring seines' used to harvest pelagic shoaling species. These were nothing but a smaller version of the larger destructive purse-seine nets. This trend created new tensions *within* traditional fishermen groups in these areas.

Quite oblivious of the economic, social or ecological implications of the above, the government actively promoted the earlier subsidy scheme for the purchase of outboard motors and introduced a new one for ring-seines. The continued conflict between fishermen using traditional fishing crafts and those using trawlers as well as the emerging conflicts between traditional fishermen themselves (over the use of nets like ring-seines), prompted the government to seriously re-examine the overall crisis in the fish economy. The government had before it the recommendations of two earlier expert committees. Most of these had not been fully implemented. It however deemed it necessary to constitute a third expert committee to review the situation once again in the light of the recommendations of the earlier committees. The main terms of reference of this committee included: a re-examination of the question of the monsoon trawling ban; an appraisal of the unprecedented increase in the number of outboard engines and their power rating; and also a review of the ecological and social impact of the rapid increase in the use of gear like ring-seines by the traditional fishermen. This committee submitted its report to the government on 26 June 1989. The government decided to immediately implement one of the recommendations made by the committee: a *total* monsoon trawling ban. The other recommendations which included restrictions on the use of ring-seines, limitations on HP rating of outboard engines, and measures for protection of estuarine areas, were kept in abeyance.

The enforcement of the total trawl ban—an effective measure to regulate access to the coastal commons—resulted in bloody confrontations between the enforcement police and the boat owners at the major trawler landing centre, Neendakara. The boat owners took the matter to the High Court and the Supreme Court. Both courts were unwilling to issue a stay order to the government's decision. This legal ruling and the unwavering stand of the government, despite the possible adverse political fallout, esured that the ban was fully effective.

The ban did result in a considerable loss of employment for the workers in the processing industry. A fair number of the fishermen from the traditional fishing communities who worked as crew on the trawlers found opportunities to go fishing on the motorized boats operated from their home villages. A large number were nevertheless unemployed. The loss of current foreign exchange earnings has not been assessed. The total monsoon trawl ban was the most important fishery management decision made by any government in the country since independence. The government also constituted an interdisciplinary task force to assess the total impact of the ban.

Two months after the ban was lifted (October 1989) very large pelagic fish harvests were reported from all over the state. It would be wrong to attribute this phenomenion *entirely* to the trawling ban though both the ruling party politicians and the traditional fishermen's unions have done so. It needs to be investigated whether the effect of enhanced rains on fluctuations of pelagic stocks has also contributed to the phenomenonal increase in fish catch. However the total ban on trawling probably did contribute significantly to this pheomenon. The non-disturbance of the aquatic milieu during the monsoon months could be an important cause for the more pronounced shoreward movement of the pelagic fish shoals in pursuit of food which is found in abundance in the in-shore water areas cooled by the inflow of rivers swollen ⸱ ⁄ith heavy monsoon rains. The ability of the motorized units—particularly those using ring-seines—to harvest whole pelagic shoals also provide an important reason for the increased harvest *given* the favourable nature-induced conditions and the after-effect of the trawl ban mentioned above.

Shore prices and retail market prices dropped drastically. Reminiscent of the 1950s, fresh fish was sold as manure for coconut plantation! It is unlikely that this bumper harvest has had a commensurate positive effect on incomes of fishermen. However it certainly provided a temporary boost to the nutritional status of fish consumers—particularly the poorer among them.

This increased harvest therefore seems to have been brought about by a combination of factors, i.e. unpredictable nature-induced processes, strong political will leading to firm management measures and the use of over-efficient harvesting technology. Only a medium-term ex-post analysis will unravel which of these factors was the determining one.

REFERENCES

Achari, T. R. T.,
1987a   The *Socio-Economic Impact of Motorisation of Country Craft in Purakkad Village: A Case Study*, Fisheries Research Cell, Trivandrum.
1987b   *Maldevelopment of a Fishery: A Case Study of Kerala State, India*, Paper presented at the FAO Indo-Pacific Fishery Commission, Darwin.

Aguero, M.,
1987   *Economic Consequences of Excessive Effort*, Paper presented at the FAO Indo-Pacific Fishery Commission, Darwin.

Berkes, F.,
1985   The Common Property Resource Problem and the Creation of Limited Property Rights *Human Ecology*, Vol 13/2.

Beverton, R. J. H. and Holt, S. J.,
1957   On the Dynamics of Exploited Fish Populations, *Fishery Investigation Series*, Vol II, 19, London.

Caddy, J. F.,
1984   An Alternative to Equilibrium Theory for Management of Fisheries , *FAO Fisheries Report* No. 289/2, Rome.

Ciriacy-Wantrup and Bishop, R. C.,
1975   Common Property as a Concept in Natural Resource Policy, *Natural Resources Journal* Vol. 15.

Chirsty, F. T.,
1966   *The Common Wealth of Ocean Fisheries: Some Problems of Growth and Economic Allocation*, John Hopkins Press.
1982   *Territorial Use Rights in Marine Fisheries*, FAO Tech Paper 227, Rome.

Dasgupta, P. S.,
1982   *The Control of Resources*, Basil Blackwell, Oxford.

George, P. C. et al,
1977   Fishery Resources of the Indian Exclusive Economic Zone, in *Souvenir*, Integrated Fisheries Project, Cochin.

George, M. J.,
1988   *Study of Shrimp Trawling in the South West Coast of India— Particularly Kerala*, Programme for Community Organisation, Trivandrum.

Gordon, H. S.,
1954   The Economic Theory of a Common Property Resource:
            the Fishery, *Journal of Political Economy,* Vol. 62,
            Chicago.
Government of India,
1971   *Evaluation of the Programme of Mechanisation of Fishing Boats,*
            Programme Evaluation Organisation, Planning Commis-
            sion, New Delhi.
1982   *Report of the Task Force on Marine Products,* Ministry of Com-
            merce, New Delhi.
Government of Kerala,
1979   *Anjengo Fisheries Development Project; An Evaluation Study,*
            Kerala State Planning Board, Trivandrum.
1985   *Economics Review 1985,* Kerala State Planning Board,
            Trivandrum.
Hannesson, R.,
1978   *Economics of Fisheries,* University-Forlaget, Bergen.
Hardin, G.,
1968   The Tragedy of the Commons, *Science,* 162.
Kalawar, A. G. et al,
1985   *Report of the Expert Committee on Fisheries in Kerala* (mimeo),
            Bombay.
Krishnakumar, S.,
1981   *Strategy and Action Programme for a Massive Thrust to Fisheries
            Development and Fishermen's Welfare in Kerala State (1978–
            83),* Government of Kerala, Trivandrum.
Kurien, J.,
1978   *Towards an Understanding of the Fish Economy of Kerala State,*
            Working Paper No. 68, Centre for Development Studies,
            Trivandrum.
1984   *Marketing of Marine Fish in Kerala State: A Preliminary Study,*
            Centre for Development Studies, Trivandrum.
1985   Technical Assistance Projects and Socio-Economic
            Change—Norwegian Intervention in Kerala's Fisheries
            Development , *Economic and Political Weekly,*Vol. 20 No. 25–6,
            Bombay.
1988   *The Economy, Energy, Entropy and Equity: with Special Refer-
            ence to Kerala's Fisheries* (mimeo).
1988a   *Studies on the Role of Fishermen's Organisation in Fisheries
            Management,* FAO Fisheries Tech Paper 300, Rome.
Kurien, J. and Achari, T. R. T.,
1988   Fisheries Development Policies and the Fishermen's
            Struggles in Kerala, *Social Action*,Vol. 38, No. 1, New Delhi.

Kurien, J. and Wilimann, R.,
1982   *Economics of Artisanal and Mechanised Fisheries In Kerala: A Study of Costs and Earnings of Fishing Units*, FAO/UNDP Publication, Madras.

Nair, K. N.,
1978   *Milk Production in Kerala: An Analysis of Past Trends and Future Prospects*, Working Paper 76, Centre for Development Studies, Trivandrum.

Oakerson, R. J.,
1988   A Model for the Analysis of Common Property Problems, *National Academy of Sciences, Proceedings of the Conference on Common Property Resource Management*, National Academy Press, Washington DC.

Panayotou, T.,
1982   *Management Concepts and Small-Scale Fisheries: Economic and Social Aspects*, FAO Fisheries Technical Paper 228, Rome.

Paul, Babu,
1982   *Report of the Committee to Study the Need for Conservation of Marine Fishery Resources During Certain Seasons of the Year and Allied Matters*, Government of Kerala, Trivandrum.

Pauly, D.,
1979   *Theory and Management of Tropical Multispecies Stocks: A Review with Emphasis on the South-East Asian Demersal Fisheries*, ICLARM, Manila.

Runge, C. F.,
1986   Common Property and Collective Action in Economic Development , *World Development*, Vol. 14, No. 5.

Schaefer, M. B.,
1954   Some Aspects of the Dynamics of Populations Important to the Management of Commercial Marine Fisheries , *Bull I-ATTCI* (2).

Schlager E. and Ostrom, E.,
1987   *Common Property, Communal Property and Natural Resources: A Conceptual Analysis*, paper presented at the Workshop on Political Theory and Policy Analysis, Indiana University.

Further Readings for Section II

Three of the readings in Section II focused on community management of natural resources—its characteristic forms, and conditions
for persistence or breakdown. Ever since Garret Hardin's essay on
the 'Tragedy of the Commons' (first published in 1968, and widely
anthologized since), there has been an outpouring of work on common property resource management, much of it aimed at either
refuting or confirming Hardin's thesis. Worth consulting are two
collections of case studies from different countries: Bonnie Mckay
and James Acheson, editors, *The Question of the Commons* (Tucson:
University of Arizona Press, 1987) and Fikret Berkes, editor, *Common Property Resources: Ecology and Community Based Sustained
Development* (London: Belhaven Press, 1989). In the Indian context,
two relevant works are Robert Wade, *Village Republics: Economic
Conditions for Collective Action in South India* (Cambridge: Cambridge University Press, 1987), a rich empirical study of co-operation among farmers in regulating grazing and allocating canal
water; and Kanchan Chopra, Gopal Kadekodi and M. N. Murty,
*Participatory Development: Approaches to Common Property Resource
Management* (New Delhi: Sage Publishers, 1989), which uses a
celebrated model of environmental renewal in a north Indian hill
village to make a more general case for decentralized development.
Where these two books use a political economy framework, a fine
study of the cultural and legal aspects of common land management is Rita Brara, *Shifting Sands: Rights in Common Pastures* (New
Delhi: Oxford University Press, forthcoming).'

Turning specifically to water management, an exceptionally rich
collection on the social organization of different irrigation systems
is E. W. Coward, editor, *Irrigation and Agricultural Development in
Asia* (Ithaca: Cornell University Press, 1980). A polemic against
canal irrigation in the United States, which has parallels with Whitcombe's work, is Donald Worster, *Rivers of Empire: Water, Aridity and
the Growth of the American West* (New York: Pantheon, 1986). Finally,
with reference to rural energy issues, an informed and comprehensive survey is Bina Agarwal, *Cold Hearths and Barren Slopes: the Wood-
fuel Crisis in the Third World* (New Delhi: Allied Publishers, 1986).

III

Competing Claims over Nature

At least three of the essays in the last section—those by Jodha, Vidyarthi and Kurien/Achari—underscored the differential access of classes and communities to nature. The essays in this section pursue this theme further, highlighting the conflicts that may arise when two or more groups covet the same resource, albeit for different reasons.

We begin with a deeply empathetic account by Verrier Elwin of the Baiga, a tribe of swidden agriculturists in central India. For the Baiga, swidden cultivation (which they called *bewar*) was not merely an economic activity vital to survival, but integral to their culture, myths and sense of self. From the late nineteenth century, colonial officials tried hard to wean the Baiga away from *bewar*—both out of a civilizing zeal wherein *bewar* was viewed as 'inferior' to plough cultivation, and due to the imperatives of commercial forestry, to which Baiga control of the forests was a hindrance. But as Elwin so movingly narrates, colonial hostility led to a deep sense of anguish among the Baiga. The economic loss apart, curbs on *bewar* led, in the anthropologist's words, to an irreparable injury to Baiga life and spirit.

A small and dispersed tribe, the Baiga were unable to effectively resist colonial policy. My own essay, also set in the colonial period, documents the history of militant peasant resistance to state forestry in the Kumaun Himalaya. In the mountains, access to woodland and pasture were crucial to agriculture and animal husbandry—here too, state takeover of forests and their subsequent working on commercial lines aroused great resentment. Thus popular movements against the new forest regime, and its intensification of forced labour operations, enjoyed widespread support. These movements form part of the 'prehistory' of the celebrated Chipko movement, which broke out in the same region half a century later.

Moving to the present, our third selection, specially written for this volume, investigates the conflicts between large mammals and human populations living in and around national parks and sanctuaries. In a sophisticated ecological analysis Sukumar locates the origins of these conflicts in habitat fragmentation and depletion, competition for resources, and mammalian social organization and foraging behaviour. He offers a number of suggestions for mitigating these conflicts, from the management of animal habitats and populations to the provision of adequate compensation to affected villagers.

It is noteworthy that all our selections pertain to conflicts around the use of forests: the first two focusing on conflicts originating in the *intensification* of forest exploitation, the last on those stemming from the *conservation* of forests and their wild life. This reflects the more general thrust of the Indian environment debate, which has hitherto been dominated by debates set in the forestry sector. As we move into the nineties and beyond, conflicts over water and minerals are likely to assume greater importance. No doubt this will in time be reflected in an outcrop of sociological studies of conflicts around those natural resources.

Civilizing the Savage

VERRIER ELWIN

What is known to the Baiga as *bewar* is extensively practised throughout the tropical and sub-tropical regions of the world. It is the common method of cultivation in the forests of South America, in many
parts of Africa and Mauritius, in Melanesia and the Atlantic Islands,
in Assam, in Ceylon, and in the remoter forest areas of South and
Central India. It is known as *sartage* in the French and Belgian
Ardennes, as *chena* by the Vedda. In India, the *dahi* and *koman* cultivation of the Bhuiya of Orissa, the *penda* of the Bastar Maria, the
jhum of the Assam hill tribes, the *podu* of the Khond of Jeypore, the
beora of the Pahari Korwa of Jashpur, the *taungya* of the Burma hill
tribes, are all, with some variations, akin to the *bewar* of the Baiga.
But so far as I have been able to discover, the only people who have
exalted this type of cultivation into a regular cultus, and have
adopted it as the symbol of their tribe, differentiating them from all
others, are the Baiga.

The Baiga were established in the practice of *bewar*[1] by Bhagavan
himself who, when he called all the tribes of the world together to
make a king, at first chose the Baiga. But Nanga Baiga begged that
the Gond, his brother, might be king in his place. Bhagavan was
pleased at this request, and, as a mark of his favour took Nanga
Baiga by the hand and placed him on his throne by his side. He
granted his prayer to make the Gond king, but he gave the Baiga an
even greater blessing.

'All the kingdoms of the world', he said:

may fall to pieces, but he who is made of earth and is Bhumiaraja, lord of
the earth, shall never forsake it. You will make your living from the earth.
You will dig roots and eat them. You will cut wood and carry it on your

Excerpted from Verrier Elwin, *The Baiga*, Chapter III, John Murray, London, 1939.

[1] The word 'bewar' is used to describe both the practice of shifting cultivation and the patches
of forest which are so cultivated.

shoulders. Your wife will pick leaves and sell them. You must not tear the breasts of your Mother the Earth with the plough like the Gond and Hindu.[2] You will cut down trees and burn them and sow your seed in the ashes. But you will never become rich, for if you did you would forsake the earth, and then there would be no one to guard it and keep its nails in place.

Then Bhagavan showed Nanga Baiga how to cut bewar and sow seed in the ashes of burnt trees; and when he had taught him every-thing, he called him to receive gifts of seed.

This legend is told, and believed, throughout the length and breadth of the Baiga country, in Mandla and Niwas, in Rewa and Dindori, in Baihar, in Bilaspur, in Pandaria. In the old days it was the foundation of the economic and social life of the tribe. Every Baiga who has yielded to the plough knows himself to be standing on *pāpi-dharti*, on sinful earth, or as we would say, is in a state of mortal sin. 'When the bewar was stopped, and we first touched the plough', says Mahatu, 'a man died in every house.' And Hothu of Taliapani confessed to me that he had at one time used a plough. 'But my children have always been weak and sickly on account of it. If even one Baiga in a village touches the plough, we are all affected!' This is a perfectly genuine religious belief, which the most vigorous propaganda has left unshaken. Dhan Singh of Pandpur once told me that if some magician were to come to him and ask him to choose the three things that he most wanted and that the Baiga most wanted in the world, he would say, 'First give us back our jungle. Then let us have free *kāndabāri* (root-planta-tions). And third, let us hunt freely once more. We do not want riches, only these three things.'

I have found the same attitude among all the sub-tribes of Baiga. Ketu, a Muria of Niwas, said to me: 'The English are giving swaraj to everyone but the Baiga: why can't they give us bewar-swaraj?' A Narotia Baiga of Balaghat said: 'It is because we commit the great sin of driving the plough that we now wear tattered clothes and have become slaves to others.' In Arhwai (in the Supkar Range) Jaggan, an old Bharotia, said: 'When we break the belly of the earth we break our own belly and all the food falls out. By stopping *bewar*, the English have turned us into naked sadhus.' And even the

---

[2] There is a curious parallel in the history of an American Indian messianic cult. Smohalla, the prophet of the Columbia River Basin, addressed his followers in 1870: 'You ask me to plough the ground. Shall I take a knife and tear my mother's bosom? You ask me to dig for stone. Shall I dig under her skin for her bones? You ask me to cut grass. But how dare I cut off my mother's hair?'—*Bureau of American Enthology*, 14th Annual Report, 1892-3, p. 716.

Binjhwar I met near Lamta sighed for the good days of *bewar* cutting and hunting.

It is commonly believed that the present poverty of the tribe is due to their disobedience of Bhagavan's command; Mother Earth is insulted when her children tear her breasts, and now refuses to supply their needs. For this reason, their magic has decayed, the crops fail, and they are subject to the vengeance of wild beasts.

Bewar, however, is still practised by the Baiga of Kawardha State, of Pandaria Zamindari, in many parts of Bilaspur, in the Baiga Chak of Mandla, and until quite recently in Rewa. The methods they adopt are not unlike those we have already described. Today, they mean by *bewar* the custom of felling and burning trees *in situ*; they give the name *dāhia* to the practice of dragging logs and brushwood into a clearing, distributing it over the space available, and then firing it. In the Mandla Settlement Report of 1868-9, Colonel Ward has given an interesting account of how *bewar* (though he calls it *dhya*) was practised in Mandla seventy years ago.

With no other instrument of agriculture but their axe and a small sickle, it is astonishing to see the extent of clearing one village of Bygas makes on the sides of the hills of which their village is located.

Until lately, it was their habit to select the spots for their *dhyas* with an utter disregard for all the rules of forest conservancy. Where the trees are largest and most numerous there will the Byga resort, and in the cold weather months will cut down sufficient wood to cover pretty closely the whole of the area he means to bring under cultivation. In May and June, just before the setting in of the rains, this wood and the brushwood in which it has fallen, is set fire to; and almost before the fire is out, the Bygas may be seen taking up the ashes and spreading them over the whole surface of their field; this is done either with a bundle of thorns, or with long bamboos, until there is a superstratum of about an inch of ashes spread over the ground.

In these ashes they sow kodon, koodkee, and, occasionally, a poor specimen of rice, called here 'bygana'. From being on the side of a hill the ashes are cut up into furrows by the action of the rains, and often much of the seed must be washed away altogether; but sufficient seems to remain for the Byga's wants. When sown, the field is fenced round very roughly, and strongly, small trees being felled so as to fall one on to the other; the interstices are filled in with bamboos, and the boughs are carefully interlaced, so that the smallest kind of deer cannot effect an entrance; in addition to this, where there is any danger of the crops being eaten up by buffaloes or bison, which push through any ordinary fence, the Bygas bury a line of broad-bladed spears, called 'dansas', in the ground at about the spot where these beasts would land if they jumped the fence. They then watch their opportunity, and, sneaking round to the opposite side, give a series of yells, which send the cattle off terrified over or through the fence. Generally more than one is wounded, and often one killed on the spot; the rest, once started, make straight away, and never visit that field again. In the fences round these *'bewurs'*, as these patches of cultivation are called, are usually two or three cunningly-contrived traps for small deer, something on the principle of the old figure of 4; and several nooses for peacocks, hares, etc. These the Byga carefully examines every morning; and great is his delight when occasionally he finds a panther crushed under one of the figure of 4 traps.

One of these *'bewurs'* lasts the Byga, at the outside, three years. He usually leaves sufficient wood on the ground the first season to last for a second season's burning. The third year, if by chance he should make up his mind to stick to one field for so long, his labour is much enhanced, as he has to cut and drag the requisite wood for some little distance and lay it over his field; in addition to this the outturn of the crops falls off every year; so that, altogether, the Byga has every inducement to change the locale of his cultivation, and, where no restriction has been put on his movements, as a rule he does so.

It takes six or seven years before one of these old *'bewurs'* is sufficiently covered with wood again to make it worth the Bygas' while to cultivate it a second time. In three years it is probably densely covered with brushwood, but this, if burnt, leaves so little ash that it has to be largely supplemented with timber; and as this has been previously cut all round the clearing, it becomes a work of supererogation to take up one of these old plots before the wood has well grown when other and more suitable land is available.

The modern Baiga prepares his *bewar* in very similar fashion. The family first goes into the jungle and selects a suitable site. When they have found one, they take some rice and throw it over a tree in the middle of the new *bewar*, and fell it with a single stroke of the axe. The head of the family takes a leaf from the tree, folds it in four, and ties it on the standing stool. This is accepted by other Baiga as evidence of occupation.

A little later, they return and cut all the grasses and brushwood. Fifteen days afterwards, they worship their axes, promising Kutki Dai or Anna Dai that if the crop is good, they will make special offerings at harvest-time. They turn the axe with the blade downwards, and recite over it a short *mantra* invoking the aid of Nanga Baiga and Nanga Baigin. Then they go to the *bewar*. Before felling, they offer a coconut to the jungle-dwellers, whose home they are now going to despoil, and then they proceed to fell all the trees within the area chosen, leaving stools about a foot high.

In May they go to burn the now dry wood and undergrowth. In the interval they have distributed the stuff fairly evenly over the *bewar*, but they have carefully observed the original tree that was felled. It is here that they are to make the Virgin Fire. It is forbidden to kindle the fire with flint and steel; it must be made by twirling a bamboo stick in a hole made in another, split, bamboo. When the fire has kindled, the bamboos are cut up, and each member of the family takes a bit and lights it. They set fire first to the original tree, and then go all over the *bewar* firing it.

The next duty is to fence the *bewar*, which they do with logs and brushwood cut round the edges, and they put snares and traps for deer and other animals.

After the first rain has fallen, they take their seed to the *bewar*, and perform a variation of the Bidri ceremony, offering special gifts to Dharti Mata. The men fill the folds of their *dhoti* with seeds, all mixed up together and scatter them anywhere and everywhere in the ashes. After a few days, they return and dibble the lines for *rahar dāl* across the middle of the field; they drop three seeds into each hole. Round the stools of the trees, they sow beans and cucumbers.

At harvest-time, they make a small imitation threshing-floor for Thakur Deo, and offer to him and Anna Dai the first-fruits of the crop and a cock or pig, whatever they had promised at the time of felling. It is vital to implement these promises; there are many grim tales of tigers devouring those who failed to do so.

The first year, the crop is gathered rather than cut; only the tops of the plants are removed, and the stalks left for next year. The second year, they burn any trees that may be left, and all the dry stalks of the previous harvest. The third year, the crop is generally poor, for there is little left to burn.

They may, however, use the third-year *bewar* as a *dāhia*-clearing, and drag logs and brushwood from the surrounding forest and spread it over the field.

Little huts are erected in the *bewar*. These are called *lāri* when they are built on the ground, and when raised on poles, *mācha*. Here the people watch their crops, and protect them from wild animals. 'We must sleep there every night; we both, husband and wife, sleep there, otherwise we would die of cold. But our wives never watch in the *bewar* during their periods.'

A threshing-floor is prepared in the *bewar*-clearing itself, or on the nearest piece of fairly level ground. The Baiga do not usually thresh with bullocks, but a line of men and women, boys and girls, go round and round in a circle stamping with their feet.[3]

Sometimes, when the crop is poor, a bundle of kodon is taken to the house and threshed there. In Jholar I saw a woman threshing kodon with her feet, on the kitchen floor. 'There was no life in the crop this year,' she said.

The winnowing is done in the usual way. A man takes the kodon in a *sūpa* and holds it up as high as his own head. He gently shakes it so that the grain falls to the ground and the chaff is blown away.

WEANING FROM THE AXE

The first serious attempt to put an end to *bewar*-cultivation was made during the Settlement operations of 1867-9. It was decided that 'according to all positive law, according to the Settlement Code, and according to the custom of the country', the Baiga had 'no title to proprietory right or to occupancy right in the tracts over which they roamed'.

What the then Chief Commissioner, Sir Richard Temple, desired was, not so much to save the forests from destruction, as 'to civilize these people and make them useful members of the Commonwealth'. In the opinion of Mr J.H. Morris, the Settlement Commissioner for the Central Provinces, and for a time Acting Chief Commissioner, this could only be achieved by inducing them to take to plough-cultivation.

So long as these people do nothing but grow kodo or koatkee on dhya patches for their own food; so long as they produce nothing at all for sale or barter to other people; and so long as they actually consume nothing except a few grains of salt from the outer world, they can never improve, they can never rise in the human scale, but must continue to be wild men of the woods as they are now.

Under Sir Richard Temple's administration the policy was 'to take one tract at a time, and bring these people down from the hill sides on which they roamed, and settle them to cultivate lands in the valleys'. But proposals to forbid *bewar* absolutely were resisted.

[3] The Maria of Bastar erect a thick bamboo railing on posts and the men (women do not take part—unlike the Baiga) range themselves in two rows on either side of the railing, holding it with their hands. Then they dance up and down, rubbing the ears of corn between their feet. Some of the Korku on the Betul border of Hoshangabad, C.P., thresh in the same way (W.V. Grigson, *The Maria Gonds of Bastar* (Oxford 1938) p. 136.

Temple refused to adopt a policy that would 'improve these poor people off the face of the earth'.

In Seoni, Captain Thomson had reported that the Baiga there 'never use the plough or till the land; but sow in the ashes of the jungle which they cut down'. In Raigarh, however, 'having been by the wasteland rules somewhat restricted in their wanderings, they had in several places taken to the use of the plough'. He had proposed stringent measures for checking *bewar* altogether, but was criticised by the Chief Commissioner for 'not treating with sufficient consideration the claims of communities belonging to the aboriginal tribes, who, in the midst of the jungle, have established some kind of village and brought under cultivation a certain amount of land'. The Chief Commissioner himself was concerned to protect 'the material interests of the wild tribes', while hoping that 'they would gradually be induced to settle down permanently into closer communication with the more civilized inhabitants and adopt more civilized ways'. He arranged, therefore, that the *bewar*-cutting tribes should be assigned tracts of country averaging a square mile or so, 'their hills being specially reserved from sale, and their right to reside and cultivate recognized in any usufruct lease granted over these hills'. I do not know how far this policy was actually carried out.

In Balaghat, the Baiga met the new rules restricting *bewar* with stubborn opposition; the district authorities moreover were not very energetic in enforcing them, and even continued to take a tax of one rupee an axe; so that ten years later only about forty families out of over four hundred had taken to the plough.

In Mandla, Colonel Ward reported that:

It had been found quite impracticable, as well as hard and impolitic, to force the Bygas to give up their dhya cultivation and take to the plough; so that the settlement with them has been simply the attempt to confine their destructive propensities within a ring fence.

Some of the Mandla Baiga, however, had already taken to the plough, 'through force of example' and were themselves 'setting an example to their wilder brethren'. But in the Ramgarh Tehsil, 'the Byga country par excellence, at the head of the Borhneyr, and the rivers which water the Pertabgurh talooqua', the situation was quite different, great damage had been done, and nothing would induce the Baiga to change their habits. However, says Colonel Ward:

If carefully looked after, the injury they cause to the forests there, may be made more negative than positive, by placing certain restrictions on their wandering habits, and keeping them within the boundaries now fixed for them; which have been selected so as to allow them wood enough for their wants, but in situations where, owing to their previous devastations, or the inaccessibility of the locality, the timber is of little value.

In Pertabgurh and Mokutpore, 7,794 acres of land were allotted to the Baiga of twelve villages.

The amount of their present cultivation roughly measured is 1,431 acres, so that a little over five times its area of cultivation has been allotted to each. Formerly the area claimed by these people amounted to over 30,000 acres. They have expressed themselves quite satisfied with the arrangement made for them. But if the country was opened up to trade, and the value of money became more known, the Bygas would soon learn wherein their own advantage lay, and would do as their brethren have done in other parts of the country—drop the axe and take to the plough; but until we have shown them what benefit it is to them, and, in fact, have created wants which their present primitive habits will not enable them to provide for, we cannot expect them to change their nature.

Ward records an amusing conversation which he had with some Baiga on this subject, in which 'he was rather put to it to reply to some of the pertinent questions of the shrewd old men' and was once entirely 'shut up' by one old grey-beard. But the Colonel evidently handled the situation with great tact, for the talk ended with his

Receiving a deputation from the tribe, requesting me to live among them, promising that I should want for nothing, and that they would supply me with four Byga wives to attend on me, and that, doubtless, under my tuition they would soon learn the art of plough cultivation. This flattering offer was declined of necessity.

Had the Colonel only been a little more adventurous, it is obvious that there would have been no problem of the Baiga Chak!

We will now trace briefly the progress of 'civilization' among the Baiga during the next twenty years. The fact that 'the marketable value of forest produce rose in something like geometrical proportions' during those years probably accounts for a shifting of emphasis from Sir Richard Temple's policy of benevolent improvement for their own sake to a frank and simple desire to better the Provincial budget. The interests of a small and savage tribe were of little account beside the necessity of commercializing the forest. The struggle between the Baiga and the administration was joined in Mandla and Balaghat. For some reason, a more liberal policy has always been followed in Bilaspur.

Balaghat is largely populated by Binjhwar Baiga, the most Hinduized section of the tribe, and even before 1868 several families of these in Pondi, Gudma and Sonkar in the Man Valley, had taken to the plough. Pondi was the earliest settlement of the kind in the whole province. But every attempt to carry out the Chief Commissioner's policy met with vigorous opposition. Up to 1870, the only new convert to the plough was Ganu, headman of Goara. He was followed by Mutira Pujari of Jaldidhar who, however, insisted on maintaining his *bewar* at the same time, 'even', he said, 'if the Deputy Commissioner cut his throat'. In 1871 a 'lucky chance' helped Colonel Bloomfield to win over a whole village of Narotia Baiga. Government had offered a reward of Rs 200 for the killing of a dangerous elephant; and the Khandarparhi Baiga headed by Ranjar Pujari, helped Bloomfield and Naylor to hunt the mad creature down, and were given the reward. As a result of this Bloomfield persuaded them to come down from the rocks of Khandarparhi and take to the plough in the good lands of Karwahi.

Colonel Bloomfield, of course, was very deeply in earnest about the uplift and civilization of the Baiga. He wrote a little pamphlet called *Notes on the Baigas* and circulated it to a number of missionary societies, his belief being that if they could be converted to Christianity all their problems would be solved.

By 1878, only about forty families, out of 441, in the Balaghat District, had been settled, and the Deputy Commissioner, Major H.M. Repton, determined to speed matters up. His view was that the slow progress made hitherto had been due to the fact that though *bewar* had been nominally forbidden, Government had continued to collect the tax of one rupee per axe, and that this had meant that the practice had in effect been winked at. In 1877, for example, no fewer than 280 axes were taxed. Major Repton determined to stop this. He abolished the tax; he forbade *bewar* throughout the district; he even went so far as to destroy standing crops on some existing *bewar*. He also obtained sanction from the Chief Commissioner for the expenditure of Rs 2,000, in Mandla and Balaghat, on the settlement of the Baiga. But the Chief Commissioner advised a policy of proceeding slowly to 'wean' the Baiga from the axe. The destruction of crops was not approved. It was proposed to mix the Baiga with Gond who would teach them the new methods of cultivation, and not to settle Baiga in villages by themselves. It is almost a tribal law, of course, that Baiga should live in separate settlements, and not mixed with other communities. The new scheme of civilization, however, was not based on anthropological principles.

By March of the following year, thirty-three families had come down into Gond villages and were putting up huts, for which they had been allowed to collect grass and bamboo free of charge. That year, a further sum, bringing the total to Rs 3,500 for Balaghat, was sanctioned for the purchase of seed and plough-cattle; and subordinate officials were ordered to see that the Baiga were not harassed, but gently persuaded to come down to the ordinary villages.

By May, 1881, seventy-five families had been settled with land, grain, bullocks and implements, at the cost of about Rs 3,000. Forty other families settled without assistance, and 485 families remained 'unreclaimed'.

In September, 1881, an annual expenditure of Rs 2,500 for four years was sanctioned.

By the end of September, 1882, the Deputy Commissioner had spent Rs 2,280 in helping 190 families to settle down to the plough, and these included a few Bharotia.

By September of the following year, this number had risen to over 300 families, and Rs 6,250 had been spent. These families were settled in twenty-three different villages, in 220 houses, and numbered 325 men, 329 women, and 488 children, a total of 1,142 persons. They were cutting 788 acres of land, and possessed 476 Government cattle in addition to eleven of their own. The majority of the new settlers were Narotia Baiga, though twenty families of the wild Bharotia were included. But that year, in face of Government pressure, many Bharotia took fright, and fifty-seven families, together with twenty-four families of Gond migrated to the Saletekri Zemindari. However, in 1884, the Deputy Commissioner of Balaghat was able to congratulate himself that on the whole the scheme had been successful, and to report that 'the Baiga I have in hand are more happy and contented than they have been for a long time'.

In Mandla some of the more civilized Binjhwar Baiga in the Mandla Tehsil had already, before 1868, taken to the plough, as is common when a tribe becomes semi-Hinduized. But, as in Balaghat, progress was slow until in 1879 a sum of Rs 800 was advanced to forty families who were settled in lands in three villages. This money was spent on bullocks, seed, implements, and the settlement of trifling debts. In their first year, these families got Gond to teach them to plough, but the next year they were able to do it for themselves. They paid one rupee per plough for the first two years, then three rupees until the Mandla Settlement expired in 1889, after which they were assessed as ordinary villagers.

In 1880, at the beginning of the cold weather, another effort was made and Rs 2,000 was spent in settling families in Silpuri near Bichia, and sixty-five families in the lands near Changaon and other villages round about Ramnagar. But as the propaganda against *bewar* increased, many Baiga fled into Kawardha State and the Zemindari of Chhattisgarh.

Thereafter the march of civilization continued year by year. In 1882, thirty-two families were settled at a cost of Rs 1,200; in 1883, an expenditure of Rs 1,550 was sanctioned. In 1884, 127 families were settled in six villages, and cost Government Rs 2,805. They had 521 acres of land, 226 cattle and 132 houses. Most of these were said to have been Bharotia.

In fact, by 1885, the Mandla Tehsil was largely free of *bewar*, and even as early as 1880 the Deputy Commissioner was able to report that the new Baiga village of Chaugaon was 'quite indistinguishable from an ordinary village of this district'.

The Ramgarh Tehsil, however, presented a much more serious problem, and it was another ten years before a solution was attempted. Shortly before 1890, however, the schemes adumbrated by Colonel Ward twenty years earlier began to be reconsidered. He had suggested confining the *bewar*-cutting Baiga within a ring-fence, and allotting to them tracts of country where, owing to previous cuttings or the inaccessibility of the locality, the timber was of little value. The forest officers did not want to prohibit *bewar*-cutting altogether, for fear that they would lose the valuable assistance of Baiga labour. For, as a Divisional Forest Officer (Mr M. Muttanah of Mandla) of the time observed:

We are entirely dependent for our labour supply on these Baiga who are by far the best wood-cutters we have in the district. Indeed it appears to me that we can scarcely get on with our work, should we lose this valuable source of labour supply. Collection of *harra* and minor products, and line clearings, would be impossible without them.

It was, therefore, decided to repeat Colonel Ward's experiment of setting aside one particular area in which *bewar* would be allowed, and to prohibit it elsewhere in the district. The original suggestion was that portions of forest known as Blocks 44 and 52 should be set aside for this purpose, but they were found on enquiry to be unsuitable, and instead a tract of 23,920 acres was carved out of Block 54. The Deputy Commissioner of Mandla at this time was Colonel Hogg, who was inclined to treat the Baigas liberally, and say to them, 'You have got all that you may expect, and now you will get no more.'

THE BAIGA CHAK

The tract chosen was in the wild uplands of the Mandla Hills, and was described by Colonel Hogg as 'a hilly tract practically hemmed in on all sides by wild and uninhabitable hills. It is perfectly inaccessible and is therefore useless as a timber-producing area'. This Baiga Chak, as it was now to be called, was bounded on the east by the Narbada and Rewa State; on the south by Bilaspur District; on the west by Mandla Tehsil; and on the north by *ryatwari* areas only recently excised from Government forest. The Chak was established by a letter (No. 2,860/221 of the 13th May, 1890) from Mr L.K. Laurie, officiating Secretary to the Chief Commissioner, to the Commissioner of the Jubbulpore Division.

After much discussion

So runs the text of the letter—

it is now proposed to confine all the bewar-cutting Baigas to an area to be carved out of Block 54, amounting to 23,920 acres (of the Ramgarh Tehsil). . . . . This is the only tract in Mandla in which *bewar* cultivation shall in future be permitted. The area will be known as the 'Baiga Reserve'. All the bewar-cutting families now residing outside that area must be warned forthwith that, if they wish to practise *bewar*, they must move into the Reserve before the next cultivating season; and *bewar* must be put a stop to in all other parts of the Tehsil. None but Baigas must be allowed to settle in the Reserve.
The Chief Commissioner entirely agrees that it should be the policy of the Administration to convert the Baigas—so far as they can be induced to settle to regular cultivation—into forest-workers; and that their management should, therefore, be entrusted in the main to the Forest Department . . . .
The Baigas should be told that though they are to be allowed to practice *bewar* within the Reserve, they can only do so in such localities as may from time to time (and as required) be pointed out to them by the Forest Officer. The latter will be responsible that *bewar* is not allowed on ridges enclosing the head waters of important streams, or where it would be detrimental to the water supply of the country.
Furthermore, the Baigas should be made to understand that the Administration, while permitting the practise of *bewar* within the Reserve, does not

look with favour upon this form of cultivation. As an indication of its disapproval, it will demand—and recover through the Forest Department—a tax of Re 1 per annum for every axe employed in felling wood for bewar. As an encouragement to them to seek other means of support, plots of land within the Reserve will be allotted on ten years' leases—of which the first three will be rent-free, and the remaining seven at the rate of 4 annas per acre—to all the Baigas who are willing to settle down to regular cultivation. Any Baiga family wishing to take up land outside the Reserve, will be given plots on the same terms. Advances of money, free of interest, for the purchase of plough-cattle and seed will be given by the Deputy Commissioner to any Baigas who take leases of plots (either within or without the Reserve) upon these conditions. Employment will also be found by the Forest Department for all who may agree to work in the forests under the orders of the forest officers. Baigas undertaking to work in this way will be settled in forest villages, helped to build, and given plots for home cultivation.

In order to provide labour for those who are willing to work, it should be arranged that in the extracting of timber for the Department and for purchasers, and in the collecting of *harra* and other minor produce, Baigas should be preferentially employed. All contracts relating to the produce of the forest in the neighbourhood of the Reserve must stipulate for this preferential employment.'

Malguzars were also to be encouraged to accept Baiga in their villages. When Baiga cultivators had been settled for five years, the Malguzar would receive a *sanad* entitling him to have such lands valued at half rates at settlement. In Mandla Tehsil, all the *bewar*-cutting Baiga lived in Malguzari villages, and though in Mandla the clause (XVI) in the Wajib-ul-arz regarding forests did not bind Malguzars to manage these in accordance with the directions of Government, it did prohibit the cutting of *sal*, teak and *shisham* without permission. This restriction, if properly insisted on, would probably suffice to stop *bewar* in Malguzari villages. It should be enforced by the Deputy Commissioner universally, so far as the conditions of the Settlement allow: and *bewar*-cultivation should be stayed, wherever possible, in the Mandla as well as in the Ramgarh Tehsil.

The Chak was not, therefore, as sometimes has been supposed, a sort of National Park where the Baiga would be allowed to carry on their ancient tribal life, but a Reformatory where the Baiga, under strict supervision and increasing official pressure, would be slowly 'weaned' from their primitive habits.

Inside the area demarcated for the Chak there were already a number of Baiga villages, Daharkata, Silpuri, Dhaba, Ajgar, Jhilung, Lamota and Rajni Sarai. Here 1,551 Baiga were living. Outside the Chak, all the Baiga were ordered either to abandon *bewar* or move into the Reserve. It is notable that there was practically no migration into the Reserve, though many Baiga went into the neighbouring States. The rest refused to leave their villages, and agreed to adopt

plough cultivation if advances of money for seed and cattle were
given them. These Baiga were now definitely settled in seven forest
villages, specially constituted for the purpose, Chauradadar,
Karadih, Dadargaon, Daldal, Udhor, Jagatpur, Pandpur; and at
the same time three villages of Gond were established at Tuichidih,
Pandripani and Tirchula. The first five of the Baiga villages were
already largely occupied by Gond, who were in possession of the
best land. Udhor and Pandpur had only poor land, and Udhor was
soon closed. Pandpur remains a fairly flourishing Baiga settlement.

Unfortunately, it does not seem to have been agreed whether
the Forest Department or the Deputy Commissioner was really
responsible for the reformation of the Baiga, and for the next three
years very little was done beyond the enforcement of the order
prohibiting *bewar*. The Secretariat Letter we have just quoted
had contemplated a generous scheme of compensation for Baiga
both within and outside the Chak, but for three years this was not
forthcoming. During these years the condition of the Baiga of Ramgarh Tehsil was deplorable. Suddenly deprived of their ancestral
means of livelihood, threatened with expulsion from the forests
they had known from childhood, prevented even from growing
root-crops for fear this should divert their attention from the
plough, forced to adopt a mode of cultivation forbidden by their
religion, yet unprovided with the means of purchasing ploughs
and cattle, these Baiga endured some years of utter poverty and
destitution. Those days are still vividly remembered. 'There was
no food, there were no bullocks, there was no money. The Ranger
tried to help us, but what could he do?' It is good to note that the
names of Mr Muttanah, the D.F.O. and Mohan Lal, the Ranger,
are still gratefully remembered by the Baiga for the sympathy and
help they gave during those hard years. Ranger Mohan Lal in fact
sent a letter to the D.F.O., Mandla, which by its quaint humanity
brightens the dull pages of the official file in which it is preserved.

'The poor Baiga', he wrote, 'is a race that is admitted on all hands as living
from hand to mouth, and having even no sufficient cloth to cover their
loins with. They could not be allowed to make new *bewars* nor have they
been supplied with other means of support. So death is staring these poor
helpless people in their faces as it were, and these innocent loyal creatures
are at the mercy of district authorities.'

Mohan Lal proposed that the Baiga should be allowed to sow
their old *bewar* for one year at least so that they should not fall into

the hands of the money-lenders. But though Colonel Grace now came to advise Colonel Hogg, nothing was done.

At the end of 1892, a number of Baiga, eleven in Pandpur, thirty-four in Udhor, twelve in Karadih and seven in Dadargaon, began cutting *bewar* again, saying that otherwise they were faced with certain starvation. They were severely reprimanded, but under the circumstances criminal action was not taken against them. It was not until 1894 that, after a great deal of correspondence, a sum of Rs 800 was advanced and fifty-six bullocks were supplied to the Baiga. One pair of bullocks was given on loan to every two families, together with as much seed as they wanted.

Progress, however, had been slow. After three years, only seventeen out of the ninety-four families in Block 62 had settled to plough cultivation, and of these only seven owned their own bullocks. The administration of the Chak was strongly criticised by Colonel Grace. In 1893, therefore, the Chief Commissioner decided on a new drive to free the country of *bewar* altogether. He transferred the management of the Chak—to its great advantage—to the Forest Department; he decided not to extend the Reserve, but 'to take up in real earnest the work of settling Baigas down to a regular plough cultivation in forest villages', and asked for the submission of a scheme that would effect this purpose.

At this time there were ninety-four Baiga families in what was known as Block 62, thirty families in Block 54, some sixty families in the surrounding Malguzari villages, and 362 families in the Chak. The greatest difficulty was experienced in dealing with the families living in Malguzari villages, the Deputy Commissioner reporting that 'they clung like a spoilt child to their axe and fire'. To combat this, a policy was adopted of mixing Gond with Baiga; Gond were encouraged to settle among the Baiga and given advantageous grants of land when they did so, and they were asked to take Baiga as agricultural labourers and train them to the plough. In the end, however, we find many Baiga who have nominally accepted the plough, never actually touching it, but employing Gond as their servants, while they themselves carry on their ancient duties of sorcery with an occasional excursion into the woods for roots.

This policy succeeded almost everywhere, though in the Ghugri Malguzari, from 1894 to 1898, *bewar* was permitted over an area of no less than 6,172 acres, being cut by 610 families who made 1,153 clearings at one rupee four annas the axe. Elsewhere, however, by

1895, the Baiga had generally settled down to the new conditions—
the name of Forester Mannu Tiwari should be remembered as one
of the apostles of civilization in the Mandla District.

Within the Chak itself, the Baiga were put under discipline. A
Forester was placed in charge of the Chak, and the *bewar*-plots
were strictly delimited. The Baiga seem to have been found rather
difficult to manage; they could not understand why they could
only cut *bewar* in the plots allotted to them. They claimed that they
could go anywhere they liked. They seem to have resented the
propaganda against *bewar*. A famous Dewar named Mahtu, the
headman of Dharkata, set his face against all change; and although
the leader of Silpuri village, Dewan, and a number of others came
round to the official side, they dared not do anything for fear of
Mahtu's curses. At the same time, some of the officials were hardly
sympathetic. But whatever the reason, the population of the Chak
dwindled alarmingly in the course of the next ten years. In 1891 it
was 1,551; in 1901 it had sunk to 700; or from 362 families to 132. In
1903 there was a further drop of 100, for in that year Rajni Sarai was
totally deserted, the Baiga fleeing in a body on an attempt being made
to move them to the Banjar Reserve for sleeper work. Rajni Sarai
was later peopled by Gond, and is now an entirely Gond village with
a population of 114. To-day the Baiga population of the Chak is
601—the numbers have remained stationary for over thirty years.

In 1895 the policy enunciated in the Secretariat Letter of 1890 was
apparently altered, as it was felt if Gond and other cultivatorrs
were allowed to mix with the Baiga in the Chak, it would be easier
to wean the latter from their axes. Accordingly, a number of other
settlers were admitted. To-day there are eighty-one Dhoba, thirty-
seven Ahir, eighteen Agaria, 102 Panka, 132 Gond, and ten others
settled in the Chak. This is a very high proportion of the total population of 1,076; there are 475 others to 601 Baiga.

The amount of *bewar* cut has also greatly decreased. In the ten
years, 1892 to 1901, 3,354 acres were burnt for *bewar*, and at that
time it was estimated that the limitations of the Reserve were such
that only 1,000 acres remained for use. To-day there are only 194
acres under *bewar* cultivation, an area that is changed every three
years according to an official programme. This means that about 70
acres a year are all that are required. On the other hand, the area
has recouped itself remarkably since 1901 when there were only
1,000 acres available for *bewar*. It is now estimated that 5,500 acres

are ready for immediate *bewar*, and a further 4,740 acres will be available after twenty or thirty years. There are also 4,124 acres of fields under plough cultivation.

In Daharkata, out of twenty-eight families of Baiga, twenty-two *bewar* are cut by twenty-one families. In Silpuri, out of twenty-three families, twelve and a half *bewar* are cut by fifteen families. In Ajgar, out of twenty-nine families, only thirteen cut *bewar*. Less than fifty *bewar* are thus being cut throughout the Chak.

No new Baiga are allowed to enter the Chak, and once a Baiga has surrendered his *bewar*, he cannot recover it. Only those who have the hereditary right are now allowed to practise it.

We have now almost reached the end of our survey. It remains to state that to-day *bewar* is permitted in certain States, notably Kawardha and Bastar—it has recently been prohibited in Rewa to the great distress of the Baiga there—and in some of the great Zemindari. It is permitted in the Southern Circle of Bilaspur, on condition that only bamboo and mixed forest areas that are free of *sal* are used, that notice is given before firing, that the Baiga are responsible for clearing a line round their *bewar* to prevent the fires from spreading, and that they keep to each *bewar* for three years.

THE CASE FOR BEWAR

What is real case against *bewar*? Sir Richard Temple thought that so long as the Baiga practised it, they would remain wild men of the hills and never rise in the social scale. Forest officers have very naturally deplored the destruction of the trees—Mahatu recalls how Mr Muttanah and his wife visited a *bewar* clearing in Karadih about 1890 and actually wept at the sight of such devastation. His wife embraced the trees and said they were her children. 'It is sad', says Colonel Ward,

To see the havoc that has been made among the forests by the Baiga axes. . . . In many places the hills have been swept clean of forests for miles; in others, the Byga marks are tall, blackened, charred stems standing in hundreds among the green forests; these are the trees killed by the Baiga for the sake of the resin.

And again: 'It is really difficult to believe that so few people could sweep the face of the earth so clear of timber as they have done.' Forsyth says: 'The Byga is the most terrible enemy to the forests we have anywhere in these hills. Thousands of square miles of *sal* forest have been clean destroyed by them in the progress of their *dhya* cultivation.' Others fear the possible effects of *bewar* on rainfall and the rivers. Desiccation and erosion have long been the bugbears of the administration. *Bewar* is also condemned as a lazy method of cultivation.

Waste and idleness, erosion and the failure of the water supply, a primitive and uneconomic method—these are the expressions that the course of time have transformed into clichés, representing unquestioned and unquestionable facts.

What is there to say on the other side? In the first place we must remember that shifting cultivation is regarded in other parts of the world as the mark of a comparatively advanced stage of civilization. Tribes like the Punan of Borneo, the Kubu of Sumatra, the Sakai of Malay, many Indian tribes in America, most of the Australian aboriginals have no form of cultivation at all, and live by hunting and gathering food. The Government of Ceylon actually put pressure on the Vedda to take to *chena* shifting cultivation in order to raise them in the scale of humanity. The 'mound-culture' of America and the 'ditch-culture' of ancient Peru and the hoe-tillage of Africa and the South Seas are all more primitive than *bewar*. In fact, the plough is characteristic only of the European and the dominant Asiatic civilizations; in opposition to *bewar* it has been exalted into a sort of fetish. The plough is undoubtedly the mark of the ever-advancing Hindu-European civilization which will soon finally overwhelm the old culture of the axe.

Authorities are by no means agreed about the extent of the damage done to the forest by *bewar*-cultivation. The opinions of Ward and Forsyth are undoubtedly exaggerated. Waste there is, but much of that waste is recouped in time.

'There is much misconception', says *The Mandla District Gazetteer*,

As to the amount of permanent damage done to the forests by the axe cultivation of the Baigas, which has been blamed for the denudation of the sources of the Upper Nerbudda and her tributaries. Mr Bell discussed this matter at length with many Baigas, and the allegation is not in accordance with either their assertions or his own observation. They claim that the jungle only grows the thicker and stronger after the abandonment of a *bewar*, and they have shown not one, but fifty abandoned *bewars* where the *sal* reproduction was strong and luxuriant enough even to impede progress. It is the *dahia* cultivation of the Gonds, they assert, which has denuded the forests. The reason for this is that the Gonds cultivate only below the line of frost. The *sal* once cut in those regions can only reproduce small shoots, which are destroyed by the annually recurring frosts. As frost comes as early as the middle of November, the Baiga crops, which as a rule are late ripeners, must be sown where they will not suffer from it. The Baigas, therefore, choose a site well above the line of frost for their *bewar*, and in such sites the *sal* can freely reproduce. The Gond inflicts a permanent, the Baiga only a temporary, injury to the forests.

In 1909, a notable report was written on this subject by Mr A. P. Percival, who had been D.F.O. in Balaghat for several years and was then in Mandla. 'I think', he says,

That the importance of the whole matter has been exaggerated, and there is a general want of perspective when so much can be talked and written about the Baiga Chak, and far more important and urgent questions such as the fire protection and working of several hundred square miles of pure *sal* forest, and the truly serious state of affairs in the reserved forest in and around Dindori plain are ignored or passed by without comment, or any serious attempt to improve matters.

The old *bewars* are invariably situated on *dadars*, on tops of hills, and on the middle and upper slopes, always well above the frost zone. The reason is that their wild crops do not ripen before frost, and to *bewar* on low ground means frost-ruin. Also, on lower ground a dense coarse grass grows up and chokes the crop. The lower ground also has not enough tree-growth. It is thus certain that the ruined aspect of many low-lying frost-bitten areas and the black cotton *maidan* lands below them, are in no way due to the Baigas; occasionally they may be due to the Gonds, but in my own opinion it is mainly a question of soils.

Percival considered that an area was fit to be re-*bewared* after twelve to fifteen years.

I had some difficulty in getting through the dense thickets of *sal* saplings on twelve-year-old *bewars* on an elephant. Nobody can possibly inspect past *bewar* areas as I have done, and not be struck with the extraordinary regrowth that springs up within a few years.[4]

If *bewar* leads inevitably to denudation and ruined forests how can we explain

The often wonderful regrowth of *sal* in all stages from seedlings through saplings to poles that is to be seen stretching in an almost unbroken line of forest from the Baiga Chak to Karadih towards Amarkantak, say twenty square miles, the like of which I have rarely seen in the whole of the Balaghat,

[4] 'There is a popular idea that jhuming tribes fell and destroy virgin forest every year. This is, of course, absurd. All suitable land in the Rengma country was taken up generations ago, and now lies fallow under secondary jungle for the six to twelve years rotation on which each block is cut.'—J.P. Mills: *The Rengma Nagas* (London, 1937), p. 76.

Motinala or Banjar Sal forests, and of which there is no possibility of doubting that the majority are old *bewar* areas?

Up to three years after an area has been abandoned the regrowth is scanty, by the end of six years it is freely filling up, at the end of twelve years regeneration is usually complete. If there are any exceptions it is on comparatively small areas where rocky ground is to be found and the Biagas say there never was forest growth nor *bewar*, which is obviously correct, as on recent low-lying *bewar* given out on wrong principles by the very people who are inveighing against the damage wrought by *bewar*.

Percival concludes by pointing out that if it were a matter of exploiting the forest commercially, and cutting timber on a large scale, one would say anything about the damage and denudation of the forest:

Perhaps I can best make my point by saying that were the Chak situated near a railway station with a demand for timber and fuel, we should not professionally hesitate a moment in constituting felling series and working over a fixed area of probably 200 to 300 acres annually.

But all that the Baiga in the Chak at that time required was 161 acres, and Percival thought at least 5,000 acres were available.

Ten years earlier, the illicit *bewar*-cutting in the Ghugri estate in Mandla had attracted the attention of Government. The manager, Narbada Prasad, acting for his aunt, Parbati Bai, the Malguzarin, had allowed *bewar* to be cut from 1894 to 1898. No fewer than 610 people had taken advantage of the opportunity, and had cut 1,153 *bewar* between them. Narbada Prasad levied a tax of Re. 1.40 per axe from the Baiga and something a little in excess of the usual plough rate from the Gond.

The *bewar*-cutting came to a natural end as a result of the famine of 1897, when over half the Baiga population of Ghugri died, and the orders of Government prohibiting it were hardly necessary. But Mr C.M. McCrie who was then D.F.O. of Mandla sent a competent Ranger to examine the estate and see how much damage had actually been done. McCrie reported that

The figures clearly show that *bewar*-cutting does not entail the permanent extinction of forest growth on the areas on which it is practised. Indeed it would probably do little harm or permanent damage if old *bewar* were allowed sufficient rest before being again attacked, and if due precautions were taken to prevent the whole forest being burned annually at the time when the *bewars* for the year are fired.

He considered that the *bewar* did have an adverse effect on the commercial value of the forest, as the trees grew up again in a pollard state and were not fit for working, but he did not think they had any real effect in causing denudation and the ruin of the water-supply.

I will call three more witnesses in the Baiga's defence, Dr J.H. Hutton, Mr W.V. Grigson and the late Sir Bampfylde Fuller. Dr Hutton places the problem on the broadest basis.

'Afforestation', he says,

Is a frequent grievance, and in forests which were common property under a tribal regime it becomes a punishable offence to exercise what the tribe regards as an inalienable right. Thus, under the Assam Forest Regulations tribal land used for *jhuming* is held to be Unclassed State Forest, and as such at the absolute disposal of Government. It can be taken and its possessors ousted without any sort of compensation. But this land has by the great majority of hill tribes been regarded for many generations as their most valuable real property .... In the Madras Agency Tracts again the same attitude has been taken towards *jhum*, there called *podu*, and has been carried to the extent of the prohibition of cultivation, twice bringing the Sawara tribe to the verge of open rebellion. *Dahia* (or *bewar*), as it is there called, is similarly forbidden in the Central Provinces, compelling the forest tribes to cultivate only under the Land Settlement system which is in many cases unsuited to them. Primitive systems of agriculture are frequently extremely wasteful of forest land and may in hill country prove damaging to adjoining plains on account of denudation, the too rapid escape of rain, and consequent inundation below. At the same time, wasteful cultivation of this kind is often the only known means of subsistence. It cannot be abandoned in a day for other methods with which the cultivator, whose knowledge is traditional, is unfamiliar.

Mr W.V. Grigson, writing about the Maria Gond of Bastar State, points out that even if there has been damage to the forest, most of this has occurred in places so inaccessible that they could not be exploited for commercial purposes.

'This shifting cultivation', he says,

Is criticised from two points of view. The forestry enthusiast laments the passing of much fine forest, and foretells desiccation and erosion. Others condemn *penda* as a lazy method of cultivation. The former forgets that in most of this area the forests have been too remote and inaccessible ever to be exploited, and that, even though some fine timber has been sacrificed, much that has gone was hopelessly over-mature .... Few signs are apparent of erosion, save in the more open parts of the Bison-horn country where *erka* has cleared the plains below the hills of forest, and there are no signs of any reduction in the heavy rainfall .... It is a superficial criticism that condemns *penda* cultivation as lazy. The clearing of the land, especially if it be covered with heavy timber, is most arduous. Remote and sometimes almost perpendicular slopes two or three miles from the village have to be cleared; the wood and scrub spread over the ground; field-houses, sheds and watching platforms have to be built on the *penda* slopes. The firing of the *penda* is particularly arduous: the stumps have to be cleared of the shoots that spring up when the rains have set in: and where deer or bison are numerous the clearings have to be fenced with heavy timber fencing.

Life in the *bewar*, in fact, is not only arduous, but dangerous, as the long roll of Baiga killed by bear, panther, or tiger testifies. The *bewar* calls out the best in a man; he is summoned to a desperate battle with the forces of nature; the *bewar* preserves something of the romance and adventure of the days of old.

No administrator, not even Ward or Bloomfield, has shown greater or more intelligent appreciation of the needs of the Baiga than Sir Bampfylde Fuller. From 1893 to 1901 and afterwards he was actively interested in their problems. At the end of 1893 he was Commissioner of Settlements and Agriculture in the Central Provinces. In that capacity he toured widely among the Baiga of Mandla and the Lormi Range in Bilaspur, and also among the Muria of Bastar. 'I believe', he says, 'that the settlement of *bewar*-cutting Baigas to cultivation will be a far more difficult task than has sometimes been anticipated. Baigas will be found to take land. But they will rarely be of the *bewar*-cutting class.'

'The recent orders of Government', he continues,

Have really brought the *bewar*-cutting Baigas of Mandla and Bilaspur to a state of destitution. Their cultivation with the axe and mattock is of an entirely different type to plough-cultivation, and they cannot more reasonably be forced to a plough than a weaver can be forced to service in a cotton mill.

The Bhumias of Bilaspur complained bitterly to me of the hardships they were put to for bare subsistence .... When I was in the Mandla uplands tigers were giving great trouble and I was told that the current report was that the Baigas in revenge for their treatment by Government had withdrawn the spells by which they keep the tigers in check and that numerous deaths from tigers might be expected. The Bhumias of Lormi obliged me by an exhibition of dancing, but they refused for some time my presents of money, eagerly asking instead for their lost bewars.

Fuller goes on to doubt whether the reasons for stopping *bewar* were as clear and cogent as they were usually assumed to be. He suggested that the timber cut was of no great value and was situated in so remote and difficult localities that it would never pay to transport it. Secondly he questioned 'whether *bewars* under certain conditions of soil and rainfall do denude the hills provided that they are not concentrated on too small an area. In this matter', he adds,

A great deal too much has been taken for granted.
I have been told that in Mauritius the forests are regularly cut and burnt
. . . . The people I asked declared that in some respects forest growth was
improved by *bewar*, and that a *bewar*-clearing would ordinarily be under
dense jungle in eight or ten years. I was shown hills in Mandla which were
said to have been stripped by *bewar* twenty-five years ago, but were now
thickly clothed with high forest. In Bastar where jungle is almost universally cut and burnt as a preparation for plough-cultivation, I saw really fine
patches of young *sal* forest on land which I was informed had been cleared
only three years previously, and looking to the number of years during
which *bewar* has been practised unchecked it seems necessary to conclude
that almost the whole of our Forest Reserves have been under *bewar*-culti-
vation at some time or other.
There are circumstances which justify a Government calling on its subjects
to reform or perish. But the reform must be supported by very strong
reasons, and the more numerous the people affected the stronger must be
the case against them. With these people there are, moreover, sentimental
reasons for kind treatment. They are relics of old time; they live in places
which no others would dare to inhabit; and it seems hard to deny them
their customary food in order to lengthen the life of valueless jungle.

Again, when Commissioner of the Jubbulpore Division in 1898,
Fuller returned to the charge.

I am under the impression, that in the past rather exaggerated ideas
have been entertained of the injurious effects of *bewar*, especially in a
country of heavy rainfall where its effects seem often to be not the permanent denudation of the land, but the substitution of one kind of forest
growth for another.

And finally, most cogently of all, in 1901, he said:

It is of much more importance that a tribe of people should live in peace
and comfort, than that a certain area of land should grow trees of one sort
or another, or indeed should grow trees at all.
The practise of *bewar* undoubtedly changes the character of the jungle,
substituting bamboos for trees. But bamboos are, speaking generally, the
most useful forest product we can grow.

I have quoted enough to show that there is, among those who
have served the Baiga best and loved them most, a considerable
body of opinion that considers that *bewar* should not be regarded as
quite the bogey that it has been assumed to be, that the damage it
causes has been exaggerated, that given proper conditions the
forest often recovers itself in time, and that in the case of a small
tribe like the Baiga the effect on erosion and the rainfall is not a very
serious danger. After all, there are only some 40,000 Baiga, and even
if all of these began to cut *bewar* again, they could hardly—spread

as they would be over a very large area—make a great deal of difference to the climatic conditions of the country.

On wider grounds, it may be argued that the Baiga have a very legitimate grievance. It is sometimes said that no one has ever criticized the justice of the anti-*bewar* policy. This is not correct. For the last seventy years, the Baiga have constantly and bitterly criticized the inequity of their treatment. But they have had no champion to fight for them, no spokesman to voice their grievances. When the Chak was first founded a great many petitions were sent to Government, of which the following is a specimen. It was presented by Dholi Baiga of Udhor in 1892. 'Now that *bewar* has been stopped', he says,

We daily starve, having had no food grain in our possession. The only wealth we possess is our axe. We have no clothes to cover our body with, but we pass cold nights by the fire-side. We are now dying for want of food .... We cannot go elsewhere, as the British Government is everywhere. What fault have we done that the Government does not take care of us? Prisoners are supplied with ample food in jail. A cultivator of the grass is not deprived of his holding, but the Government does not give us our right who have lived here for generations past.

And in the famine of 1897, Guhra and Ramsingh, Baiga of Kukrapani, begged that at a time when Government was helping everyone, they might be allowed to cut *bewar* in the forest near their village. 'We are dying of starvation. Beside *bewar* we have no other profession'. Both these petitions, and most of the others that were received, had to be rejected in accordance with the accepted policy.

I have recorded two songs which vividly describe the feelings of the Baiga when their *bewar*-cutting is prohibited.

Such a calamity had never been before!
Some he beats, some he catches by the ear,
Some he drives out of the village.
He robs us of our axes, he robs us of our jungle.
He beats the Gond; he drives the Baiga and Baigin from their jungle.
The police come with orders to catch us like dogs.
O such a calamity had never been before!

And again:

In this Raja's reign we all are dying of hunger.
He robs us of our axes, he robs us of our jungle.
The Baigin says to the Baiga, Come let us dig some roots.

We will fetch them in a small basket,
And feed our little children,
But secretly or else the police will take them from us.
From village to village go the Raja's men,
They make roads, but not for us; the roads are for the Raja.
He steals the Baiga's bewar.
We are all dying of hunger during this Raja's reign.

Both these songs were entirely spontaneous, and were not prompted by any political agitation, of which the Baiga are wholly ignorant.

The extraordinary importance of the *bewar* in the social, religious and economic life of the tribe is clear. It is their own special possession; it makes them different from all others; it is their right and duty, laid on them from the beginning of the world. The contrast between a *bewar*-cutting village and a 'civilized' village is astonishing; the social and religious life of the latter is emasculated, void of reality and vigour. Materially, it may be better off, but the inner life of the people is dying, and the Baiga of these villages will soon sink to the dead level of apathy and futility of their semi-civilized neighbours. Even Colonel Ward, hostile as he was to *bewar*, was struck by the difference between the Baiga of Mandla who were 'getting over gradually their dislike to ploughs and cattle, and where they have the means, show no objection to the plough' and 'the real Baigas' of the hills of the Maikal Range.

Wild as the forests they live in, they have none of that cringing fear of people in authority which is shown so much by the Gonds and Bygas of Mundlah. They are independent, high-spirited, finer specimens of humanity than their brethren farther west, very well behaved, ready to oblige, and deserving every consideration for their orderly manner of life.

And this is only to be expected, for it is impossible to deprive primitive people of a vital part of their economy,[5] to tear a page out

---

[5] Experience in Africa has emphasized the great caution needed in any interference with old-established tribal customs: there may well be a sound technological basis for their survival. For example, Mr Dudley Stamp has shown that the African has probably discovered in his 'dirty farming' the most efficient method of cultivation in a climate where 'it is almost impossible to protect the long plow farrow from the most destructive and virulent forms of soil erosion.' 'It is to be hoped that Southern Nigeria may long be spared the dangers of the plow'. And Dr Leakey has defended the Kikuyu method of irregular planting of different crops mixed up, in precisely Baiga fashion in the same patch. He shows how this custom, condemned by the European agriculturalist, conserves the moisture and prevents soil-erosion. See Leakey: *Kenya Contrasts and Problems* (London, 1936), pp. 118 ff.

of their mythology, to force them into a way of life repugnant to them by tradition, inclination, and tribal law, without irreparably injuring their life and spirit.

Colonialism and Conflict in the Himalayan Forest

RAMACHANDRA GUHA

This essay examines the trajectory of social protest in Kumaun during the early decades of this century. Since 1973, Kumaun has been the epicentre of the Chipko Andolan, possibly the best known contemporary movement against the exploitation of forests by an outside agency. Nonetheless, Chipko is only one—though undoubtedly the most organized—in a series of protests against commercial forestry dating from the earliest days of state intervention. While the absence of popular protest in the first century of British rule had given rise to the stereotype of the 'simple and law abiding hillman', the reservation of the Kumaun forests in 1911-17 'met with violent and sustained opposition', culminating in 1921 when within the space of a few months the administration was paralysed, first by a strike against *utar* (statutory labour) and then through a systematic campaign in which the Himalayan pine forests 'were swept by incendiary fires almost from end to end'.

Recent research has shown that world ecology was profoundly altered by Western capitalism, in whose dynamic expansion, from the fifteenth century onwards, other ecosystems were disrupted, first by European trade and later by colonialism. Such interventions virtually reshaped the societies into whose habitat they intruded. In India, too, the exogenously induced changes engendered by colonialism and the usurpation of natural resources by the state undermined the traditional social fabric in a variety of ways. In her pioneering study, Elizabeth Whitcombe shows how the reorientation of agricultural production towards the export market and the construction of large irrigation works which increased soil salinity by

Excerpted from Ramachandra Guha, 'Forestry and Social Protest in British Kumaun c 1893–1921', in Ramajit Guha, ed., *Subaltern Studies IV*, OUP, New Delhi, 1985.
    Notes and References have been omitted. Editor

obstructing natural drainage led to an unprecedented strain in the rural economy of the Doab. The adaptation of farming techniques to cope with these rapid changes was further hampered by the deforestation caused by the use of wood-fuel by railway companies. In south Bihar, the deterioration of the system of social management of irrigation—which, it is argued, was one factor behind the rise of the Kisan Sabha in the 1930s—could be traced to the commercialization of agriculture and the affirmation of state control over water resources. As Sengupta points out, ownership and land control, though undoubtedly very significant, are only one aspect of social relations within the agrarian population.

These works notwithstanding, the neglect of the study of the ecological dimensions of social conflict in India is almost embarrassingly complete. It is time to amend this neglect, first because a study of forest policy and law may help to modify the theories based on the ideological presuppositions of colonial policy, and second because the transformation of social relations brought about by commercial forestry was one whose repercussions continue to be felt today. The history of deforestation has assumed an additional importance in view of the continuing struggles of tribals and other forest dwellers, and can help illuminate the forms such conflicts have previously taken in different parts of the country.

Conflicts over forest and grazing rights were a recurrent feature in pre-capitalist and early-capitalist Europe as well. The enclosure of common woodland, for hunting reserves and later for rationalized timber production, was an imposition keenly resented by the peasantry. However, the nature of social conflict in the transition to industrial capitalism in Europe inevitably differed from that of the endemic conflict over forest rights which was germane to the artificially induced capitalism under colonial rule. B.H. Baden-Powell, one of the architects of Indian forest policy, pointed to this distinction when he observed that in Europe, 'in a more advanced state of social life and occupation it has become more and more easy to alter an occupation that could not be continued if a forest right was taken away'.

KUMAUN: ECONOMY AND SOCIETY

Although ruled by different dynasties during the medieval period, the social structures of Kumaun[1] and Garhwal share marked similarities. The largest ethnic stratum is made up of the Khasa or Khasiya who comprise the traditional peasantry, while the next largest stratum consists of the Doms serving the cultivating body as artisans and farm servants. Numerically the smallest but ritually the highest group are the Thuljat-Brahmins and Rajputs claiming to be descendants of later immigrants from the plains. It has been conjectured that the Doms are the original inhabitants of the hills who were conquered and enslaved by the Khasas. While the Khasas were a widespread race in prehistoric Asia, the origins of the hill Khasas are obscure. They have, however, adhered to a Vedantic form of Hinduism at least since the eighth century AD. With caste restrictions and other rules of orthodox Hinduism being singularly lax in the hills, over time the Khasas have merged with the Thuljat.

The independent chiefdoms of Garhwal were first subjugated by Ajayapal in the thirteenth century, while the unification of Kumaun took place under Som Chand around 960 AD. Exempt from the payment of tribute to the Muslim dynasties of north India, these isolated hill tracts were conquered by adjoining Nepal between 1793 and 1804. The system of military assignments under Gurkha rule introduced certain changes in the agrarian structure built around strong village communities, with most members enjoying a hereditary interest in land. The Anglo-Gurkha wars culminated in the treaty of 1815, by which the East India Company annexed both Kumaun and Garhwal. Retaining Kumaun and eastern Garhwal, the British restored the western portion (known as Tehri Garhwal, after the king's new capital) to the son of the last Garhwali ruler.

The boundaries of the treaty of 1815 were fixed with a view to controlling the route to Tibet and the passes used for trade. It was the prospect of commercial intercourse with Tibet and not considerations of revenue that induced Lord Hastings to embark on the hill campaign. Its location, strategic from the viewpoint of both defensive security and trade, played an important part in the evolution of British land policy in Kumaun.

[1] In this article, Kumaun refers to the British civil division comprising the districts of British Garhwal, Almora, and Naini Tal. Historically the latter two districts constituted Kumaun. I shall, however, use Kumaun to include Garhwal as did the official sources from which I have largely drawn. The Kumaun Division (hereafter KD) was separated from Nepal in the east by the river Kali; from Tibet in the north by the Himalaya; from the state of Tehri Garhwal in the west by the Alakananda and Mandakini rivers and from the adjoining division of Rohilkhand in the south by the outer hills.

The Central Himalaya is composed of two distinct ecological zones: the monsoon-affected areas at middle and low altitudes, and the high valleys of the north, inhabited until 1962 by the Bhotiya herdsmen who had been engaged in trade with Tibet for centuries. Along the river valleys cultivation was carried out, limited only by the steepness of land and more frequently by the difficulty of irrigation. Two and sometimes three harvests were possible throughout the last century, wheat, rice, and millets being the chief cereals grown. The system of tillage and methods of crop rotation bore the mark of the hillmen's natural environment. With production oriented towards subsistence needs, which were comfortably met, there remained a surplus of grain for export to Tibet and southwards to the plains. Usually having six months stock of grain at hand, and with their diet supplemented by fish, fruit, vegetables, and animal flesh, the hill cultivators were described by Henry Ramsay, commissioner from 1856-84, as 'probably better off than any peasantry in India'.

The absence of sharp inequalities in land ownership among the cultivating proprietors who formed the bulk of the population was the basis of solidarity within the village community. Single-caste villages were not uncommon, and in these the village *panchayat*—an institution quite different from the caste *panchayat* of the plains—dealt with social disputes, arrangements for festivals, etc., with every adult member having a voice in its affairs. The establishment of British rule notwithstanding, *panchayats* frequently continued to deal internally with matters technically under the jurisdiction of civil and criminal courts.

The hill land-tenure system inherited by the British differed no less strikingly from that in the plains. The first commissioner, G.W. Traill, observed that at least three-fourths of the villages were *hissedari*, i.e. wholly cultivated by the actual proprietors of the land; the revenue demand on them was restricted to their respective shares of the village assessment. The remaining villages were divided into (i) those in which the right of property was vested in earlier recipients of land grants (many dating only from the period of Gurkha rule) while the hereditary right of cultivation remained with the original occupants (called *khaikhar*), and (ii) a handful of villages owned by a single individual, where again individual tenants (called *khurnee*), were able to wrest easy terms owing to the unfavourable land-man ratio. As even the most important landowners depended not on any legal right but on the actual influence they exercised over village communities, there was not one estate which could be termed 'pure zamindari'. Government revenue and certain customary fees were collected by the *elected* village *pradhan* (headman), who reported in turn to a higher revenue official (called the *patwari*, in charge of a *patti* or group of villages) entrusted with police duties and the responsibility of collecting statutory labour for public works. While over time much of the class of *khurnee* merged with that of *khaikhar*, the latter differed from the *hissedar* only in that he could not transfer land and had to pay a fixed sum as *malikhana* to the proprietor—this sum representing the conversion into cash of all previously-levied cesses and perquisites. But by the end of the century, fully nine-tenths of all hillmen were estimated to be *hissedars*, cultivating proprietors with full ownership rights.

Some evidence from census returns is given in Table 1. Not strictly comparable with the other mountainous districts, Naini Tal comprised a few hill *pattis* and a large area of Terai which had begun to be settled by the end of the nineteenth century. Within the hill districts proper, one observes that around 60 per cent of the agrarian population were owner-cultivators. Having already noted the position of *khaikhari* tenures (Category IIb), we can conclude that around 80 per cent of the total population farmed largely with the help of family labour. The extraordinarily low proportion of agricultural labour confirms the picture of an egalitarian peasant community—a picture used more often as an analytical construct than believed to exist in reality.

The best class of cultivation was to be found in villages between 3 and 5000 feet above sea level, having access on the one hand to good forest and grazing ground, and on the other to riparian fields in the depths of the valley. Village sites were usually chosen halfway up the spur, below oak forests and the perennial springs associated with them, and above the cultivated fields along the river bed. In such a situation all crops could be 'raised to perfection', a healthy elevated site was available for houses, and herds of cattle could be comfortably maintained. Until 1910 most villages came close to this ideal.

With animal husbandry being as important to their economy as grain cultivation, the hillmen and their cattle migrated annually to the grass-rich areas of the forest. Temporary cattle sheds (*kharaks*) were constructed and the cultivation of small patches carried out.

Table 1

Occupational Classification of the Agricultural Households in Kumaun, 1911–21
(Workers + Dependants)

Category		District					
		Naini Tal		Almora		British Garhwal	
		1911	1921	1911	1921	1911	1921
Those whose income is:							
I.	Primarily from rent:						
	a) Landlords	3023		681		102	
	b) Occupancy tenants	5025		21		2	
	c) Ordinary tenants	15199		22		17	
	Total Class I	23247	722	724	530	121	155
		(9.98)	(0.35)	(0.15)	(0.11)	(0.03)	(0.03)
II.	From cultivation of their holdings:						
	a) Landlords	48887		287952		292649	
		(20.80)		(59.31)		(66.60)	
	b) Occupancy tenants	22449		107519		104793	
		(9.55)		(22.15)		(23.85)	
	c) Ordinary tenants	118411		88337		34799	
		(50.38)		(17.16)		(7.92)	
	Total Class II	189747	184276	478808	486776	432241	448649
		(80.73)	(89.15)	(98.62)	(98.04)	(98.37)	(99.11)
III	Farm servants and field labourers	14212	15261	1771	2411	3917	1744
		(6.05)	(7.38)	(0.36)	(0.49)	(0.89)	(0.39)
IV	Goatherds, shepherds and herdsmen	4886	3741	3151	6035	1507	642
		(2.07)	(1.81)	(0.65)	(1.21)	(0.34)	(0.14)
V	Others (including forestry)	2956	2698	1053	763	1609	642
		(1.26)	(1.31)	(0.22)	(0.15)	(0.37)	(0.14)
VI	Agriculture and pasture (Total)	235028	206698	485507	496517	439395	452692
VII	Total population	323519	276875	525104	530338	480167	485186
VIII	VI as % of VII	72.65	74.65	92.46	93.62	91.51	93.30

Source: *Census of India*, 1911 and 1921

Note i) A simpler classification was adopted in 1921 owing to the Non-Cooperation Movement.

ii) Figures in parentheses denote percentage of agricultural population (VI)

In the permanent hamlets, oak forests provided both fodder and fertilizer. Green and dry leaves, which served the cattle as litter, were mixed with the excreta of the animals and fermented to give manure to the fields. Thus the forest augmented the nutritive value of the fields, directly through its foliage and indirectly through the excreta of the cattle fed with fodder leaves and forest grass. Broad-leaved trees also provided the villagers with fuel and agricultural implements.

In the lower hills the extensive *chir* forests served for pasture. Every year the dry grass and pine-needle litter in the *chir* forest was burnt to make room for a fresh crop of luxuriant grass. Simultaneously the needle litter, whose soapy surface endangered the otherwise sure-footed hill cattle, was destroyed. Very resistant to fire, *chir* was used for building houses and as torchwood. In certain parts where pasture was scarce, trees were grown and preserved for fodder.

Its isolated position and status as a recruiting ground for army personnel were reflected in the administrative policies followed in Kumaun. Recruitment had started by the mid-nineteenth century, and both Kumauni and Garhwali soldiers were drafted into Gurkha units. The Garhwali Regiment, with headquarters at Lansdowne in the outer hills, was formed in 1890 and became the 39th Garhwal Rifles in 1901. Essentially peasant farmers who returned to culti-vate their holdings on retirement, hill soldiers enjoyed an enviable record for their bravery. In these circumstances British land-revenue assessment was extraordinarily light—around Rs 3 per family—and its revision barely kept up with the increase in population. A rapid expansion of the cultivated area was watched over by a highly per-sonalized administration under Henry Ramsay, whom fellow Englishmen hailed as the uncrowned King of Kumaun.

At one stage the hills had afforded distinct possibilities for tea cultivation. In 1862-3 over 35,000 lbs. of tea was produced in Dehradun and Kumaun, and an estimate of waste land fit for tea cultivation revealed that it was feasible to match the entire export trade of China from this region alone. The refusal of the hill peasant to shed his subsistence orientation and the opposition anticipated at the introduction of white settlers led to these plans being shelved. In later years, state intervention in the form of induced commer-cialization of agriculture was conspicuously absent. In the odd year when the monsoon failed, grain was imported by the authorities and sold at remunerative prices—a measure, it was stressed, necessitated not by the poverty of the population (which could well afford to buy grain) but by the inaccessibility of many villages and the lack of markets in an economy characterized by the absence of traders in foodgrains. Such measures may help to explain why no agitations related to revenue occurred in either the nineteenth or the twentieth century.

THE DEVELOPMENT OF ORGANIZED FORESTRY IN KUMANUN

Stable forest cover on any terrain is established through the process of ecological succession. This succession can generally be divided into three stages: (i) the initial stage, in which certain species of trees, usually with small or light seeds, take possession of newly exposed ground; (ii) the transitional stages, in which changes take place on ground already clothed with some vegetative cover; (iii) the climactic stage, which represents the farthest advance towards a hygrophilous (i.e. adapted to plentiful water supply) type of vegetation which the locality is capable of supporting. While it could be said that in the Himalaya the oaks and other broad-leaved species represent stage (iii) and the conifers stage (ii), in the days before forest management mixed forests were the norm. In general, the more favourable the locality is for vegetation the greater the number of species struggling for existence in it.

Two points may be noted. First, while the oaks (and other broad-leaved species) are more valuable for hill agriculture on both ecological and economic grounds, the conifers have had, since the inception of 'scientific' management, a variety of commercial uses. Second, while 'progressive' succession—from stage (i) to (ii) to (iii)—occurs in nature, 'retrogressive' succession—from stage (iii) to (ii) to (i)—can be caused by man, either accidentally or deliberately. Foresters are cautioned that in many cases 'the natural trend of this succession may be diametrically opposed to what is desirable from an economic point of view'.

The importance of forests in hill life gave rise to a 'natural system of conservancy' that took different forms. Through religion, folklore and tradition the Khasa communities drew a protective ring around the forests. Often, hill tops were dedicated to local deities and the trees around the summit and on the slopes were preserved. Many wooded areas were not of spontaneous growth and bore marks of plantation and preservation. Particularly in eastern Kumaun, and around temples, *deodar* plantations had become naturalized. Temple groves of *deodar* varied in extent from a few trees to woods of several hundred acres. As late as 1953 it was reported that the finest strands of *deodar*, found near temples, were venerated and protected from injury. An officer newly posted to the hills in the 1920s was struck by the way communal action continued to survive in the considerable areas which served as village grazing ground, and by the fact that fuel and fodder reserves were walled in and well looked after. Traditionally, many villages had fuel reserves even on *gaon sanjait* (common) land measured by the government, which the villagers cut over in regular rotation by common consent. Chaundkot *pargana* in Garhwal was singled out for its forests within village boundaries, called 'banis', where branches and trees were only cut at specified times and with the permission of the entire village community. Cooperation of a high order was also manifest in the fixed boundaries adhered to by every village—boundaries existing from the time of Indian rulers and recognized by Traill in the settlement of 1823. Within these boundaries the inhabitants of each village exercised various proprietary and other rights of user. In some areas a group of villages had joint rights of grazing and fuel, secured by long usage and custom.

Since an analogous situation existed in many other forest areas, the inception of commercial forestry disrupted existing patterns of resource utilization. The landmark in the history of Indian forestry is undoubtedly the building of the railway network. The large-scale destruction of accessible forests in the early years of railway expansion led to the hasty creation of a forest department, set up with the help of German experts in 1864. The first task before the new department was to identify the sources of supply of strong and durable timbers—such as *sal*, teak and *deodar*—which could be used as railway sleepers. As *sal* and teak were very heavily worked out, search parties were sent to explore the *deodar* forests of the Sutlej and Jamuna valleys. Intensive felling in these forests—1.3 million *deodar* sleepers were exported from the Jamuna valley between 1865 and 1878—forced the government to rely on the import of wood from Europe. But with emphasis placed on substituting indigenous sleepers for imported ones, particularly in the inland districts of north India, the department began to consider the utilization of the Himalayan pines if they responded adequately to antiseptic treatment.

Successful forest administration required checking the deforestation of the past decades, and for this the assertion of state monopoly right was considered essential. A prolonged debate within the colonial bureaucracy on whether to treat the customary use of the forest as based on 'right' or on 'privilege' was settled by the selective use of precedent and the principle that 'the right of conquest is the strongest of all rights—it is a right against which there is no appeal'. Since an initial attempt at asserting state monopoly through the Forest Act of 1865 was found wanting, a comprehensive all-India act was drafted thirteen years later. This act provided for the constitution of 'reserved' (i.e. closed) forests, divested of existing rights of user to enable sustained timber production. The 1878 Act provided for an elaborate procedure of forest settlement to deal with all claims of user, which, if upheld, could be transferred to a second class of forest designated as 'protected'. While the burden of proof to establish 'legally established rights' was on the people, the state could grant both 'non-established rights' and 'terminable concessions' at its discretion.

The systematic management of the Kumaun hill forests commenced with the constitution of small blocks of reserved forests to furnish a permanent supply of fuel and timber to the administrattive centres of Naini Tal and Almora and the cantonment town of Ranikhet. A survey was commissioned to report on the detailed composition of the hill forests, particularly those within 'reasonable distance' of land and water, and select sites for roads and saw mills. This was followed in 1893 by the declaration of all unmeasured land in the Kumaun division as 'district protected forest' (DPF). What was thought 'of primary importance was to assert the proprietary right of Government in these forests and lay down certain limits to the hitherto unregulated action of right-holders'. Official interest in these forests—dominated by the long-leaved or *chir* pine—quickened further when two important scientific developments were reported by Indian forest officials. The tapping of *chir* pine for oleo-resin had been started on an experimental basis in the 1890s, and by 1912 methods of distillation had been evolved which would enable the products to compete with the American and French varieties that had hitherto ruled the market. At the same time, fifty years of experimentation on a process to prolong the life of certain Indian woods for use as railway sleepers through chemical treatment finally bore fruit. Of the timbers successfully treated, the *chir* and blue pines were both found suitable and available in substantial quantities, and could be marketed at a sufficiently low price.

Four distinct phases, representing the progressive diminution of villagers' rights in the forests of Kumaun, can be distinguished.

(i) Between 1815 and 1878, when the state concentrated on the submontane *sal* forests of the Bhabhar, while the forests of Kumaun proper were left untouched. However, the forests around Naini Tal were demarcated in the 1850s and those around Ranikhet and Almora in 1873 and 1875 respectively.

(ii) Between 1878 and 1893, when the above forests were notified as reserved under the 1878 Act, while grants of forest made to Iron Companies and several other tracts in Almora and Garhwal districts were declared reserved or protected forests.

(iii) On 17 October, 1893 all waste land not forming part of the measured area of villages or of the forests earlier reserved was declared to be protected forest under the Act, although the necessary enquiry (*vide* Section 28) had not been made. Thus DPF comprised tree-covered lands, snow-clad peaks, ridges and cliffs, river beds, lakes, buildings, temple lands, camping and pasture grounds, and roads and shops. A skeletal forest staff was employed, and on 24 October, 1894 eight types of trees, including *deodar, chir* and *sal,* were reserved. Rules were framed for regulating the lopping of trees for fuel and fodder and claims for timber, and trade by villagers in any form of forest produce was prohibited. On 5 April, 1903 the Kumaun DPF were divided into two classes: (a) Closed Civil Forests, which the state considered necessary for reproduction or protection, and (b) Open Civil Forests, where villagers could exercise their rights subject to the rules prescribed in 1894.

(iv) All these cumulative incursions culminated in 1911 with the decision to carve extensive reserves out of the DPF. Forest settlements set up in the three districts between 1911 and 1917 resulted in the constitution of almost 3,000 square miles of reserved forest in the Kumaun division. Elaborate rules were framed for the exercise of rights, specifying the number of cattle to be grazed and amount of timber and fuelwood allotted to each rightholder. Villagers had to indent in advance for timber for construction of houses and for agricultural implements, which would be supplied by the Divisional Forest Officer (DFO) from a notified list of species. The annual practice of burning the forest floor for a fresh crop of grass was

banned within one mile of reserved forests; but as this excluded
few habitations in these heavily forested hills, the prohibition
virtually made the practice illegal.

Within a few years of commercial working the Kumaun forests
had become a paying proposition. When one full fifteen-year cycle
(1896–1911) had revealed that resin tapping did not permanently
harm trees, attempts were made 'to develop the resin industry as
completely and rapidly as possible'. Between 1910 and 1920 the
number of resin channels tapped rose from 260,000 to 2,135,000, a
rate of increase matched by the production of resin and turpentine
(Table 2). When the construction of a new factory at Bareilly was

Table 2

Imports into and Production in India of Resin and Turpentine, 1907–23

Year April to March	Resin			Turpentine		
	Imports	Indian production	Total (cwts)	Imports	Indian production	Total (gallons)
1907–08	76,200	4,845	81,045	225,560	16,086	241,646
1910–11	41,600	6,625	48,225	197,720	17,051	214,771
1913–14	45,769	20,100	65,869	193,937	58,803	252,740
1916–17	18,760	43,500	62,260	80,000	125,663	205,663
1919–20	13,855	46,700	60,555	113,638	148,680	262,318
1921–22	10,602	57,200	67,802	70,369	163,151	233,520
1922–23*	18,037	82,000	100,037	90,364	279,100	369,404

Source: Smythies, 'India's Forest Wealth', p. 83.
* Calendar Year 1922.

completed in 1920—with a rated capacity of 64,000 cwts of resin
and 240,000 gallons of turpentine, a capacity that could be easily
expanded fourfold—production was outstripping Indian demand.
This put under active consideration proposals for the export of
resin and turpentine to the United Kingdom and the Far East. Indeed,
the only impediment to increased production was the inadequacy
of means of communication. The extensive pine forests in the interior
had to remain untapped, with extraction restricted to areas well
served by mule tracks and sufficiently close to rail-heads.

The War provided a fillip to the production of *chir* sleepers. The
cessation of antiseptic imports proved a 'blessing in disguise' when
the Munitions Board requisitioned untreated sleepers. Almost 4 lakh

sleepers were supplied during 1916-18, and the Kumaun circle began to show a financial surplus for the first time, with all stocks cleared. The government saw-mill was unable to deal with all the indents it received. Nevertheless, over 5,000 *chir* trees were felled and sawn annually. For the Forest Department, its activities during the war were adequate justification of the recent and controversial forest settlement in the hills.

Begar IN KUMAUN

The system of forced labour in Kumaun, was known by various names during the colonial period (*coolie utar, bardaish, begar, godam*). The British in fact operated the system, a legacy of the petty hill chiefs who preceded them, from Darjeeling to Simla, on grounds of administrative convenience in tracts whose physical situation made both commercial transport and boarding houses economically unattractive. As embodied in their settlement agreements, landholders were required to provide several sets of services for all government officials on tour and for white travellers (e.g. *shikaris* and mountaineers). The most common of these involved carrying loads and building *chappars* (temporary rest huts), and the supply of provisions (*bardaish*) such as milk, food, grass, wood and cooking vessels. Although only *hissedars* and *khaikhars* were technically liable to be called upon to provide coolie-*bardaish*, *sirtans* were also held liable 'as a matter of custom and convenience'. Other forms of statutory labour included the collection of material and levelling of sites for buildings, roads, and other public works, transporting the luggage of regiments moving from Lansdowne, and the carrying of iron and wood for the building of bridges in the interior. Old men and widows were exempt from these burdens at the discretion of the DC; otherwise, remissions were rarely granted. According to the settlement villagers were to be reimbursed for these services, but in actual practice they were often rendered free. While convinced of the 'inequity of the practice' as early as 1850, the government had concluded after an enquiry that there existed no available substitute.

The incidence of *utar* was comparatively slight in the first century of British rule. Nevertheless, its impressment was resisted in various ways. The village *pradhan* (himself exempt) occasionally concealed some of the *hissedars* in his village; or, as travellers who indented for coolies often found out, the headman was 'openly defied' by his villagers, who refused to supply labour or provisions. When census returns from Garhwal reported a large excess of males over females in the 10-14 age group, this discrepancy was traced to the age (16 years) at which men were called upon to carry loads or furnish *bardaish*. Thus all those whose age could possibly be understated were reported to be under 16. Officials commented too that the hillman's aversion to work under compulsion had led to an undeserved reputation for indolence. While he worked hard enough in his fields, coolie labour, especially during the agricultural season, was performed in a manner that made his resentment apparent. Travellers and soldiers thus often found themselves stranded when villagers failed to oblige in carrying their luggage. Ramsay had to levy a fine of Rs 500 on a village near Someshwar in Almora district which struck against *utar*. Another strike in 1903 led to the imprisonment of fourteen villagers of Khatyadi. Concurrently, opposition to the *begar* system was expressed in newspapers, edited by nationalists of the Gokhale school, from Almora, Naini Tal and Dehradun. The Kumaun Parishad based in Almora took up both the *begar* and forest issues, and asked the Forest Department to hire its own coolies and build more roads.

With the advent of the Forest Department, the burden of these services on the Kumaun villager dramatically increased. The reservation of the forest and its future supervision involved extensive touring by forest officials who took *utar* and *bardaish* for granted. Coming close on the heels of the demarcation of the forests, the additional burdens created by the new department evoked a predictable response. Forest officers touring in the interior of Garhwal were unable to obtain grain, as villagers, even where they had surplus stock, refused to supply to a department they regarded 'as disagreeable interlopers to be thwarted if possible'. *Utar*, in the words of the Kumaun Forest Grievances Committee 'one of the greatest grievances which the residents of Kumaun had against the forest settlement'—when coupled with the curtailment of community control over forests represented an imposition unprecedented in its scope and swiftness. Villagers looked back, not altogether without justification, to a 'golden age' when they had full freedom to roam over their forest habitat, and state interference was at its minimum. These emotions were beautifully expressed by a government clerk who applied for exemption from *begar* and *bardaish* thus:

In days gone by every necessities of life were in abundance to villagers than to others (and) there were no such Government laws and regulations prohibiting the free use of unsurveyed land and forest by them as they have now. The time itself has now become very hard and it has been made still harder by the imposition of different laws, regulations, and taxes on them and by increasing the land revenue. Now the village life has been shadowed by all the miseries and inconveniences of the present day laws and regulations. They are not allowed to fell down a tree to get fuels from its for their daily use and they cannot cut leaves of trees beyond certain portion of them for fodder to their animals. But the touring officials, still view the present situation with an eye of the past and press them to supply good grass for their horses, fuels for their kitchens, and milk for themselves and their (retinue) without even thinking of making any payment for these things to them who after spending their time, money and labour can hardly procure them for their own use. In short, all the privileges of village life, as they were twenty years ago, are nowhere to be found now, still the officials hanker after the system of yore when there were everything in abundance and within the reach of villagers.*

As one can discern from this petition, the new laws and regulations were already beginning to threaten the considerable autonomy enjoyed by the Khasa village community. Here, as elsewhere in colonial South and South East Asia, unusual exactions and other forms of state encroachment upon the privileges of individuals or communities were regarded as transgressing the traditional relationship between ruler and ruled. By clashing with his notions of economic justice, increased state intervention breached the 'moral economy' of the peasant. Anticipating that the hillman would react by 'throwing his Forest loads down the *khud* and some day an unfortunate Forest Officer may go after them', Wyndham, the commissioner of Kumaun, believed that the only way to prolong the life of the *utar* system would be for forest officials to use pack ponies. Government could hardly defend the use of *utar* by a money-making department which, if it continued to avail of *begar*, would hasten the end of the system. Echoing the commissioner's sentiments, the Garhwal lawyer and Legislative Council member Taradutt Gairola pleaded for a 'vigorous policy of reform', failing which 'trouble (would) arise' at the revision of the revenue settlement.

These warnings were to prove prophetic, but in the meantime the state hoped to rely on a series of ameliorative measures. The

---

* Language and grammar as in original.

Lieutenant-Governor had in 1916 rejected the possibility of the *utar* system itself being scrapped; while it had caused 'hardship' in certain areas the government, he emphasized, was concerned merely 'with checking any abuses of the system'. In a move initiated by Gairola, coolie agencies were started in parts of Garhwal: by paying money into a common fund from which transport and supplies were arranged, villagers were not required to perform these tasks themselves. In other parts, registers were introduced to ensure that the *utar* burden did not fall disproportionately on any individual or village. Officers were advised to camp only at fixed places and procure grain from merchants subsidized by the government. Rules were framed prescribing what kinds of supplies could be indented for, and loads restricted to 25 seers per coolie. In a bid to 'raise the status of the soldier', retired and serving members of the Garhwal regiments were granted personal exemption from *utar* in 1900, although they were required to provide a substitute. This was extended during World War I into an unconditional exemption for all combatant members of the 39th Garhwalis, and for the direct heirs of soldiers killed in battle. The introduction of these 'palliatives which afford a considerable measure of relief', it was hoped, would ensure the continuance of the system itself.

EARLY RESISTANCE TO FOREST MANAGEMENT

It is important to understand the dislocations in agrarian practice consequent on the imposition of forest management. The working of a forest for commercial purposes necessitates its division into blocks or coupes, which are completely closed after the trees are felled to allow regeneration to take place. Closure to men and cattle is regarded as integral to successful reproduction, and grazing and lopping, if allowed, are regulated in the interests of the reproduction of favoured species of trees. Further, protection from fire is necessary to ensure the regeneration and growth to maturity of young saplings. Thus the practice of firing the forests had to be regulated or stopped in the interests of sustained production of *chir* pine. While the exercise of rights, where allowed, was specified in elaborate detail, rightholders had the onerous responsibility, under Section 78 of the Act, of furnishing knowledge of forest offences to the nearest authority and of extinguishing fires, however caused, in the state forests. In general, as endorsed by the stringent provisions of the Forest Act, considerations of control were paramount.

We find evidence of protest at the contravention of traditional rights well before the introduction of forest management. Charcoal required for smelting iron in the mines of Kumaun was brought from neighbouring forests, and where these lay within the boundaries of villages the inhabitants prevented wood being cut without the payment of *malikhana*. And in the years following the constitution of the DPF in 1893, the Deputy Commissioner (DC) of Garhwal reported that 'forest administration consists for most part in a running fight with the villagers'.

Even where discontent did not manifest itself in overt protest, the loss of control over forests was acutely felt. The forest settlement officer of British Garhwal, at the time of the constitution of the reserved forests, commented:

[The] notion obstinately persists in the minds of all, from the highest to the lowest, that Government is taking away their forests from them and is robbing them of their own property. The notion seems to have grown up from the complete lack of restriction or control over the use by the people of waste land and forest during the first 80 years after the British occupation. The oldest inhabitant therefore, and he naturally is regarded as the greatest authority, is the most assured of the antiquity of the people's right to uncontrolled use of the forest; and to a rural community there appears no difference between uncontrolled use and proprietary right. Subsequent regulations—and these regulations are all very recent—only appear to them as a gradual encroachment on their rights, culminating now in a final act of confiscation. . . [My] best efforts however have, I fear, failed to get the people generally to grasp the change in conditions or to believe in the historical fact of government ownership.

This brings out quite clearly that alternative conceptions of property and ownership lay at the root of the conflict between the state and hill villagers over forest rights. There did not exist a developed notion of private property among these peasant communities, a notion particularly inapplicable to communally-owned and managed woods and pasture land. In contrast, the state's assertion of monopoly over forests was undertaken at the expense of what British officials insisted were *individually* claimed rights of user. With the 'waste and forest lands never having attracted the attention of former governments' there existed strong historical justification for the popular belief that all forests within village boundaries were 'the property of *the villagers*'.

The affirmation of state control—and its obverse, the diminution of customary rights—had an unfortunate effect, with the loss of control contributing to a growing alienation of man from forest. The demarcation of reserved forests having given rise to the speculation that the state would take away other wooded areas from their control, villagers were in certain cases deforesting woodland. But where ownership was still vested in the community, forests continued to be well looked after, such as the twenty-mile stretch between Rudraprayag and Karanprayag in the Alakananda valley, where the government had explicitly made over these forests to the neighbouring villages. As later developments indicated, the small extent of forests under the control of village *panchayats* was invariably well managed.

Discontent with the new forest regulations manifested itself in various other ways. Desertion was considered by a group of villagers belonging to Tindarpur *patti* in Garhwal, who approached an English planter for land 'as the new forest regulations and restrictions were pressing on them so severely that they wished to migrate into another district and climate rather than put up with them any longer'. Another time-honoured form of protest—non-compliance with imposed regulations—was evident when villagers gave misleading information at the time of the fixation of rights. As villagers were 'not in a frame of mind to give much voluntary assistance', one DFO predicted accurately their 'active resentment' at the fire protection of large areas and their closure to grazing and other rights.

The year 1916 witnessed a number of 'malicious' fires in the newly constituted reserved forests. In May the forests in the Gaula range of Naini Tal division were set ablaze. The damage reported was exclusively in *chir* forests, and 28,000 trees which were burnt had to be prematurely felled. For the circle as a whole it was estimated that at least 64 per cent of the 441 fires which burnt 388 square miles (as against 188 fires that had burnt 35 square miles in the preceding year) were 'intentional'.

The 'deliberate and organized incendiarism' of the summer of 1916 brought home to the state the unpopularity of the forest settlement and the virtual impossibility of tracing those who were responsible for the fires. Numerous fires broke out simultaneously over large areas, and often the occurrence of a fire was the signal for general 'firing' in the whole neighbourhood. Forty-four fires occurred in north Garhwal division, almost all in order to obtain a fresh crop of grass. In Naini Tal and in the old reserves of Airadeo and Binsar of Almora district—areas which had been fire protected for many years—an established crop of seedlings was wiped out. The areas chosen for attack had been under both felling and resin-tapping operations. In Airadeo the fire continued for three days and two nights, with 'new fires being started time after time directly a counterfiring line was successfully completed'. As a result of such 'incendiarism', several thousand acres of forest were closed to all rights for a period of ten years.

The protests against the forest settlement were viewed with apprehension in Lucknow, where the Lieutenant-Governor, anticipating the conclusion of World War I, observed that 'it would be a pity for the 39th Garhwalis to come home and find their villages seething with discontent'. Reporting on the situation, the DC of Garhwal concluded somewhat self-evidently that the government could not but affect village life in every *patti* by taking over the forests. The people's 'dislike of the Forest Department and the horde of new underlings let loose on the district' was shared by the soldiers, one of whom stated that if the war had ended before they left Europe, they could have petitioned the King to rescind the settlement. The soldiers' discontent was evidently disturbing, for, as the district officer put it, 'if we can get them on our side it will be a great thing. . .They are already a power in the land and will be still more a power after the war'. The Forest Department continued to be complacent about the possibilities of such discontent blowing over when the villagers had 'greater familiarity with the true aims of the department'. They pointed, alternatively, to the strategic and financial results obtained in a few years of commercial working. But the commissioner of Kumaun, Percy Wyndham, the senior official entrusted with law and order, was considerably less sanguine. He preferred that the hills should continue to provide 'excellent men for sepoys, police and all such jobs'—a prospect jeopardized by the Forest Department which had demarcated the 39th Garhwali villages as if 'the world were made for growing trees and men were vermin to be shut in'. In a situation where the 'Revenue Department holds the whole country by bluff' without the help of regular police, Wyndham was clearly not prepared to enforce new rules on a 'dissatisfied people' and preferred to do away with forest rules and staff altogether.

Contravention of the new regulations concerning lopping, grazing and the duties of rightholders was, as Table 3 indicates, perhaps the most tangible evidence of the continuing friction. Figures from

Table 3

Breaches of Forest Law in UP, 1911–22

Circle Year	Western Circle		Eastern Circle		Kumaun Circle[1]	
	A[2]	B[2]	A	B	A	B
1911–12	786	1798	1167	2306	958	2159
1912–13	881	2182	1230	2424	1203	3374
1913–14	1006	2091	1365	2905	1309	3864
1914–15	1248	2681	1646	3293	1671	5857
1915–16	1401	2662	1514	3029	1610	5796
1916–17	1368	2517	1636	2944	2023	10264
1917–18	1242	2364	1530	2777	2197	11046
1918–19	1153	2058	1723	3167	2167	11024
1919–20	1162	2120	1378	2773	2136	13457
1920–21	926	1618	901	2154	1723	10328
1921–22	1248	2437	1622	839	2070	3799[3]

Source: Annual Progress Report of the United Provinces Forest Development, relevant years.

Note: (1) The total area of reserved forest in U.P. equalled 4.32 million acres, of which 1.91 million acres lay in the Kumaun Circle.

(2) A = Cases; B = Convictions (persons).

(3) Cases dropped due to the recommendation of the Kumaun Forest Grievances Committee.

other forest circles are given by way of comparison. While the number of yearly convictions in the Kumaun circle far exceeded those obtained elsewhere, a comparison with 'Criminal Justice' in Kumaun itself is no less revealing. Over a ten-year period (1898–8), an average of only 416 persons was convicted annually in Almora district on account of cognizable crime of all kinds, ranging from non-payment of excise to murder. Indeed, with the absence of an adequate patrolling staff, many breaches of the forest law went undetected.

The continuing opposition to forest administration bore a strong similarity to traditional methods of social protest in Kumaun and Garhwal. Known as *dhandak*, peasant movements had typically encompassed two major forms of protest. First of all, peasants refused to comply with imposed rules and the officials who enforced these. Occasionally, when the demands grew excessive and were backed by force, villagers fled to the jungles or across political frontiers into British territory. Alternatively, they would catch hold of an offending official, shave his head and moustache, put him on a donkey with his face towards the tail and drive him out of the state. Such non-co-operation at a local level often culminated in a gathering of men drawn from neighbouring villages. Having decided not to cultivate their fields or pay revenue, peasants marched to the capital, accompanied by the beating of drums. Here they demanded an audience with the king and the repeal of the new laws.

In the *dhandak*, physical violence (barring isolated attacks on officials) was conspicuous by its absence. Its socio-cultural idiom was predicated firstly on the traditional relationship between *raja* and *praja*, and secondly on the democratic character of these peasant communities. By protesting in such a manner, peasants actually believed that they were helping the king—to whom they accorded a quasi-divine status—restore justice. Once punishment was inflicted thus on erring officials, the *dhandak* invariably subsided— only to flare up again when fresh cases of tyranny occurred.

The *dhandak* essentially represents a right to revolt which is sanctioned by custom. Hindu scriptures urged obedience to the sovereign as well as the right to revolt when the king failed to protect his people. A form of rebellion sanctioned by customary law has existed in many pre-capitalist societies, from medieval Europe to twentieth-century African kingdoms. In the words of Weber, 'opposition is never directed against the system as such—it is a case of "traditionalist" revolution', the accusation against the ruler being that he failed to observe the traditional limits to his power. In the area covered by my study, the *dhandak* embodied, however, a distinctive form of social protest which continued to be used, albeit with variations, during the colonial period. Vestiges of this form of collective resistance can be found in contemporary peasant movements as well.

THE *Utar* AND FOREST MOVEMENTS, 1921

Meanwhile, village opposition to the *begar* system was matched organizationally by the establishment of the Kumaun Parishad in 1916. This association of local journalists, lawyers and intellectuals, chaired in its initial years by Rai Bahadurs professing loyalty to the King Emperor, underwent a rapid transformation with the onset of the Forest Department and the enhancement of the customary services. The impact of village-level protest and indirectly the upsurges elsewhere in India contributed to a growing radicalization of the Parishad, best exemplified in the person of Badridutt Pande of Almora. As Shekhar Pathak has compellingly shown, Pande, far more than other Kumaun nationalists (such as Govind Ballabh Pant), was acutely aware of the growing discontent among the peasantry. (However, most Parishad leaders were small landholders, like the majority of their kinsmen, and perhaps less alienated from the villages than urban nationalists in many other parts of India). Convinced of the futility of memoranda presented to government by a few individuals based in Almora, Pande and his associates sought to establish branches of the Parishad in the villages of Kumaun. Simultaneously, his weekly *Shakti*, published from Almora, became an important forum in which the begar system and forest rules were made the butt of strident criticism.

In 1920 *Shakti* reported a strike against *utar* by villages in Patti Kairarao, with villagers refusing to pay the fine levied to them. At the annual session of the Kumaun Parishad, held at Kashipur in December 1920, a major conflict arose between those who still hoped to negotiate with the state and village representatives who pressed for direct action. After the reformists had walked out, the latter urged Badridutt Pande and other Parishad leaders to come to the Uttaraini fair. Held in mid-January at Bageshwar (a temple town at the confluence of the Saryu and Gomati rivers), this fair annually attracted 15 to 20,000 pilgrims from all over the hills.

Here matters came to a head. In early January the Conservator of Forests was refused coolies at Dwarahat and Ganai, and anticipating a strike the DC (District Commissioner) of Almora, W.C. Dible, urgently asked the government for a declaration of its future policy (a request summarily dismissed). At Bageshwar a crowd of over ten thousand heard Badridutt pass on a message from Mahatma Gandhi that 'he would come and save them from oppression as he did in Champaran'. When almost everyone responded to a call to raise their hands to show that they would refuse *utar*, Pande continued: 'After abolishing coolie utar' they would agitate for the forests. He would ask them not to extract resin, or saw sleepers, or take forest contracts. They should give up service as forest guard which involves insulting their sisters and snatching their sickles'. Slogans in praise of Mahatma Gandhi and 'Swatantra Bharat' and cries that the government was *anniyayi* (unjust) rent the air. In a dramatic gesture, village headmen flung their coolie registers into the Saryu.

In the weeks following the fair, several officials were stranded when the villages neighbouring Bageshwar declined to supply coolies. Elsewhere, only *khushkharid* (i.e. on payment) coolies were available at extraordinarily high rates. With school masters and other government functionaries extending their support to the movement, Dible hastily summoned the regular police. Pathak has uncovered evidence of at least 146 anti-*begar* meetings in different villages of Garhwal and Kumaun between January and April 1921. When the DFO of Almora complained of the continuing difficulties faced by touring officials, he was tersely told that the district administration was not in a position to 'give you or your department one *utar* coolie'. Requests for *utar* were not made in tracts where they were likely to be refused. In a matter of weeks the state's determination not to dispense with the system itself had broken down, and its abolition followed. In the following year, over 1.6 lakh rupees were spent by the exchequer on the transport and stores of touring officials in the hills. . . .

Following Uttaraini, Pande and his colleagues toured the different *pattis* of Almora, establishing local *sabhas* of the Parishad. Inspired by the success of the anti-*utar* campaign, Pande in his speeches urged the need for direct action in order to recover lost rights over forests. For the 'Government that sells the forest produce is not liable to be called a real Government'—indeed it was precisely these mercenary motives which had made God send Gandhi 'as an incarnation in the form of [a] Bania to conquer Bania Government'. As the reference to Gandhi's caste indicates, the term 'bania' evoked images of power as well as deception: by selling forest produce the state was hastening the erosion of the legitimacy it had once enjoyed in the eyes of the peasantry. At Bageshwar, Badridutt had depicted this transition in tellingly effective symbols. When forest resources and grass were plentiful and easily available, villagers had an abundance of food and drink; but now, he said, 'in place of tins of ghee the Forest Department gives them tins of resin'. Sensing the peasantry's mood after the *utar* strike, Dible had with uncanny prescience predicted the shape of the impending agitation: '[The] next move will be against the Forest Department. Agitators will make a dead set for resin coolies and contractor's coolies engaged in sleeper work, and try to drive them from this work. The people will be incited to commit Forest offences and we shall have serious trouble with fires'. In the coming months breaches of the forest law increased daily, and these included not merely the firing of forests for grass but also 'wholesale cutting of trees'. In Garhwal, too, the popular feeling against the forest policy continued to be 'very bitter'.

The summer of 1921 was one of the driest on record. The failure of the winter rains had contributted to a poor *rabi* crop and money was sanctioned as subsistence *taccavi* in the hill districts. In Totashiling, where the campaign was to be at its most intense, the local branch of the Kumaun Parishad passed a resolution that the people were themselves to decide whether or not to set fire to forest land falling within *san assi* boundaries. From the last week of April a systematic campaign, especially in Almora district, was launched for firing the forest. Instead of assisting in extinguishing these blazes, when called upon to do so under Section 78 of the Forest Act, the villagers directed their energy towards helping the fires to spread. As a consequence the attempted fire protection by the Forest Department of commercially worked areas was a major failure. Of 4 lakh acres of forest in which fire protection was attempted, 2.46 lakh acres were burnt over. The machinery for control of forest offences 'more or less broke down', and an estimated total of 819 offences occurred, of which 395 were definitely known to be 'incendiary'.

Several features of a form of social protest, summarily labelled by the state as 'incendiarism', merit comment. On the one hand this represented an assertion of traditionally exercised rights—the annual firing of the forest floor—circumscribed by the state in the interests of commercial forestry. On the other the areas burnt over were almost exclusively *chir* pine forests being worked for both timber and resin. This wholesale burning of the *chir* reserves represented, according to Wyndham, a 'direct challenge to Government to relax their control over forests'. The intensification of the campaign in Almora and Naini Tal was confined to areas that had been under commercial working for some time and were well served by a network of roads. When fires swept through nearly all the areas being logged, young regeneration was wiped out. Covering nearly 320 square miles of forest, these fires destroyed 11.5 lakh resin channels and 65,000 maunds of resin. At the same time, there is no evidence that the vast extent of broad-leaved forests, also under state control, were affected at all. As in other societies in different historical epochs, this destruction by arson was not simply a nihilistic release but carefully selective in the targets attacked. As Hobsbawm has argued, such destruction is never indiscriminate, for 'what is useful for poor men'—in this instance broad-leaved species, far more than *chir*—is spared.

But, as the analysis of court cases by the collector of Almora indicates, the act of burning the *chir* forests represented a direct confrontation with the colonial authorities. The decision to burn the commercially-worked areas was predicated not merely on their containing the locally almost useless (i.e. in comparison with oak) *chir* pine. For, as Badridutt Pande well understood, the export of forest produce by the state clashed strongly with the subsistence orientation of the hill peasant. In the collector's classification, typical in its detail of the concern on the part of the colonial state to understand—with a view to suppressing—any sign of protest, the fire cases were broken down into the categories shown in Table 4.

Table 4

Fire Cases in Almora, 1921

Category	No. of cases	No. of persons involved
I. *INTENTIONAL*		
A) To paralyse Forest Department (FD) by destroying valuable areas	8	21
B) To cause loss to FD by way of revenge due to hatred	26	45
C) To have good grass for cattle	11	17
D) To cause loss to resin mates out of enmity	2	3
E) To spite another out of enmity	3	5
F) Whose agitation was direct cause of fire	(not available)	13
Total:	50	104
II. *ACCIDENTAL* (This includes smoking or carrying fire within the reserves, the spread of fire from cultivated fields or waste land not under government, etc.)	23	45

Further details which may reveal more about the nature of protest can be gleaned from summary accounts of the court cases. Gangua, aged 16, was one of the several youths 'put up by non-co-operators' to destroy 'valuable regeneration areas' by fire. Nor was participation restricted to men. Thus Durga was sentenced to one month in jail when she 'deliberately set fire to Thaklori forest'. In at least four different instances, witnesses set up by the prosecution were 'won over' by non-co-operators and the cases had to be dropped. Chanar Singh and four others of the Tagnia clan of Doba Talla Katyur were 'affected by lectures' by 'Non-co-operators and a Jogi' and set fire to regeneration areas. This tantalizingly brief reference to the yogi (who was eventually prosecuted) leads one to speculate that the peasantry sought (as in the Uttaraini *mela*) a moral-religious sanction for their acts. No such sanction was required by Padam Singh and Dharam Singh of Katyur, awarded the maximum sentence of seven years rigorous imprisonment, who expressed their opposition to state monopoly in no uncertain terms. In the words of the magistrate: 'The compartment fired was near the village and used by them. They resented the work of the Department in this compartment since it interfered with their use of the compartment. Therefore, they set fire to it deliberately'.

The firing of pine needles for grass occurred in Garhwal as well. With commercial forestry and the protection of regeneration areas from grazing and fire as yet restricted in its operations, the damage to state-controlled forests was not as widespread as in Almora. Yet the DC had convicted 549 persons, 45 for 'direct or indirect incendiarism', and 504 for refusing to extinguish fires, before the recommendations of the Grievances Committee led to all pending cases being dropped. Fires were reported to be most acute in the areas bordering Almora, and in the southern *pattis* of Lansdowne subdivision in the outer hills. With resin-tapping in its infancy, fires were most often started with a view to obtaining fresh grass.

While all social groups participated, the involvement of soldiers in the forest movement of 1921—in the same way as the participation of village headmen in the *utar* campaign—bore witness to the failure of the colonial government's attempt to assimilate them as a part of the indigenous collaborating élite. In Garhwal the fires were most often started by soldiers on leave, but as '99 per cent of the population sympathized with them', their apprehension by the authorities became an impossible task. Four soldiers of the 39th Garhwalis were arrested for threatening or assaulting forest officials.

After the Uttaraini *mela*, ex-soldiers were active among those who helped the Kumaun Parishad form *sabhas* in the villages of the Kosi valley. One soldier said in his speeches that 'Government was not a Raja, but a Bania and Rakshasi Raj and the King Emperor was Ravan'. Recounting his experiences in Europe, where he was wounded, the pensioner described the visit of the King Emperor to his hospital bedside. Asked to state his grievances, 'he complained against *patwaris* and forest guards, but instead of removal of these grievances all that has been given is the Rowlatt Act and Martial Law'. No longer was the king perceived as being bestowed with quasi-divine powers of intervention in order to restore justice and a harmonious relationship between the state and the peasant. As expressed through the symbolism of the epics, the government now embodied not merely the rapacious *bania* but the evil-intentioned demons of Hindu mythology. Ravan, the very personification of evil, was equated with the King Emperor, whose failure (or inability) to stem the expansive growth of the Forest Department and its minions had led to a rapid fall from grace.

For the Kumaun peasant the cohesion and collective spirit of the village community provided the mainspring of political action. The wide-ranging campaign of 1921, though different from a modern social movement in its aims and methods, was far from being a spontaneous outburst of an illiterate peasantry representing a blind reaction to the expropriation of a resource crucial to its subsistence. It expressed, albeit in a far more heightened way, the motivations which underlay the sporadic and localized protests in the early years of forest administration. Expressed through the medium of popular protest were conflicting theories of social relationships that virtually amounted to two world-views. One can meaningfully contrast state monopoly right with the free use of forest by members of the village community as sanctioned by custom—a pattern of use, moreover, regulated by the community as a whole. The exploitation of the pine forests on grounds of commercial profitability and strategic imperial needs was at variance, too with the use of natural resources in an economy wholly oriented towards subsistence. The invocation of the symbols of *bania* and *rakshas*, with all that they stood for, was a natural consequence of this discrepancy. As the paternalist state transormed itself into an agency intruding more and more into the daily life of its subjec population, so its claim to legitimacy floundered. Peasant opposition to this encroachment took the form of consciously determined actions—actions incomprehensible to an observer unfamiliar with the social and cultural heritage of the Kumaun peasant. But set in their socio-historical context, these actions become intelligible and are seen to represent a frontal challenge to state authority, something of which the seemingly docile peasantry had been thought incapable.

Wildlife—Human Conflict in India: An Ecological and Social Perspective

R. SUKUMAR

INTRODUCTION

'Elephants Invade City' screamed the newspaper headlines on 29 January, 1985. The previous morning the students of an engineering college in the suburbs of Bangalore had woken up to find a herd of nine elephants outside their hostel building. The elephants had walked some 15 km through cultivation during the night from the forests of Bannerghatta before entering the college campus. This unusual incident made headlines partly because it happened near a big city. But elephant incursion into human habitation is not something unusual or new. It has been going on ever since man took to agriculture within elephant habitat. The *Gajasastra* (or elephant lore) that can be traced back to the fifth or sixth century BC, narrates that wild elephants invaded the kingdom of Anga and caused considerable damage, a reference no doubt to crop raiding. People in the Indian sub-continent have dealt with 'rogue' elephants and man-eating tigers through the ages in a manner that can only be described as relatively tolerant; otherwise these animals would simply not have survived to this day given the long history of settlement and the large human population. Elsewhere people have often solved their problem by simply wiping out an offending species; an example of this is the extermination of the wolf, a predator on sheep, from Great Britain during the nineteenth century. Religious taboos no doubt played a role in the past in this tolerance towards other creatures. However, in the present context of a rapidly changing society such traditional attitudes to nature are unlikely to sustain the conservation ethos for long. It is both unrealistic and

This paper has been specially written for this volume. Editor.

unjust to expect only a certain section of society, the marginal farmers and tribals, to bear the entire cost of depredatory animals. We have to work towards ameliorating the impact of wildlife on people if conservation of wildlife and their habitats is to gain acceptance among such people who interact with these in their daily lives.

Why conserve wildlife in the first place? There are strong ethical, ecological, economic and aesthetic arguments as to why wildlife has to be conserved (Ehrlich and Ehrlich 1981). The ethical argument is basically that living creatures have an intrinsic right to exist, irrespective of their utility or otherwise to humans. From an ecological view point, large mammals such as the elephant or the tiger play a dominant role in an ecosystem by virtue of their large biomass or position at the summit of an intricate food web. Disappearance of such key species could lead to the disruption of ecosystem functioning, perhaps resulting in extinctions of other species. Economic justifications include the direct value of wild animals as sources of food for people (game ranching), returns from wildlife-oriented tourism and so on. Lastly, wildlife is a source of considerable pleasure for many people, thereby having a therapeutic value in promoting human well-being.

This essay describes the nature of the conflict between large mammals and people, provides ecological explanations for the origins of such conflicts, examines their socio-economic implications and discusses measures that can help in minimizing the impact of animals on people. It illustrates these conflicts by focussing on two mammals, the Asian elephant which is a herbivore and the tiger which is a carnivore.

2. THE NATURE OF THE CONFLICT

Large mammals come into conflict with human interests by destroying crops, livestock or property and sometimes by even killing people.

2.1 *Crop and livestock depredation*: A variety of mammals including elephants, wild pig, deer, rhino and monkeys are known to damage cultivated crops. Damage by wild pig is probably the most widespread because this species is found in almost all forested habitats including highly degraded and fragmented ones. Pigs are commonly killed for this reason but this is not a major conservation issue anywhere. On a more localized scale the damage caused by elephants to crops can be considerable. All cereal and millet crops such as paddy, sorghum, maize and finger millet are potential targets for elephants, as are sugar cane, banana, mango, jack fruit, coconut, oil palm and various legumes. A few estimates are available of the economic loss due to elephants. The loss of crops due to elephants in Palamau, Bihar, was estimated to be Rs 40,000 during 1969–70 (Mishra 1971). In southern India, which has a wild elephant population of 6000–7000, the damage to crops was estimated to be about Rs 6.5 million during 1981–3 (Sukumar 1989). In the north-eastern states of West Bengal, Assam, Arunachal and Meghalaya the loss seems to be much greater (Lahiri Choudhury 1980). Compared to these the loss to highly commercial agricultural ventures may be even greater; in peninsular Malaysia the damage to oil palm and rubber plantations by elephants runs into millions of dollars annually, averaging some 20 million dollars for a single agency FELDA (Blair *et al.* 1979). In addition to feeding on crops, elephants may also damage or destroy houses and other property occasionally.

Carnivores such as tiger, leopard, lion and wild dog prey upon domestic livestock either by entering settlements in the vicinity of their habitat or when these come into the jungle for grazing. The Project Tiger authorities paid compensation for 622 cattle killed by tigers or leopards during 1974–83 near the Bandipur reserve. The Melghat Project Tiger authorities pay compensation for about 250–300 livestock kills every year (M. Watwe, pers. comm.). Many more cattle, buffaloes, sheep and goats would have fallen prey in other forest areas. The buffaloes kept by the Maldharis in the vicinity of the Gir Sanctuary of Gujarat form a substantial proportion of the diet of the lions there (R. Chellam, pers. comm.). Similarly, domestic livestock constitute 30 per cent of the tiger kills near the boundary of the Chitawan National Park in Nepal (Mishra 1982).

2.2 *Manslaughter*: Of greater concern than loss to crops or livestock is the incidence of human kills by large mammals. Wild elephants kill on average 30–50 people in south India, 30–50 in West Bengal, 5–10 in Uttar Pradesh, over 50 in Assam and perhaps another 50 in other states each year. A study in southern India showed that about 45 per cent of the incidents occurred within settlements when elephants came to raid crops and the rest occurred inside the forest (Sukumar 1989).

The man-eating tiger has been a problem historically in certain regions of the sub-continent such as Bengal, Central India and the *terai* tract along the Himalayan foothills (McDougal 1987). Tigers killed 57 people on the average each year during 1975–84 in the Sundarbans of India and Bangladesh (Khan 1987, Sanyal 1987). Most of the victims here have been fishermen and honey collectors. Elsewhere in the sub-continent another 10–20 people are killed annually. We must, however, remember that the incidence of man-eating by tigers in the sub-continent has come down substantially during the past two centuries due to elimination of over 95 per cent of the tiger population. In the year 1822 over 500 people were killed by wild animals, chiefly tigers, in a single district, the Khandesh of Bombay Presidency (McDougal 1987). In 1877 the tiger claimed 798 human victims in British India, while the figure was 909 during 1908.

The Asiatic lion is today confined to a single location, the Gir Sanctuary in Gujarat. In the past lions have not been a serious threat to human life but in recent years there have been incidents of lions straying far away from their habitat and mauling people.

3. An Ecological Perspective to the Conflict

Why do elephants raid crops or why do tigers take to man-eating? Although we do not have all the answers as yet, the basic causes of such behaviour can now be deduced from ecological theory and a knowledge of the social life of these mammals. These can be explained both in proximate terms (i.e. the immediate compulsion for an action) and in the ultimate (i.e. evolutionary) sense.

3.1 *Habitat and resource depletion*: As people continue to occupy more and more forest land for settlement, agriculture, building dams and other forms of development, the shrinking habitat area compresses the wildlife populations to levels beyond its carrying capacity. The carrying capacity is the number of individuals or biomass of a population that can be supported given the area and productivity of the habitat. When the carrying capacity is exceeded the interaction between people and wildlife is intensified in many ways. In the first place the increase in the length of the 'boundary' between forest and human settlement on a local scale means that animals would make more frequent contact with settlement due to chance alone. Large mammals such as tiger and elephant move long distances both daily and seasonally. It is not unusual for them to move 10 or 15 km a day or have a home range of over 100 square kilometers. Small or fragmented habitats surrounded by cultivation are simply incompatible with the conservation of large mammals. Often new settlements spring up along traditional migration paths of elephant herds and these are naturally subject to damage before the animals find other routes or restrict their extensive seasonal movements.

Apart from restricting the area, and thus the amount of resources, available for wildlife populations, human exploitation of the forest for timber, fuel wood and fodder may also degrade the habitat and lower the resource base considerably. This would be especially true if resources flow out of a region without a corresponding input. Bamboo stocks for instance have been overexploited over much of country's forests for use by paper mills (Prasad and Gadgil 1981). To a limited extent the exploitation of primary forest does not necessarily lower habitat quality for large mammals. Typically the highest biomass of large mammals is found in forest and grassland under some human use (Bell 1971) but this trend does not continue indefinitely. For example, shifting cultivation practised on a small scale with sufficient interval between rotation of sites does not seem to have any adverse impact on wildlife populations. On the other hand, the expansion of human populations has increased the area under shifting cultivation and decreased the period between rotation of sites to less than five years in many states in the northeast and in Orissa. The result is that the land remains perpetually as low quality grassland dominated by weedy plants such as *Imperata, Chromolaena* and *Lantana* with no tree cover. This has been disastrous for elephant populations here because elephants need not only grassland but also forest for meeting their nutritional requirements (Lahiri Choudhury 1980, Sukumar 1989). Elephants may also be subject to heat stress in the absence of adequate shade in pure grasslands.

Competition between people and wildlife for resources may also occur indirectly. Large numbers of domestic livestock held in the vicinity of wildlife areas compete with the herbivores for forage. There have been no quantitative studies to clearly evaluate the impact of livestock on wildlife populations in India but this can be often deduced from subjective observations. Overgrazing by livestock reduces the amount of forage available for wild herbivores both directly and indirectly by causing adverse changes to soil properties through trampling. Ungulates such as deer, antelopes and gaur, which have a high degree of food niche overlap with livestock, seem to be the most affected by this competition. Reduction in ungulate prey for the carnivores would force them to hunt domestic livestock.

When wildlife populations exceed the carrying capacity of their habitat, either due to reduction in its area or reduction in food resources through competition from people, they would tend to spill over into settlements, if their numbers are not being correspondingly reduced artificially or by natural processes. A natural reduction in a population may occur through lower fertility and or higher mortality, although in large mammals there is usually considerable time lag before this actually takes place. On the other hand, more commonly the reduction has occurred through hunting (as of the tiger) or capture (as of the elephant).

3.2 *Optimum foraging theory and conflict*: Ecological theory predicts that animals would tend to feed in a manner that maximizes their nutrient (energy, protein, minerals, etc.) intake in the minimum possible time (reviewed by Pyke *et al.* 1977). A tiger should, therefore, hunt prey that will provide it sufficient meat (that is, nutrients) with the least possible effort. It is easy to see that cattle, adapted to a relatively secure life under domestication, would fall prey to a carnivore far more easily than their wild cousin, the gaur, or the fleet-footed antelopes.

A study on crop raiding by elephants showed that cultivated grasses such as paddy and finger millet provide more protein, calcium and sodium than the wild grasses consumed during the corresponding season (Sukumar 1989, 1990). It is important to realize here that the proximate reason for elephants to prefer cultivated crops is their higher palatability. Succulent finger millet plants or sweet sugar canes would surely appeal to the elephant's palate much more than fibrous and siliceous grasses found in the wild. Herbivores are also able to detect minerals such as calcium and sodium by taste; hence they often eat soils rich in such minerals. But such an ability to seek out the most nutritious plants or parts is also adaptive in that it promotes better health and ultimately better reproduction. Thus, crop raiding by elephants or predation on domestic livestock by tigers can be thought of simply as an outcome of their foraging strategy shaped by evolution. This has important implications in planning for the control of such depredations. A certain level of depredation would still persist even if the wildlife species concerned had adequate food resources in the wild.

3.3 *Animal social organization and conflict*: The social organization of the animal may play a role in promoting its conflict with people. Many large mammals are polygynous and some males tend to sire a large number of offspring while other males may fail to reproduce; by contrast the females would contribute more equally to the next generation (Trivers 1985). Evolution has favoured in such species a dimorphism between the sexes, with the male being typically larger in size than the female. A large body size is important for the male to dominate other males in the competition for mates and thus reproduce more successfully. Good nutrition and body condition are also essential for a male during the 'rut' when most of the breeding occurs. The male of the species thus has a greater stake in obtaining the nutrition necessary for growing large and healthy, and its willingness to take greater risks to achieve this goal may result in a more intensified conflict with human interests (Sukumar, in press).

The adult male elephant for instance raids crops about five to six times more frequently than does an average number of a female-led family group (Sukumar & Gadgil 1988, Sukumar 1989). Because of its larger body size and food requirements, the male elephant also consumes about twice as much crops per raid as a family herd member. Added to this the adult male may also damage the economically more valuable crops such as coconut. The net result is that the average adult male elephant ends up causing over 20 times as much damage in economic terms as compared to that inflicted by an average member of a family herd. An adult male caused damage worth Rs 6700 per year compared to only Rs 320 by a herd member (Sukumar 1989).

The male elephant is also the chief culprit in cases of manslaughter. An investigation of over 150 such cases in southern India revealed that sub-adult and adult male elephants (above 10 years of age) were responsible for over 80 per cent of the killings even though they made up less than 10 per cent of the total elephant population. Nearly half the incidents occurred within cultivation (and the rest inside forest) and most of these were due to raiding male elephants.

The social organization of tigers may also drive the males into a more intense conflict with people. Male tigers have to establish and defend territories if they are to breed successfully (Sunquist 1981). When a male tiger is ousted from its territory by a rival male it may move into peripheral habitats adjoining settlements where it is likely to come into frequent contact with people. Male tigers with wounds or a 'wounded pride' can be expected to be aggressive. Some of the incidents of manslaughter by tigers near the Royal Chitwan National Park in Nepal seem to have been due to this reason (McDougal 1987). A study of the man-eating phenomenon in the Sundarbans showed that 10 out of 13 man-eating tigers were males and these accounted for 86 per cent of the victims (Hendrichs 1975). It is however not absolutely clear from other accounts of man-eaters that the male tiger is always the *bete noire*; there have been many notorious female man-eaters as well (e.g. see Corbett 1944).

4. MANAGEMENT OF ANIMAL-HUMAN CONFLICTS

The impact of wildlife on people has to be minimized through a variety of methods, ranging from creating wildlife proof barriers to selectively culling offending individuals to providing a measure of social security for people.

4.1 *Barriers to wildlife movement*: Physical barriers to prevent animals from crossing into human settlements may be feasible only in few cases. A barrier against elephants would be very expensive to create. Trenching the boundary of cultivation with forest is the most common method used in the country, but the costs may range from Rs 25,000 to 50,000 per kilometer. There would be additional maintenance costs. If a trench is even slightly shallower than the minimum depth of 7 feet needed to keep away elephants, a large bull might negotiate it. Even otherwise elephants might cross a trench by digging the soil with their feet, or more commonly the trench eventually fills up with soil washed down by rain. In actual practice most trenches fail due to improper maintenance, unless they surround a small piece of land.

4.2 *Psychological warfare*: Animals learn much of their behaviour during their lifetime and it may be possible to deceive them into learning to fear people or objects that protect them. The most successful example of this 'psychological warfare' is the imaginative use of electrified dummies and masks against tigers in the Sundarbans of West Bengal (Sanyal 1987, Rishi 1988). Tigers were conditioned to associate humans with pain by allowing them to attack electrified clay models placed in natural settings inside the jungle. These dummies resembling fishermen and honey-collectors are dressed in used clothing to give them a human smell and wrapped in wire. The wire is connected to a 12-volt battery through an energizer which delivered a current of 230 volts. Man-eaters attacking the dummies receive a shock but a safety fuse and a low current of 20-25 milliamps ensure that this is not fatal to the animal (Sanyal 1987). The incidence of man-eating reduced by half, from an average of 45 per year during 1975–82 to 21 per year during 1983–5. Since then the tiger has been tricked by another simple, cheap device—a mask resembling a human face worn at the *back* of the head. Tigers generally attack their victims from behind, catching them off-guard. A mask worn in this fashion gives the predator an impression that it is being watched and hence it may be reluctant to attack. Some 2500 masks made of a rubberized plastic were distributed during November 1986–October 1987 among honey-collectors, fishermen and wood-cutters permitted to work inside the buffer zone of the Sundarbans reserve. Not a single person using the mask fell victim to a tiger. On the other hand, all the 30 people killed during this period were not using a mask (Rishi 1988). Although it is too early to say whether the tiger can be continued to be fooled in this manner, the success of these techniques is remarkable.

Electrified barriers against elephants have also been parttly successful. A high-voltage electric fence typically consists of two or three wires appropriately strung on hard wood or stone posts and connected to an energizer which draws power from the mains or a battery. A current of 5000 volts is given in pulses of very short duration, about 1/3000 second. An elephant coming in contact with the wire would receive a severe shock but is in no danger because of the short duration of the current. Electric fences in oil palm plantations in Malaysia are reported to have a 80 per cent success rate. They are also considerably cheaper than trenches, although some feel that in a country like India a labour-intensive method like trenching is more appropriate. In the course of time elephants also learn

.that the tusks and the soles of the feet are poor conductors and use these to break down electrified fences in order to enter cultivation.

4.3 *Habitat management*: The impact of wildlife on people can be ameliorated to some extent by proper management of its habitat. Such management has to be balanced between the needs of wildlife and people. Land-use for agriculture or other forms of development near wildlife areas has often proceeded in a haphazard fashion. To take an example the cultivation of sugar cane near forest often draws prey animals and tigers behind them. Tigers may even give birth in sugar cane fields which resemble their natural tall grassland habitats. The stage is thus set for confrontation between tigers and people. Sugar cane is also too great a temptation for elephants. Not only should attention be paid in future to the type of agriculture being encouraged near wildlife habitats but also to maintaining the integrity of the habitat. It is better to have a single compact block of natural habitat for wildlife with the minimum interface with human settlement, rather than have a fragmented habitat of equal area interspersed with cultivation. This may inevitably mean that some settlements in certain problematic areas have to be translocated.

Use of forests for human needs has to be properly regulated. All too often the natural habitat for wildlife has been devastated through indiscriminate cutting of trees, raising monoculture plantations of exotic species such as eucalyptus, mining, construction of dams and overgrazing by livestock. Illegal hunting of prey species such as deer has to be curbed in order to provide an adequate food base for the carnivores. When the carrying capacity of the habitat is reduced the excess animals tend to spill over into human settlements. On the other hand, the opposite trend has also occurred in some places. The creation of reservoirs through dam construction has provided perennial water sources for wildlife, thereby increasing their populations artificially beyond the normal carrying capacity of the habitat, and causing them to intrude into settlements. It is beyond the scope of this essay to go into specific details of habitat management; each region has to be obviously dealt with according to the peculiar conditions prevailing there.

4.4 *Animal population management*: Wildlife populations that come into severe conflict with human interests may have to be directly managed to keep their levels below tolerable limits. This will involve removal of problem animals from the population. A proper under-standing of the demography of the species is important if one is to ensure that a viable population is maintained. One example of how elephant populations can be managed to minimize conflict and yet maintain their viability can be outlined from a synthesis of our knowledge of social organization, demography and population genetics of the species. It is clear that the adult male elephants are inherently more predisposed to raiding crops as a consequence of social organization. The removal of an adult male elephant from the population would have a far greater effect in reducing crop-damage (by a factor of 20 in economic terms) and saving human lives than the removal of an elephant from a family herd. Our under-standing of demographic processes in such polygynous species also show that the loss of a certain proportion of males is not likely to affect the intrinsic rate of growth of the population (Sukumar 1989). The removal of females from the population would certainly reduce its growth rate. Hence, the selective culling of male elephants identified as inveterate crop raiders or rogues would be the best form of population management. Some of this culling can simply be cap-ture for domestication. A successful example of this is the capture of nine elephants by chemical immobilization in the Kattepura Forest Reserve of Karnataka during 1986 (Appayya 1989). All the elephants were males which had moved into this small forest patch, isolated by a reservoir, and were in regular conflict with nearby settlements.

Beyond a certain point the distorted sex ratio, with a predomi-nance of females, caused by selective removal of males may lead to genetic problems such as loss of variation and inbreeding depression if population sizes are small (Frankel and Soulé 1981). In southern India the high rates of poaching of male elephants for tusks has created some of the most unequal sex ratios known for elephant populations anywhere. Further culling of males here may not be justified other than in exceptional cases. Other elephant populations such as those in northeast India have a high proportion of tuskless males (up to 80 per cent of the male segment). These can be expected to have a more equal sex ratio and hence can tolerate a certain amount of selective male removal (Sukumar, in press).

Similar arguments may be applicable to other polygynous mam-mals that come into conflict with people. The tiger is highly endan-gered and every effort should be made to avoid culling of these animals. However, there would be no other option but to capture or shoot identified man-eaters. The decision to cull should be easier to take if the offender is known to be a male tiger.

4.5 *Social security*: To mitigate the impact of wildlife on people, a variety of social security schemes should be made a part of conservation plans. Project Tiger did take this into account by providing compensation for livestock killed by tigers or leopards near reserves. Many schemes are in operation now but in practice some of these are not adequate. States such as Karnataka and West Bengal do have schemes for compensating damage to crops by elephants, but others such as Tamilnadu do not. Crop insurance has yet to be seriously tried out anywhere. Moreover, a serious problem with social welfare schemes in a country like India is that they are prone to abuse through corruption.

Compensation for loss of life is generally made in most states but here again the amounts are low. The maximum amount paid is about Rs 15,000 while in states like Tamilnadu this may be as low as Rs 2000. The compensation for people killed by elephants within cultivation should be higher than for those who fall victim inside the forest; the reasoning here is that the elephant had no business to enter legal settlement. Under the law a person can probably kill an elephant within settlement and get away by pleading self-defence, although people hardly ever resort to this. In some states such as Tamilnadu, the tribals engaged in forestry operations or collection of minor produce are insured under the Janatha Accident Insurance Scheme. An annual premium of Rs 12 provides a cover for Rs 15,000 against accidental death. Such insurance schemes must be popularized in regions where people face the risk of being killed by animals. These can be promoted through co-operative societies as is being done in Tamilnadu.

CONCLUSIONS:

There is a pressing need both to conserve wildlife and to minimize its impact on human lives and property. We live in a rapidly changing society. On the one hand a highly materialistic culture is arising—witness the advertising culture particularly over television which reaches a large section of the population—while on the other the majority of people barely manage to survive. When the rich and middle classes are caught up in the consumerist boom (really an antithesis of conservation), it will be too much to expect the poor to remain as silent spectators. Conflict over access to natural resources is bound to only increase in future. Conservation can succeed only if the legitimate aspirations of people dependent on forests for their livelihood can be met by the rest of society. To cite an example of the prevailing attitude—when officials tried to explain to villagers in the Gir Sanctuary the need to protect lions, they were told to take all the lions with them to Delhi!

Today the local people see sanctuaries or national parks as simply the pleasure resorts of the affluent. There is urgent need to reorient management of our wildlife reserves so as to pass on economic benefits to local communities. This can be done in many ways. In the Chitwan Park of Nepal, an attempt is being made to balance the needs of people and wildlife by allowing people to remove tall grass from the park in a fashion that does not cause any adverse impact (Mishra 1982). About 30,000–50,000 permits are issued each year and the value of the produce removed during 1978–82 was about 3 million US dollars. Thus the Chitwan people recognize that most of the tall grass outside the park has disappeared, but the reserve is protecting those left in the district.

Wildlife reserves have enormous potential for generating income from tourism, but so far the benefits from this have not reached the local people in the way it should have. If an adequate proportion of the income derived from tourism is retained by the local economy there would be increased motivation for people to value wildlife and their habitats rather than deplete them through over-grazing, wood cutting or illegal hunting. Such schemes have been successfully tried out in the Luangwa valley of Zambia (Lewis *et al.* 1990). Not only do the resident villagers participate in wildlife management, considerable revenues generated through wildlife *safaris* are retained by the local communities. As a result poaching has dropped dramatically and village attitudes toward wildlife conservation become more positive. It is time that we also take bold new approaches towards reconciling economic development with conservation. In the words of ecologist Norman Myers, 'Conservation should not only sustain the spirit but also the stomach'.

References

Appayya, M. K.,
1989   Destroy the Jungle, Move the Elephants, *Sanctuary*,9 (No. 3), 48–51.

Bell, R. H. V.,
1971   A Grazing Ecosystem in the Serengeti, *Scientific American*, 224, 86–93.

Blair, J. A. S., Boon, G. G. & Noor, N. M.,
1979   Conservation or Cultivation: The Confrontation between the Asian Elephant and Land Development in Peninsular Malaysia, *Land Development Digest* 2, 27–59.

Corbett, J.,
1944   *The Man-Eaters of Kumaon*, Oxford University Press, London.

Ehrlich, P. R., & Ehrlich, A. H.,
1981   *Extinction : The Causes and Consequences of the Disappearance of Species*, Random House.

Frankel, O. H., & Soulé, M. E.,
1981   *Conservation and Evolution*, Cambridge University Press, Cambridge, U. K.

Hendrichs, H.,
1975   The Status of the Tiger *Panthera tigris* (Linn., 1758) in the Sundarbans Mangrove forest (Bay of Bengal). *Saugetieri-kundliche Mitteilungen*, 23, 161–99.

Khan, M. A. R.,
1987   The Problem Tiger of Bangladesh, in *Tigers of the World: The Biology, Biopolitics, Management and Conservation of an Endangered Species*, ed. R. L. Tilson & U. S. Seal, Noyes Publications, Park Ridge, New Jersey, pp. 92–6.

Lahiri Choudhury, D. K.,
1980   An Interim Report on the Status and Distribution of Elephants in Northeast India, in *The Status of the Asian Elephant in the Indian Sub-continent* (IUCN/SSC Report), ed. J. C. Daniel, pp. 43–58, Bombay Natural History Society, Bombay.

Lewis, D., Kaweche, G. B. & Myenya, A.,
1990   Wildlife Conservation Outside Protected Areas—Lessons from an Experiment in Zambia, *Conservation Biology*, 4, 171–80.

McDougal, C.,
1987   The Man-eating Tiger in Geographical and Historical Perspective. In *Tigers of the World : The Biology, Biopolitics, Management and Conservation of an Endangered Species*, ed. R. L. Tilson & U. S. Seal, Noyes Publications, Park Ridge, New Jersey, pp. 435–48.

Mishra, H. R.,
1982   Balancing Human Needs in Nepal's Royal Chitwan Park, *Ambio* 11(5), 246–51.

Mishra, J.,
1971   An Assessment of Annual Damage to Crops by Elephants in Palamau District, Bihar, *Journal of the Bombay Natural History Society*, 68, 307–10.

Prasad, S. N., & Gadgil, M.,
1981   *Conservation of Bamboo Resources of Karnataka*, Karnataka State Council for Science and Technology, Bangalore.

Pyke, G. H., Pulliam, H. R. & Charnov, E. L.,
1977   Optimal Foraging: A Selective Review of Theory and Test, *Quarterly Review of Biology*, 52, 137–53.

Rishi, V.,
1988   Man, Mask and Maneater, *Tigerpaper* Jul–Sep. 1988, pp. 9–14.

Sanyal, P.,
1987   Managing the Man-eaters in the Sundarbans Tiger Reserve of India—A Case Study, in *Tigers of the World: The Biology, Biopolitics, Management and Conservation of an Endangered Species*, ed. R. L. Tilson & U. S. Seal, Noyes Publications, Park Ridge, New Jersey, pp. 427–34.

Sukumar, R.,
1989   *The Asian Elephant : Ecology and Management*, Cambridge University Press, Cambridge, U. K.

Sukumar, R.,
1990   Ecology of the Asian Elephant in Southern India. II. Feeding Habits and Crop Raiding Patterns, *Journal of Tropical Ecology*, 6, 33–53.

Sukumar, R.,
(In Press)   The Management of Large Mammals in Relation to Male Strategies and Conflict with People, *Biological Conservation*.

Sunquist, M. E.,
1981   The Social Organization of Tigers (*Panthera tigris*) in Royal Chitwan National Park, Nepal, *Smithsonian Contributions to Zoology*, 336, 1–98.

Trivers, R. L.,
1985   *Social Evolution*, Benjamin/Cummings, Menlo Park, California.

Further Readings for Section III

As we have observed, studies of the sociology and history of conflicts over nature in India have been dominated by work on forest
conflicts, though in the wake of popular movements against large
dams, water conflicts are now attracting scholarly attention. A
countrywide analysis of forest-based resistance in colonial India
may be found in Ramachandra Guha and Madhav Gadgil, 'State
Forestry and Social Conflict in British India', *Past and Present*,
number 123, May 1989 (also reproduced in David Hardiman, editor,
Peasant Resistance in India, 1858–1914 (New Delhi : Oxford University
Press, 1992)). Going much further back in time, an interesting 'ecological' interpretation of the conflict between forest peoples and
agro-pastoralists can be found in the chapter titled 'The Palace of
Maya' in Irawati Karve's study of the Mahabharata, *Yuganta : the
End of an Epoch* (1968 : reprint New Delhi : Disha Books, 1992).
   Outside the subcontinent there is a wide range of studies to
draw upon. William Cronon's *Changes in the Land : Indians, Colonists
and the Ecology of New England* (New York : Hill and Wang, 1983)
explores the ecological roots of the conflicts between native Ameri-
cans and European colonists in the northeastern United States. In
its skilful integration of ecological, economic and social factors,
Cronon's book could well serve as a model for regional ecological
histories of India. A fine study of the links between colonialism
and socio-ecological change in Africa, likewise of much relevance
to the Indian context, is Helge Kjekshus' *Ecology Control and
Economic Development in East African History* (Berkeley: University
of California Press, 1977). Also set in that continent is Richard
Grove and David Anderson, editors, *Conservation in Africa* (Cambridge: Cambridge University Press, 1989), with a particularly valuable section on the social implications of national park management.

IV

Towards Environmental Renewal

The bulk of the selections in previous sections focussed on a particular region or resource. Our two concluding essays have a far wider sweep. At once reflective and programmatic, they offer acute diagnoses of the social processes behind ecological degradation even as they outline the elements of an environmentally benign, and socially humane, strategy of development.

In his contribution, A.K.N. Reddy uses technology choice as an entry point into the environment-development debate. He argues that many modern technologies tend to centralize power, save labour, degrade the environment, and intensify social inequalities. He thus cautions against the wholesale import of modern technology into the developing world. Finally, Reddy offers a comprehensive set of criteria by which various technological options can be assessed, and choices made in keeping with the imperatives of development, equity, local self reliance, social control, and environmental sustainability.

While broadly sharing Reddy's outlook on the interactions between technology, society and the environment, Anil Agarwal's essay is illustrative rather than analytical. He uses a wide array of examples from different resource sectors in highlighting the intimate links between intensification of resource use, environmental degradation and poverty. Sensitive to the class and gender dimensions of inequality, the essay speaks of a deep engagement with patterns of resource use and abuse in urban and rural India. On the conceptual plane, he offers the notion of 'Gross Nature Product' as being a more accurate indicator, compared to the conventional Gross National Product, of levels of development and prosperity in a biomass based economy.

The selections in this section are notable for two other reasons. While concerned primarily with the developing world, both essays contain a series of suggestive comparisons between environmental concerns in rich and poor, or First and Third World, countries. Again, while penned by an energy scientist and environmental writer respectively, both contributions combine a sure grasp of the ecological context with a nuanced understanding of changing social structures. In the end, it is this ability to transcend the boundary between biophysical and socio-cultural approaches that marks out social ecology from orthodox social science.

Technology, Development and the Environment: An Analytical Framework

A. K. N. REDDY

CRITICISMS OF MODERN TECHNOLOGY

Over the past few years, the case for environmentally sound and appropriate technologies has been repeatedly stated in different ways and from various standpoints. This quest for alternatives has invariably been based on implicit or explicit criticisms of the pattern of technologies now current in the industrialized, developed countries and in the process of massive transfer to the developing countries. These are the technologies which have been developed with staggering and increasing rapidity, particularly over the past thirty years. . . .

The mounting criticisms of modern technology that have emerged not only from the developing countries, but as strongly from the developed countries, constitute the basis for the recommendation of an alternative pattern of technologies. Hence, a description of these criticisms must serve as an introduction to the concept of environmentally sound and appropriate technologies.

The various criticisms of modern technology can be classified into three broad categories: (1) Environmental; (2) Economic; and (3) Social; but the overlap between these categories prevents an unambiguous classification. Further, it is often difficult to establish the precise extent to which modern technology is the sole causal factor responsible for the effects eliciting the criticisms, and the

Excerpted from A. K. N. Reddy, *Technology, Development and the Environment: A Reappraisal*, United Nations Evironment Programme, 1979.

Notes and References omitted. Editor.

extent to which the overall social structure in which technology operates is in fact the crucial factor. But such difficulties are inevitable when two systems, such as technology and society, are closely interrelated, strongly interacting and dynamically involved. Thus, in many respects, the classification of criticisms is essentially heuristic.

DEVELOPED COUNTRIES

Environmental Criticisms

The prolific advances of modern technology in the developed countries have led to spectacular increases in affluence, but it has been asserted that this affluence has not necessarily resulted in an environment more conducive to the physical and mental well-being of man. Indeed, with the increasing deployment of modern technology, man's welfare has been threatened by escalating levels of pollution—pollution of the air that he breathes, the water that he drinks, the food that he eats, the quietness that he needs (instead of 'the decibel inferno') and the beauty of nature that he enjoys. This tragedy of progress in technology being associated with deterioration of the environment has been too well documented to need repetition here. . . .

At the same time, the nature of these technologies (their scale, their demands on energy, water, etc.) has a determining influence on the structure and functioning of human settlements. In particular, urban gigantism has become increasingly predominant; and with it, has followed the aggravation of psychological stresses and social tensions, until many a famous metropolis has been left with a decaying core of slums, crime and insecurity. Simultaneously, these giant cities have had major environmental impacts arising from their exorbitant demands for water, energy, sanitation, transportation and housing.

All this hyper-activity of production and consumption has involved a scale of 'exploitation of natural resources'—the telling phrase used in common parlance—unprecedented in human history. The word 'exploitation', which accurately describes the essence of the man-nature relationship implicit in modern technology, connotes the very opposite of efficient resource management. No wonder there is alarm at the rapid rate with which non-renewable resources are being depleted. The story can be and has been illustrated with innumerable examples, [such as], petroleum and minerals. This mismanagement, which it is argued is an inherent feature of modern technology, extends even to the renewable resources of air, water and land. In short, modern technology has been criticised because it is based on the assumption that nature is an inexhaustible source for the satisfaction of man's escalating resource needs and a limitless sink for his wastes. Modern technologies do not explicitly concern themselves with 'the full and heavy responsibility of managing all the resources—human and natural—of this planet'.

The effects of this irresponsibility are already evident in the disturbance of the finely adjusted ecological balances of nature through pollution, reckless use of resources, elimination or near elimination of various species (blue whales, for instance), destruction of forests, etc. The question is not one of the intrinsic value of stability in ecosystems, but of the inevitably engendered risks that modern technology brings in its wake. These risks derive from the fact that the effects of these technologies are invariably multiple, often uncontrolled and rarely predictable and foreseen. Further, the gravity of the risks vary from relatively trivial ones like automobile accidents to potentially catastrophic ones such as all-out nuclear warfare or destruction of the life-sustaining properties of the biosphere. Some of these risks may be cumulative, such as the build-up of nuclear wastes or of optically active pollutants in the atmosphere, or they may be discrete risks, like genetic engineering accidents. . . .

According to the critics, these diverse, but deleterious, environmental consequences stem from the following fundamental characteristics of modern technology:

i) its pursuit of economies of scale leads to an ever-increasing size of the productive units; and this obsession with large-scale production results in a constantly increasing magnitude of perturbation of natural ecosystems through the spatial localization of pollutant sources and the temporal increase of the rate of emission and discharge of these pollutants;

ii) These gigantic productive units are highly interdependent by way of inputs and outputs, and they also place stringent demands on infrastructures; hence, these units must be agglomerated into small areas of intense industrialization, and thus compel the concentration of millions of working people into crowded metropolises which then display the well-known environmental problems of excessively large human settlements;

iii) The constant urge to satisfy the needs of individual consumption and sustain the large productive units results in a continuous drive to develop and distribute luxury products, which are ever changing in appearance and form, but essentially similar in function and content; and this obsession with product technology is the root cause of the rape and exhaustion of resources, the high degree of product obsolescence and the culture of throw-away objects;

iv) The major role of military objectives in determining the development of technology has resulted in the arsenals of many developed countries being filled with weapons so terrible that, if ever used, all life on earth can be destroyed;

v) Its growing energy intensiveness leads, on the one hand, to centralized energy production with an increasing environmental impact, and on the other hand, to a reckless profligacy in the use of energy sources, particularly fossil fuels.

Economic Criticisms

From the economic point of view, the major criticism of modern technology is that it tends to magnify inequalities between countries, and within countries (including developed ones). Thus, it plays a crucial role in making inequality recursive and increase with time.

The contention underlying this criticism is that an inequality in the distribution of purchasing power leads to a skewed demand structure, which in turn influences technology to respond more avidly to the needs of the rich while assigning lower priority to the needs of those who exert weaker demand. The result is the emergence of technologies of products, technologies of production and technologies of resource use that are more responsive and accessible to the privileged than to the underprivileged. And thus, one comes to the next turn of the spiral . . . the increased inequality resulting from the initially unequal access to the new technologies stimulates the development of further advances in technology which will then accentuate the inequalities even more.

Technology has perhaps always played this divisive role, but in the past, the low levels of capital and energy intensity characteristic of primitive technology facilitated virtually equal access. In contrast, modern technology, associated as it is with its high capital and energy intensiveness, tends to be intrinsically incompatible with equality of access.

This inequality-magnifying effect of modern technology has become particularly evident in the relationship between developed and developing countries, which has its historical roots in the era of the exploitative domination by imperial powers over colonies. Today, modern technology has become the principal instrument for widening the disparities between these two sets of countries and for exacerbating their relationship into an irrational and unjust economic order. This economic order involves a 'world market system. . . (which) . . . has continually operated to increase the power and wealth of the rich (countries) and maintain the relative deprivation of the poor (countries)', according to the Cocoyoc Declaration. And, in this world market system, those who control modern technology acquire the power to dictate prices. Thus, the volume of exports by the poor world increased by one-third over the past 20 years, yet the value of these exports increased by only 4 per cent.

Further, the development and control of modern technolgy today is largely in the hands of the multinational corporations, which originate from and often represent the developed countries, but are increasingly taking assistance of profit-motivated, self-interested independence with respect to their countries of origin. The necessity of bridling these multinational corporations and redressing. the inequality and injustice in the relationship between developed and developing countries, has led the poor nations of the world to demand the establishment of a New International Economic Order, but this demand has not yet exposed the umbilical link between the current economic order and modern technology.

It is not as if modern technology has not had its tell-tale inequality-magnifying effect within the developed countries too. It has been argued that almost every developed country has its own poor (these may be racial minorities, or immigrant workers or inhabitants of a backward region), and the disparities between the rich and the poor in affluent countries are accentuated by modern technologies which tend to cater to the privileged. The underprivileged are thus 'left behind to observe vicariously on television how the lucky three-quarters live'. The social effects of this process are another matter which will be discussed below.

There are two other criticisms of the economic consequences of modern technology which deserve mention. Firstly, modern technology has been designed to process cheap raw materials, which are mostly imported from the developing countries. It has also been wedded—as pointed out earlier—to economies of scale, and has, therefore, resulted in the gigantism of highly capital and energy-intensive production units. These units because of their very size cannot adjust to sudden or prolonged cessation in raw material or energy supplies, or for that matter to major escalations in the prices of these supplies. And thus modern technology has conferred upon the industries based on this technology a vulnerability to drastic changes in international trade. For the same reason, the industries are equally vulnerable to internal disturbances, for example, strikes and sabotage.

Secondly, notwithstanding the apparent economic efficiency of production units based on modern technology, the fact remains that the calculus can be misleading and many costs are ignored because they are externalized and borne by society or by future generations. For example, a factory may discharge its wastes into a river, leaving a township downstream with the cost of purifying the water; or a mine may reduce the cost of mining by working the richest or most accessible strata, but such a procedure only results in future increases in extraction costs which are not reckoned with in the costing.

The economic criticisms outlined above have reiterated a point which emerged from the environmental criticisms: the trend of modern technology to establish larger and larger production units in the name of 'reduction of unit costs' sets off a number of unwelcome consequences. In addition, it appears that the capital-and energy-intensiveness of modern technology; and the orientation of its product technology towards luxury goods for private consumption, give it the highly undesirable characteristic of accentuating economic inequalities between and within countries, and of increasing disparities between the rich and the poor.

Social Criticisms

The tendency of modern technology to respond to the needs of the rich and to accentuate inequalities has proved a highly divisive and disruptive force in the societies of developed countries. By denying the under-privileged access to its constantly publicized benefits, and at the same time forcing them to live cheek by jowl with its unpleasant features such as pollution, modern technology aggravates their feelings of being dispossessed. The ensuring social stresses and tensions constitute an ideal breeding ground for violence. And when these people are also forced by the technology of transportation and human settlements to concentrate in central slums, the city begins a process of decay which spreads outwards from the core. 'The turn of the century could see total disintegration in many of the world's already troubled cities'.

To worsen the whole situation, modern production technology has relentlessly pursued the so-called economies of mass production and automation. In doing so, it has generated a highly-skewed pattern of demand for skills, in which only a few are required to possess a high degree of intellectual capability and/or manual skills, while only the barest minimum of intelligence and dexterity is expected from the vast majority of the working force. To this majority, 'soul destroying, meaningless, mechanical, monotonous, moronic work is an insult to human nature which must necessarily and inevitably produce either escapism or aggression'.

The successful exclusion of craftsmanship and creativity from work in factories based on modern technology results in the sharp separation of work from leisure, and facilitates the spread of the technology of automated entertainment, where participants are replaced by spectators.

The picture is not much rosier at the opposite end of the income spectrum. Modern product technology is specifically designed, on the one hand, to respond to, and on the other hand, to deliberately evoke and stimulate, demands from those privileged with purchasing power. The result is the proliferation of luxury goods for individual consumption and the generation of overly consumption-oriented lifestyles. But 'Man has a limited capacity to absorb material goods. It does not help us to produce and consume more and more if the result is an ever-increasing need for tranquilizers and mental hospitals'.

At the same time, there looms in the background the technology-power equation.

The preoccupation with military technology which confers on

those who control technology a disproportionate share in the exercise of power—power for the external coercion of recalcitrant countries and the internal control of dissenting groups.

DEVELOPING COUNTRIES

Environmental Criticisms

One would not expect the environmental effects of modern technology to be as serious in developing countries, which are not as heavily industrialized. However, this expectation is not borne out in reality. This is because the industrialization of most developing countries has been based on the import of modern technology, which by being highly capital and energy-intensive gravitates to regions where such capital and energy are best mustered, i.e., the urban metropolises. One observes, therefore, large concentrations of modern technology in the cities, and in these limited regions the intensity of industrialization can be of the same order as in the developed countries. As a consequence, such urban concentrations of modern technology often have levels of pollution as high as in the developed countries.

In some cases, the levels of pollution are even higher than in the developed countries because not only is there much less lobbying against environmental degradation, but there may in fact be a view that . . . 'all (debate over) environmental problems may . . . be potential threats to . . . domestic development' and that developing countries 'must not and will not allow themselves to be distracted from the imperatives of economic development and growth by the illusory dream of an atmosphere free from smoke or a landscape innocent of chimney stacks . . .' Such views bring to mind a century-old statement from the then industrializing, now polluted, developed countries: 'Smoke is an indication of work . . . Therefore, we are proud of our smoke'.

The viewpoint that environmental degradation is a necessary and unavoidable stage in development can be criticised on two counts. Firstly, it implies the questionable assumption that development must inescapably follow the path used by the developed countries and involve the deployment of modern technologies; and secondly, it does not reckon with the fact that the poverty-stricken inhabitants of developing countries are more adversely affected by pollution because of their much lower level of nutrition and health. Hence, the under-privileged in poor countries can afford pollution even less than the healthier and better nourished people in rich countries.

Further, the non-existent or far weaker environmental lobbies in the developing countries permit many modern technologies based on the plant or mineral resources of the region to use these resources irrationally and wastefully. Serious environmental effects follow, e.g., rayon factories denuding a whole region of its bamboo forests. Such environmentally unsound irrational and wasteful use of resources can also arise from another effect of the introduction of modern technology in developing countries. This effect stems from the creation of urban markets for rural products coming in the wake of rural impoverishment to upset the ecologically sound traditions of resource management. A revealing example of this process is the way urban markets for charcoal have led (and are leading) to rapid deforestation, soil erosion and desertification, and the manner in which metropolitan demand for cash crops have resulted in taking away land from food crops and using it for cash crops.

Finally, the introduction of modern technologies into developing countries has also been claimed to be directly responsible, through the well-known sequence of rural impoverishment, mass migration to cities and uncontrolled urbanization, for festering slums which have become major problems from the human settlements and environmental point of view. . . .

Economic Criticisms

The most significant criticism of the establishment of modern technology in a developing country is that it triggers off a chain of consequences, the most direct one being a shattering of the traditional rural industries. As a result, many of the occupations traditional in the countryside cease to exist, and vast numbers of people are thrown out of work. The problem is then aggravated by the fact that the urban industries are based on imported modern technology, which by being highly capital-intensive and labour-saving restricts the increase of employment per unit of extra investment. Since unemployment aggravates poverty, and since it is only employment at the higher levels of the capital-intensive modern sector that permits entry into the market of the luxury goods produced by modern industry, the gap between the affluent and the poor increases. Modern technologies of consumption are increasingly energy-intensive, and the inability of the poor to enter the market for commercial energy accentuates disparities. And thus, one observes the well-known phenomenon in the developing countries of inequalities growing with increasing industrialization on the basis of modern technology. Further, rural impoverishment leads to increasing mass migration to the metropolitan centres. This aggravates the problem of slums and shanty towns, which are festering sores of unbelievable poverty frustrating the best intentions of urban planners.

Simultaneously, the traditionally simple and contented ways of life succumb before the onslaught of the consumption-oriented lifestyles stimulated and catered to by modern technology. The demand for a new product-mix gets generated, and this product-mix invariably has a higher import content than the traditional mass-consumption goods which are usually based on local resources. Thus, the balance-of-payments situation of developing countries worsens with increasing industrialization along modern lines. At the same time, the import of modern technology requires payment— for technical fees, royalties, services of foreign experts, license fees, etc. And with the continuous advance of modern technology, the number of payments for the import of technology keeps on escalating. With increasing technical dependence, self-reliance is thwarted more and more. . . .

In the last analysis, this [process] originates from the fact that capital-intensive, labour-saving modern technology is fundamentally inconsistent with the factor proportions of most developing countries, *viz.*, a shortage of capital and an abundance of manpower. The deal is worsened due to two further features of the technology of developed countries: firstly, this technology relies on a global resource-base, rather than on locally available resources, and therefore, a developing country which adopts this technology has necessarily to import many raw materials; secondly, the deliberate bias of this technology towards meeting elite demand has the twin effect of accentuating disparities in consumption and increasing imports. In short, the content of the package deal makes modern technology incompatible with development.

It is the realization of these harsh facts that has moved local and national groups in developing and developed countries, and also many international agencies, to urge an alternative strategy of development based on a pattern of technologies different from modern technology.

Social Criticisms

Further criticisms of modern technology arise from the social effects that it produces in developing countries. These criticisms focus on two main processes: (1) the disintegration of established social forms of organization which have been interwoven through centuries of evolution with ancient modes of production; and (2) the generation of a dual society involving urban islands of affluence amidst vast seas of rural poverty.

The disruption of traditional social forms resulting from the drastic changes in modes of production introduced by modern technology has a telling effect on the family (e.g., the trend away from extended families with their type of social security and towards nuclear families), on structures of authority (e.g. the displacement of village elders by literate entrepreneurs), on traditions of village self-reliance (e.g., the strength of collective self-help giving way to the weakness of dependence on urban-based aid and external development agencies), on social mores (e.g., contentment with one's lot being rejected in favour of acquisitive greed), and so on. It is not suggested here that all was perfect in the ancient social forms, but that usually the 'good' in traditional societies has also been rejected along with the 'bad' and that modernization (customarily equated with westernization) is not necessarily conducive to social harmony and individual peace.

The dissolution of the traditional society through the process of modernization is associated with the polarization into a dual society: a society, mainly urban, of the affluent 10–20 per cent of the population, and a society of the underprivileged 80–90 per cent, consisting mainly of the rural poor but also including the urban slum-dwellers. The elite largely controls the political decision-making machinery, with so-called 'politics' becoming equivalent to wrangles between various sections of this elite. The market economy, the social services and the educational system are almost wholly dominated by the elite, leaving the poor (in particular the poorest 50 per cent) in abject poverty with regard to essential goods, services and knowledge. It has been argued that this polarization is the consequence of all modern technologies for goods or services (e.g., health, transport, education) being accessible only to those with purchasing power, which renders all modern technologies, therefore, inherently elitist.

The polarization of the society of a developing country into a dual society with a small, affluent, acquisitive, conspicuously consuming, city-centred elite drawing its ideas, values and lifestyles from the developed countries, and a large mass of poor people left out of the circle of production and consumption by the lack of employment and purchasing power, is an intrinsically unstable situation. It is fertile soil for alienation, tension and aggression. The instability is amplified by the constant exposure to the overwhelmingly greater affluence of the elite who practise conspicuously a philosophy which can be summed up thus: 'all that is rural is bad, all that is urban is better, and all that is foreign is best'. Several obvious questions follow: 'Can we rationally suppose that (the poor) will accept a world 'half slave, half free', half plunged in consumptive pleasure, half deprived of the bare decencies of life? Can we hope that the protest of the dispossessed will not erupt into local conflicts and widening unrest?' If social participation and control over their future cannot assume peaceful forms, it can only lead to explosions of violence.

These potentially explosive social effects of modern technology originate mainly from the incompatibility of modern technology with the factor proportions of a developing country. The exorbitant demands which these technologies make on scarce capital and energy resources has the inevitable result of developing urban pockets at the expense of the countryside, and it is this unevenness in development which is the causal basis for the polarization into a dual society. At the same time, the absence of an evolutionary link between modern and traditional technologies leads to the destruction of traditional rural industries, and thus to the damage of the fabric of social life. This damage is aggravated by the intrinsic tendency of modern technology to respond to, and stimulate, lifestyles modelled on those prevalent in the developed countries. But, the inherently inequality-magnifying feature of these technologies mean that they can only be accessible to an elite. Thus, modern technology spreads the desire for affluent life styles while restricting to a small elite the means of satisfying these stimulated desires, and thereby lays the foundation for alienation and social conflict.

ENVIRONMENTALLY SOUND AND APPROPRIATE TECHNOLOGY

The gathering storm of criticism of modern technology has resulted in an increasing number of appeals and demands for a new pattern of technologies, and therefore in a proliferation of new terms to designate it. Apart from 'alternative', 'appropriate' and 'intermediate' technologies, some of the other adjectival terms in use are 'soft', 'humane', 'liberatory', 'rational', 'equilibrium', 'convivial', 'careful', 'radical', 'inequality-reducing', 'people's', 'progress', 'utopian', 'environmentally sound' and 'low- and non-waste'. This affluence of jargon can prove an embarrassment, because the various terms differ in the characteristics considered essential for the new technology to be proposed as a contrast to modern technology; and even more because the set of complete characteristics associated with each term is difficult to identify amidst explicit statements and implicit views to be read between the lines. . . .

Fortunately, it is not necessary to enter the morass of terminology because, notwithstanding the many differences of emphasis, priority and strategy, there is a 'shifting core' of agreement underlying the various terms. In particular, it is the agreement that technologies must be chosen by taking into account environmental, economic and social goals.

There is also a broad domain of implicit accord regarding these goals: harmony with the environment, reduction of inequalities (between and within countries) and participation and control by the people are the environmental, economic and social goals.

Such a thrust is very much in tune with the emerging view of the relationship between environment and development. According to this view, the relationship between environment and development is inevitable, intimate and inseparable. If concerns are restricted purely to development objectives, and the environmental context of society is disregarded, then the consequential deterioration of the habitat leads to an indirect, but nevertheless serious, frustration of those very objectives. Thus, if environmental considerations are ignored, development cannot be sustained in the long run, and development goals are imperilled.

There is also another side to the coin. If the sole preoccupation is with the physical environment, and the society which pursues its aims and endeavours in that milieu is amorally forgotten, then the prevailing economic disparities between and within countries may lead to a situation where both the affluent and the needy despoil the environment. The affluent often damage their surroundings through irrational and wasteful consumption, and the poverty-stricken may have to ensure their survival even at the expense of the environment. Both luxury and poverty can have undesirable environmental consequences. Thus, if development tasks are forsaken, the environment is jeopardized.

It is such a view of the environment-development nexus which has led to a re-statement of development objectives. According to this re-statement, development must be directed primarily towards: a) the satisfaction of basic human needs (material and non-material), starting with the needs of the neediest, in order to achieve a reduction of inequalities between and within countries; b) endogenous self-reliance in order to promote social participation and control; and c) ecological soundness in order to attain harmony with the environment and make development sustainable over the long term.

This view of development is fundamentally different from one in which development is equated with growth. It is focused on human beings, rather than only on goods and services. It is principally concerned with the quality of life, and not merely with the quantity of goods and services. It is deliberately directed towards the neediest, instead of hoping that the benefits of growth will automatically and spontaneously trickle down to the under-privileged. Not merely growth (and the magnitude of the GNP), but also the structure and benefits of growth (and the composition and distribution of the GNP) are of central importance.

This view of development is global in scope and validity. It is as applicable to the industrialized countries as to the developing countries, though the precise priorities and programmes for these two categories will obviously be profoundly different. Thus the industrialized countries, which have already satisfied the minimum material needs of their populations, have major development tasks pertaining to basic non-material needs; while developing countries must necessarily place over-riding emphasis on the satisfaction of minimum elementary needs such as food, clothing, shelter, health, education and employment. . . .

It is in this context that technology has an essential role to play, for it is man's crucial instrument for introducing environmental concerns and for the achievement of socio-economic objectives. However, there is widespread concern that many of the technologies currently being used and generated in diverse parts of the world are unsatisfactory. It is not merely that these technologies make insufficient use of local factors (which is the usual formulation of the concern), but also that their environmental impacts are often highly unpleasant and undesirable, and that they are associated with many social effects which are considered to be unwelcome. Further, it is sometimes argued that these technologies are umbilically linked to the old international economic order between developed and developing countries and also to the dual societies into which many developing countries are polarized.

SOME CONCEPTUAL CLARIFICATIONS

Though the clamour for the deployment of appropriate/alternative/intermediate and so on, technologies has been rising over the past decade or two, the concept of environmentally sound and appropriate technologies is of recent origin. It is no surprise, therefore, that the concept has sometimes led to unforeseen apprehensions and unintended impressions. Some clarification is, therefore, in order.

At the outset, there are the semantic issues arising from the word 'appropriate', which acquires meaning only when one specifies 'appropriate to what or to whom?'. Too often, the sole concern is with appropriateness in relation to the capital and labour endowments of a region or country, but this purely economic view is a narrow, restricted and one-dimensional theory of appropriateness. In contrast, the assessment of appropriateness from the standpoint of development objectives necessitates a three-dimensional view in which the environmental and social dimensions are no less important than the economic one.

Sometimes it has been assumed that the case for environmentally sound and appropriate technologies, particularly for developing countries, is built upon a rejection of industry and industrialization. Nothing could be farther from the truth. In fact, it is considered self-evident that industrialization is essential for meeting the basic needs of growing populations. It is implicit in such a view that a great deal will have to be learnt from the industrialization process of the developed countries. But, that process—it must be noted—includes both successes and failures, with corresponding lessons. Hence, development does not have to consist of a slavish imitation of the type of industrialization followed by the developed countries.

Similarly, it has often been assumed that the proponents of environmentally sound and appropriate technology demand a total rejection of the so-called 'modern' technology of the developed countries. In fact, what is demanded is a careful scrutiny of the economic, social and environmental implications of modern technology from the standpoint of the objectives of Development and the New International Economic Order, and an unqualified acceptance of such of these technologies (in original or adapted forms) which advance those objectives. Thus, what is rejected is the blind faith that all the technologies of the developed countries are universally appropriate, despite the specificity of the historical circumstances which spawned them and the particularity of the demands in response to which they were evolved. Also discarded is the naive belief that these technologies are always an unmitigated blessing, equally satisfying the interests of those who sponsor, hawk, and vend them, as of those who intend to use them to fulfil national development objectives.

In some quarters, the argument for environmentally sound and appropriate technologies has been misunderstood as a plea for a total return to, and dependence on, the traditional technologies of ancient peoples. In fact, the plea is quite different. Traditional technologies have undergone a selection process over centuries of empirical testing; hence, they are very likely to represent optimum solutions. But they are optimum only for the particular conditions, constraints, materials, and needs in response to which they were developed. With the emergence of new conditions, constraints, materials and needs, it is likely that their applicability will have been eroded and the technology rendered invalid. Nevertheless, it is quite possible that these traditional technologies can undergo qualitative changes through minor modifications. These improvements can be brought about by the use of modern science and engineering to understand and clarify the rational core of ancient practices. Such transformed traditional technologies may well qualify as environmentally sound and appropriate.

In addition to the possibility of 'modern' technologies and transformed traditional technologies being environmentally sound and appropriate, there is also the possibilty of alternative technologies being specifically designed *ab initio* to meet the criteria of environmental soundness and appropriateness.

Since there are three main sources for the selection of environmentally sound and appropriate technologies, viz., 'modern', transformed traditional, and alternative technologies, it is very likely that the optimum pattern of technologies to advance the development objectives of a country will consist of a mix or blend of technologies from the various sources. The possibility of this mix making up the whole package of environmentally sound and appropriate technologies refutes the alleged bias wholly in favour of traditional technologies or wholly against modern technology.

Another important clarification relates to the dynamic nature of the concepts of environmental soundness and appropriateness. This dynamism follows inevitably from the continuously changing nature, on the one hand, of the physical environment in a country, and on the other hand, of the structure of its development goals. Thus, what is environmentally sound and appropriate at one juncture of history may not be so at a later time. As a result, the concepts of environmental soundness and appropriateness cannot be static; they must evolve with the state of the environment and with the nature of development tasks. It also follows that the composition of the mix that constitutes the total package of environmentally sound and appropriate technologies may have to change with the passage of time.

Finally, some votaries of appropriate technology have themselves been responsible for creating the impression that technology alone can remove poverty, redress injustice, solve development problems, and prove a universal panacea (provided it is the right brand!). But, technology is only a sub-system of society, and the development of society hinges not only on technology, but also on the other crucial sub-systems—the political, economic and social sub-systems—as well as on the physical environment of society.

In other words, technology is only an instrument for the development of society. Like all instruments, it must be specifically chosen and/or designed to fulfill its intended function. But, the will to use the instrument and the skill to wield it effectively does not depend so much on the instrument itself as upon the user.

Thus, the right type of technology (an environmentally sound and appropriate technology) is a necessary condition for development, but not a sufficient condition. It is also essential that the political structure and the socio-economic framework are both committed to development goals, and that the environmental context can sustain these goals.

Further, technology must always be seen in relation to the social setting, and the question of appropriateness is necessarily specific to the particular social context.

Technology, therefore, has both power and limits. But its power to advance development is drastically reduced if it is not environmentally sound and appropriate; hence, the paramount importance of selecting environmentally sound and appropriate technology.

CRITERIA for ENVIRONMENTAL SOUNDNESS and APPROPRIATENESS

In so far as criteria must be derived from objectives, the criteria for the choice of environmentally sound and appropriate technologies must emerge from the development objectives indicated earlier. This is undoubtedly a normative approach to the definition of criteria. The approach is based on the following value judgements:

(1) that economic development, particularly of the developing countries, is an urgent objective of the highest priority, and that this development is contingent upon the establishment of a New International Economic Order which must, above all, include a new relationship between developed and developing countries;

(2) that, in the ultimate analysis, it is a basic need of human beings to participate in the decisions and processes concerning their destiny and to exercise increasing control over these decisions and processes;

(3) that the environment is the sole irreplaceable habitat of man and must therefore be jealously protected and husbanded.

Stimulated by such a perspective, a list of preferences to be used in the choice of technology can be proposed.... One such list is presented here.

CRITERIA FOR THE SELECTION OF TECHNOLOGY

.... [I]t is in the nature of. . .lists that they generate more con-
troversy than consensus, but that is as should be, for it is by a process
of contention and testing that their revision and refinement will take
place... The [following] list of six criteria (each in turn being sub-
divided into two, making in all twelve) may well be the first of its
kind, but it is certainly not proposed with any aura of finality.

(1) SATISFACTION OF BASIC NEEDS
  (a) Does the technology contribute, directly or indirectly,
      immediately or in the near future, to the satisfaction of basic
      needs such as food, clothing, shelter, health, education, etc.?
  (b) Does it produce goods and/or services accessible particu-
      larly to those whose basic needs have been least satisfied?

(2) RESOURCE DEVELOPMENT
  (a) Does it make optimal use of local factors (manpower, capital,
      natural resources, etc.) by
      (i)   sustaining/generating employment;
      (ii)   saving/generating capital;
      (iii) saving/generating raw materials, including energy;
      (iv)   developing skills and research and development and
             engineering capabilities?
  (b) Does it increase the capacity to produce on a sustained,
      cumulative basis?

(3) SOCIETAL DEVELOPMENT
  (a) Does it reduce debilitating dependence and promote self-
      reliance based on mass participation at the local/national/
      regional levels, enabling the society to follow its own path of
      development?
  (b) Does it reduce inequalities? between occupational, ethnic,
      sex and age groups? between rural and urban communities?
      and between (groups of) countries?

(4) CULTURAL DEVELOPMENT
  (a) Does it make use of and build on endogenous technical trad-
      itions?
  (b) Does it blend with/enhance valuable elements and patterns
      in the local/national/regional culture?

(5) HUMAN DEVELOPMENT
  (a) Does it lead to creative mass involvement by being accessi-
      ble, comprehensible and flexible?

  (b) Does it liberate human beings from boring, degrading, excessively heavy or dirty work?
(6) ENVIRONMENTAL DEVELOPMENT
  (a) Does it minimize depletion and pollution by using renewable resources, through built-in waste minimization, recycling and/or re-use and blending better with existing eco-cycles?
  (b) Does it improve the natural and man-made environment by providing for a higher level of complexity and diversity of the eco-systems, thereby reducing their vulnerability?

The first criterion relates to *the satisfaction of basic needs*, of which the most important are food, clothing, shelter, health, education and transport/communication. This criterion compels a scrutiny of the products and/or services that emerge from the technology.

There is no objective justification for any particular set of products and/or services, but if the normative goal of development is accepted, then several conclusions follow.

(1) The simple development=growth equation becomes valid only after ensuring that the pattern and content of growth corresponds to increasing satisfaction of basic needs, with maximum emphasis on the needs of the neediest. Similarly, the development=production equation is justified only after confirming that the goods and/or services that are produced are accessible to those whose needs have been least satisfied.

(2) Though a vast number of technologies do not satisfy basic needs directly (e.g., energy production technologies), they can do so indirectly if their outputs (e.g. energy) can become the inputs for technologies which directly satisfy basic needs. Whether this indirect contribution to basic needs is the case or not, is the question which emerges from the first criterion.

(3) The existence of technologies (e.g. iron and steel) which lead indirectly to the satisfaction of basic needs implies that the time horizon must stretch beyond the immediate present. In other words, many technologies imply a postponed satisfaction of basic needs. It is obvious, however, that if the time horizon stretches indefinitely and the postponement is *sine die*, then the failure to fulfil basic needs is bound to prevent several other criteria on the list from being satisfied. The failure will increase inequalities, for instance, or diminish creative involvement on a mass basis, or degrade the environment. The conclusion is that the deferment in

meeting basic needs must not extend beyond the near future.

(4) Finally, the basic needs criterion implies a categorical rejection of the current practice, in countries with highly skewed income distributions, of gearing technologies to the demands of those groups with purchasing power and to ignore such needs of the under-privileged as cannot be backed up with this purchasing power.

The utilization and development of local resources is the essence of the second criterion. The term 'resources', which is intended to cover the usual economic factors of labour, capital, natural resources and land, has been deliberately chosen to emphasize that manpower too is a resource which must be utilized and developed. Within the scope of this criterion fall the usual concerns about using capital-saving, employment-generating technologies in countries with shortages of capital and abundance of manpower. But, the criterion used here is more general from several points of view.

(1) The criterion seeks to determine whether the technology makes use of all local resources including raw materials, energy and skills, as well as capital and labour.

(2) It probes into whether these resources are being developed, as distinct from being used. This aspect is particularly important for manpower (skill development) and natural resources. It is this development of resources which decides whether the capacity to produce on a sustained, cumulative basis is increasing or decreasing.

(3) The question of whether the mix of resources being used is optimum must also be scrutinized. Since different local/national/regional environments may require different resource mixes, a mix perfect for one particular environment may become less than perfect when transferred to other (and perhaps radically different) environments. The usual example cited for such an erosion in the optimum features of technologies is that of capital-intensive, labour-saving technologies generated in capital-rich, labour-short developed countries being transferred to capital-starved manpower-rich developing countries.

The third criterion concerns *societal development* and explores two categories of relationships displayed by a society:

(a) *external* relationships between the particular society under consideration and external societies with which it is in interaction; and

(b) *internal* relationships between sub-societies or groups within the society.

With regard to external relationships, the criterion seeks to determine whether the technology strengthens the society's capacity (*vis-à-vis* external societies) to determine and to follow its own path of development. This capacity is decided by the extent to which the society is self-reliant and to which its relationships with external societies do not involve a debilitating dependence. Self-reliance in turn is measured by autonomy, and by the extent to which people participate in and control the decisions which affect their lives. Of course, the possibility of mass participation in and control of decisions depends upon the size of the autonomous group, but emphasis should be placed on increasing mass participation and control. Thus, the criterion requires an examination of whether the technology promotes self-reliance by increasing mass participation in decisions and control over them.

In the matter of internal relationships between the constituent sub-societies of the society, the criterion is directed towards ascertaining whether the technology tends to reduce inequalities between the sub-societies. In particular, does the technology promote equality between occupational, ethnic, sex and age groups? Between rural and urban communities? Between (groups of) countries?

The fourth criterion concerns *the impact of technology on the cultural fabric of society*. Technology is bound to bring about changes in culture, and it is the nature of these changes that deserves consideration.

For instance, what effect does technology have on the endogenous technical traditions, i.e. the non-formalized knowledge and know-how (particularly in relation to the environment) which is invariably an acquisition of stable communities? Does technology build upon these traditions; or does it ignore them so that they are eroded and gradually lost?

Again, it is important to determine whether technology blends with and enhances, rather than disrupts and destroys, valuable elements in the local culture. For example, does technology reinforce, rather than undermine, a custom which acts as a cohesive force in the society (e.g., shared labour or shared use of facilities)?

These concerns arise from a host of anthropological and sociological studies that document the cultural damage and chaos resulting from the uncritical import and introduction of technologies from alien settings.

The fifth criterion relates to *the impact of technology on the individual man*, who is considered as the focus of interest, but living in symbiosis with his fellow-men and his environment. The criterion demands an enquiry into whether technology leads to human enrichment.

Creative involvement in social activities, be they of a physical, artistic or intellectual nature, is essential to the spiritual well-being of man, and should, in fact, be considered a basic human need (albeit a non-material one). So, the question is, does technology facilitate and promote this creative social involvement, and thereby enrich the individuals who become thus involved?

The criterion becomes especially significant in view of the importance of employment as a basic need. There should be a constant drive to make this employment meaningful. Hence, it is essential to ask whether technology tends to liberate human beings from boring, degrading, excessively heavy or demeaning work.

The sixth and final criterion involves *the preservation and development of the environment* and the impact of technology on the environment. It is necessary to ask: does technology (to use the words of an old song) 'accentuate the positive ... (and) eliminate the negative' ... environmental impacts? It is not merely a matter of technological 'fixes' which minimize pollution and resource depletion through anti-pollution and recycling measures. Technology should be inherently designed to blend with natural eco-cycles and to minimize waste at all stages of production, distribution and consumption.

All this has to do with the protection and preservation of the environment, but the objective of improving and developing the natural and man-made environment is as important. This is particularly so because a definite tendency of modern technology is to reduce the complexity and diversity of eco-systems. But, simplicity in eco-systems often leads to vulnerability and breakdown of eco-cycles. For example, the reduction of complexity associated with mono-cropping systems increase their vulnerability to attack and failure. Hence, it is important to determine whether the technology under consideration is improving the environment by enhancing complexity and diversity and thereby reducing vulnerability.

It is obvious that there is a great deal of overlap in the list of six criteria described above. The criteria are not exclusive, and one criterion may involve another through close interaction. This is inevitable, because the economic, social and environmental aspects of development are inter-related and, in fact, are components of a single process.

In so far as the process is the reality, and its resolution into components an analytical device, /the criteria must be considered together as an integral set. Thus, the strong coupling between criteria necessarily requires a holistic, rather than piece-meal or sectoral, approach to the choice of environmentally sound and appropriate technology.

Such a holistic set of criteria—of the type described above—has not been proposed hitherto. There may be several reasons for this lacuna, but one cannot ignore the fact that excessive specialization and professionalization have led to such divergent approaches of the economic, social and environmental disciplines that a common language for trans-disciplinary discussions is difficult to maintain. Yet, it is precisely such an integrated approach that must be taken to the selection of technologies designed to serve development goals, because development itself is a unified process, albeit with economic, social and environmental facets.

The six criteria constitute an extremely demanding and exacting list. Hence, an obvious objection to the list is that few technologies will satisfy all criteria, making the whole travail a worthless exercise. Such an objection is indeed tenable if the criteria are interpreted in a passive, static manner, in which selection is made from a set of existing technologies, and the issue is then closed. But, the objection subsides if the criteria are used in a dynamic perspective as a heuristic device leading to the generation of new technologies. Thus, at any one time, few technologies may satisfy all the criteria, and there may always be scope for improving them even if they do. But the testing of technologies against the criteria will reveal reasonably clear guidelines for innovation and modification. From this standpoint, the list of criteria is a long-hoped-for yardstick for innovations of environmentally sound and appropriate technology.

The obvious implication of the above discussion is that until the new or modified technologies make their appearance, the best has to be made of the 'bad bargain' of existing technologies. This can be done by weighing the criteria and settling for trade-offs amongst them. There should be little objection to such choices based on weights and trade-offs as long as all the criteria are explicitly and seriously considered and the processes of weighing and trading-off clearly revealed. But perhaps what is of greater importance is that efforts should be made to generate new technologies that allow all criteria, or a greater number of them, to be satisfied at the same time and that lessen the extent of trade-offs. In fact, since most choices of technology imply trade-offs between criteria and since most currently available technologies have been developed without reckoning with a set of criteria of the type proposed here, it is likely that more attention will have to be paid to the generation of new technologies than to the choice between existing ones.

To state the issue differently, it is almost certain that, from the standpoint of the list of criteria proposed here, few current technologies are perfectly environmentally sound and appropriate. It is only a matter of some technologies being more environmentally sound and appropriate than others. But, the revelation of the gap between the ideal and the actual provides the motivation for attempting to narrow the gap, i.e., for increasing the environmental soundness and appropriateness of technologies. In so far as the list of criteria has revealed both the goal of environmental soundness and appropriateness as well as how far away from the goal current technologies are, the list may be viewed as a distinct step forward.

An Indian Environmentalist's Credo

ANIL AGARWAL

The environment is an idea whose time has come in India. Newspapers give prominent display to environmental horror stories and editorials demand better management of natural resources. Government statements on the need to preserve the environment have become commonplace. Government programmes too are quite numerous and increasing in number day by day. There are massive schemes for afforestation, for instance. In the last four years, some 10 billion seedlings are said to have been distributed or planted. There are new laws for control of air and water pollution and for the conservation of forests. India has received plaudits all over the world for what it has done to preserve tigers. Nearly 3 per cent of India's giant land mass is now under protected national parks and wildlife sanctuaries, and there are demands to strengthen their protection and increase their area. Planning documents and most party manifestoes are equally careful to mention the importance of the environment.

But there is a major problem with this entire range of activities and concerns: it does not appear to be based on a holistic understanding of the relationship between environment and the development process taking place in the country. The programmes are *ad hoc*, without any sharp priority, and there is too much of a policeman's attitude. They seem to be based on the belief that concern for the environment essentially means protecting and conserving it, partly from development programmes but mainly from the people themselves. There is little effort to understand and modify the development process itself, in a manner that will bring it into greater

Excerpted from Anil Agarwal, 'The Fifth World Conservation Lecture: Human-Nature Interactions in a Third World Country', *The Environmentalist*, vol. 6, no. 3, 1986.

harmony with the needs of the people and with the need to maintain an ecological balance, whilst also increasing the productivity of our land, water and forest resources. This is indeed the biggest challenge before a country like India, given the state of its humanity: how do we get more from our natural resources even while we conserve them? Growth and equity have been the two major political issues of our times: the environmental movement is now adding a third—sustainability. Moreover, this issue of sustainability is raising serious questions about what kind of growth we want, and it is re-emphasizing the need for equity, both globally and locally.

The environment is not just pretty trees and tigers, threatened plants and ecosystems—it is literally the entity on which we all subsist, and on which our entire agricultural and industrial development depends. Development can take place at the cost of the environment only up to a point: beyond that point it will be like the foolish man who was trying to cut the very branch on which he was sitting. Development without a concern for the environment can only be development for the short-term. In the long term, it can only be anti-development and it can continue only at the cost of enormous human suffering, increased poverty and oppression. Countries like India are rapidly approaching that point.

THE GROWTH OF ENVIRONMENTAL GROUPS IN INDIA

Amongst the hundreds of voluntary groups working at the micro-level within the country, there has been a remarkably rapid growth of interest in environmental problems. So rapid, in fact, that we sometimes tend to describe this growth—albeit loosely—as the beginnings of an environmental movement.

There are today hundreds of grassroots groups in the country involved in environmental issues, and their experiences and interests are extremely diverse: some are interested in preventing deforestation, while others are only interested in afforestation. There are many which want to prevent the construction of one dam or another: there are others who want to prevent water pollution. There is the famous Chipko Movement in the UP Himalaya, probably the oldest and most famous of all the groups, which has played a major role in bringing the issue of deforestation to the fore of public opinion. And now there is its counterpart in the south, the Apikko Movement in the Western Ghats of Karnataka. Dams like the Silent Valley and Bedthi have already been stopped because of strong peoples' protests, and there is a major campaign against the proposed Bhopalapatnam and Inchampalli dams on the borders of MP, Andhra Pradesh and Maharashtra. The Kerala Sastra Sahitya Parishad has had a long acrimonious battle over the pollution of the Chaliyar River in Kerala by a rayon mill. The India Development Service finds itself enbroiled in another case of river pollution by another rayon mill in Karnataka. Meanwhile, the Shahdol Group has for a long time been working against the pollution of a river in the Shahdol district by a paper mill. There is, of course, the Mitti Bachao Abhiyan to organize the farmers against the water logging caused by faulty irrigation systems.

While all these are relatively well known groups and have attracted varying degrees of media attention, there are many, many others in the country who are doing excellent work in mobilizing people, both to prevent further ecological destruction (often in the face of government policies), and to bring about ecological regeneration. One thing, however, that binds most of these groups is their concern to put the environment at the service and the control of the people, the people usually being defined as the local communities who live within that environment.

Environmental protection *per se* is of least concern to most of these groups. Their main concern is about the use of the environment and who should benefit from it. This is also reflected in the fact that, unlike in the West, the environmental movement consists of only a few environmental groups. Many of these groups are old and their main concern is either civil rights, rural development, tribal welfare, appropriate technology, primary health care, or science demystification. All these groups have slowly come to see the relevance of environment to their work, to the people they work with and to the development process as a whole.

Environmental Destruction by the Rich

To understand the nature of the environmental problem in a developing country like India, it may be useful to compare and contrast certain environmental trends and concerns in India with those in the West, especially since environmental concern first began in the Western world and since many groups in India (including political parties), have for long dismissed environmental concern as a petty Western concern. There has always been the argument that too much concern for the environment can only retard economic and industrial development.

The UN Conference on the Human Environment held in Stockholm in 1972, was the landmark conference that created worldwide consciousness about the environment. Many delegations from developing countries attending that conference had argued that the solution to environmental problems lay in economic development.

'Smoke is a sign of progress', the Brazilian delegation had thundered, then representing a country witnessing an economic boom. Our own Prime Minister, Mrs Indira Gandhi, who made a major impression on the conference, is still remembered for her oft-quoted statement 'Poverty is the biggest polluter'. In all those who came from the Third World, both leftists and rightists, there was a sneaking suspicion that the Western countries were up to something. The West was simply pushing environmental concern onto an unsuspecting Third World to retard its technological modernization and industrial development. It was even argued that having got their riches and their affluent lifestyles, Westerners were now simply asking for more affluence: clean air, clean water, and large tracts of nature for enjoyment and recreation, many of which were going to be preserved in the tropical forests and savannas of Asia, Africa and South America.

But exactly ten years later, when the UN organized a meeting to commemorate the Stockholm conference, few non-governmental groups from the Third World were prepared to argue in favour of the development process as it is. All these groups recognized that the Third World today faces both an environmental crisis and a development crisis, and both these crises seem to be intensifying and interacting to reinforce each other. On the one hand, there does not seem to be any end to the problems of inequality, poverty and unemployment—the crucial problems that the development process is meant to solve. On the other, environmental destruction has grown further apace. But what is interesting is that while many environmental problems—especially those related to air and water pollution—have tended to become less severe in many parts of the industrialised world, because of the introduction of capital-intensive pollution-control technologies, these problems have continued to grow and become critical in many parts of the developing world. In other words, while the world economic development process is worsening our environmental problems, it appears to be solving them in the West. In a UN meeting in 1982, Michael Heseltine (then the UK Minister of Environment), even went so far as to say that all environmental problems in the West have been solved and they now remain mainly in the Third World.

I am sure environmentalists in the West would not agree with Heseltine's contention that all environmental problems in the West have been solved or are even on the way to being solved, but Heseltine did have a point. London, for instance, has not seen any of the smogs it saw regularly in the 1940s and 50s for years, and the Thames now even boasts of fish. However, Heseltine was also hiding something of deep significance, that is the role of the Western world in destroying the Third World environment.

The major environmental problems in the West are those arising out of waste disposal, air and water pollution, and the disposal of highly toxic, industrial and nuclear wastes. Problems of acid rain have definitely increased (and there does not yet seem to be any solution to the problem of toxic wastes), but it is true that some cities and rivers do look cleaner. In the Third World, as its own industrialization and urbanization proceeds, these waste disposal problems are getting worse day by day, but they are still not the major or only environmental problems. In the Third World, the major environmental problems are clearly those which arise out of the misuse of the natural resource base—the misuse of soils, forests and water resources.

PRESSURE AND DEMAND

These problems are created to a great extent because of the pressure to produce resources for the sustenance of the world's metropolitan system. The Third World's environment not only provides raw materials for its own industries but also for the industries of the West. For instance, the Japanese and Western timber industries have been the biggest source of forest destruction in Southeast Asia. Having turned countries like Thailand from net exporters into net importers of wood, Japanese companies are now turning to the last great wooded frontier of the world—the Amazon basin of South America.

The food needs of the Western world have played equal havoc with the lands of the Third World. No statistics on this are available, but if someone did collect them, I am sure we would find that despite the worldwide process of decolonization, there is today many times more land being used in the developing world to meet the food needs of the Western countries than in the 1940s, before the process of decolonization began. More than a quarter of all Central American forests have been destroyed since 1960 for cattle ranching. Between 85–95 per cent of the beef produced as a result has gone to the US, while domestic consumption of beef in Central America has fallen dramatically. In the US this beef has been mainly used to make tinned and pet foods and cheap hamburgers, because Central American beef is half the price of the grass-fed beef produced in the US. The price of Central American beef does not represent its correct ecological cost. Cattle ranching has proved to be the worst form of land use for the fragile soils on which these tropical moist forests existed. Within 5–7 years their productivity dropped dramatically and cattle ranchers have had to move on.

The Sahelian drought of 1968–74, which hit the world headlines and claimed the lives of approximately 100,000 nomadic people, was caused by nothing less than the French colonial policy to drive these countries into peanut farming to secure its own source of vegetable oils. Through heavy taxation policies, the French colonial authorities forced the West African peasants to grow groundnuts at the expense of subsistence crops. Groundnut cultivation rapidly depleted the soil. It soon spread to traditionally fallow and forest zones and encroached on land previously used for grazing, thereby upsetting the delicate balance between the farmers and the nomadic herders. The expansion of groundnuts was encouraged by artificially high prices, but when the US soya production began to hit the European market and vegetable oil prices began to fall, the newly independent West African countries had no alternative but to increase the groundnut area to keep up their foreign exchange reserves. As this area increased by leaps and bounds under the pressure of government policies, the nomads were slowly pushed further and further north into the desert, for which they were not prepared, their traditional relationships with the settled farmers having been totally disturbed. When the long period of drought set in and thousands of animals and human beings began to die, the nomads and their overgrazing were blamed. Nobody blamed the French or the Sahelian elite, who worked hand in glove with the French.

In a recent report, the UN Environment Programme (UNEP), points to the impact that the heavy debt burden of the Third World and high interest rates in the West has had on the environment of the Third World. The debt burden and regressive terms of trade have forced many developing countries to put enormous pressure on their natural rsources, often to the point of overexploitation. In 1981, for instance, it took one Latin American country 9.8 times as much beef to buy a barrel of oil as it did in 1961. At the end of the 1970s, profits from the export of one tonne of bananas were enough to purchase only half the steel they would have bought at the end of the 1960s. When interest rates are high there is a tendency to discount long-term issues like environment for short term gain: a one per cent increase in interest rates adds approximately £5 billion to the current debt burden of developing countries. To have increased its export earnings (not profits) by one billion dollars in 1981, South America as a whole would have had to increase its banana exports threefold, Ecuador threefold and Colombia ninefold, while leading cotton exporters like Egypt and Turkey would have had to double and triple their cotton exports, respectively. This would have meant bringing millions of additional hectares into production to grow these export crops. And, it can be added, this would have pushed millions of marginal peasants into marginal lands like desert fringes and steep hill slopes for survival, leading to accelerated desertification and soil erosion.

In [India], the first major attack on the forests of the Northeast came with the establishment of tea plantations. The current overfishing on India's coasts, as on the coasts of almost all Southeast Asian countries, is taking place because of the heavy demand for prawns in Western and Japanese markets. This overfishing is leading to considerable tensions between traditional fisherfolk and trawler owners, and violent encounters between the two are regularly reported. Recently, Indonesia completely banned the operation of trawlers from its coastal waters, and several countries including India, have set up regulations to prevent trawler operators from fishing in the first few kilometres from the coast. This zone is reserved for the traditional fisherfolk. But policing trawlers over such an extensive coastline is an expensive proposition and regulations are, therefore, seldom observed or enforced. The export of frogs' legs to cater to the palates of Western consumers, and its impact on the agricultural pest populations in affected areas, is now a well-known story.

The pattern of environment exploitation that we see on the global scale simply reproduces itself on the national scale within a country undergoing industrialization.Exactly what the Western industry does to the Third World environment, the Indian industry does to the Indian environment. Just to get an idea of how heavily dependent modern Indian industry is on the natural environment, it may be useful to point out that nearly half the industrial output in India is accounted for by industries which can be called biomass-based industries: that is, industries like cotton textiles, rayon, paper, plywood, rubber, soap, sugar, tobacco, jute, chocolate, food processing and packaging, and so on. Each of these industries exerts an enormous pressure on the country's cultivated and forest lands. They need crop lands, they need forests, and they need energy and irrigation.

The Indian paper industry has ruthlessly destroyed the forests of India. Paper companies in Karnataka, having destroyed all the bamboo forests, are now getting their raw materials from one of the last major forested frontiers of India: the Northeast. The government's own public sector paper companies are coming up in the Northeast itself. The Andhra Pradesh government has meanwhile set its sights on the virgin forests of Andamans and Nicobar Islands for a paper mill that it wants to build in Kakinada. The shortage of raw materials for wood pulp has already forced the government to liberalize import of pulp for the country's paper industry, thus adding to the pressure on the forests of other Third World countries.

The first lesson is therefore clear: the main source of environment destruction in the world is the demand for natural resources generated by the consumption of the rich (whether they are rich nations or rich individuals and groups within nations); and because of their gargantuan appetite, it is their wastes, mainly, that contribute to the global pollution load.

The Poor and their Environment

The second lesson, however, is that it is the poor who are affected

Until recently, few energy planners and government officials had any idea of the dimensions of the rural-urban fuelwood trade. Annual urban purchases of fuelwood are well over Rs 500 million in India.

Over the last ten years, Madhya Pradesh (MP), the only state left in the heart of India with any reasonable degree of forest cover, has emerged as a major supplier of fuelwood to the cities of north and western India. But as the state gets more and more deforested every year, fuelwood prices keep rising within MP itself. Madhya Pradesh has now become India's first state, and probably the world's first, to ban the export of firewood. As a result, Delhi, which uses about Rs 15 million worth of firewood on the retail market, is now getting less firewood from MP, and an increasingly higher proportion from Assam, the same place from which paper mills are now getting their bamboo. What happens when Assam also says no?

LOSS OF LIFESTYLE . . . LOSS OF LIVELIHOOD

Biomass resources not only meet crucial household needs but they also provide a range of raw materials for traditional occupations and crafts and are thus a major source of employment: firewood and cowdung are important sources of fuel for potters; bullock carts and catamarans are made from wood; bamboo is a vital raw material for basket weavers, and so on. Traditional crafts are not just being threatened by the introduction of modern products but also by the acute shortage of biomass-based raw materials. A study from the Indian Institute of Science—the first in India on the changing market of bullock carts—reports that people in Ungra village in Karnataka can now no longer afford to buy new bullock carts with the traditional wood wheel because wood has become extremely expensive. A recent report from the Murugappa Chettiar Research Centre from Madras reports that traditional fisherfolk now find it very difficult to make catamarans because the special wood they use is extremely scarce and expensive.

Several reports from all over the country—from MP, from Maharashtra, from Tamil Nadu—portray the extreme difficulty of hundreds of thousands of basket weavers in eking out a bare existence because of the acute shortage of bamboo. In the Bhandara and Chandrapur districts of Maharashtra, nearly 70000 basket weavers have been protesting against discriminatory prices and small quotas of bamboos given to them, whereas big paper mills have been leased out large bamboo forests.

In Karnataka, Madhav Gadgil and S. N. Prasad undertook a study of the use of the state's bamboo forests by paper mills, after a series of protests by basket weavers. They found that whereas bamboo was available to paper mills at Rs 15 a tonne, it was available to basket weavers and other small bamboo users in the market at Rs 1200 a tonne. Social activists in Saharanpur have pointed out the travails of *baan* makers who have now been deprived of their earlier sources of bhabhar grass. The UP Forest Development Corporation discriminates in favour of paper mills and this policy has turned thousands of baan workers into destitutes, landless labourers and urban migrants. Wood is now difficult to get even for making agricultural implements like the plough, especially wood that has been traditionally used for these implements. Few people know that one of the things that led to the Chipko movement was the anger of the local people over the forest department's refusal to provide ash wood, traditionally used for making ploughs, whereas the forest department happily allocated the same wood to sports goods manufacturers.

Even biomass resources like thatch have become so difficult that maintenance of mud and thatch huts has become difficult. A government report from Bastar, of all places (as it is still one of the heavily forested districts in the country), points out a village where no new hut has been built over the last two decades because the entire area around the village has been deforested. Traditional mud roofs have disappeared from many parts of the country because of the large quantities of timber needed by them. They are being replaced by tiled roofs, but baking of tiles still requires large quantities of firewood.

Fodder is another vital resource that is in acute shortage. With only 2.45 per cent of the world's land mass, India supports 15 per cent of its cattle, 52 per cent of its buffaloes, and 15 per cent of its goats. All these animals play an extremely important role in the integrated system of agriculture and animal husbandry that Indian farmers practise. As a study from the tribal areas of Gujarat shows, shortage of fodder, especially from public lands, means that poor landless households and marginal farmers do not benefit much from the milk co-operatives and animal improvement schemes in the region.

have been protesting against discriminatory prices and small quotas of bamboos given to them, whereas big paper mills have been leased out large bamboo forests.

In Karnataka, Madhav Gadgil and S. N. Prasad undertook a study of the use of the state's bamboo forests by paper mills, after a series of protests by basket weavers. They found that whereas bamboo was available to paper mills at Rs 15 a tonne, it was available to basket weavers and other small bamboo users in the market at Rs 1200 a tonne. Social activists in Saharanpur have pointed out the travails of *baan* makers who have now been deprived of their earlier sources of bhabhar grass. The UP Forest Development Corporation discriminates in favour of paper mills and this policy has turned thousands of baan workers into destitutes, landless labourers and urban migrants. Wood is now difficult to get even for making agricultural implements like the plough, especially wood that has been traditionally used for these implements. Few people know that one of the things that led to the Chipko movement was the anger of the local people over the forest department's refusal to provide ash wood, traditionally used for making ploughs, whereas the forest department happily allocated the same wood to sports goods manufacturers.

Even biomass resources like thatch have become so difficult that maintenance of mud and thatch huts has become difficult. A government report from Bastar, of all places (as it is still one of the heavily forested districts in the country), points out a village where no new hut has been built over the last two decades because the entire area around the village has been deforested. Traditional mud roofs have disappeared from many parts of the country because of the large quantities of timber needed by them. They are being replaced by tiled roofs, but baking of tiles still requires large quantities of firewood.

Fodder is another vital resource that is in acute shortage. With only 2.45 per cent of the world's land mass, India supports 15 per cent of its cattle, 52 per cent of its buffaloes, and 15 per cent of its goats. All these animals play an extremely important role in the integrated system of agriculture and animal husbandry that Indian farmers practise. As a study from the tribal areas of Gujarat shows, shortage of fodder, especially from public lands, means that poor landless households and marginal farmers do not benefit much from the milk co-operatives and animal improvement schemes in the region.

In such a situation, where millions of people are heavily dependent on biomass sources for their daily existence, the destruction of the environment or any policy that reduces access to biomass resources—like the creation of a wildlife sanctuary or enforcement of forest conservation legislation—will have an extremely adverse impact on the daily lives of the people.

The Transformation of Nature

Despite this near-total reliance on biomass resources for bare survival, nature in India has steadily undergone a major transformation. There are two major pressures operating on the country's natural resources today. The first, generated by population growth and leading to increased household demand for biomass resources like firewood, has been widely talked about. The poor often get blamed for the destruction of the environment. But the second set of pressures, generated by modernization, industrialization and the general penetration of the cash economy, are seldom talked about, at least in policy making circles.

Modernization affects nature in two ways. Firstly, it is extremely destructive of the environment both in its search for cheap biomass-based raw materials and in its search for cheap opportunities for waste disposal. Unless there are strong laws which are equally strongly implemented, no attempt is made to internalize environmental costs—both public and private industrialists prefer to pass them on to the society. State governments are also happy to give away large tracts of forests for a pittance, and throw water pollution control laws to the winds to get a few more factories.

Apart from the destruction of the environment, modernization affects nature in yet another way, by steadily transforming the very character of nature. In biological terms, the tendency is to reduce the diversity in nature and transform it into high-yielding monocultures. The ecological role of the original nature is usually disregarded in this transformation. In social terms, the transformation is generally away from a nature that has traditionally come to support household and communty needs, and towards a nature that is geared to meeting urban and industrial needs, a nature that is essentially cash generating. Excellent examples of such transformation are the pine forests in place of the old oak forests in the

Himalaya; the teak forests in place of the sal forests in the Chotta-
nagpur Plateau; eucalyptus plantations in place of natural forests
in the Western Ghats, and now the proposal to grow oil palm in
place of the tropical forests in the Great Nicobar Islands. Both these
phenomena—the destruction of the original nature and the creation
of a new, commercially-oriented nature—have been taking place
simultaneously in the Indian environment and on a massive scale.

The effect of this massive environmental change has been disastrous for the people, especially when we realize that in a country
like India, where on the one hand we have an extremely high level
of poverty and on the other a reasonably high level of population
density, there is hardly any ecological space left in the physical
environment which is not occupied by one human group or another
for its sustenance. Now, if in the name of economic development,
any human activity results in the destruction of an ecological space
or in its transformation into something that benefits the more powerful groups in society, then inevitably those who were earlier dependent on that space will suffer. Development in this case leads to
displacement and dispossession and will inevitably raise questions
of social injustice and conflict. The experience of microlevel groups
shows clearly that it is rare to find a case in which environmental
destruction does not go hand in hand with social injustice, almost
like two sides of the same coin.

FORESTS, FISHERIES AND GRAZING LANDS

Let us look at a few cases of how the destruction of nature has
affected the lives of people. One very dramatic area where government policies have consistently increased conflicts is forests. The
entire tribal population, and millions of other forest dwelling people,
depend on the forests for their very existence. Destruction of forests
has meant social, cultural and economic destruction of the tribal
populations in particular. Beginning with the British and continuing
on with free India, the government has decided to control the forest
resources itself, leaving little or no control in the hands of the forests
dwellers. The government control over forests has definitely meant
a reallocation of forest resources away from the needs of local communities and into the hands of urban and industrial India. The end
result is both increased social conflict and increased destruction of
the ecological resource itself.

Yet another major component of the country's physical environment is grazing lands. The destruction of the grazing lands has meant enormous hardships for poor people, especially for the nomadic groups in the country. Few people know that India has nearly 200 castes engaged in pastoral nomadism which, when added up, number up to six per cent of India's population. India is unique in the world in terms of the diversity of animals associated with pastoral nomadism. There are herders of camels in Rajasthan and in Gujarat, of donkeys in Maharashtra, of yaks in Ladakh, of pigs in Andhra Pradesh, and even of ducks in southern India. Sheep, goats and cattle are of course the main animals used for nomadism.

A number of factors, including land reform and development programmes (which have promoted expansion of agriculture on to marginal lands), have steadily led to an erosion of grazing lands. The Rajasthan Canal is a fine example of a government programme that has transformed extensive grazing lands into agricultural lands. No effort was made by the government to ensure that the nomads who used these grazing lands earlier would benefit from the canal on a priority basis. In almost every village, the *panchayat* lands traditionally used as *gauchar* lands, have been encroached upon by powerful interest groups and privatized. Nomadic groups have been increasingly impoverished over the last 30 years and an ever increasing number is being forced to give up their traditional occupations, to become landless labourers or migrants.

Riverine fisherfolk constitute another group that has suffered immensely with environmental destruction. Riverine fisheries are being seriously affected with increasing water pollution. Large scale fish kills are regularly reported. In the 158 km stretch of the Hooghly, the average yield of fish is just about a sixth in the polluted zones as compared to the unpolluted zones. Growing water pollution is thus affecting thousands of riverine fisherfolk in the country, yet little data is available on their plight. Rivers have now become a resource for urban and industrial India, to be used as cheap dumpyards for their wastes, and all this is sanctioned in the name of economic development.

'COMMERCIALISED' NATURE

The new, commercial nature that is being created is also of little help to village communities and their daily needs. There are people's protests in many parts of the country against the conversion of oak forests into pine forests and of sal forests into teak forests. Neither pine nor teak is of any interest to local communities. In the Singbhum area of Bihar there is even a movement to destroy the new teak forests. Equally, there is a strong protest in Karnataka against the planting of eucalyptus on farmers' fields.

The planting of eucalyptus on farmers' fields—and even on so-called barren fields—is an excellent example of the adverse biomass conversion (adverse to the people) promoted by modernization. What happens to the poor people when eucalyptus is planted on a farmer's field? We have a concrete example from a village in Punjab, where a rich farmer and a former Governor, with over 100 hectares of land has stopped growing cotton and has switched to eucalyptus. As long as he grew cotton, enormous quantities of cotton sticks were available for the landless labourers in the village to use as fuel. Because of the shortage of firewood, crop wastes from the landlords' fields were the major—and almost the only—source of fuel for these poor landless villagers. Now with eucalyptus growing, their main source of fuel has dried up, putting them in a precarious position. This is a case where afforestation has actually created a fuel famine for the neediest community.

What happens when eucalyptus is grown on a barren piece of land? Usually no land is barren, unless of course it is highly eroded (in which case even eucalyptus cannot be grown on it). Generally barren lands have large quantities of weeds growing on them. With the destruction of our original vegetation, a few aggressive weeds like Lantana, Parthenium and Eupatorium have literally started taking over the country. None of these weeds are palatable to animals and they therefore survive the pressure of grazing.

If we look at the firewood statistics in the country, we find there is a huge gaping hole in these statistics. The officially produced firewood does not account for even one-fifth of the total estimated demand of some 130 million tonnes of firewood a year. When this was first discovered in the early 1970s, it was immediately concluded that the rural people must be stealing wood from the forests on an enormous scale. Later, however, it was found that over three-quarters of the fuel used in rural areas is in the form of twigs and little branches, and there need not be any felling of trees to get this wood. But even today we do not know what vegetation is actually providing this massive quantity of twigs and branches. My guess is that weeds are now playing an extremely important role in the vital supply of cooking fuel for the poor, and in all my travels across India, this guess has been confirmed.

A weed is defined as a plant which has no economic value, but in the socio-economic reality of India, Lantana, Parthenium and Eupatorium are weeds only for revenue-earning forest departments of the government. For poor households, who have no lands of their own, weeds growing on public lands are extremely useful, because of the very fact that they are not wanted by the modern sector of the economy. Once they acquire an economic value, they will go out of their hands—like bamboo which was for long described as a weed by foresters.

Thus, when a patch of barren land is planted with eucalyptus, even the weeds are no longer available to poor landless households and their fuel crisis intensifies. Not surprisingly foresters report from all over the country, in the form of a complaint, that women even take away dry eucalyptus leaves from eucalyptus plantations for use as fuel, thus destroying, as the foresters say, any chance of the leaves breaking down into humus and enriching the soil. But what else can these energy-starved women do?

Thus what we see in India today is growing conflict over the use of natural resources and, in particular, over biomass between the two sectors of the country's economy: the cash economy—or the modern sector—on one hand, and the non-monetized, biomass-based subsistence economy—the traditional sector—on the other.

As the growing stock of biomass goes down, the demand for biomass from the cash economy goes up, and as demand begins to exceed supply, the pressures to exploit the remaining biomass increase enormously; biomass prices rise, and destructive processes accelerate because of sheer market forces. Illegal timber felling is today a major activity in the country undertaken with the full support of political interests. Stealing a few dozen trucks of timber is the surest and easiest way to become rich. Recently no less than a Chief Minister had to resign because of his family's involvement in timber smuggling.

As even those forms of biomass that are used by the poor become commercialized, the access of the poor to those biomass sources automatically becomes reduced because of limited purchasing power. The trend towards commercialization of firewood has been so rapid in the last 15 years that it is now rare to find poor households using much firewood, especially in the shape of logs. Firewood is no longer a fuel of the poor but of the relatively rich. The poor now subsist on qualitatively inferior sources of biomass fuels: crop residues, weeds, twigs, cowdung and whatever organic wastes they can find. In fact, if one goes to a village, one will see that even firewood, crop wastes and cowdung are fuels used according to the family's economic status— crop residues usually being at the lowest end of the pecking order. Unfortunately, several scientific agencies, thinking that 'crop wastes' are actually wastes, have begun to undertake research on commercial utilization of crop residues. Technologies like fuel briquetting plants and small scale paper mills based on crop residues are being heavily promoted by the government. This raises the prices of fuel and fodder and directly hits poor landless peasants, who now have to rely heavily on the mercy of landed farmers to allow them to take these residues away, which they will do only as long as they are non-commercial entities for them.

In fact, in many parts of Haryana and Punjab, farmers are already insisting that crop residues be taken by their labourers in exchange for wages. In one district of Haryana we found that a common practice now is to let a woman pick an acre of cotton in exchange for the cotton sticks from the acre. There is no additional payment. The commercialization of biomass and its drain towards those who have the power to purchase, will inevitably harm the poor and erode the non-monetized, biomass-based, subsistence economy.

Environment and Women

The destruction of the environment clearly poses the biggest threat to marginal cultures and occupations like that of tribals, nomads, fisherfolk and artisans, which have always been heavily dependent on their immediate environment for their survival. But the maximum impact of the destruction of biomass sources is on women. Women in all rural cultures are affected, especially women from poor landless, marginal and small farming families. Seen from the point of view of these women, it can be argued that all development is ignorant of women's needs, and often anti-women, literally designed to increase their work burden.

Given the culturally accepted division of labour within the family, the collection of household needs like fuel, fodder and water is left to women. As the environment degrades, and survival needs become increasingly difficult to collect, women have to spend an extraordinary amount of time foraging for fuel, fodder and water in addition to household work, agricultural work and caring for animals. There is almost no data which shows how the time spent by women on their daily household activities is increasing and how this increase differs across different ecoclimatic zones of India. But the data that is already available on the existing work burden is downright shocking. In many parts of India, women spend 14–16 hours working everyday and it does not matter whether they are young, old or pregnant and whether it is a Sunday or any other holiday. Day after weary day, the routine repeats itself and year after weary year, fuel and fodder collection time increases. In many parts of India, the women have literally reached their 'carrying capacities'.

The worst situation is in the arid and semi-arid parts of the country and in the hill and mountain villages. In all these areas trees and forests have been steadily destroyed. Because of a number of factors—soil and climatic conditions, very small land holdings, lack of irrigation, etc.—the Green Revolution has not reached these areas unlike Punjab and Haryana, where trees are few but the green revolution has meant an enormous increase in biomass from croplands. As a result, there is now an acute biomass famine in these areas. In all such areas women can spend as much as 5–6 hours everyday, and in some households as much as ten hours everyday, just collecting fuel and fodder. On the contrary, in a state like Kerala, where ecoclimatic conditions permit a rich green cover, the work burden of women is much smaller, probably the least in the country. Even the minimal land reforms, in which landless families have been distributed one tenth of an acre as homestead plots, has meant access to a few dozen coconut trees, which helps to provide at least half the annual fuel requirements.

But in the rest of the country, the increasing work burden on women, caused by deforestation, is affecting everything else in their lives. A study from the Indian Institute of Management in Ahmedabad shows that five times more men than women seek treatment at primary health centres. Women do not have time to seek health care even when they are ill. A study by the Operations Research Group found that in western UP even pregnant women work for 14 hours a day. They do this almost till a few hours before the delivery and begin normal work 3–4 days thereafter. One woman told the ORG researchers: 'We are too much loaded with family chores. Hospitals, injections, etc., are too time consuming business for us'.

Another study from rural Punjab recently described the problems faced by poor women after the tubectomy operation. Nine out of ten women from agricultural labour households in the villages who had undergone tubectomy complained about postoperative pains. All of them wanted to take rest but none of them could. Collecting fodder alone took three hours. There was hardly any source of freely available fodder in the village. Most women had to dig grass and other weeds from between wheat plants in the fields. Many farmers would not allow this and landless women had to go from one field to another. Firewood meant still more work and another journey. The bending and stretching increased the pain. The women wanted to pass on their work to others, especially their children. They then ran into conflicts with their husbands and their children, who wanted to play rather than work. One woman kicked and punched her daughter so hard for not working with her that she died. Such viciousness may be rare but increased family tensions are commonplace.

MALE TREES AND FEMALE TREES

The penetration of the cash economy is affecting the relationships between the men and the women in a peculiar way, and is creating a real dichotomy in their respective relationships with nature. Men have become more involved with the cash economy than women. Women continue to deal with the non-monetized, biomass-based subsistence economy of the household. Even within the same household, we can find cases of men happy to destroy nature to earn cash even though it could create greater hardships for the women in collecting daily fuel and fodder needs.

The Chipko Movement has given us numerous examples of this dichotomy in male-female interests, and the role of the women in preventing deforestation has been paramount in this movement. Even the Chipko experience with afforestation confirms this dichotomy between men and women and stresses the role of women in ecological regeneration. Even though many crucial household needs could be met by rehabilitating the local village ecosystem—by planting fuel and fodder trees, for instance—the men do not show much interest in doing so. It is women who are doing most of the afforestation work organized by the Chipko Movement.

The new culture created by the penetration of the cash economy has slowly but steadily alienated the men from their ecosystem. Employment for them means work which can bring cash in their hands. This employment can be found mainly in the city, hence mass male migration. Even when the men are in the village, a job is still something that must earn cash.

There are few of the caste and class barriers in the Himalayan villages which prevent people from working together as a community. But still women continue to walk miles and miles over arduous paths to fetch fuel, fodder and water every day, while men sit idle without doing anything to plant trees in the denuded areas arounded them.

It is not surprising that the eucalyptus based 'social forestry', trotted out to be such a great success by the World Bank and the government forest departments, is all in the hands of men, all planting trees with the cash motive. Other than employing women as cheap labour in nurseries, these agencies have nothing to show in terms of the involvement of women—the very people who deal with fuel and fodder—and the government, too, still gives this the name of 'social forestry'.

Male migration further increases the work burden of women, who then have to take care not only of household needs but also have to devote more time to family's agricultural fields. But as the time needed to collect fuel and fodder grows, agriculture must get neglected. A study of three villages in the Kumaon region of UP, for instance, shows that the ratio of human energy spent in collecting fuel and fodder is already 2.5 times more than the energy spent on agriculture. As time for fuel and fodder collection grows and firewood becomes scarcer, the traditional practice of manuring these fragile soils will be exhausted very soon. It will be a disastrous situation both for the local people and the environment.

I recently came across another study which makes the same point. This is a study on Ratnagiri district, a major source of male workers for the city of Bombay. Ratnagiri is one of the few districts in the country where the sex ratio is in favour of women. It has far more women than men. Says Rajani Desai, who conducted the study:

The women do many of the men's jobs in the villages, or they learn to manage without the fruits of such labour. Thus, land must somehow be tilled or allowed to lie fallow. The cultivable waste is as high as 21 per cent of the total land under cultivation (according to the agricultural census, 1970–1), whereas it was 3.7 per cent for Maharashtra as a whole. But the wonder is that it is not far higher for, as we found with interview after interview, land cultivation was having to be less intensive (than before and than desired), or even abandoned, because manpower (or, more accurately, female power) in families was inadequate.

Because of the increasing intensity of floods, there has been considerable talk in recent years about integrated watershed management in the Himalaya and in the Ghats. The Himalaya are being described as one of the most threatened ecosystems in the world, which in turn determines the fate of several hundred million people in the Indo-Gangetic plains. But if any action for ecological reconstruction has to be taken in the hills, it cannot be done without the involvement of women. The census data of 1981 shows that all the districts in the country which have high rates of female work participation, are situated in the Himalaya or in the Ghats. In the Himalaya most women workers are also classifed as cultivators. Therefore, any programme which aims at ecological rehabilitation in these areas will have to involve heavily overworked women unless, of course, labour is brought into these areas from outside, which will create tensions of another kind.

Fortunately, the experience of the Chipko Movement shows that women in these parts, despite their 14–16 hour back-breaking work schedule, are extremely keen to participate in such work, especially in tree planting. Once the women are organized and mobilized, the evidence is that they work with great keenness and they fight any obstacle that may be created by men; and we get as a result some of the highest tree survival rates found in afforestation efforts. It has also been found that when women become involved in afforestation, they tend to demand fuel and fodder trees, trees which can meet household needs, whereas men demand trees that can generate cash. The best ally in the demand for an ecologicaly and socially sound nature is, therefore, womankind.

As similar experiences have been noted in East and West Africa, in Kenya and in the Sahelian countries, there is every reason to believe that this differential interest in nature between men and women is cross-cultural in character. Male trees and female trees are now becoming something of a jargon amongst those interested in involving communities in afforestation.

CASH SHORTAGE AND HEADLOADING

All this should not be taken to construe that poor rural households do not have any need for cash. The unfortunate thing is that much of the cash generated by the men is not spent on household needs. Instead a reasonable proportion of this cash gets spent on products like alcohol and tobacco and artefacts of modernization like transistor radios.

This situation is creating a new demand on the time of the poor women and, in some cases, it is resulting in a new militancy against nature. Women now have to go out and also earn some cash. Millions of rural women today sell firewood in the towns and cities. If we look at the quantum of firewood consumed in the cities, we can say that at least 2–3 million people must be doing headloading—bringing wood on their heads to sell in the towns. This should make the rural-urban firewood trade the largest employer in the commercial energy sector of the country. Surveys show that selling firewood is a profession that has grown rapidly in the last 10–15 years with the growth in landlessness and joblessness. Most of these headloaders are women, and mostly tribal women. Selling firewood is backbreaking work and brings extremely little money. But the women do this because they cannot rely on their men to bring any cash back home. The big advantage with headloading is that this work is generally available round the year. So when no other work is available, headloading at least provides some income.

The life of the headloaders of Ranchi shows how difficult this entire business . . . is. The women wake up early in the morning, at about 4 a. m. and soon after they begin their trek to the forest. On reaching the forest, some 8–10 km away, they begin collecting firewood. By the afternoon, having collected the firewood, they do not return home but go off to Ranchi on a train. They spend the night at the Ranchi railway station, which these days is an extraordinary sight. Then early morning they sell the wood, a load of some 20–25 kg. For this entire load they get Rs 5–6, a third of which they lose in bribing the forest guard (on a fixed weekly rate) and the train conductors, who allow them a free ride. With the remaining money, the women buy some salt, kerosene for lighting, and other vital household necessities and return home. That evening they cook food and eat the first freshly cooked meal in two days. Next morning the two day cycle begins afresh.

Every headloading woman knows that the forests will soon be destroyed and even this horrible occupation will come to an end. But they are afraid that if they do not take advantage of the forests now, the foresters will soon sell them off to a contractor. The forest departments are extremely keen to get headloading banned. They have made no study of the phenomenon of headloading nor have they made any plans to meet the firewood needs of the cities: obviously they have not made any efforts to connect the two issues. Foresters say that these women destroy young trees, lop trees excessively, and therefore should be banned. No wonder forest rights are a major issue in most tribal agitations.

If we take a head count at this stage, we will find that the destruction of the environment and its transformation is affecting on an immediate and on a daily basis, at least the following groups: artisans, nomads, tribals, fisherfolk and women from landless, marginal and small farm households. These groups add up to no less than half to three-quarters of the country's entire rural population. And, unlike the situation in the West, the question of environmental destruction is not an issue related to quality of life—it is a question of survival.

Towards Holistic Management

If these are the problems, then what do we do about them?

First of all, there must be a much more holistic approach regarding the management of our land and water resources, and this will not be easy unless a determined effort is made. For all the talk about the need for a scientific temper, it must be recognized that the current methodology of scientific analysis carries within itself an extremely unscientific practice, that of reductionism. It is this reductionist approach that has today produced both natural and social scientists who know more and more about less and less, who know how to cure a disease but create another disease in the process.

Ecology is the first scientific discipline that has actually forced people to integrate and not reduce.

Let me illustrate this by describing what is happening to the three major components of our land: our forest lands, our crop lands and our grazing lands.

The destruction of forests has a major impact on the productivity of our croplands. This happens in two ways. Soil erosion increases manifold and the soil literally gets washed away, leading to an accentuated cycle of floods and droughts. But equally important is the impact of the shortage of firewood on the productivity of croplands. When firewood becomes scarce, people begin to burn cowdung and crop residues. In many places cowdung and crop residues are now the major sources of cooking energy. Thus, slowly, every part of the plant gets used and nothing goes back to the soil. Over a period of time, this nutrient drain affects crop productivity. Add to this the technology of the green revolution—the technology of growing high yielding varieties on a limited diet of chemical fertilizers like nitrogen, phosphates and potash. The total biomass production goes up and so does the drain of the nutrients from the soil. Plants need some twenty five odd elements to grow, not just N, P and K. They keep taking out these nutrients from the soil and the more intensive the agriculture, without any manure and crop residues going back to the soil, the faster is the nutrient drain. Today, the district of Ludhiana in Punjab has the highest yields of many cereals but it also has the highest deficiencies of many micronutrients in its soils. In Punjab, many farmers have begun to use zinc routinely as a fertilizer: soon it will be sulphur, manganese and iron. The micronutrient fertilizer industry, already a Rs 100 million industry, is sure to become the boom industry of the future. But the net result is that Indian agriculture, because of this and many other factors (all of them mostly related to ecological factors), is showing a consistently declining trend in output when compared to the rapidly rising levels of inputs.

If existing crop lands and irrigation water resources are not used well, then faced with a rising population the demand for colonization of marginal lands for agriculture will grow. As large parts of the country have excellent soils and enormous sunlight and the only shortage is of water, government programmes have also promoted the cultivation of marginal lands, especially through spread of irrigation. Fortunately, the rate of expansion of the cropped area has now come down as compared to the 1950s and 60s, but enormous ecological damage has already been done. Even more than forest lands, crop lands have expanded on to grazing lands. This has, in turn, led to the overstocking of grazing lands, destroying their productivity and impoverishing the graziers in the process. The graziers have taken recourse to two strategies in such a situation. As the environment becomes more and more hostile, they get rid of the more vulnerable cattle and start keeping goats. The number of goats in Rajasthan has expanded dramatically—much faster than any other livestock. Environmentalists may howl that the goat is highly destructive of the environment, but it is better suited to the hostile environment we human beings are creating in the arid and semi-arid areas of Rajasthan, Gujarat and Maharashtra. It makes economic sense for the grazier to reduce his risk during a period of drought, which is common in these areas.

The herders try to solve their problems in yet another way: they begin to use forests as grazing lands. This infuriates foresters who see goats and cattle as the worst evil that ever existed. It is true that India's forests are among the most heavily grazed forests in the world. As forests are now disappearing in Rajasthan and Gujarat, nomads from these states now enter Madhya Pradesh in large numbers, still a heavily forested state.

Threatened by this invasion, MP's foresters banned these 'foreign' invaders, but the Supreme Court struck down the ban saying that Indians cannot be restricted from going from one state to another. So the interstate movement goes on, but clashes are accelerating. MP's foresters killed 5000 sheep in one extremely brutal event on the MP-Rajasthan border last year and local politicians rushed to rouse passions against these nomads, making every effort to break down the highly synergistic relationship that once prevailed between the nomads and the settled farmers. The nomadic animals would bring manure to the fields of settled farmers. Like a walking vacuum cleaner, these animals would gather nutrients from all over and dump them on to the farmers' fields where they would rest, and the nomad would even be paid for this service. But today there is open hostility.

MP's forest secretary recently wrote an article in the *Times of India* saying: 'For the love of . . ., please keep these animals out of our forests'. If only the animals could be kept out, the forests would regenerate themselves. But such despair is no answer. Obviously animals cannot be kept out without creating extraordinary conflicts.

THE CYCLE OF DESTRUCTION

Meanwhile, however, the foresters have found an ingenious solution: plant trees like eucalyptus which cannot be browsed by animals. Eucalyptus is loved by foresters exactly for this reason. There are many who doubt the ability of eucalyptus to produce more wood than many indigenous species. But it is indeed ironic that when the country faces an acute fodder crisis, foresters can only plant eucalyptus and produce non-browsable biomass, that is, we do exactly the opposite of what the people need. In fact, eucalyptus is the true weed from the point of view of the landless. It is non-browsable, like all fast-spreading weeds, and does not benefit the poor unless they own land.

But in this manner the cycle of destruction is complete. The forest departments have destroyed forests by selling off timber to the industrial and urban interests. The firewood shortage and the resulting soil erosion is keeping the productivity of India's agricultural lands low. Crop lands have expanded on to marginal lands and have reduced grazing lands. Animals have moved into forests and are preventing regeneration. All the chickens are coming to roost. Meanwhile as landlessness and joblessness grown, even groups like the tribals—who from time immemorial have lived in total harmony with forests—are turning against forests and want to sell them off as fast as they can.

Experts sit in grand isolation. Foresters have no interest in fuelwood or in crop lands. Agricultural experts have no interest in animals or in grazing lands. Animal husbandry people never tell foresters that they must produce fodder banks.

In the life of the proverbial last person of Gandhi, all this isolated thinking brings havoc. Life for the poor becomes terrible. Finally, even nature turns against itself. Once denuded, the high solar energy and temperatures—the very factors that can bring high productivity and high prosperity—begin to bring high dessication, erosion, destruction, and social and ecological poverty. FAO figures show that the effect of unchecked soil erosion on soil productivity is one of the highest in the world given the ecoclimate conditions of South and Southeast Asia.

Improving the Country's Gross Nature Product

Nothing could be more important for planners and politicians today
than to rebuild nature. But this can only be done if we re-establish
a healthy relationship between the people and their environment.
Only then can a nature that is useful to the millions—not for making
millions—be re-established. Regardless of what happens in the
West, for all its electronics, biotechnology, communications satel-
lites, efforts to mine the oceans, solar cells and windmills, and
regardless of how much we may want to catch up with the West in
the name of modernization, rebuilding nature and rebuilding its
relationship with the people will remain the only way to solve the
problem of poverty and possibly even unemployment. It is estimated
that India today has some 100–150 million hectares of wasteland
and with the crying need to produce biomass, this country can never
get a better opportunity to harness the power of its people to the
power of its land, to strike at the roots of landlessness, poverty and
unemployment, all at the same time.

Activities needed to develop the country's ecological infrastructure—like soil and water conservation programmes, afforestation,
building of protection walls, and digging of ponds and tanks—all
require extraordinary levels of labour. No such calculations have
been made, but I would conjecture that if a nationwide programme
for ecological regeneration was undertaken, the country would
reach a stage of full employment —a dream for all national planners. Maharashtra is today the only state in the country which
guarantees the right to work. Anyone demanding a job has to be
provided with one by the district authorities. At the moment, these
authorities employ people mainly on the job of constructing a
road. In one infamous case against which there are now widespread protests, they have even sanctioned the construction of a
road at the expense of a majestic forest.

Few efforts have been made to create employment through
afforestation or watershed development activities, because there
are no off-the-shelf schemes that have been made available to district authorities for ecodevelopment of specific regions. In Rajasthan,
however, where the Aravali range now lies in a devastated state with
extensive deforestation, the Forest Department has responded to
the request of a social worker to undertake afforestation work on an
urgent basis in order to save further deforestation. The Forest

Department was told by this individual last year that during drought conditions, impoverished villagers have no option left for a livelihood except to sell more wood to the nearby city of Udaipur. Programmes for alternate employment were therefore urgently needed and, of course, what could be better than to employ these impoverished villagers in afforestation work—something that would benefit them on a long-term basis? The Forest Department responded immediately and this small effort is today, to my mind, a national model for employment generation during drought and famine conditions. The social worker mobilized the villagers while the Forest Department provided the necessary resources. Apart from employment, within a few months the protected enclosures began to yield large quantities of grass, which not only saved the animals of the villagers from starvation, but the villagers were also able to sell some grass. In a few years many trees will start bearing fruit and the villagers will also be able to sell bamboo. But these kinds of schemes will be possible only if the government prepares plans for biomass generation, literally for every village of India.

The availability of biomass would have a major impact on the poverty of the people. If enough biomass was available, poverty—that is, lack of cash (as defined by economists and by modern civilization)—would not disappear. But without doubt, the increasing rigours of poverty and the increasing susceptibility to natural emergencies like floods and droughts, would be arrested. In fact, conventional measurements of poverty based on income data or on food calories are clearly inadequate in a situation where the rest of the biomass needs are becoming increasingly difficult to meet, and collecting them on a daily basis constitutes the worst (and growing) drudgery humankind—especially womankind—has ever known. These calculations are not only inadequate, but they also reflect a strong gender-bias because they deal mainly with those aspects of poverty (lack of cash) that the male is generally concerned with, but not with those aspects of poverty that the woman deals with (lack of fuel, fodder, water, etc.).

If we were to construct a concept like Gross Nature Product, we would find that for the poor it is this indicator which is many times more important than the conventional Gross National Product. In fact, we can even say that those who do not get much from conventional GNP—the poor—are the ones who are most critically dependent on the Gross Nature Product. The Gross National Product cannot be allowed to destroy or transform the Gross Nature Product.

The Importance of Diversity in Nature

Just as the economists get very worried about the structure of the Gross National Product, it is equally important, if they have the poor in mind, that they worry about the structure of the Gross Nature Product. It is not just the quantity of biomass that is important for meeting basic households needs, but also its diversity. Sources of biomass within any village ecosystem must be diverse enough to meet the diverse household needs of fuel, fodder, building materials, etc. and of artisans.

The diversity in nature has also acted as an insurance during periods of emergency by reducing societal vulnerability. During periods of drought and resulting crop failures—which are recurring phenomena in many parts of India—roots, leaves and wild animals in the forests, used to become an important, alternative source of nutrition. In 1983, the tribals of Chotanagpur survived a drought not because of government assistance but despite government callousness. It is the forests which gave them their nutrition. Surviving on the forests during a drought is common in Bastar. Madhav Gadgil and his co-workers have reported many castes in Maharashtra which once survived on wild animals in the forests. Now that the forests have disappeared, these castes have increasingly taken to theft, prostitution and begging. The combination of trees, grasses, crops, animals and ponds which we found in almost every village, was an extraordinarily interactive and resilient system to natural emergencies. Instead of destroying this complex and interrelated system, science must be used to build on it.

In other words, it is not enough to preserve biological diversity just in those areas of our country where the flora and fauna are genetically rich and diverse by setting up biosphere reserves and national parks; instead we must ensure that biological diversity is preserved and/or recreated in every village ecosystem. Concentrating on the production of a few commodities (cereals, for instance) is totally inadequate in a society which is only partly monetized and where the vast majority still has to depend on access to free biomass resources from the immediate environment. Every village has to become a biosphere reserve.

Knowledge of the Gross Nature Product and how it is changing within the national ecological space (or shall we say, national economy) is extremely limited, despite its crucial importance for the poor. Unfortunately we do not know as yet how to construct such an indicator. But I am sure that if we did, we would find that while the conventional GNP has gone up, the Gross Nature Product has steadily gone down, the former acting as a parasite on the latter.

THE NEEDS OF THE POOR: A PRIORITY

The answer to India's immediate problem of poverty, therefore, lies in increasing the biomass available in nature, and moreover, increasing it in such a manner that access to it is ensured on an equitable basis. But given a 'green cover' to the country—the real green revolution—would probably require the most holistic thinking that planners, economists and scientists have ever known. The conflicting and complementary nature of existing land use patterns have to be extremely well understood, otherwise land-use patterns will remain as chaotic as today. Poorer peasants will continue to oppose planting trees on community lands under so-called social forestry programmes because they are afraid this will take away their grazing lands. Forest Departments and richer peasants will only plant those trees which animals cannot touch (like eucalyptus), even though there is a stark fodder crisis all around. Nothing could take us closer to Gandhiji's concept of *gram swarajya* than striving to create village ecosystems which are biologically diverse and self-reliant in their local biomass needs to the maximum extent possible. This will clearly demand an extremely intensive use of our natural resources, like land and water, to create a huge and diverse stock of biomass. Any science which teaches how to do this will truly have the right to be called a people's science.

Easy availability of biomass, leading to a reduction in women's work burden, could create the appropriate conditions for many desirable social changes. Kerala, for instance, is often cited as an interesting case of an economically poor state moving ahead with its demographic transition. But is Kerala poor in environmental terms also? The availability of biomass in Kerala, in fact, appears to be the maximum in India, and women's work burden low. This may sound an exaggerated proposition but could it not be surmised that, among many other things, it was the easy availability of biomass and relatively lower work burden in Kerala that created the appropriate conditions for state literacy programmes for women to succeed? If women in Kerala had to spend as much time as women do in large parts of Rajasthan, Uttar Pradesh and Bihar, wouldn't there have ᵇeen immense male pressure to keep women working in crucial household activities and away from schools?

The biggest challenge lies before social workers and politicians who have to play a crucial role in ensuring that people can participate in a biomass-based development process. No biomass-based strategy can suceed without the involvement of the people, especially women, without whom this work cannot be dₒ.ne. The role of women in recreating a healthy and useful environment cannot be overstressed.

The country must recognize immediately that there is a desperate need for a clear biomass policy, which recognizes the competing uses for biomass in society, especially between biomass-based industry and poor households, and sets clear priorities on the use of biomass in a situation of scarcity. The needs of the poor must be specified as a priority use of biomass in the existing situation of environmental degradation.

Enriching the Alienated Commons

While talking about the importance of the Gross Nature Product, it is important to deliberate on the question: why do the poor, who suffer so much from the shortage of biomass, not plant all the trees and grasses they need? Why does one-third to one-half of India increasingly become a wasteland? It is crucial that we find a clear answer to these questions because only then will we be able to devise appropriate and feasible policies.

To my mind the answer really lies in the alienation created by the modern state amongst village communities from their commons. Croplands are almost entirely private property. Before the advent of the modern state, grazing lands, forest lands and water bodies were mostly common property and village communities played an important role in their use and management. The British were, however, the first to nationalize these resources and bring them under the management of government bureaucracies. In other words, the British initiated the policy of converting common property resources into government property resources. The management of forests was taken over in the name of conservation of forests. But in reality, both in British and in post-independent India, the common resources have been ruthlessly exploited almost to the point of their decimation. This exploitation has been mainly to met the needs of the elite, whereas the needs of the poor—who survived on these resources—were neglected, and the poor were repeatedly blamed for the ecological destruction. Thus, both colonial and post-colonial governments have expropriated the common resources from the poor and reallocated them to the more powerful in society. This perfidy towards the poor can even be noticed in the terminology that officialdom uses. For people dependent on forest fruits, medicinal herbs, small timber for building purposes, firewood and fodder, all such things were major forest produce. But government forest departments call them minor forest produce whereas timber is called the major forest produce. Forest dwellers seldom have any need for timber, except for minor building purposes: timber is the major forest produce for the modern urban-industrial system.

This expropriation has clearly alienated the people from their commons and has started a free-for-all. Today India's tribals, who have lived in harmony with the forests for centuries, are so alienated that they do not feel anything in felling a green tree to sell it off for a pittance. Repeatedly we have been asked, what is the point in saving the forests, because if the poor didn't take them first, the forest contractors would take them away. The desperate economic condition of the poor, made worse by the ecological destruction, has left them with no other option but to cut the trees.

In a region of the Aravalis, near the idyllic city Udaipur, we recently came across a tribal village in which no forests are left. The people there are extremely poor and men regularly migrate in search of jobs to Udaipur. The women are left to survive by scrounging around for weeds and twigs. Even headloading of firewood came to a halt in this village nearly seven to eight years ago because of the scarcity of wood. When we asked, 'Where have all the forests gone?', the women replied, 'They have gone away to Udaipur'. We then asked, 'If your lives are so dependent on the forests, why did you allow them to be cut so ruthlessly?' They replied, 'But at that time everyone was doing so, *including the government* .' Today the alienation from common resources is total.

The Chipko Movement was the first major ecological movement in the country to assert the rights of the village communities. When, in 1974, the women of the Reni village prevented the felling of the Reni forest, they were saying; 'This may be a government forest, but we live next to it, and our needs (of ecological security from landslides, of basic needs like water, fuel and fodder) have priority'.

Unless people's alienation from their commons can be arrested and reversed, there cannot be any proper afforestation on common lands. In a country like India where agriculture and animal husbandary are closely intertwined activities and the animal pressure is extremely high, plantations and grasslands will have to be protected from animals, especially if the biomass that is sought to be grown is multipurpose—that is, capable of meeting the crucial need of fodder. Any attempt to enclose an area of land will be strongly resented by the people, however underproductive it may be, for fear of loss of grazing land. And all such attempts will be subverted by them unless they are fully assured that the biomass which is grown inside those enclosures will meet their felt needs on a priority basis. If public participation is not available, then either the survival rates will be very poor, or anti-social, non-browsable plants like eucalyptus will be planted—a technical fix for a social problem.

COMMUNITY INVOLVEMENT

That people must be involved in afforestation is now widely accepted. But how is this to be done? This is a million dollar question and the manner in which it is answered could determine the future of poverty in the country.

There are two basic ways of dealing with this problem. First, that common lands be privatized and parcelled off as small plots to landless and marginal peasants, who will then take a special interest in developing and enriching those lands. Concepts like tree *pattas* (that is, lease of trees and tree produce instead of lease of land) can be developed. But the problem with this approach is that it will only accelerate the current process of privatizing the commons and, as there clearly isn't enough land to benefit all the poor, there will always be some poor people who will be left out. And these poor would have no commons left to survive on. Furthermore, if at some time politicians were to intervene, to get cheap votes or whatever, these privatized landholdings could easily adopt adverse land use practices and, with little control left over them, ecology would suffer greatly. There are several afforestation schemes in Indian states in which government forest lands have been leased to landless or marginal landholding peasants for afforestation. The schemes include a monthly stipend for five years for afforesting a piece of degraded land and for taking care of it. Every year an additional piece of land is given to the household for afforestation, and in this way these poor families can come to control over ten hectares of government forest land under a lease. The beneficiary family has full rights to the grass and all other produce from the trees it plants, except the timber, which the forest department shares in return for the monthly stipends it pays.

The big difficulty with these schemes in areas where the commons are already dwindling, is that the beneficiary family becomes a big target for those in the community who can no longer benefit from the privatized common land. We came across a case in Rajasthan where an entire hillside had been extremely well afforested and taken care of. But the beneficiary family had been excommunicated from the village community and could not participate in community dinners and festivals. We can expect similar resentment wherever the commons are already under heavy pressure and scarce, and further privatization is legally permitted to undertake ecological enrichment. The World Bank is keen to push such privatization schemes.

The second, more difficult option is to retain and manage the commons as commons, by organizing and mobilizing village communities to develop the commons as a community enterprise. This is socially the best option but clearly very difficult. It requires great social enterpreneurship.

Experience in India shows that it can be done provided the following three principles are observed:

1. The commons must be brought under the control of the village communities. This means divesting government agencies of their control of the commons;
2. The entire community must be involved in the protection of the commons under its control. If only a section of the community is involved in the protection of a part of the commons, then that community must be homogeneous and it must gain clear control over that part of the commons. In other words, whichever group controls whatever portion of the commons, it must control it completely and protect it jointly. If only a few

members of a group are left to protect a common resource against the wishes of the rest, they will probably fail;

3. All members of a group expected to protect a common resource will do so only if all of them benefit from the commons equally.

These principles of control, co-operation and equity may sound extremely difficult to implement in practice. Community management systems have usually been failures. But it is my strong belief that the environment crisis, and the associated human crisis has gone so deep that—given the right leadership—any number of village communities will today be prepared to organize themselves along the above lines.

COMMON LAND, COMMON RESOURCES

There are two outstanding projects near Chandigarh in which villages have been organized on these principles and the results are outstanding. The Shivaliks are a young mountain range, where the rock still crumbles like lumps of mud. Overgrazing and deforestation has left the mountains bare. The monsoon literally washes away the mountains every year. The erosion has to be seen to be believed. All efforts to educate this community of shepherds about the need for self-imposed restraints on grazing failed repeatedly, until it was realized that these gullies provided a very valuable product—water. An earthen dam was built to impound the water, but the community was given the water only after it had agreed to stop grazing in the watershed area. All members of the community agreed to protect the watershed only when it was ensured that water would be given equally to each member of the community, including those who had no land. The landless could sell their water to the landed or take a share in the produce. Nowadays, water is a resource of the commons that is allocated according to the unequal landholding structures. But in these villages it is different. The common resource is equally distributed and today the entire community in these villages protects the watershed. The protection has lead to increased production of grass. The increased availability of fodder has lead to increased production and sales of milk. People have replaced goats by high quality milch animals. The village community sells the grass from the watershed. The purpose of afforestation is not just to yield firewood and more fodder but also raw materials for small scale industry like ropemaking, so that non-agricultural employment can be generated. And, most of all, from the water impounded behind the earthen dams, the croplands have begun to yield two to three crops and total production of cereals has increased five to six-fold, and increased the resilience to droughts. This is indeed the finest approach to self-reliant rural development that we can come across. In Chipko, too, there is greater equity and community participation, and conservation of the commons has led to increased production of basic necessities.

The village people have constantly set their own priorities. Conservation work first began in the Chipko villages not by protecting trees, but by building walls around the agricultural fields to protect them from wild animals. This was their first priority. But as grass grew up quickly in the protected space between the fields and the walls, and as this benefit became clear to the village women, they began to organize themselves readily for protecting and afforesting other patches of common lands. While trees take many years to bear fruit, grasses grow fast in a protected area and can provide fodder in less than six months. The Chipko women have devised a very simple technique for sharing this produce from the commons equally. Once a month the head of the village Mahila Mangal Dal (women's welfare group) announces a particular day on which one member from each family can take away as much grass as he or she can.

In one case, there was a clash between the Mahila Mangal Dal (an informal organisation), and the head of the panchayat (village council) which legally controls the commons, over the right to the grass. The clash resulted in a police case, but the women took the matter up to the highest district authorities: in consequence the police case had to be withdrawn and the panchayat had to relent. The women thus asserted their right to control the piece of the commons that they had jointly undertaken to enrich, to care for, and whose produce they were sharing equitably: an illegal assertion in the current order of administration, but a path-breaking assertion which shows how things ought to be done and will have to be done in the future.

Given the increasing population pressure and the pressure generated by the demands for a higher standard of living, it is evident that the already heavy pressure on the natural resource base will have to be increased even further. Not only do we have to produce more biomass, but we also have to produce it on a sustainable basis. This is definitely possible—definitely at least in the case of

India. India has one of the world's largest expanses of highly productive soils, an enormous water potential and excellent sunlight.
With our crop yields less than a tonne per hectare in most parts of
India, and nearly half of India literally lying waste, India has more
untapped potential today than possibly any other country in the
world. But even if a fraction of this potential has to be realized on a
sustainable basis, without mining our soils and turning more of
our forest and grazing lands into vast tracts of wastelands, we will
have to care for our natural resource base and respect ecological
principles as never before.

Nothing in this emphasis on the Gross Nature Product as compared to the Gross National Product implies a demand for 'back to
nature', as critics often tend to point out. On the contrary, we need
much more sophisticated inputs of science and technology and
equally sophisticated forms of social organization than we have .
seen until now. We have to organize our village communities to
manage the commons as commons, and push our scientists away
from highly simplistic monocultures to complex polycultures for
integrated production of crucial biomass needs. As a minister of
the environment said, 'You are asking for a revolution in community
organisation.' When pressed hard a forester in Delhi argued back:
'You are talking about a revolution in forestry sciences. We know
little about polycultures.' Indeed, that is just what we are talking
about! The minister knew what a disastrous failure the political system has been and still is, especially at its lowest levels. However,
neither the politicians nor the scientists have shown adequate cour-
age to grasp the nettle that issues of equity and sustainability pose.

The 'Recreation' of Nature

All this sophisticated social organization, science and technology
will not work unless we look back into our culture and revive those
values and beliefs that made us respect nature. All over India there
were numerous traditional practices born out of a respect for
nature: the sacred groves of Maharashtra and the Chotanagpur
plateau, and the sacred *orans* of Rajasthan are just a few examples.
Instead of understanding the ecological basis of these practices,
and lifting them up through appropriate education from a substratum
of supernatural beliefs to a higher plane of secular understanding

and respect we have, in the name of modernization, dismissed all of them as superstition.

Let me tell you about a common Indian myth that my mother once told me, and whose ecological implication I understood only recently. There is a very famous myth in India about the descent of the Goddess Ganga from the heavens. King Bhagirath wanted the goddess to come down to earth to wash off the sins of his forefathers. After a lot of prayer, Ganga agreed to come down to the earth but told Bhagirath that she could do so only if somebody was prepared to tie her up. 'If I am not tied down,' she said, 'I will not be the lifegiving source that you expect me to be, but I will create enormous chaos and destruction on earth'. Bhagirath then looked around and finally found the only person who could tie down the mighty Ganga, the powerful God, Shiva. He went into another period of prayer, this time praying to Lord Shiva to tie up the Ganga as she descended to earth. Shiva finally agreed, and Ganga descended into the locks of his hair, from whence she comes out as a little trickle to give life to the vast plains of northern India. This is the myth, which is embedded even today in the minds of over 500 million Indians.

But look at the myth in another way. The monsoon is a life giving system for the Indian subcontinent, which to my mind is nothing but the descent of the Ganga every year. Shiva in many ways is synonymous with the Himalaya, and if you agree with that, then the forests of the Himalaya are synonymous with the locks of Shiva. These locks of Shiva tie the Ganga down ever year, year after year, and turn it into a lifegiving source by regulating its water flow. The biggest change, however, is that over the last 150 years, human beings have acquired the temerity to start cutting down the locks of Shiva, and it is not surprising that the Ganga is now turning into the fury the myth had said it would become. Today there are more floods and more droughts.

It is clear from what I have said that the challenges before us are great and difficult, and they become even greater when we realize that for all this to work, the change has to come first in the very metropolitan sector to which we all belong. If India, for instance, fails to recreate nature on a massive scale, in a manner that generates employment and equity, not only its villages but also its cities will become unlivable. Many people prefer to call the urban migrants economic refugees from the countryside. But to my mind many of them are really ecological refugees, displaced by dams, mines, deforestation, destruction of grazing lands, floods, by droughts, urban expansion, and other such factors. We have today the world's fourth largest urban population: before the end of the century we will be the largest. Managing this huge urban population will call for extraordinary political and managerial sagacity and completely new approaches—something we cannot learn from the rest of the world. But one thing is definite: if the process of urbanization continues to create the same demands on our rural environment for natural resources, it will only accelerate the destruction of the rural environment and in turn make the urban environment impossibly large to manage. India cannot survive without a low-energy, low-resource input urbanization. These technology choices will be crucial in the twenty-first century. People have widely talked about alternative rural development—from Gandhi to Mao to Nyerere. But it has now become crucial that we also talk about—and implement—an alternative urban development strategy. Because if we don't, nothing will survive in the villages of the Third World.

Further Readings for Section IV

Two kinds of writings are relevant here; work on the environmental movement, and philosophical or policy oriented studies of environmental reform. In both categories, Indian work is meagre in comparison with work set in other geographical regions. The literature on Western environmentalism is abundant—worth reading, for a start, are Roderick Nash's illuminating history of American environmental ideas, *Wilderness and the American Mind* (New Haven: Yale University Press, 1982), and Philip Lowe and Jane Goyder's keen sociological analysis of British environmental organizations, *Environmental Groups in Politics* (London: George Allen and Unwin, 1983). In coming years studies are bound to emerge of Third World environmentalism, with implict or explicit contrasts with the Western experience.

More reflective, and at times sobering analyses of where the human and natural worlds are heading can be found in two persuasive works unlikely to date easily: E. F. Schumacher, *Small is Beautiful: A Study of Economics as if People Mattered* (London: Abacus, 1973); and Rudolph Bahro, *From Red to Green: Interviews with New Left Review* (London: Verso, 1984). A policy oriented work of environmental reform, based on a set of commissioned studies, is Robert Repetto, *World Enough and Time: Successful Strategies for Resource Management* (New Haven: Yale University Press, 1986). A handy study of two important resource sectors in India, written by three highly experienced pracitioners, is Robert Chambers, N. C. Saxena and Tushaar Shah, *To the Hands of the Poor: Water and Trees* (New Delhi: Oxford and IBH, 1989).

Index